ACT OF CREATION

The Founding of the United Nations

ALSO BY STEPHEN C. SCHLESINGER

The New Reformers:
Forces for Change in American Politics (1975)

Bitter Fruit:
The Story of the American Coup in Guatemala
(with Stephen Kinzer, 1982)

ACT OF CREATION

The Founding of the United Nations

A Story of Superpowers, Secret Agents,
Wartime Allies and Enemies, and
Their Quest for a Peaceful World

STEPHEN C. SCHLESINGER

A Member of the Perseus Books Group

Copyright © 2003 by Stephen C. Schlesinger

Published in the United States of America by Westview Press, A Member of the Perseus Books Group, 5500 Central Avenue, Boulder, Colorado 80301–2877, and in the United Kingdom by Westview Press, 12 Hid's Copse Road, Cumnor Hill, Oxford OX2 9JJ.

Find us on the world wide web at www.westviewpress.com

Westview Press books are available at special discounts for bulk purchases in the United States by corporations, institutions, and other organizations. For more information, please contact the Special Markets Department at the Perseus Books Group, 11 Cambridge Center, Cambridge, MA 02142, or call (617) 252–5298, (800) 255–1514 or email j.mccrary@perseusbooks.com.

Library of Congress Cataloging-in-Publication Data
Schlesinger, Stephen C.
    Act of creation : the founding of the United Nations : a story of superpowers, secret agents, wartime allies and enemies, and their quest for a peaceful world / Stephen Schlesinger.
        p.   cm.
    Includes bibliographical references and index.
    ISBN 0-8133-3324-5 (hbk. : alk. paper)
    1. United Nations—History. I. Title.
JZ4986.S358   2003
341.23'09'044—dc21

                                                                    2003014600

The paper used in this publication meets the requirements of the American National Standard for Permanence of Paper for Printed Library Materials Z39.48–1984.

Text design by Brent Wilcox
Typeface used in this text: 11.5-point Apollo MT

10   9   8   7   6   5   4   3   2

To my mother and my father

They performed a great task of creation.

ADLAI STEVENSON
Chicago Bar Association
June 28, 1945

CONTENTS

ACKNOWLEDGMENTS

This book had a lengthy gestation period. I first began to contemplate it when I read a *New York Times* story dated August 11, 1993, revealing that the United States had undertaken spying at the founding conference of the United Nations in San Francisco in the spring of 1945. The disclosure had come about almost incidentally to a Freedom of Information request by the historian Gar Alperovitz seeking information from the National Security Agency about America's decision to drop the atomic bomb. Although Mr. Alperovitz did not pursue the U.N. angle, I had had a long-standing regard for the United Nations—especially its origins. So this new information especially piqued my curiosity. I divined that, as far as the creation of the U.N. was concerned, surely there had to be more to the tale than just the U.S. surveillance activities.

I made my decision to write this book based on the *Times* piece. My first step was to get hold of the recently released Alperovitz documents. I wrote to the National Security Agency in early fall 1993, and promptly received about 627 pages of information detailing the operations of our nation's army agents in surreptitiously following the preparations of other nations for the San Francisco Conference. Much of the information was blacked out for "security" considerations, but enough of it was still readable to allow me to gain a broad understanding of how extensive and meticulous was the gumshoe work that went on in that California city.

Concomitantly, I began to spend my lunch hours when I worked for Governor Mario Cuomo in offices in Times Square at the nearby New York Public Library. I commenced to search the computerized files for all the books that had ever been written about the San Francisco Conference. I discovered that there was not one full-length account of that historic event anywhere in the collection. This redoubled my fascination with the topic. Soon, I compiled a list of works that at least touched on the meeting or devoted some portion of their text to evaluating the proceedings. Meanwhile, I began Xeroxing all the *New York Times* articles about the two-month conference running from April 25, 1945, to June 26, 1945. I was especially respectful of the *Times* coverage since the principals at the conclave talked at their daily gatherings almost exclusively about what the *Times* was saying.

The copying assignment at the New York Public Library turned out to be a mammoth one. I became an expert in how to handle microfilm—skillfully inserting the round cartridges in cranky old machines and threading the spools, arranging the film so that it unwound in the right chronological direction, peering at page after page to assay the San Francisco–related articles, and carefully photographing the appropriate pieces. It was a laborious task—but over the period of about six months, I managed to accumulate the entire public story of the conference; this gave me a real sense for the first time of how crises erupted and died away at San Francisco, of the constant flow of commentary and analysis that influenced events, of who was or wasn't a key figure at various public sessions.

In due course, I also supplemented my research with the private notes of the participants at two libraries, the Truman Presidential Library and the Stettinius Archives at the University of Virginia. Although I was not able to visit either personally, through the genius of our technological age, I made use of these repositories though Xeroxes, faxes, Fed-Ex, e-mails, and phone calls. At the first institution, the Truman Presidential Library in Independence, Missouri, Archivist Dennis Bilger was of particular help to me in arranging for me to receive documents relating to Truman's involvement in the San Francisco event. Later at the University of Virginia in Charlottesville, Virginia, Mr. Gregory Johnson, who works in the Albert and Shirley Small Special Collections Library, was of estimable assistance in gaining me access to hundreds of reports, memoranda, and telephone summaries generated by Stettinius and his staff. Ms. Vesta Lee Gordon undertook the actual research into the Special Collections Library to harvest these documents for me—a wonderful achievement and an important contribution.

In the course of my efforts, I began to look around for a publisher who might be willing to take on my book project. Little did I know at the time that I would be engaging in a problematical quest. At first, I wrote a substantial outline, which, in retrospect, was perhaps not as persuasive as it could have been, though, in my defense, at that time I did not know the true dimensions or novelty of the story. My intrepid agent, Sterling Lord, who always praised my venture and kept up my spirits, circulated my outline to a series of publishing houses, but elicited scant reaction. Such indifference continued for so long—almost two years—that I began to realize that something was amiss. In due course I learned that the mere mention of the word "United Nations" for publishing industry folk was the equivalent of biting on an especially bitter lemon. For the organization was automatically associated with dreaded research reports, tedious academic works, lengthy and unread studies, boring surveys, and otherwise worthy but neglected white papers. In short, by publishing standards, the body was considered a snooze. But after a drawn-out period, one firm did show appreciation for my proposal and was willing to take a chance on it through its senior editor, Peter Kracht—Westview Press. Then, years after, I had the fortunate experience of being placed in the very good hands of my editor, Steve Catalano.

Midway through this time, I decided to publish my preliminary findings drawn on the Freedom of Information documents detailing the secret intelligence operations of the Roosevelt administration in San Francisco. In the fall of 1994, I wrote a piece for the *World Policy Journal* titled "FDR's Five Policemen: Creating the United Nations." That led to a query from the historian of spycraft David Kahn about what exactly was the nature of the clandestine methodology employed by the federal operatives. Mr. Kahn convinced me to rewrite and broaden the piece by explaining precisely how the scheme was mounted. Eventually, I wrote an elongated study on the operation for the July 1995 issue of *Cryptologia* under the title "Cryptanalysis for Peacetime: Codebreakers and the Birth and Structure of the United Nations." This essay was picked up by the *New York Times* and published on April 23, 1995, as a breaking story titled "War Decoding Helped U.S. to form U.N." It quoted Mr. Kahn as saying that mine was "one of the most important articles in the history of cryptology" because it detailed only the second-known instance where cryptanalysis affected a significant peacetime event.

By now I had broadened my research. I applied under the Freedom of Information Act for all documents related to FBI surveillance in San Francisco. The agency released over one hundred pages of messages and memoranda to me on October 27, 1998—much of it blacked out. Yet there was enough material to permit me to obtain an idea of how the bureau handled the various groups and individuals—mostly Americans—attending the sessions. I also found, most important, the bible of the conference's documentation, the Foreign Relations of the United States, volume I, 1945, "The United Nations Conference," published in 1967, containing the almost daily transcription of U.S. delegation meetings. Soon thereafter, I visited the Library of Congress, where I delved into the diaries of Edward Stettinius and Senator Arthur Vandenberg, and the files of Leo Pasvolsky—invaluable guides to strategic debates and ideas that guided and illuminated the conference. In addition, I had the opportunity to interview Harold Stassen by phone on November 19, 1997. His mind was as sharp as a knife's blade at age ninety. A young student, Neil Abrams, from the University of Pennsylvania, also helped prepare background materials for me on U.S. relations with both Poland and Argentina during the war, for which I am grateful. Shashi Tharoor, William Van Den Heuvel, and Richard Gardner shared helpful comments on the epilogue. The United Nations Photo Archives Division generously supplied most of the photographs in the book. Ray Naldo of the Division was of particular help.

During all this, I was holding down a series of jobs—with Governor Cuomo, later at the United Nations Habitat agency, and finally as Director of the World Policy Institute at the New School University. In between, for a two-year period, Dr. Mitchell Moss, Director of Taub Urban Research Center at New York University, lent me an office—a generous gesture for which I am truly appreciative. I worked on weekends, in the evenings, on vacation, or at other odd hours I could find, to complete my book. My model for this sort of feverish activity was James Chace, one-time editor of the *World Policy Journal,* who managed with considerable agility to craft a superb biography of Dean Acheson while holding down a full-time teaching position at Bard, editing the *Journal,* writing important pieces for magazines, and performing dozens of other professional tasks.

This venture was of considerable sacrifice to my family life. In the end, I could not have completed this book without the sustaining support of my understanding and loving wife, Judy, and my sweet daughter, Sarah. Both tolerated my antic habits with equanimity and forbearance far beyond the call of household loyalty. I also want to thank my loving father for his support and advice—and for his willingness to comment on and edit this text. To him, I am immeasurably grateful. And I want to thank my mother and the rest of my family for their encouragement. The responsibility for this work, though, is all my own.

I hope that over the long run my book may contribute to a better understanding and more profound sympathy for the United Nations—and for a deeper comprehension of the historic role of the United States in creating this organization. For a nation rightly proud of its innumerable accomplishments, this unique achievement should always be at the top of its illustrious roster.

INTRODUCTION

"Four times in the modern age," English historian John Keegan has written, "men have sat down to reorder the world—at the Peace of Westphalia in 1648 after the Thirty Years War, at the Congress of Vienna in 1815 after the Napoleonic Wars, in Paris in 1919 after World War I, and in San Francisco in 1945 after World War II."[1] Such is the march of human history that all these events—except for the most recent one—collapsed in disagreements that eventually led to renewed wars. The fortunes of the last of these, the San Francisco Conference, are still not known. However, what happened in that California city that produced the last of these grand compacts has already had an enormous impact over the past six decades. Indeed, the founding of the United Nations, in far more sinister circumstances than faced any of the U.N.'s predecessors—namely, the age of nuclear weaponry—is affecting the survival or demise of humanity.

I decided to write this book for one reason—to relate the tale of the origins of this unusual organization and explain to people in our own time why it must be preserved. In today's world, though, few really know the story. Indeed, the U.N. is so much a part of our lives that few individuals have ever felt the need to search for its beginnings. In some ways, the U.N. is a tedious subject—until, that is, one enters the General Assembly in New York City and observes with awe all the nations of the world gathered together in one chamber. The U.N. and its labors are, in fact, the background noise of our global age—sometimes loud, sometimes soft, but always emitting a hum. One cannot pick up any major newspaper or watch any network newscast or listen to any radio news show or consult any media Web site in the United States and not hear or see the name of the U.N. invoked regularly by a broadcaster or written down in a daily report by a journalist. The name of the U.N. has become as commonplace for us as that of the White House or Congress. Yet people forget that just over a half-century ago there was no U.N.— just a creaky and faltering institution called the League of Nations universally derided for its incompetence and ineffectiveness.

Today, the U.N. is regarded as a resilient, if aging, organism, despite its dearth of financial resources and the brickbats tossed at it by American politicians. Still, few citizens can explain from whence it hailed and why. Some believe it sprang fully clothed onto the world stage, others that it evolved along with the globalization of the planet. Once one begins to trace the birth of the United Nations back to its nativity in San Francisco, though, one realizes that this body had a difficult if not perilous delivery. It was certainly not an ineluctable happenstance. Its creation, indeed, as this account reveals, was akin to a series of near-death experiences.

Cognizant of the U.N.'s difficult birth pains, I initially wondered why there had never been a full-length study done on the climactic conference in San Francisco. There was, of course, Ruth Russell's pioneering and monumental report on the creation of the U.N., *A History of the United Nations Charter,* published in 1958, which devotes the entire second half of its chronicle to San Francisco. Otherwise, however, there have been only glancing references to the gathering in America's West Coast city in the spring of 1945. Yet the drama of the U.N.'s inception— and its special meaning for our time—should, in my view, be riveting people's attention, for the U.N. today holds the broadest, if most fragile, guardianship over the geopolitical situation.

In searching through the libraries and repositories of U.N. documents, I discovered a raft of books, personal records, government documents, memoirs, newspaper reports, oral interviews, and diaries that allowed me to flesh out the story almost on a day-by-day, sometimes hour-by-hour, basis. I reconstructed the tale mainly from the U.S. point of view, which, without putting too much of a gloss on it, was the most important. For it was the Americans who designed the body, writing the U.N. Charter within the State Department, using as their inspiration

President Woodrow Wilson's League of Nations, the U.S. offering to the international community in 1918. Washington also prepared an elaborate spying scheme in San Francisco to guarantee its control over the conclave and to assure its favorable outcome. Although this latter stratagem was hardly a moral thing, both it and the authorship of the charter demonstrated how determined the U.S. government was to make a reality of its model for world security.

It was also not until I plunged fully into the story, though, that I discovered the pivotal role that Secretary of State Edward Stettinius played in forging the consensus that ultimately prevailed at the U.N. meeting. I learned, in addition, about another unsung American stalwart, Leo Pasvolsky, the behind-the-scenes intellectual powerhouse for global organizations, who proved to be the key player in weaving together the intricate and often conflicting ideas behind the U.N. Charter. His first boss—until he took left in 1943—was also an estimable planner for the United Nations, Undersecretary of State Sumner Welles. Finally, the most extraordinary visionary of them all was President Franklin Roosevelt—followed by his equally heroic vice president, Harry Truman, who helped realize Roosevelt's dream.

What shines through today for Americans in our more cynical age is the unusual intellect and honest idealism of these founding fathers and mothers of the U.N.—particularly, the seven members of the U.S. delegation to San Francisco. These individuals, balancing peace with cold-eyed realism, especially with regard to the veto, erected a formidable structure. There were Democrats, including Senator Tom Connally and Adlai Stevenson, and Republicans, ranging from Senator Arthur Vandenberg, John Foster Dulles, and Nelson Rockefeller to Harold Stassen. Having endured the most calamitous war in human history, this generation extracted from the human propensity for devastation the right lesson for our time—the need for world organization to oversee and guide state craft toward a peaceful future. That these men and women could fashion such a righteous journey in light of the League's collapse, delegates' squabbles, and a war itself, was remarkable.

An additional intriguing feature of the San Francisco Conference was the role of the U.S. media. Despite abiding sympathy among thousands of the press corps, most correspondents refused to compromise on their reportage. Indeed, the *New York Times* under James Reston served as the official "leak central" during the entire affair. Reston reported in an unvarnished tone on the inevitable tussles, the strains felt by participants, the clashes between delegations, the struggles between Washington and Moscow. Yet he, like the others, seemed to realize that the sum in San Francisco was greater than its separate parts, and could very well determine the destiny of humankind.

There were also many nongovernmental organizations. In unprecedented fashion, civic groups around the nation—in business, in labor, in academia, in social clubs, and among professionals—organized themselves to enlist in the fight for the United Nations. Disparate associations and networks lobbied Congress in the early 1940s for the passage of a global institution and carried forth the mission of "one world" around the public arena. They raised the U.N. banner to U.S. citizens after the conference, and helped wage the successful struggle for ratification.

The pitfalls of San Francisco were manifold, the obstacles forbidding, the ending uncertain. The tale of that Golden Gate city, as you will see in the pages to come, was really one of how an inexperienced but agile U.S. delegation, led by an underrated secretary of state, was able to surmount crisis after crisis over the charter for almost fourteen straight weeks, flex its muscle when necessary, act with a certainty when not being sure of the outcome, persevere toward a creation that would limit the enormous power of the United States, yet strive for the good of peoples everywhere and for our country's security. This is, in the end, the story of thoughtful and courageous representation by the United States, living up to and embodying its country's ideals. Whatever the flaws of the United Nations, it measures up well with the values of that American heritage.

CHAPTER 1

THE TAKEOVER

The president of the United States, Franklin Roosevelt, was seated in his living room on a leather chair near the fireplace at the Little White House in Warms Spring, Georgia. It was a warm sunny morning on April 12, 1945, the air scented by the early spring foliage outside. Roosevelt—unseasonably aging at sixty-three years old, his eyes wearied by many burdens, his face pallid but his mind still sharp—was perusing official papers, including secret reports from General Bill Donovan's Office of Strategic Services (OSS), which were resting on a card table in front of him. Madame Elizabeth Shoumatoff, a Russian-born artist, was drawing his countenance for a watercolor portrait arranged by his long-time friend and occasional companion of three decades, Lucy Mercer Rutherford.

The fires of war were just then starting to abate. The battle of Berlin was nearing its climax. The Ninth Army was making its way across the Elbe River just west of the capital. Russian troops were assembling on the sides of the Oder River preparing for an assault on the German city fifty miles away. In the Pacific, hundreds of B-29 Superfortresses were dropping bombs on Tokyo while U.S. soldiers were in bloody combat to flush out the Japanese in Okinawa—an island agonizingly near the Japanese homeland. And in just thirteen days, the people of San Francisco were preparing to greet delegations from some forty-six nations around the world meeting to establish a global organization to bring an end to all wars.

Mrs. Rutherford sat on a couch near Roosevelt. Two cousins were present—Margaret Suckley, who was knitting, and Laura Delano, who was arranging roses in a vase. Nearby, a house boy from the Philippines was getting lunch ready. It was now one o'clock in the afternoon. Roosevelt told the artist that he could spare only fifteen more minutes. As the time elapsed, the president placed his hand on his temple and uttered, "I have a terrific headache," and he slumped forward, gasping. Breathing heavily, the Filipino youth and Roosevelt's valet, Arthur Prettyman, lifted the president into his bedroom. A U.S. Navy cardiologist named Howard Bruenn, summoned immediately, arrived within a half hour. He promptly injected Roosevelt with amyl nitrate and papaverine. By 3:35 P.M., the president had stopped breathing. The doctor told the small group that Roosevelt was dead.[1]

At this dramatic moment, the vice president of the United States, the sixty-year-old Harry Truman, was presiding over a debate in the Senate about a water treaty with Mexico. It was his eighty-third day in office. Ninety minutes after Roosevelt's collapse, no news of his passing having yet arrived, the Senate adjourned at 5:00 P.M. Washington time. Dressed in a double-breasted gray suit and wearing a polka-dot tie and steel-framed glasses, Truman ambled over to the secret hideaway of House Speaker Sam Rayburn to talk to the congressional leader and others about pending legislation and discuss the world situation generally. This private sanctum on the ground floor of the Capitol, called by insiders the "Board of Education," was the place where the Speaker entertained congressional leaders. On seeing Truman, Lewis Deschler, the House parliamentarian, prompted Rayburn to tell Truman about his need to return a phone call from Roosevelt's White House press secretary, Steve Early. Truman dialed Early. Speaking in an unusually urgent tone, Early said, "Please come right over and come through the main Pennsylvania Avenue entrance and as quietly as you can."

That was a departure from routine. Truman normally entered the White House through the East Executive Avenue entrance, where he could visit Roosevelt unobserved. Truman turned pale. "Jesus Christ and General Jackson," he said to Rayburn. "Boys, this is in the room. Something must have happened." Truman excused himself, telling Rayburn he would be back shortly and asking him not to tell anyone about his trip to the White House. Truman ran through the basement of the

Capitol, losing his Secret Service guards. He instructed his driver to deliver him speedily to the front entrance. He arrived about 5:25 P.M. on a misty, rainy April eve.

Two ushers took him to the elevator to the second floor, where he was brought to Mrs. Roosevelt's study. Colonel John and Mrs. Anna Roosevelt Boettiger and Steve Early, along with the first lady, were present. The mood was deeply sad, the expressions stricken. He knew something terrible had taken place. Mrs. Roosevelt was calm and dignified. She stepped forward and placed her arm gently about Truman's shoulder.

"Harry," she said quietly, "the president is dead."[2]

Truman stared silently ahead in shock. He had had little inkling that Roosevelt, whom he had last seen two weeks ago, just before the president departed for Warm Springs, was so near the end. Nor apparently had his family or his personal physician, none of whom was with the president. Although Roosevelt had not looked robust in recent months, he also had not appeared in mortal decline.

Finally, Truman said, "Is there anything I can do for you?"

Mrs. Roosevelt, loyal to an innate sense of duty that never left her, replied, "Is there anything we can do for you? For you are the one in trouble now."

There was a truth in her statement. In the midst of some of the most searing conflicts and profound strategic troubles ever to affect an American leader, the vice president was a man at this moment without a clear guide. In his twelve-week tenure as Roosevelt's second in command, Truman had remained an outsider. According to appointment records, Truman had seen the president officially only eight times (and a few unreported impromptu meetings) during the year before he died.

Truman had never been inside the Map Room of the White House, where Roosevelt directed the war effort. He did not know of the existence of the atom bomb. He had only hints of Roosevelt's growing problems with the Russians over Poland and other nations. Nor had Roosevelt taken him to the decisive Yalta Conference just two months earlier where, with Josef Stalin and Winston Churchill, the president had decided, among other matters, that their three nations (along with France) would occupy Germany, that Russia would enter the war

against Japan, and, finally, that on April 25 the major powers would in-
augurate the session in San Francisco to establish a global body. As
Truman noted in his diary for April 12, "I knew the president had a
great many meetings with Churchill and Stalin. I was not familiar with
any of these things." Several years later, he told his daughter, Margaret,
that Roosevelt "never did talk to me confidentially about the war, or
about foreign affairs or what he had in mind for peace after the war."[3]

Yet the vice president was also not as naïve a man as some Americans
suspected, nor was he a hack from the Pendergast political machine of
Missouri, which others feared. A self-educated man who never attended college, he had an almost ravenous interest in history. In his
memoirs, he reports that as a boy he indulged in "endless reading of
history," a passion he continued as an adult. "I wanted to know what
caused the successes or the failures of all the famous leaders of history."
He had perused Plutarch's *Lives,* spent time on Abbott's biographies of
famous men, explored accounts of ancient Egypt, the Mesopotamian
civilizations, studied Greece and Rome, ruminated on cultures of the
Orient, read widely about modern nations, and tracked the drama of
America's birth and growth.

Although his teachers at Independence (Missouri) High School, his
highest educational attainment, instructed him in the traditional texts
of Cicero, Caesar, and Marcus Aurelius, they also introduced him to
English and American writers and poets. At the age of fifteen, for example, he wrote a short essay on courage, commencing with a quote
from Ralph Waldo Emerson: "Behavior is the Mirror in which each man
shows his image." He read all of Mark Twain's books, which he freely
quoted throughout his life. His education gave him a solid grounding
in his early years. But his need to earn a living soon eclipsed his academic pursuits; a career in business intervened. When he was thirty-
three, however, and not having enjoyed great success, he quit his commercial work and went to France to fight in the World War I. He rose to
the rank of captain. That extraordinary and trying experience proved
to him that he had leadership abilities.[4]

All this was a part of Truman's intellectual heritage when Edward
Stettinius, the secretary of state, knocked on Mrs. Roosevelt's study

door and entered, his eyes red and swollen. Only in his post for five and one-half months, Stettinius was now the keeper of the Great Seal of the United States and therefore responsible for proclaiming the president's passing. Truman, who barely knew Stettinius, soberly greeted him and then, on the latter's advice, quickly agreed to convene a cabinet meeting after his swearing-in. Truman asked Stettinius to round up the cabinet officials who would attend the emergency session. Meantime, he telephoned his wife and daughter and asked them join him for the ceremonial oath-taking. While officials of the government and congressional leaders arrived at the White House over the next half-hour, Steve Early and other searched for a Bible on which Truman could affirm his allegiance to the Constitution and the nation. Chief Justice Harlan Fiske Stone arrived to administer the swearing-in oath. At 7:09 that evening, surrounded by family and colleagues, Harry Truman was sworn in as president. An official photo was snapped. Then everybody but the cabinet officers left.

As Truman's session with his administration officialdom was just beginning, Steve Early stuck his head in and asked Truman what he should tell the press corps clamoring outside and urgently wanting to know whether the new president was going to postpone the San Francisco Conference. The media's concern had been triggered by a hasty statement just issued by Senator Tom Connally (D-Texas), chairman of the Senate Foreign Relations Committee and one of the leaders of the U.S. delegation to San Francisco, predicting a delay in the meeting. Given the advent of a new and untried leader, the press was apparently growing apprehensive about the fate of the world assembly just days away.

What this interest also revealed, though, was the obvious ignorance among the journalists and correspondents about the new president's views toward the global organization (though it must be said that the beliefs of most vice presidents have always remained ciphers to the media). No one in the journalistic community knew that the new president carried folded in his wallet several stanzas of his favorite poem, "Lockesley Hall" by Alfred, Lord Tennyson, and had done so since he was a young man:

For I dipt into the future, far as human eye could see,
Saw the Vision of the world, and all the wonders that would be;
Saw the heavens fill with commerce, argosies of magic sails,
Pilots of the purple twilight, dropping down with costly bails;
Heard the heavens fill with shouting, and there rained a ghastly dew
From the nations' airy navies grappling in the central blue;
Far along the world-wide whisper of the south-wind rushing warm,
With the standards of the people plunging thro the thunderstorm;
Till the war-drum throbbed no longer, and the battle-flags were furl'd
In the Parliament of Man, the Federation of the World.
There the common sense of most shall hold a fretful realm in awe,
And the kindly earth shall slumber, lapt in universal law.

Tennyson's poem, with its sense of the grandeur of a united human-ity, foreshadowed a signal preoccupation of Truman's career. Truman once described how he had studied the "Grand Design" of King Henry IV of France, who ruled in the sixteenth century. The king's plan had envisaged a sort of federation of sovereign Protestant countries within Europe to prevent them from being swallowed up by the Catholic House of Hapsburg. Truman envisaged the same design as a model for his own era to avert wars. Truman ardently followed all of Woodrow Wilson's writings and speeches on the League of Nations. He was one of many Americans who despaired at the "willful men" in the Senate who eventually sank the League.

As a first-term senator, Truman had in October 1939 called on Roo-sevelt to revise the Neutrality Act of 1936 and allow U.S. arms sales to "our friends" in Europe. Truman was also deeply angered by the isola-tionist arguments made by the America First movement and speeches delivered by Charles Lindbergh. In September 1941, he voted for the first peacetime draft. And at a huge rally in Chicago in April 1943, long before the liberation of the death camps, he urged help for the doomed Jews in Europe.

Throughout much of the war, Truman also chaired the Senate Special Committee to Investigate the National Defense Program (later called the Truman Committee). His probe into excessive cost-plus contracts and other instances of misuse of taxpayer dollars by defense companies resulted in Justice Department inquiries and large-scale savings—$250 million alone on army camp construction. The fame Truman earned from these hearings, as well as Truman's own popularity in the Senate, was what attracted Roosevelt's attention in 1944 when he was looking for a replacement to Henry Wallace as his vice-presidential running-mate in that election year.[5]

As early as March 1943, Truman had also championed a Senate resolution calling on President Roosevelt to endorse a worldwide assembly for peace and security. Throughout that year, indeed, he had tenaciously sought to win a majority of Congress behind this pronouncement. He even went on a bipartisan speaking tour with others from Congress in twenty-six states arranged by long-time advocates for a global body. His stubborn battle stirred up a ruckus because many political observers believed that Truman and his cohorts were forcing the president's hand before he was ready to act.

Roosevelt later asked Vice President Truman to serve as the "go-between" on world organization between the Senate and the White House. Just seven weeks before Roosevelt's death, on February 22, following the Yalta Conference, Truman had spoken in Jefferson City, Missouri, urging his fellow citizens to enlist in the crusade for a global association. He observed: "The policy we hope and believe will emerge from the San Francisco Conference and others to follow will embody cooperation among nations to keep down aggressors." He warned: "The only rational alternative to existing international anarchy lies in some reasonable form of international organization among so-called sovereign states. This is merely an extension of local and national practices to an international plane." And, on a radio broadcast the next day, he said: "America can no longer sit smugly behind a mental Maginot line."[6]

In response to Early's question, therefore, Truman did not hesitate. As the first decision of his presidency, he instructed the press secretary to tell the media that the San Francisco Conference would go forward as planned. As he later wrote in the opening chapters of his memoirs: "I wanted to make it clear that I attached the greatest importance to the establishment of international machinery for the prevention of war and the maintenance of peace. I knew many of the pitfalls and stumbling blocks that we would encounter in setting up such an organization, but I also know that in a world without such machinery we would be forever doomed to the fear of destruction." He concluded: "It was important for us to make a start, no matter how imperfect."

In retrospect, the only thing that might have prevented Truman from approving that starting date was not opposition to the project but inability to deal with the enormous burdens suddenly thrust upon him. As he told the press corps the next day, it was as if "the moon, the stars, and all the planets had fallen on me." With just two weeks to go before San Francisco, he had not only to catch up with five years of decisions made by Roosevelt during the greatest war in human history but also to face immediate questions about how to end the Pacific War, placate restive Soviet allies, overcome the chaotic postwar situation in Europe, exert leadership in Congress, and construct an enduring peace.

Still, he was intensely aware of the public yearning for some sort of international body. The polls had shown it. Since Roosevelt's Yalta meeting, over 80 percent of the American people had expressed a desire for U.S. participation in a world assembly with the power to assure the peace. He knew that invitations had already been sent out by the four convening powers—the United States, Great Britain, China, and the Soviet Union—to some forty-two other nations asking them to meet in the Pacific city on April 25. Countries around the globe were genuinely astir about the event, believing it might finally provide the global legal and military authority that would protect them from future aggression. All were looking intently to the United States, the only nation in the world in 1945 to have its forces still intact and its economy practically untouched, to lead the way.[7]

He was aware, too, that neither Winston Churchill of Great Britain nor Josef Stalin of the Soviet Union was terribly enthusiastic about the venture. Stalin, indeed, had declined even to send his foreign minister, Vyacheslav Molotov, to San Francisco. On more than one occasion, Roosevelt had ruefully acknowledged the resistance of both leaders to the idea. There was also the public controversy over the two extra votes for the Soviet Union in the world organization that Stalin had recently demanded at Yalta. There were hints in the newspapers of potential quarrels at San Francisco over the fate of colonial possessions, the admissibility of rogue nations, the right of the big powers to possess a veto, and sundry other items. Last, the shadow of a failed League of Nations hung heavily over the project. The U.S. Senate might again conceivably reject a role for the United States in a global council.

Nonetheless, hovering over Truman was the great legacy of Franklin Roosevelt. President Roosevelt, the larger-than-life steward of a progressive America, had determinedly steered the idea of a world association through all sorts of political hazards and had fiercely surmounted all kinds of security obstacles in a relentless push for its creation before the war ended and the nations of the world lost interest. And, ultimately, there was also Truman's own deep commitment to such a federation expressed in the Tennyson poem that he had kept in his wallet all these years and reflecting a mind constantly tinkering with how to bring countries together to create peace.

Truman went a step further. Shortly after his brief cabinet meeting, Truman, sitting with his wife and daughter in the Oval Office, invited Stettinius, Steve Early, and his own press secretary, Jonathan Daniels, to stay for a moment. He asked them what he could further do regarding the United Nations situation, for he was still anxious that he had not said enough. All three urged him to issue a formal statement reassuring the U.S. allies on the San Francisco meeting. Truman immediately authorized Stettinius, whom Roosevelt had several months earlier designated to lead the U.S. delegation to San Francisco, to make a public declaration on his behalf. As Truman later wrote, "I wanted to scotch any rumors or fears . . . that there would be any changes in the plans that had been made." Stettinius was impressed: Truman seemed to him "a simple sincere person, bewildered, but who is going to do everything in his power to meet this emergency." He sensed "no feeling of weakness whatever." He immediately notified the press about Truman's firm commitment to San Francisco.[8]

The next morning, Friday, April 13, the day after Roosevelt's death, Truman reaffirmed yet again his support for the United Nations meeting. Truman had another meeting—this one lasting forty-five minutes—

with Secretary of State Stettinius, to go over the world matters of the day. Truman, preoccupied by the upcoming conference, instructed Stettinius to issue still another pronouncement to reassure global allies that there would not be any change from his predecessor's foreign policy and to reemphasize his intention to press forward "toward the establishment of a world organization endowed with strength to keep the peace for generations and to give security and wider opportunity to all men." But hemmed in by immediate problems in Washington, Truman also told Stettinius that he had decided himself not to go to San Francisco, as President Roosevelt had planned to do, believing instead that Stettinius could "conduct the meeting with great success." Truman said he planned to address the opening by radio.

Once they had discussed those issues, Stettinius brought up other questions that would likely affect the conference, including America's deteriorating relationship with the Soviet Union since Yalta. He blamed the darkening skies on Stalin's "political problems" in his own country. Truman responded, according to Stettinius, by suggesting that it was high time to "stand up to the Russians," implying perhaps that Washington had been too easy with them. Charles Bohlen, the State Department's expert on Russia, who joined in the discussion, described in detail the Russian attempt to set up its own provisional Communist-dominated regime in Poland, which effectively elbowed aside both the Polish government in exile in London and the Big Powers agreement in Yalta for coalition rule. Bothered by his limited knowledge on these matters, Truman asked Stettinius for several memoranda summarizing all the diplomatic questions he would have to face in the coming weeks, including the Polish and San Francisco matters, and he urged Stettinius to bring them back to him by the end of that day.[9]

Truman sandwiched in a quick meeting with his military leaders, who warned him that the war in Europe could drag on for another six months and the one in the Pacific by another eighteen months (they would be proved wrong on both counts), and at noon traveled to Capitol Hill for a luncheon with congressional leaders to inform them of his decision to address Congress on Monday, April 16, following Roosevelt's weekend funeral. There, one of the leading Senate Republicans on international affairs, Senator Arthur Vandenberg of Michigan, also one of the members of the U.S. delegation, "heartily applauded" Truman's decision to proceed with the San Francisco Conference.

After the Hill visit, Truman, back at the White House, saw James Byrnes, the former Supreme Court justice and U.S. senator, who had aspired to be Roosevelt's running mate in 1944. Truman had admired for Byrnes for years, having known him in his Senate days, during his high court service, and while he headed war mobilization in Roosevelt's administration. The two spent much of their time ranging over Roosevelt's foreign policy meetings during the war. Fearful that he did not fully comprehend the record of what had happened at Yalta, Truman asked Byrnes to give him a memorandum about what the Yalta Conference had decided. Byrnes, who had gone to Yalta at Roosevelt's urging, took ten days to complete the memo, to Truman's later chagrin.

More important, Truman told Byrnes that he was now reorganizing the entire foreign policy team and wanted to name him secretary of state after the San Francisco Conference. Truman was concerned that the secretary of state was the next person in line for the presidency after the vice president—and Truman wanted an elected official in that position. Besides, Truman privately felt guilty about Byrnes's failure to obtain the vice presidency and wanted to "balance things up." Byrnes was eager for the job. Margaret Truman later called the Byrnes selection the "first miscalculation" of Truman's presidency, for Byrnes had scant regard for Truman's abilities and high regard for his own. In any event, soon after the session, Byrnes or Truman or somebody in the know leaked the story of Byrnes's imminent designation, and for days afterward, rumors swept Washington that Secretary of State Stettinius's days were numbered. The speculation clouded Stettinius's performance in San Francisco.[10]

Shortly after Byrnes's departure, around 3:30 P.M., Stettinius returned to the White House, accompanied by Charles Bohlen, bearing several memos he had promised Truman. First, he conveyed an important message to the new president from the American ambassador to the USSR, Averell Harriman, stating that Josef Stalin, shaken by Roosevelt's death, had now agreed to dispatch Soviet Foreign Minister Molotov to Washington and thence to the San Francisco Conference as a gesture of friendship to the new leader. Harriman, a formidable emissary from a wealthy New York family, had aggressively seized the occasion of Roosevelt's sudden passing to urge Stalin to reverse his original decision canceling Molotov's presence at the conference. Stalin now agreed on the Molotov trip, but he wanted Truman's approval for the request. Truman gave Stettinius the go-ahead.

Stettinius moved on to explore the Polish crisis further with Truman. From his brief reading of the secret correspondence between Stalin, Churchill, and Roosevelt, and close attention to Bohlen's presentation, Truman had begun to educate himself on the Polish imbroglio. He now understood that the Soviets had established a Communist regime in Lublin and were refusing to include democratic Poles in exile in London or in the Polish underground; this was in spite of an agreement at Yalta between Roosevelt, Stalin, and Churchill that the so-called Lublin regime should be broadened into a coalition encompassing the differing factions of the Polish political scene and would thereafter hold elections on the basis of universal suffrage and the secret ballot. The impasse was threatening to turn a simmering diplomatic conflict into a potential civil war.

Churchill that day was urging Truman to sign a joint statement opposing the Soviets on the matter. Truman, however, told Stettinius that he opposed a public statement, apprehensive that it might hurt military collaboration with the Russians. Instead, he told Stettinius, he wanted to persuade Churchill to send a joint private telegram to Stalin. With Stettinius acting as intermediary, both leaders soon began working on a text asking that three Poles from London and four from Warsaw be invited to Moscow to establish a formula for a government of national unity. There was yet another disquietude in the offing, though, when Stettinius raised with Truman the fact that the Russians were hinting they were going to insist the Lublin government be represented at the San Francisco Conference without prior settlement of the dispute. That posture could potentially snarl the U.N. meeting.

On departing, Stettinius left behind his two memoranda for Truman. The first was a tour d'horizon of America's global agenda in the spring of 1945. Besides the expected military issues, Stettinius dwelled at length on his worries that, since the Yalta Conference, "the Soviet

Government has taken a firm and uncompromising position on nearly every major question that has arisen in our relations." He listed prominently the Polish matter and its relation to the San Francisco Conference, and also noted that the Soviets were not permitting democratic elections in Hungary, Romania, and Bulgaria.

Stettinius' second memo outlined in greater detail some of the key points relating to the U.N. Conference, now twelve days away. He indicated that there would be a few changes in the recommendations of the 1944 Dumbarton Oaks Conference held by the United States, Great Britain, Russia, and later China, which produced the framework proposal for the United Nations Charter. Senator Vandenberg, for example, wanted to add certain references to justice and international law in the charter. Stettinius advised Truman, though, that alterations would be minimal and that the seven-person U.S. delegation would forward them to the president before they departed for San Francisco.

Stettinius's memo went on to remind Truman of other potentially awkward, if not truly grave, disagreements still facing the organizers of the conference. In one of the more serious disputes, the Soviet Union was trying to change the president of the conference. The Russians were insisting that the four sponsoring governments (China, the United States, Great Britain, and the USSR) rotate as the conference head. Washington, as the host nation, argued that it alone should assume the presidency; the other big powers would serve as vice presidents. The Russians were demanding also that the United States must agree, by the lights of the Yalta Conference, that two additional Soviet republics— White Russia (now known as Belarus), and Ukraine, which Roosevelt had reluctantly agreed were extra votes for the USSR—be represented at the conference. The United States was adamant that it was up to the conference itself to decide that issue, not the Big Three. Last, on the issue of conquered territories, Stettinius pointed out that, at Yalta, Roosevelt had also agreed to setting up "machinery" to control trusteeships of lands without naming specific areas, but that the U.S. military now wanted to retract or amend this agreement.[11]

On Saturday morning, April 14, Truman rose at dawn to prepare for Roosevelt's funeral ceremony. In that morning's *New York Times,* James

Reston, who had won the Pulitzer Prize a year earlier for breaking the tale of the then-secret Dumbarton Oaks proposals in 1944, produced a story stating that, in his view, six major problems still faced the San Francisco Conference. Reston included the quarrels over Poland and the two extra votes for the Soviet Union, the questions relating to trusteeship as well as the veto powers of the Big Four, the right of regional organizations to have a role in the United Nations, and the allocation of six nonpermanent seats on the Security Council. His story, together with the Stettinius memo and some other news accounts, indicated that contentious issues were already starting to undermine the U.S. government's strategy at San Francisco and might threaten the meeting's eventual success.

Truman met the train bearing Roosevelt's body at Union Station and accompanied the hearse in a long, slow, tearful procession down Pennsylvania Avenue to the White House, where the body lay in state in the East Room for the entire day. Shortly afterward, Truman asked Harry Hopkins, Roosevelt's closest aide, who had left a sickbed in the Mayo Clinic in Rochester, Minnesota, to attend the funeral, to meet with him around lunchtime in the Oval Office. As Truman noted in his memoirs, "I wanted to go over the whole situation with Hopkins in regard to Russia and Poland and the United Nations." They conversed for two hours, Hopkins giving Truman the details of agreements reached at various Roosevelt encounters over the past five years.

That night Truman and his family took the overnight train that carried Roosevelt's body to Hyde Park, New York. After the Sunday morning service and burial, Truman took the train back to Washington. He spent much of his time on the return trip working on his speech to Congress. Members of the Roosevelt administration and legislative leaders on the train contributed to the address. To still public doubts about his commitment, Truman paid a great deal of attention to the phrasing he would use to express his strong backing for the San Francisco meeting.

On Monday, April 16, 1945, Truman spent a busy morning in the White House before leaving for Congress to give his speech at 1:00 P.M. On his arrival at 8:00 A.M., he saw Secretary of State Stettinius yet again. Stettinius handed him the summary of another telegram from

Ambassador Harriman analyzing the latest on the Polish problem. Harriman accused Stalin of contributing "little of a concrete nature toward a solution" and he argued strenuously that the U.S. government should not accept a "whitewash of the Warsaw regime" set up by the Soviets. He said the Soviets knew their puppet regime had little support among the Polish people.

Next, Truman met with Anthony Eden, the British foreign secretary, and Lord Halifax, the British ambassador to the United States. They discussed a final text of the joint communication that he and Churchill were going to send to Stalin concerning Poland. The message stated that it was time to "correct the completely erroneous impression" that the Western Allies wished to exclude the Lublin regime from a coalition government. The two leaders emphasized that all they opposed was the power of the Soviet-supported Polish government to veto individual representatives of the exiled Poles for the unity cabinet. The letter provided the names of a handful of free Poles that the two Western governments recommended be chosen for consultative talks in Moscow.[12]

At midday, Truman arrived in the House chamber to sustained applause by members of both parties. He was introduced to renewed cheers and clapping. Dressed in a dark suit with a black tie, a white handkerchief tucked into his suit pocket, Truman read his speech from a large black loose-leaf notebook. Truman made a central appeal to all Americans "regardless of party, race, creed or color, to support our efforts to build a strong and lasting United Nations organization." He spoke proudly of how, within an hour of his taking office, he had ordered that the San Francisco meeting proceed.

He reminded his listeners that "the task of creating a sound international organization is complicated and difficult. Yet, without such an organization, the rights of men on earth cannot be protected. Machinery for the just settlement of international differences must be found. Without such machinery, the entire world will have to remain an armed camp." He concluded by saying that although the Big States "have a special responsibility to enforce the peace, their responsibility is based upon the obligations resting upon all states, large and small, not to use

force in international relations except in the defense of law. The responsibility of the Great States is to serve and not dominate the world."
Applauded loudly in his peroration, Truman stood for a moment with
his hands in his pockets, obviously moved. He quickly recovered, nodded, smiled, and left the chamber.

As Truman's speech ended, Moscow Radio reported that the Soviet
government was now insisting that the admission of the Polish Provisional regime to the conference was a condition for the Soviet Union's
attendance. The Polish government in exile in London, in its turn,
raised the question whether democratic Poles who had gone to Warsaw
a month earlier were now missing. The difficulties of Poland were now
growing, not receding, exacerbating the already unpleasant atmosphere cited in Stettinius's memo to Truman and Reston's article about
the U.N. Truman's forceful attempt to recall Roosevelt's vision in Congress amounted to using his Missouri grit to vault over all obstacles to
the creation of this world assembly.[13]

Truman still faced enormous challenges as an untried leader, cut off
from major geopolitical policy decisions by President Roosevelt and
barely acquainted with FDR's foreign policy team. He had never managed a worldwide conference—much less one that was 3,000 miles away.
Though he had long studied the idea of international organizations, he
did not know yet all the nuances and tricky interpretative problems associated with the U.N. Charter. He hadn't even traveled to Europe since
his service in World War I. There were only ten days to go before the
San Francisco meeting, and he was trying to settle the wars on the continent and in the Pacific, reach out to the Allies, master pressing domestic legislation, meet with congressional leaders, and address the American people—all in less than a hundred hours. And now he, as president,
had also inherited his predecessor's most formidable problem, one
deeply embedded in the global psyche: a historic resistance by the nations of the earth to joining any world-wide organization that might
tread on their sovereignty—a resistance that had surfaced just twenty-
five years earlier in its most virulent form in America.

CHAPTER 2

THE LEAGUE FOLLIES
Wilson and Roosevelt

From its inception, the United States has always prided itself on its geographical distance from the conflicts and corruption of Europe and of Asia. Separated by two vast oceans from the Old World and the Orient, successive American leaders treated their unique territorial status as an ideological imperative, namely, avoiding involvement of any sort with foreign powers, except in the event of a direct threat to national survival. George Washington admonished his countrymen to "steer clear of permanent alliances," and Thomas Jefferson warned them against "entangling alliances." This doctrine was not all-encompassing: U.S. merchant ships still plied the seven seas; our culture imbibed freely of influences from abroad. But the tradition of apartness became an abiding measure of the country's birthright.

The desire to maintain the purity of national sovereignty was, for the most part, a trait shared with the rest of the world. Though states had from time immemorial forged partnerships with one another, as recorded in the written accounts of the Chinese Bamboo Annals almost a thousand years before Christ, by Greek historians such as Thucydides writing on the Peloponnesian Wars, and in biblical tales, they had only fitfully moved toward larger confederations. When the Peace of Westphalia was signed in 1648, the modern state system came into being. Westphalia brought an end to the Thirty Years' War, a religious battle between Catholicism and Protestantism and the most savage struggle in European history until then, in which an estimated 10 million people may have died. The pact represented an entirely new kind of diplomatic agreement and helped to make possible peaceful relations on a regional scale. It was the model for emerging global organizations.

In 1795, nearly 150 years later, the philosopher Immanuel Kant wrote *Toward Perpetual Peace,* an essay that set forth more broadly the intellectual reasoning for global federations. His treatise analyzed the ethical and moral basis for a broad union of free states cooperating to maintain peace. Kant contended that humanity would best be served by a republican form of government because the state would not depend on a hereditary monarchy or aristocracy that grabbed domains by royal fiat and pitted proprietary privilege against public right. On an international level, Kant argued, representative governments working together through a world federation could conceivably banish conflict forever.

Bolstered by the Kantian logic (though without its democratic moorings), Europe in the nineteenth century reformulated the Westphalia archetype. In response to the devastation created by the Napoleonic Wars, the major lands of Europe held four conferences between 1815 and 1822, beginning with the Congress of Vienna. Through the rest of the century, the chieftains of Europe's leading states, referred to as the Concert of Europe, gathered an additional thirty times to discuss urgent political issues. By the twentieth century, the idea of a worldwide assemblage had taken hold. Nations from around the globe, including the United States, met twice in so-called international peace conferences in the Hague. The first, held in 1899 with twenty-six countries, established the Permanent Court of International Arbitration; the second, in 1907 with forty-four nations, including most states of Latin America, adopted the Drago Doctrine, which held that European nations should not use force to collect debts owed by Latin American countries.

The advent of the World War I broke down the Concert of Europe and irrevocably shattered the balance of power in Europe that had protected the United States and the Hemisphere for over a century from threats from abroad. The collapse of the Concert redefined the nature of national sovereignty and noninvolvement for all countries—especially the United States. Now, for the first time, the United States, which had tried with increasing difficulty to maintain a semblance of neutrality toward the European conflict, grew more and more concerned that the intensifying war would directly imperil its interests. It was possible that a single power could seize the continent and invade the United States—or, at the very least, gravely jeopardize its commercial relations with the states of Europe.

Under President Woodrow Wilson, the United States revised its thinking and, in April 1917, came to the conclusion that it must abandon neutrality and intervene overseas to save its own democracy. Wilson reached this position despite winning reelection to the presidency in 1916 on the slogan, "He kept us out of war." He justified his change of mind as a response to the German government's resumption of unrestricted submarine warfare against U.S. vessels and, further, as a consequence of learning through British intercepts that Germany was plotting to incite Mexico and Japan to rise against the United States. The European war was about to entangle the United States.

Wilson now propounded a doctrine that, deliberately or not, replaced the Founding Fathers' credo of independence with a new credo of interdependence. Confronting doubts within his own nation—for there was no groundswell for such a radical departure from hoary tradition—he began to speak about a global role for the United States. Indeed, within a year or so, he could send a message to a convention of teachers stating that the United States was now going to be the "chief interpreter to the world of those democratic principles, which can rid the world of injustice and bring peace and happiness."[1] He was ineluctably starting an educational process to convince his own countrymen of the importance of global organization—a task that was eventually to take him and Democratic successors a quarter of a century to complete.

As early as May 1916, President Wilson offered for the first time his vision of the country's international mission—namely the founding of a league of nations to secure peace for the world. The next year, he dispatched U.S. soldiers to France. And in January 1918, Wilson enshrined his concept of the League as part of his celebrated Fourteen Points peace proposal to the Germans. Much of his plan was based on studies prepared by a secret group set up by his closest advisor, Colonel Edward House; called "The Inquiry," the crew consisted of geographers, historians, political scientists, and other specialists on Europe (one of those members was Walter Lippmann, the soon-to-be-famous journalist.) Six of Wilson's points related to the general principles of diplomacy, including an important pledge to keep open agreements openly arrived at, to safeguard the freedom of the seas, and to seek a fair settlement of colonial claims. Eight points pertained to the notion of national self-determination. The final point called for forming "a general assembly of nations" to afford "mutual guarantees of political independence and territorial integrity"—the future League of Nations.

As the year 1918 wound down, Wilson, preparing for peace talks, asked the American people for a broad endorsement of his policies in the midterm congressional elections. He made a partisan assault, irritating Republicans already disenchanted with Wilson's increasingly high-handed moral dictates, and they won both houses of Congress. The new Senate had the power to defeat any peace treaty. As he was headed into the January 1919 peace parley in France, Wilson arrived with a weakened hand and confronted ever more skeptical European partners.

Wilson compounded his woes at home by failing to appoint an influential Republican to his five-member peace delegation. His token Republican was a congenial career diplomat named Henry White, but White was hardly a figure of political stature. Wilson also ignored members of Congress and women. His other judgments, although controversial, were at least understandable. He decided to attend the conclave himself as the leader of the U.S. delegation. In some eyes, that move reduced him from being a supreme arbiter above the fray to that of mere negotiator, but, in practice, he proved to be an able and effective bargainer. He was also determined to tie the League to the fate of the peace treaty, which meant that he risked involving the world organization with potentially poisonous disputes over the division of spoils among the victors as well as other narrowly nationalistic preoccupations. Yet it seems unlikely that he could have been able to negotiate the two accords separately. Most of the Allies cared only about a peace pact and might not have attended a summit for the League.

Wilson was greeted by rapturous crowds from the moment he alighted in Brest on December 13, 1918. During his first appearance at the Versailles Conference the following month, Wilson, with an enthusiasm brightened by his reception, pressed for the creation of the League. The organization, as he envisaged it, would be an assemblage of states, each having a vote and a veto. A Body of Delegates would provide every signatory a seat; there would also be a smaller nine-member Executive Council with the authority to decide issues of peace and security. The latter group would consist of five permanent states, the United States, the British Empire, France, Italy, and Japan, and four nations selected by the Body of Delegates. Because a single dissent could block any action in any of the League's forums, every country would wield a weapon. The treaty also set up a secretariat as well as an international Bureau of Labor and a mandate system to oversee seized enemy territories.

The primary goal of the League, in Wilson's eyes, was to maintain the peace. To achieve that aim, the concordat obliged countries, before they resorted to war, to submit disputes either to inquiry by the Executive Council or to arbitration by the Permanent Court of International Justice, which the council was to create. If a member resorted to war in disregard of the charter, the aggression would be deemed an act of war against the League's entire roster. In such eventualities, members agreed to penalize outlaw states by cutting off economic ties. The council could also recommend that League members contribute military and naval units to uphold the organization's provisions. It was the council's duty to provide advice on the means by which to ensure that member nations lived up to Article 10, the central feature of the League's charter in Wilson's view. This clause bound nations "to respect and preserve against external aggression the territorial integrity and existing political independence of all members of the League."

Wilson wanted the Versailles participants to break with all past precedents of noninvolvement or dependence on bilateral treaties by relying solely on the League. Although not creating a world government, they would be fashioning a lasting global body to deter war and provide a forum for states to discuss solutions to potential conflicts. But, even under Wilson's formula, the League could still merely "recommend," not compel, military intervention; indeed, the authority possessed by member states, especially the veto, might be used to perpetuate the status quo rather than change it. Nonetheless, the League was, in Wilson's words, "a living thing," capable of being remolded, chiseled, expanded, and reformulated, as the years went on.

The charter for Wilson's League was heavily influenced by one of the British representatives, Jan Smuts of South Africa. Smuts, a hero of the Boer War, had contributed one of the original drafts for the League from which Wilson had borrowed substantially. Smuts's version included the concept of a permanent secretariat, a small executive council and a larger deliberative body, a system of mandates to handle territorial war booty, and provisions for labor and minority rights. On February 14, 1919, after the Versailles committee had vetted the charter, Wilson presented the League report to the Plenary Session. He contended that the organization would be chiefly dependent on "the moral force of the public opinion of the world"—though he reminded the delegates that it would also have the capacity to use force after the processes of discussion, arbitration, and economic boycott had been exhausted. The reaction of the leaders at Versailles was promising, suggesting that at least publicly they were willing to back the League.[2]

During a quick trip home in February 1919, Woodrow Wilson began to encounter the first signs of domestic opposition to the League. On the Senate floor, on February 28, Republican Senator Henry Cabot Lodge launched a harsh attack, calling the treaty incompatible with the sovereignty of the United States, the Monroe Doctrine, and the traditional policy of nonentanglement. Wilson took Lodge's criticisms and those of several other senators into account. When he returned to Versailles the following month for the second phase of the peace talks, he negotiated three more amendments: every nation would have the right to withdraw from the League if it wished; domestic issues would be exempted from the League's jurisdiction; and the inviolability of the Monroe Doctrine would be preserved.[3]

By the time Wilson returned to the states to start his final fight for the treaty, he seemed to be in a position of potential strength. Fully thirty-five Republicans (out of forty-nine party members) were now willing to cast their votes for the accord, but with some modest reservations—such as allowing Congress (1) to judge whether the United States should accept a territorial mandate; and (2) to decide whether the United States should withdraw from the League. Only fourteen Republicans, the so-called irreconcilables, adamantly opposed the accord except with more rigid reservations. Allied with the moderate Republican group, Wilson might have quickly forged a coalition with a majority of the other forty-seven Democrats and, with a few minimal modifications, ratified the treaty by the two-thirds Senate majority required by the U.S. Constitution. But Woodrow Wilson, his temper aroused by the incessant derogation by his foes, was now increasingly distrustful of the opposition—any opposition—especially that emanating from Senator Lodge and his allies.

Consequently, Wilson barely consulted with the Senate. He stubbornly refused to consider all but a few of the reservations put forward by leading Republican senators; most of the others he viewed essentially as "amendments" that would have required him to renegotiate the accord (though the British, the French, and the State Department did not think this was necessarily true). In the end, he regarded the entire exercise as a personal assault on himself; in addition, he failed to reach out to civic groups and professional organizations that might have rallied public opinion to his side.[4]

Wilson was exceptionally upset by one reservation in particular— Senator Lodge's opposition to Article 10, the obligation of member nations to come to the aid of other states against external aggression. Actually, an increasing number of senators were coming to believe the article conflicted with Congress's constitutional authority to declare war. Article 10 meant, or seemed to mean to these concerned Senators, that U.S. soldiers might be sent into combat not just in defense of the United States but in defense of a generalized world order. The League, in short, could be dispatching Americans at some time in the future to die for what most countrymen might see as an abstraction when the country was neither in peril nor was its national interest engaged. This assumption, though, belied the fact that the United States had the right to veto any League action it opposed at any time.

Nonetheless, Lodge inserted a reservation stating flatly that the United States would assume no duty to preserve the territorial integrity or political independence of any other country without the approval of Congress. This requirement already happened to be true under the Constitution. But Lodge apparently feared that any moral obligation as outlined by Article 10 could be so compelling that, willy-nilly, it would automatically bring on U.S. involvement. Wilson, on the other hand, regarded that specific qualification to be what it said it was—a "moral" responsibility to protect the peace, but one that was not legally binding. He perceived it to be the essential spirit of the League and thought that Lodge's unyielding opposition violated the life-force of the agreement.[5]

The troubles Wilson faced over Article 10 now coalesced not simply on the right, but also on the left. Walter Lippmann, for example, brusquely turned against the treaty over Article 10 and suddenly resigned from the Wilson camp to become an editor of the *New Republic.* Lippmann contended, as soon more and more liberals would, that the article, by consecrating the territorial sanctity of member states, solidified a basically unjust status quo and prevented real change. He railed against ratification every week in the *New Republic,* and even joined cause on occasion with the oppositionist isolationists in the Senate. Then in October 1919, John Maynard Keynes published *Economic Consequences of the Peace;* the book asserted that the Versailles agreement would subject Germany to complete and utter economic devastation and painted Wilson not as an idealist but as a duplicitous and sometimes fumbling statesman. The attack added to the growing sense of dismay in the Wilson ranks.[6]

Wilson's base of support was eroding. Suddenly, on September 26, 1919, during a speaking tour of the West, his health broke and he suffered a nervous collapse. A stroke further crippled him on October 2, paralyzing his left side. He was not able to meet with his cabinet for the next six months. These catastrophic events precipitously diminished his ability to influence public opinion and impaired his capacity to consider in any levelheaded way accommodations with his opponents. Instead, Wilson hardened his posture. Thus, on the climatic day of the vote, November 19, 1919, the Senate Democrats, on his direct instructions, blocked a Lodge-backed version of the League; and then that same day, the Republicans, in turn, killed an unamended version of the treaty introduced by the Democrats. Those votes sounded the death knell for Wilson's global organization. In retrospect, many observers— even many within Wilson's own ranks—felt that accepting Lodge's qualifications might have been less damaging than killing it off altogether. But Wilson remained obdurate to the end, even though he said of the League's demise, "I can predict with absolute certainty that within another generation there will be another world war."[7]

The Democrats and their candidate, James Cox, tried to resurrect the League as an issue in the 1920 presidential race against Warren Harding. One of the main speakers in favor of it was the young vice-presidential nominee, Franklin Roosevelt. Shortly after his designation at the Democratic Convention in San Francisco, Roosevelt told a press conference that he regarded the League as "the dominant issue of the campaign." And in the hundreds of speeches he delivered during the campaign, the majority were on behalf of the League. Roosevelt's approach was to shed some of Wilson's glittering idealism to make a more gritty argument for the League as a "practical necessity." He even suggested that he would be open to amendments. And at various points along the campaign trail, he warned audiences that if the United States did not enlist in the League, the body "would degenerate into a new Holy Alliance" dominated by Europe. But nothing changed.[8]

In the end, whether U.S. membership would have made any difference in the League remains a speculative question. The League officially came into being in January 1920, in Geneva, Switzerland. Around that time began a long retreat from world affairs by three successive U.S. administrations in the 1920s. Washington was not likely to have been an especially active partner in the enterprise anyway. And the League itself was premised on such shaky constitutional grounds that U.S. membership may have been even less than a force. On security matters, though, the League actually had some early successes, although only as long as its decisions were resolutions, not troop deployments. When Finland and Sweden had a border dispute, for example, the League successfully resolved the disagreement. It persuaded Greek and Yugoslav forces not to invade the new country of Albania. It also convinced Greece to withdraw its forces from Bulgaria in 1925 and pay Sofia compensation for an incident. It settled a frontier conflict between Turkey and Iraq over Mosul. And in 1934, it actually dispatched a tiny peacekeeping force to hold onto a buffer zone between Colombia and Peru.[9]

But the League proved itself incapable of handling any cases that required serious military action. The first crisis it faced that might have necessitated armed response was in 1931, when Japan invaded Manchuria. China called for immediate help from the League. Japan, a permanent member of the Executive Council, vetoed a resolution for a League police role, demonstrating how easily a single member could smother the League's minimal enforcement powers. Then, in 1932, a League Commission of Inquiry named Japan the aggressor in Manchuria and demanded that Japan withdraw its forces. In an expression of contempt, Japan quit the League in 1933 and kept its troops in China. Germany, which had joined the League in 1926, resigned from it in 1933 under its new chancellor, Adolf Hitler. Three years later, it reoccupied the Rhineland in a clear violation of the Versailles Treaty, brushing aside protests from the League. Over the next few years, it annexed Austria and Czechoslovakia, showing no concern for the League's views.

In 1935, the dictator of Italy, Benito Mussolini, invaded Ethiopia, a fellow League member. In an unusual gesture of collective anger, the League agreed to impose economic sanctions on Italy. The measures included, first, a halt to all exports of arms and war material (though not oil); second, a refusal of credit to the Italian government and companies; and third, an end to all imports from Italy. But Germany and Japan, among other nations, did not adhere to the embargo. The United States, not a League member, attempted to impose its own independent arms embargo within the boundaries of its 1935 Neutrality Act that prohibited the sale abroad of any U.S. weapons. But the act made no distinction between victim and aggressor, so while it could bar shipments to Italy, it could not permit them to Ethiopia either. Washington, nonetheless, tried to initiate a "moral embargo" on other exports like oil. But eventually, by mid-1936, once Italy had consolidated its hold over Ethiopia, the

League dropped all of its prohibitions on trade with the fascist regime. And the United States gave up. Soon after Italy quit the organization.

Meantime, the League issued pronouncements denouncing the involvement of foreign armies in the next European showdown, the Spanish Civil War, but showed no ability to do anything. And in the winter of 1940 just as World War II was beginning, the Soviet Union, which had joined the League in 1934 out of alarm over the rising Nazi and Japanese threats, suddenly seized the territory of a fellow League member, Finland. This led to one of the few punitive acts by the League toward one of its own. In December, 1940, it expelled Russia for violating the ban on aggression against a League compatriot. This extraordinary blow by an essentially ineffectual body was the last dying gesture of the League. It left an enduring scar on Russia's leader, Josef Stalin.

The signal weakness of the League was that it could, at most, under article 16, impose an absolute obligation on member states—namely, to sever economic and communications ties to nations that had gone to war in defiance of the League's covenant. If such embargoes failed, then the council could do little else except, at best, "recommend" to governments the use of military, naval, or air forces. Article 10, on which the League foundered in the United States, proved ineffectual because it rested on a "moral" duty that few states felt any obligation to heed. Because countries were not willing to place their troops at risk in battles that did not relate directly to their national interests, they refused to get involved.

The other primary weakness of the League was its inability to extend its range beyond security matters. As League observers were increasingly wont to point out, many nations were plunging into wars for economic reasons. To the extent that a world organization could help ease financial and social woes, war might begin to vanish. The League did take a few steps toward dealing with labor issues through the International Labor Organization, by working to control epidemics, by endeavoring to limit slavery and narcotics—but these were all on a small scale. The League never mounted serious foreign aid programs. The one innovation that lasted was the so-called mandate system whereby territories of Germany and Turkey, the defeated powers in World War I, were given to victorious states under League oversight. While its role was supervisory, the League did establish the principle of accountability for nations holding such possessions.[10]

Even as the League floundered, the United States sank deeper into isolationalism. Franklin Roosevelt was now president—but his commitment to the League had withered since his 1920 campaign. In 1932, while running for the first time for the presidency, Roosevelt, subject to intense pressure from publisher William Randolph Hearst, publicly repudiated the League in exchange for Hearst's influential backing. Ultimately, Roosevelt gave a speech to the New York State Grange in February 1932 in which he stated that the League had often been "a mere meeting place for the political discussion of strictly European political national difficulties. In these the United States should have no part." He concluded: "American participation in the League would not serve the highest purpose of the prevention of war and a settlement of international difficulties in accordance with fundamental American ideals." Therefore, he did "not favor American participation." That year the Democratic Party platform, too, for the first time did not urge membership in the League.[11]

After his election, Roosevelt did not totally forswear internationalism. He continued to mention the League, albeit with some diffidence and ambivalence. In December 1933, he told guests at a Woodrow Wilson Foundation dinner that President Wilson should be commended for his efforts on behalf of peace and said the League of Nations was a "prop in the world peace structure" that "must remain." The United States was not a member, he said, and did not "contemplate membership," but nonetheless was "giving cooperation to the League in every matter which is not primarily political and in every matter which obviously represents the views and the good of the peoples of the world as distinguished from the views and the good of political leaders, of privileged classes and of imperialistic aims."[12]

In the spring of 1933, Roosevelt even directed the U.S. emissary in Geneva to assert that, if a global accord could bring about a substantial reduction in armaments, the United States was ready to consult with other nations in the event of a threat to peace. Eventually, the Senate suggested that Roosevelt might be dropping U.S. commitment to neutrality in favor of collective security and passed a restrictive amendment that nullified his pledge. Isolationist attitudes were so deeply embedded in the fabric of discourse that, just two years later, the Senate even refused Roosevelt's recommendation that the United States join the World Court. As Roosevelt wrote to Elihu Root, who had advanced the idea of a global court at the Hague a generation before, "Today, quite frankly, the wind blows against us." Preoccupied by the Depression, Roosevelt did not seek the votes to challenge the prevailing Senate sentiment.[13]

Roosevelt was nonetheless too much of a sophisticate with a world view to abandon deeply held convictions. He had made thirteen visits to Europe and spent almost three years of his life there. His experience as Wilson's assistant secretary of the navy had early in his life helped him forge a strategic vision of the globe. He had stacked his own State Department and embassies abroad with passionate Wilsonians: Secretary of State Cordell Hull, Undersecretary of State Sumner Welles, Ambassador Joseph Davies, and others; isolationists such as Raymond Moley did not last long at the State Department.[14]

In 1937, after Japanese forces ruthlessly marched into China and pillaged Nanking and other cities, Roosevelt spoke out again about the obligations of nations to act together to preserve democracy. In October, he urged the "decent" members of the global community to "quarantine" predatory nations. His words were aimed also at forestalling a quickening European debacle. But the country was not ready for a broader assumption of responsibility. The address had the curious countervailing impact of provoking a new wave of isolationism, as Undersecretary of State Sumner Welles later noted, undermining any possibility of even a limited interventionist policy. Nonetheless, the disputes of faraway lands could not be avoided much longer.[15]

Outspoken intellectuals and religious leaders warned about the growing forces of aggression overseas and the need to restrain them. Clark Eichelberger was the hard-driving executive director of the League of Nations Association, a lobbying group set up to keep Wilson's dream of a global organization alive. Over the years from 1936 until late 1944, Eichelberger periodically visited Roosevelt at the White House to press for a global organization. He now put together a Committee to Defend America by Aiding the Allies to start an effort to repeal the Neutrality Act. James T. Shotwell, a Columbia professor and one of the leaders in the fight for the League of Nations, actually quit the League Association because he believed it was no longer able to act with sufficient authority. Shotwall formed the Commission to Study the Organization of Peace and enlisted leaders in politics, academia, and journalism, among them Republican John Foster Dulles, Virginia Gildersleeve, Owen Lattimore, Max Lerner, and William Allen White. In January 1940, the group inaugurated fifteen-minute radio shows on Sunday evenings titled "Which Way to a Lasting Peace?" Some ninety CBS stations carried the programs, which argued for some sort of international law structure to control the wayward criminal appetites of nations. John Foster Dulles, a major foreign policy figure in his party, also convened a venture under the auspices of the Federal Council of Churches—named the Commission to Study the Bases of a Just and Durable Peace—to examine various peace initiatives.[16]

In the fall of 1939, Germany attacked Poland, drawing France and England into the battle, almost at the same moment the League of Nations in Geneva was honoring the memory of Woodrow Wilson by placing a large bronze sphere on the terrace of its headquarters. Simultaneously, President Roosevelt achieved his first victory in steering Congress toward world responsibility when it amended the Neutrality Law to permit France and Great Britain to purchase U.S. arms so long as they paid for them in cash and picked them up themselves. As the pace of events accelerated, Roosevelt made the decision to seek an unprecedented third term as president and maneuvered to put America on a war footing for a possible coming conflict.[17]

By mid–1940, during his reelection campaign, Roosevelt significantly widened his nation's obligations. With Winston Churchill as prime minister of England in April 1940, the possibility of genuine resistance to the Nazis gave Roosevelt hope. That August, Roosevelt persuaded Congress to enact a Selective Service Act to draft new soldiers. In September, he stretched constitutional boundaries when he made a deal with Churchill to exchange a batch of aging U.S. destroyers for U.S. bases in British colonial lands. In November, he won the White House by an electoral landslide of 449–82 over Wendell Willkie. In December, he proclaimed the United States the "arsenal of democracy" for the stricken nations of the world.

Finally, in January 1941, at his State of the Union address to a joint session of Congress, Roosevelt began to outline his aims for a global peace. In a clarion call that reminded some of Roosevelt's old League idealism, he told a cheering Congress that there are four essential human freedoms: freedom of speech and expression; freedom of religion; freedom from want; and freedom from fear. We should not seek this promise for a "distant millennium," he said, but as a "definite basis for a kind of world attainable in our own time and generation." He was unmistakably summoning his people to a full-bodied crusade that embodied a Wilsonian vision. William Allen White, the renowned newspaper editor, observed that the president had given the world "a new Magna Carta of democracy." Though he no longer heralded the League, Roosevelt was beginning a long march toward a new global architecture of some sort, its outcome ever uncertain.[18]

CHAPTER 3

THE UNLIKELY PILGRIMAGE
OF LEO PASVOLSKY

By the fall of 1939, the State Department had already started to prepare secret plans for the postwar period. Acting in response to President Roosevelt's cautionary words to the American people about a possible war and the need for a "final peace," Secretary of State Cordell Hull proposed an in-house research team on a global security plan. Roosevelt consented to this proposition because, unlike President Wilson, he wanted to keep all postwar blueprints within his administration to avoid the confusion that had led to the defeat of the League of Nations. Roosevelt also sought to keep postwar planning under wraps for fear of stirring up the isolationists and diverting focus from the war. To lead the planning, Hull chose his long-time personal assistant, Leo Pasvolsky, a Russian-born economist, as special aide for the problems of peace and gave him the authority to direct a departmental operational group.[1]

Pasvolsky was a quiet, methodical individual of unprepossessing appearance; indeed, he looked like a bank clerk. At age fifty-two, he stood five feet, five inches and weighed over two hundred pounds; he had an inordinately large, egg-shaped head, a small mustache, and he puffed on a pipe. He was a man of prodigious knowledge, and one sarcastic accolade that circulated called him "the brain that walked like a man." He was a one-man think tank for Hull, also a doughty infighter. His own aide observed of him: "He reminded me of the third little pig in Disney's version of that fairy tale—the one whose house could not be blown down." Hull called him "Friar Tuck," and Pasvolsky himself joked that

33

it might have been easier for him to roll than to walk. He was the perfect choice for a confidential mission. By inclination, he preferred staying in the background. One observer wrote: "Pasvolsky can dodge more reporters than any man in government. One swore once he saw him move in answer to a question but others said it must have been the building."[2]

He possessed formidable and indefatigable work habits. For the seven years between 1939 and 1945—under two presidents, three secretaries of state, and three undersecretaries of state—he directed most of the department's committees preparing an international charter, immersed himself in every facet of the review process inside and outside the government, assisted in resolving disputes over the organization, and continuously briefed U.S. and foreign officials about the progress on the assembly's construction. He was a brilliant negotiator. Observers called him "the chess player in operation." He nurtured the organization's first seeds in Washington and, by 1945, presided over its full flowering in San Francisco.

Pasvolsky, who was born in Pavlograd, Russia, in 1893, had fled to the United States in 1905 with his anti-Czarist parents. He attended night school at City College of New York and pursued graduate work in political science at Columbia University. His fluency in Russian led him to serve as the editor of the English-language *Russian Review* and later as the editor of the Russian-language daily newspaper, *Amerikansky Viestnik*. He plunged into the political fights that engulfed émigré circles at the time. He recounted debating Leon Trotsky during the Russian revolutionary's brief visit to New York in 1916. With the accession to power by the moderate socialist regime of Aleksandr Kerensky in early 1917, Pasvolsky divined a new start for Russia, but Lenin's violent coup later that year quickly embittered him and led him to express strongly anti-Communist views.

In 1919, Pasvolsky covered the Paris Peace Conference for several New York City newspapers, including the *New York Tribune* and the *Brooklyn Eagle,* and two years later, the Washington Arms Conference for the *Baltimore Sun.* Those experiences bolstered his increasingly pro-Wilsonian views favoring international cooperation and free trade as the basis for a peaceful world. He soon tempered his feelings toward the Soviet Union, now arguing that the United States should recognize the USSR and help bring her into the family of nations, including the League of Nations, thereby correcting a signal "tragedy of Versailles." He began attending the annual sessions of the League of Nations, and, by 1936, served as the alternate U.S. member of a League of Nations economic committee.[3]

In 1922, he took a job as an economist on the research staff of the Brookings Institution in Washington, D.C., the organization that was to become his home on and off until his death in 1953. During Roosevelt's first term, Secretary Hull took him on as his special assistant. Pasvolsky stayed only two years before returning to Brookings. As the international skies darkened, Hull persuaded him to return in 1936. Hull soon grew to depend heavily on this determined, tenacious man, who drove himself endlessly, often to the point of illness. Pasvolsky was a perfect public servant for Hull, endowed with a sharp analytical talent, a nonconfrontational but principled personality, a library-like mind on global issues, a faith in free trade, and a passion to remain invisible. One journalist noted that, among Pasvolsky's formidable talents, was his ability to "pull out his protocol pencil and 'tut-tut' his Tartar-tongued boss. . . . He can usually weed out enough of the Tennessean's blazing vernacular to make some parts printable." In his memoirs, Hull frequently wrote about the breadth and variety of Pasvolsky's work, at one point penning a brief encomium: "His capacities were splendid, his service exceedingly valuable."[4]

On September 16, 1939, Hull formally assigned Pasvolsky to the peace portfolio. Shortly afterward, Pasvolsky wrote a memorandum to the secretary suggesting that a broader committee on "problems of peace and reconstruction" be created to review the "basic principles" that should "underlie a desirable world order." He suggested that it might even be based on the model of Wilson's Inquiry, but this time be retained within the department. Heeding Pasvolsky's call, on December 27, 1939, Hull established an Advisory Committee on Problems of Foreign Relations and named Undersecretary Welles its chairman; the committee was composed of fifteen members, including several outsiders, and Pasvolsky headed its subcommittee on economics. Hull announced the formation of the group in a press release the following month, but, aware of Roosevelt's great sensitivity about disclosing plans for a world body, limited its mandate to examining "overseas war measures."[5]

This was to be first of numerous department committees on global organizations established by Hull—all of which he eventually reorganized, abolished, revived, renamed, neglected, or championed. Because the war took precedence over internal planning, purposeful deliberations were often disrupted. Another chronic problem was that Hull couldn't spare people for assignments due to his limited State Department staff. A further difficulty was that Hull often differed with the conclusions of some of his own committees, especially those run by Sumner Welles, with whom he had a simmering rivalry. Yet another problem was that other agencies of the government wanted a piece of the United Nations action—for example, Vice President Henry Wallace's Board of Economic Warfare. Finally, perhaps the largest source of the commotion and perplexity for Hull was President Roosevelt's personal conduct of foreign policy. FDR liked to keep his options open and, in the early years of the war, shunned public association with the idea of a world organization lest it avert the attention of Americans from the conflict and arouse the wrath of America Firsters.[6]

Within this shifting, labyrinthine context, the Advisory Committee began its stumbling first effort at inventing a world organization. The committee's initial tentative ideas revived several of the League's features. A preliminary sketch included an embryonic "Executive Council" and a larger "General Assembly," but the two chambers were assigned differing levels of powers. The Advisory Committee suggested that the old League's rule of unanimity be replaced by some form of majority rule; that nine separate blocs of nations be represented in the assembly (a special cause of Sumner Welles, who favored a regional approach for the global body); and, finally, that an independent police force be set up. The Advisory Committee never got anywhere with its recommendations, however, because Europe's so-called phony war erupted into a real one in the spring of 1940 and effectively sidelined it.[7]

With the Advisory Committee now on the rocks, Pasvolsky waited until the fall of 1940. In a November memo to Hull, he suggested that the time was ripe for the revival of a planning board. Following Roosevelt's Four Freedoms message to Congress in January 1941, the moment seemed more appropriate than ever. In early February 1941, Hull eschewed an official committee and without public notice created the Division of Special Research and gave it a wide-ranging mandate to undertake "special studies" in foreign relations. People within the department knew that its purpose was to study plans for a world assembly or, as Hull put it, "a future world order." Hull once again chose Pasvolsky to be the chief of the new division. The unit quickly began an assessment of various policy approaches suggested by foreign governments, think tanks, and other professionals. But the Research Division rapidly bogged down because of insufficient staff and, by April 1941, Pasvolsky was urging a return to a more expansive Advisory Committee concept.[8]

In mid-August 1941, President Roosevelt's dramatic meeting at sea with British Prime Minister Winston Churchill, in Argentia Bay off the coast of Newfoundland, brought new attention to a world organization. Roosevelt first demurred from Churchill's suggestion that the two men issue a proclamation, known later as the Atlantic Charter, that would refer to the setting up of an "effective international organization." Under pressure from his aides, including Harry Hopkins and Sumner Welles, as well as from Churchill himself, Roosevelt finally embraced a somewhat different if muddier formulation, calling for the disarmament of the aggressors "pending the establishment of a wider and permanent system of general security." This latter statement, relatively innocuous at the time, soon became the key intellectual underpinning for the State Department's covert labors.[9]

Pasvolsky still had to press for a more concrete plan of action. On September 12, 1941, he once more counseled Hull to consider a new approach to the three most important postwar questions: political and territorial settlements, arms pacts, and trade and financial issues. He advised that the State Department should take the lead on organizing a heavyweight commission of governmental officials and private citizens to study all possible ideas on these matters—independent of the day-to-day problems of the war. In October, prodded by Pasvolsky, Hull and Welles spoke with Roosevelt about making the department the exclusive clearinghouse for postwar planning. The president "heartily" approved. Hull quickly appointed a new Advisory Committee on Post-war Foreign Policy.[10]

The fourteen-person committee, of which Pasvolsky was a member, convened for the first time on February 12, 1942, just nine weeks after the devastating Japanese attack on Pearl Harbor and six weeks after twenty-six nations had assembled in Washington, with Winston Churchill present, and signed a United Nations Declaration affirming their determination to conquer the Axis powers and fulfill the Atlantic Charter. Roosevelt had by now privately proposed the name "United Nations" to Churchill; indeed, in his eagerness to suggest the name and to win Churchill's approval, Roosevelt had burst in on the prime minister in his bedroom at the White House and found him taking a bath. The new committee was mainly composed of governmental officials, including Dean Acheson and Herbert Feis, but there were four outsiders—Norman Davis, president of the Council on Foreign Relations and chairman of the American Red Cross; Hamilton Fish Armstrong, the editor of *Foreign Affairs* magazine; Isaiah Bowman, the president of Johns Hopkins University; and Anne O'Hare McCormick, a member of the *New York Times*'s editorial staff.[11]

The Advisory Committee immediately established several subcommittees, all under the direction of Pasvolsky, to examine political problems, economic reconstruction, territorial matters, legal questions, and the creation of an international organization. Hull could not supervise the group because he suffered from mild diabetes, as well as the aftereffects of tuberculosis, and had to leave for an eight-week vacation. While he was away, more personnel were added to the Advisory Committee from other departments, changes that hampered the group's ability to keep its conclusions secret. On his return in late April 1942, Hull decided to disband the committee after only four sessions, determining instead to rely on its smaller subcommittees.[12]

Sumner Welles, who had been running the department during Hull's two-month absence, now became the most active of the United Nations planners, convening sixty weekly sessions over the next year. By April 4, Welles's venture had produced a preliminary outline for an "interim U.N." The outline once again copied, in many essentials, the design used for the League of Nations. Welles proposed an organization made up of the twenty-six signers of the U.N. Declaration. He divided it into an executive committee of the four major powers (who had policing duties), five regional representatives, and a U.N. "Authority" consisting of all the member states. However, Pasvolsky, an old Wilsonian with a yen for a strongly centralized U.N., opposed the "regional" nature of the executive committee and soon came to the conclusion that Welles's draft was too hastily put together. Upon Hull's return, he persuaded the secretary of state to oppose it. Hull, who had his own doubts about the plan's regional character and its vague military components, promptly killed the proposal. Roosevelt backed Hull over Welles.[13]

Welles was not dismayed. In June, he set up another special subcommittee on international organization that was a substratum of his Political Committee—and Pasvolsky was placed on it as a gesture to Hull. It met some forty-five times during the years 1942–1943, beginning on July 17, 1942; it issued a preliminary draft on March 26, 1943, and held a final session on June 26, 1943. During this time, Welles consulted regularly with President Roosevelt, sometimes with Hull present, often by himself. Disputes arose in this subcommittee between Welles and Pasvolsky over the attributes of the U.N., including Pasvolsky's objections to Welles's advocacy of regional representation. Pasvolsky persisted in preferring a full-bodied universal organization to one that was decentralized. Pasvolsky also served on a parallel commission on security that probed the vexing question of a standing U.N. army. He was becoming a decided, if still low-key, opponent of Welles. Although Pasvolsky was undoubtedly acting in some ways as an agent of Hull's, he was also reflecting his own deeply held convictions.[14]

Franklin Roosevelt was not sure in which direction he wanted to go. Sometimes he expressed more sympathy to regionalism, a position also held by Winston Churchill, who, as a balance-of-power partisan, wanted councils for Asia, Europe, and the Americas. At other times, FDR drifted in the direction of the unitary global body proposed by Pasvolsky and Hull. No matter how he was ultimately going to decide, though, Roosevelt adhered unswervingly to one central realpolitik tenet derived from his disillusion with the League's enforcement operations, that the four major powers—China, the Soviet Union, Great Britain, and the United States—should act as policemen and provide the security for any world organization.

Roosevelt made his feelings clear on this subject repeatedly, beginning as early as New Year's Day, 1942, during the signing of the U.N. Declaration. As if to emphasize the higher status of the Four Powers, the president arranged for their representatives to sign the Declaration in front of those representing the other twenty-two countries. In May 1942, at a meeting with Soviet Foreign Minister Molotov, he reiterated his "Four Policemen" philosophy, knowing that it would appeal to Stalin. In an interview he gave in April 1943 to the *Saturday Evening Post,* he barely mentioned his interest in a global organization and said that he opposed the revival of a League of Nations. He restated his credo that the Big Four should be responsible for maintaining the peace.[15]

In the face of Roosevelt's continuing twists and turns over the world organization, Welles pressed forward with a new flow of suggestions and initiatives. Pasvolsky was present at most of Welles's meetings, politely offering his views, directing the staff on research for Welles, and serving always as a liaison to Hull. Hull, meantime, by his own choice, remained on the sidelines. Every once in a while, he would resurface to reclaim the mantle of chief foreign policy officer. For example, Hull delivered a radio address to the nation on July 23, 1942, broadcast worldwide, in which he called for the creation of an "international agency" to keep the peace "by force, if necessary." Pasvolsky helped craft the pronouncement. Still, it was Welles who propelled the planning process forward throughout 1942. By October, Welles had gained President Roosevelt's approval to complete a full-blown U.N. Charter. By the turn of the new year, Welles produced a full draft, and for two hours one afternoon in late January he discussed it with Roosevelt.[16]

Welles's proposal fleshed out many of the details of the plan he had unsuccessfully presented to Roosevelt the year before. As in the earlier plan, Welles carefully incorporated the Big Four in an Executive Council, but he now gave them a less than absolute veto by including representatives from global regions (this time seven regions, not five). Roosevelt wondered whether Stalin would accept the more limited veto and expressed doubts that amorphous entities such as the Pacific and the Middle East could be properly organized to serve as Security Council members. He urged Welles to do some more work on the plan.

By late March 1943, Welles had a more complete draft of the United Nations Charter in hand. Roosevelt now invited Welles (accompanied by Hull) to show it to the visiting British foreign minister, Anthony Eden, at the White House. The discussion was extended but inconclusive. Shortly afterwards, Welles, with Roosevelt's assent, also privately gave an update on his work to those senators, including Joseph Ball (R-Minn., author later of the Ball Resolution for a Global Assembly), who had been growing restive over the lack of movement by Washington toward peace aims and were drafting a resolution in favor of a global security organization. Though Roosevelt earlier that month had warned legislators that they were moving too quickly for the American public, he also wanted to co-opt them.[17]

Welles's growing activism in and dominance over U.N. planning were starting to embitter Hull. As a former senator, Hull saw himself as the point man in dealing with Congress, and regarded Welles, a nonelected appointee, to be a naïve interloper. Roosevelt's closeness to Welles—Welles had served as a page boy at Roosevelt's wedding and had attended both of Roosevelt's alma maters, Groton and Harvard—and the president's obvious appreciation of Welles's incisive mind grated on Hull, just as the president's own ill-disguised impatience with Hull's plodding ways upset the secretary. The president's habit of consulting Welles without informing Hull—and Welles's use of this same backdoor access to Roosevelt to impart his views—deeply poisoned their relationship.

In addition, because of Hull's illness, the president had invited Welles but not Hull to the Atlantic Charter meeting with Churchill. The two had also had an angry run-in over a conference of Latin American nations in Rio de Janeiro in mid-January 1942; Welles had persuaded most of the Hemisphere nations to "recommend" a break with the Axis powers, but Hull did not feel that the commitment Welles procured on severing links was strong enough. Roosevelt had overruled Hull on this matter. In addition, at Roosevelt's urging, Welles had now begun to deliver speeches over a "permanent system of general security," much of the time without Hull's knowledge—a further annoyance to the secretary of state. And, of course, there were widening policy differences over a "regional" U.N.[18]

When Hull returned from his annual vacation in Florida in mid-April 1943, he sensed that events were dangerously passing him by. He complained to one intimate that he still felt "very much in the dark" about the department's plans for a global organization. He griped that no one had told him about what was going on, "yet he was entirely responsible for the outcome." He was also convinced that Welles had confused the Senate over the putative Ball Resolution, now under consideration and stirring up controversy, by not giving "at least a month of careful preparation." Welles, he said, had "spent twenty-five minutes" in the chamber compared to his own "twenty-five years." What profoundly irritated Hull, too, was that, on his return, the president had denied even seeing a plan for the U.N. drafted by Welles—but "he believed otherwise."[19]

Hull also wondered why Leo Pasvolsky had not paid more attention "to these important matters," especially as he served on Welles's subcommittee. He thought Pasvolsky was making too many speeches and seeing too many unimportant people. Implicit in his laments was a hint that Pasvolsky was not paying sufficient attention to protecting the secretary's interests. Moreover, he was concerned that Pasvolsky's effectiveness might be impaired by failing health. He indicated now that he wanted to start attending all future meetings on postwar organizational planning. And, despite Welles's draft proposal, he insisted on getting "the ideas of everybody before talking about some definite plan."[20]

Hull immediately began a series of executive actions to seize back authority from Welles. First, he instructed Welles's subcommittee to focus on a "universal rather than a regional basis" for the postwar assembly. The committee quickly agreed. Next, he began to lobby Roosevelt directly to change his views about regional autonomy. He began to visit the White House "frequently," bringing Pasvolsky as well as other aides on these excursions. As he recalls in his memoirs, "We argued with the president to induce him to change his ideas, but for some time without avail. . . . As summer arrived he began to turn toward our point of view." Basically, Hull and his entourage contended that regional councils might break up the Big Four coalition, could dilute the U.N.'s authority, and would undoubtedly interfere with the capacity of the world body to deter war—as well as diminish the enthusiasm of Americans for the U.N.[21]

Hull stepped up the pace of his reprisals. He abruptly adjourned all the subcommittees, including Welles's own—this edict issuing shortly after Welles boldly presented his last recommendation to Roosevelt on the United Nations Charter in mid-June 1943, again with a regional bias. Then Hull administered a final lethal blow to Welles's status. As early as January 1943, he had raised with Roosevelt rumors of Welles's alleged homosexual activities, which, he warned, would create a political storm. Roosevelt had waved away the issue. But, in early August, 1943, the *New York Times* ran a story reporting that the State Department was suffering from a "lack of a cohesive policy" due to an angry and "well-known" feud between Welles and Hull. The piece placed most of the blame on Hull. A furious Hull went to the White House on August 10 and demanded that Roosevelt fire Welles—and eventually Roosevelt, though desperate to keep Welles, agreed, aware of his greater need for Hull in helping win Senate approval on a U.N. treaty. Welles resigned on August 22.[22]

With Welles out, Hull now assumed full responsibility for U.N. planning and immediately named Pasvolsky as his sole consigliere to direct the drafting operations and compose "a brief and simple instrument" for the global body. Pasvolsky swiftly gathered together a rump group of aides, known as the Informal Agenda Group, to delve into the old Welles archives, former League provisions, past proposed language, and published and unpublished proposals from independent groups and foreign countries (the British government, for example, had sent an aide-mémoire to Roosevelt in mid-July). By early July, Pasvolsky was seeking additional answers from his staff on such matters as the powers of a global body, voting arrangements, organs within the assembly, judicial machinery, control of arms, trusteeships, social welfare, human rights, and other related issues.

In August, Pasvolsky put together a tentative draft charter. It was in some respects a departure from Welles's schema in that it played down the regional concept, but it also retained some familiar features, including the Security Council, the General Assembly, and the Secretariat, all of which Pasvolsky and Welles had originally agreed upon. Whether this draft got to the president's desk right away is the subject of some dispute; Welles's document was apparently still circulating at the White House. But the new draft with Pasvolsky's distinctive imprimatur began to supersede the Welles version. In the ultimate reckoning, Pasvolsky became the person most responsible for the American language in its U.N. instrument. Although the ideas were certainly not original to him, Pasvolsky chose where to place the words and how to define the most important concepts; thus he significantly molded the contours of the organization. As Senator Tom Connally, one of the U.S. delegates to San Francisco, later wrote in his memoirs, "Certainly he had more to do with writing the framework of the charter than anyone else."[23]

Now, as the war was turning in the favor of the Allies, Secretary Hull and President Roosevelt also became intent on outlining a set of postwar aims around which the president's Four Policemen could rally publicly. Roosevelt regarded an agreement among these nations as a necessary precondition to any global conference. Soon after Hull and a lame-duck Welles met with Roosevelt (along with Pasvolsky, who was, by now, a regular at these sessions) on August 10, 1943, to agree on a Four Powers statement, Hull assigned Pasvolsky to draw up a list of goals, based, in part, on the U.N. Charter he had largely overseen. Known later as the Four Powers Agreement, Pasvolsky's enumerated objectives were basically a collection of pieties, but ones that bound the four partners together to work toward a preliminary joint, four-way conference for a "system of general security."[24]

There next followed a series of summit conferences in the fall of 1943 among the four major states—for which Pasvolsky and his team did much of the preparatory labor on the side of the United States. First, in late August, came a tête-à-tête between Roosevelt and Churchill in Quebec, where both leaders endorsed the global assembly concept while putting off a tentative plan for an interim U.N.; next, Secretary Hull met with his two fellow foreign ministers (China was absent) in Moscow in October, where a formal Four Nations Declaration was issued also endorsing the world body; the following month, Roosevelt, Churchill, and Chiang Kai-shek caucused in Cairo to assure China's participation in such a conclave; at the end of November and beginning of December, Roosevelt and Churchill met with Stalin in Tehran. Here, Roosevelt convinced Stalin to back a centralized organization with a heavy Big Four presence in place of the regional-based body that Churchill (and Stalin) had long sought.[25]

Almost simultaneously, the U.S. Congress passed two resolutions in favor of a global assembly; these gave public sanction to the process. First, on September 21, 1943, the House of Representatives passed the so-called Fulbright Resolution "favoring the creation of appropriate international machinery" to maintain the peace; and then on November 5, 1943, the Senate enacted the Connally Resolution (named after the head of the Senate Foreign Relations Committee), which was a variation of the original Ball statement and called for the establishment of "international authority with power to prevent aggression" in the form of a "general international organization." Cordell Hull later stated in his memoirs that, in his view, the two proclamations "cleared the path at home" for U.S. involvement in a multilateral body and ended twenty years of isolationism—a process, he noted, that had earlier been reinforced when the United States participated in the International Food and Agricultural Conference at Hot Springs, Virginia, in the spring of 1943, and had arranged the Relief and Rehabilitation Conference in Atlantic City the fall of that same year.[26]

Roosevelt, on his return from Tehran, now asked Hull to give him the newest edition of a U.N. Charter with which he could begin to tinker and perhaps rework. Hull, who by now had reconstituted Pasvolsky's ad hoc unit into the Informal Political Agenda Group, dutifully presented Roosevelt with Pasvolsky's latest draft on December 29, 1943. The proposal once again embodied the idea of a small Executive Council, with veto power held by the Big Four, to handle security matters; a General Assembly that would be a forum for all nations; a Secretariat, various U.N. subagencies, and a World Court. Within two months, on February 3, 1944, the president formally cleared Hull to use this draft as the basis of the U.S. government's proposal for the soon-to-be-determined meeting of the Big Four. Pasvolsky's operation commenced a series of discussions over the next seven months—some seventy in all—to prepare the document for the Big Powers' preparatory event.[27]

Meantime, Edward Stettinius, who had replaced Sumner Welles as undersecretary of state in late September 1943, was undertaking a major reorganization of the State Department in January 1944 on Hull's instructions—in response to the criticism that Hull's stewardship had been lackluster and directionless. Stettinius, who at forty-two was a former chairman of U.S. Steel and former administrator of the Lend-Lease Program, promptly used the authority Hull delegated to him to elevate postwar planning to the same status as the department's other responsibilities and, with Hull's assent, consolidated Pasvolsky's authority by promoting him to the new post of executive director of the Committee on Postwar Programs. Stettinius, who knew little about global organizations, and, unlike his strong-minded predecessor, had even fewer opinions about them, deferred to the greater expertise of Pasvolsky in this arrangement.[28]

Hull and Pasvolsky met with Roosevelt again on February 3. In what was later seen as a historic turning point, Roosevelt placed his official imprimatur on the latest Pasvolsky draft, which Hull had sent him just after Christmas. He accepted two of Pasvolsky's most important modifications: first, lodging authority over security matters in the eleven-member Security Council rather than in the Four Policemen that Roosevelt had long wanted, thereby reducing the domination of the council by a "dictatorship of four"; and, second, assigning exclusive jurisdiction for security issues to the council while giving the General Assembly, where all states had a vote, all nonsecurity questions—a singular change from the approach of the old League of Nations, which had invested security responsibilities in both its council and assembly. Roosevelt also told Hull and Pasvolsky that he thought the General Assembly should elect smaller states to council membership—which meant, as Pasvolsky put it, that "the regional principle goes out." Finally, Roosevelt asked Hull now to invite the other Big Powers to the formal drafting synod, now scheduled for the Dumbarton Oaks estate in Washington, D.C., in the summer.[29]

Through the spring, Hull and Pasvolsky exchanged notes with the British, Russian, and Chinese governments, working on specific dates for the conference, and continued to fine-tune the U.N. Charter recommendations. Hull, in addition, revived his Advisory Committee on Problems of Foreign Relations, an outside citizen's group, to give him a continuing flow of independent ideas and advice. Sensitive, too, to the demise of the League of Nations in the Senate, Hull in April simultaneously started meeting with a small eight-person group of Republican and Democratic senators from the Foreign Relations Committee to brief them on the U.N. Charter and its provisions. One of the most conservative members of the consultative group, Senator Arthur Vandenberg (R-Mich.), pronounced himself thrilled that Hull had, with the inclusion of the veto power for the Big Four, devised a plan that was "so conservative from a nationalist standpoint." Hull also delivered several addresses to the nation written by Pasvolsky in which he sketched out in more detail the U.S. proposals. In addition, he urged Roosevelt to identify himself with the preparations. Thus, on June 15, in a somewhat vague statement also written by Pasvolsky, FDR told the American people for the first time that he had been conferring with State Department officials for eighteen months and that he completely endorsed Secretary Hull's roadmap.[30]

By now, Roosevelt, Hull, and Pasvolsky had gained agreement with the Big Four on a late August 1944 conclave. There was one hitch—the Russians objected to sitting down with the Chinese because they had not yet declared war on Japan. Consequently, Roosevelt consented to two successive meetings: the first with the British and Russians, a later one with the British and the Chinese. But neither the British, the Russians, nor the Chinese seemed to take the preparatory work very seriously. Each of the governments sent Roosevelt some general thoughts on a global body, but, except for some lengthy British notations titled "Future World Organization," nothing of serious consequence. The result was that, as Robert Hilderbrand, author of the standard work on Dumbarton Oaks, later wrote, the Pasvolsky proposal, "which was by far the most complete and detailed of the three, became—albeit unofficially—the basic frame of reference for building a plan of world organization." Another U.N. specialist, Edward Luard, also concluded after an exhaustive analysis of the meeting that the U.S proposal "to a large extent, formed the basis for discussions" at the conference. So, too, Hull himself observed in his memoirs that "all the essential points in the tentative draft" that he had originally handed to the Russians and the British before the conference "were incorporated in the draft now accepted by the conference."[31]

Pasvolsky became a dominant figure at Dumbarton Oaks. His influence, apart from that of President Roosevelt and Undersecretary Stettinius, who led the U.S. delegation to Dumbarton Oaks, clearly was immense. Hilderbrand cites Pasvolsky sixty-eight times in his index—more than anybody else aside from FDR and Stettinius. Why? Because Pasvolsky had prepared the text of the charter and knew the meaning of practically every clause and paragraph. He could tell immediately the impact a single word change made in the document. As a member of the exclusive Joint Steering Committee, he was also present at the drafting sessions. He participated in most of the arguments within the U.S. delegation and between the various representatives of Moscow, London, and Washington over the writing of the charter. He exercised an outsized intellectual hold over the participants, especially Stettinius and Hull. As Gladwyn Jebb, the British representative, remarked of him in his memoirs, Pasvolsky and his research colleagues were "anything save experts of the first order. . . . Pasvolsky appeared to be on the up grade" because his planning body "was large and impressive and was seemingly capable . . . of coping with the individualistic, not to say wayward approach to postwar problems of the great men" involved in the meeting. Or, as the *Washington Post* noted simply: "Atop the heap sits Leo."[32]

Pasvolsky, working vigorously behind the scenes, weighed in on the most important matters of the conference. The Big Three nations early on accepted the basic framework for the world organization inherited from the League of Nations, including an eleven-member Security Council (with five permanent seats), a General Assembly, a Secretariat, and various subagencies—as well as a Military Staff Committee composed of officers from the five permanent states to direct all U.N. enforcement actions.

The discussions in the meetings mainly centered on how to distribute powers among the various branches. Pasvolsky tried to persuade the Russians to accept an Economic and Social Council to deal with the causes of war, such as poverty and famine, arguing, though, that it should remain separate from the already overburdened Security Council. The British liked the idea. Eventually the Soviets agreed.[33]

Next, the British and Americans reached a compromise (later accepted by the Russians) on the question of regionalism based on a paper presented by Pasvolsky titled "Role of Local and Regional Agencies." Pasvolsky had originally emphasized the subordination of regional groupings to the Security Council, but the U.S. delegation finally gave way somewhat to the British position, which favored a higher profile for regional assemblies. It accepted language stating that "nothing in the Charter should preclude the existence of regional arrangements or agencies." Washington, struggling to accommodate to its own regional Pan-American Congress, was, in any event, in an ambivalent frame of mind about the matter. In acquiescing to the amended phraseology, it was, in effect, mildly discouraging regional bodies but also somewhat enhancing their autonomy.[34]

On the matter of the Security Council, Pasvolsky played a significant role in helping to define that body's responsibilities. He persuaded Undersecretary Stettinius to oppose the designation of Brazil as the sixth permanent member of the Security Council, a cause pressed by Roosevelt to quell impending Latin American discontent over representation. Stettinius used many of the arguments in Pasvolsky's memo, including the question of whether Brazil really amounted to a Great Power, to convince Roosevelt ultimately to drop the notion of Brazil. And Pasvolsky argued successfully for the council to stay in continuous session at the U.N. to handle crises.

Third, he aggressively fought a Russian proposal to give an absolute veto to the five permanent members, a posture that would have allowed them to block attempts at discussion of an issue or peacefully settling disputes in which they themselves were involved. This was a viewpoint that his own boss, Cordell Hull, had at first supported. Pasvolsky regarded such an outsized veto as giving the Big Nations far too much power, much of which could probably be abused by the Soviets; and, as well, it would place the major states unfairly on a higher plane than smaller nations regarding conflict settlement. Eventually, Hull changed his mind, as Hilderbrand put it, worn down by Pasvolsky's sheer "perseverance." On September 13, along with his two junior counterparts, Gladwyn Jebb of Great Britain and Arkadei Sobelov of the USSR, Pasvolsky developed a tentative compromise formula whereby the veto could be used only on enforcement or "substantive" issues, not on matters of discussion or peaceful settlement, which were viewed as "procedural" issues. However, when this notion was presented to Stalin, the Soviet leader stuck unswervingly to his original stand; he was later joined by Churchill, further complicating the U.S. position.[35]

Toward the end of the conference, the Soviets suddenly demanded that all sixteen Soviet republics become members. The Russian representative, Andrei Gromyko, pressed this proposal, apparently because of Stalin's fear that the Western powers, with their fellow democracies, would always outvote the USSR. Taken aback by the suggestion, and fearful that it would damage the U.N.'s chances in the Senate, Roosevelt instructed Stettinius to give the Russians the impression that the United States would give their idea serious consideration; but privately he would attempt to derail it. Stettinius swore the U.S. delegation to secrecy about the Roosevelt strategy, informing no other official but Pasvolsky and another fellow operative on the Joint Steering Committee. Gromyko eventually withdrew his notion temporarily, hoping for unspecified future action on it. Pasvolsky later circulated a list of proposed states for U.N. membership (excluding the sixteen Soviet republics) that left Gromyko disgruntled again. He opposed including nations that had not yet declared war on the Axis, such as Argentina. Pasvolsky's initiative only increased the Soviet resistance to any deal.[36]

Pasvolsky did not succeed in persuading the Soviets to reconsider their stance on either the extra votes or on the veto. For all his remarkable talents, there were certain questions that he (and the U.S. mission) was simply unable to resolve at Dumbarton Oaks. The lingering issues were the absolute veto; the membership list; further delineation of the authority of the Economic and Social Council, and more broadly, the

General Assembly; the role of regional groups; congressional authorization of U.S. troops under U.N. command; the creation of a Trusteeship Council (a subject not brought up because of U.S. military opposition); the statute of the World Court; a site for the U.N. headquarters; the transfer of League of Nations property to the U.N.; and a budget for the new body. By the end of the conference, although it was clear that much had been accomplished at Dumbarton Oaks, there was an evident consensus that the host of undecided issues must now be bucked up to the highest authorities in the United States, Great Britain, and the Soviet Union for resolution. (This same conclusion was strengthened later in the second China phase of the meeting.)

On September 21, at a White House meeting with Roosevelt, the president asked his officials to bring Dumbarton Oaks to a close and hold all unsettled questions in abeyance until his own get-together with Stalin and Churchill. Pasvolsky returned to his research position in the State Department.[37]

CHAPTER 4

YALTA AND AFTERMATH
Roosevelt's Last Acts

W ith victory in Europe in sight, President Roosevelt was growing more and more preoccupied with assuring the creation of
his United Nations organization before the fighting ended and the nations of the world, including his own countrymen, lost interest in the
enterprise. Through the fall of 1944, he pressed his State Department
team for new approaches to the Security Council voting formula in advance of his meeting with Joseph Stalin and Winston Churchill, now
scheduled for the Crimea in mid-February 1945. He wanted to make
sure that Latin American allies were consulted and were on board. He
instructed his advisors to prepare Congress and the American public
for a major campaign to establish the organization.[1]

The State Department, with broad approval from the White House,
soon did something it had never done before—it initiated a nationwide
public relations blitz for the United Nations. Already, private groups
had moved on their own to shape public opinion, even before Dumbarton Oaks ended. With the State Department's knowledge and tacit assent, Clark Eichelberger, one of the leaders of the Commission to Study
the Organization of Peace, on September 28, 1944, invited over fifty organizations to meet in New York City to discuss pro-U.N. strategy. Forty
groups assembled at the Woodrow Wilson Library on October 6, 1944,
and agreed to back a common campaign for the organization.[2]

On October 1, the head of the State Department's Office of Public
Affairs, John Dickey, wrote a confidential memo to Secretary Hull

proposing the department begin its own full-blown PR crusade for the United Nations. Stettinius met on October 7 with over one hundred representatives from various world affairs organizations in an off-the-record briefing. Subsequently, acting on Stettinius's advice, and in coordination with nongovernmental groups, Hull authorized a virtually unprecedented and massive information drive. On Hull's instruction, in early November, Stettinius circulated a memo to department employees saying that this "public information job [is] of the highest importance" and that "it is imperative that we exert ourselves to satisfy the earnest public demand for information and guidance on these proposals." By late December 1944, Roosevelt had persuaded Archibald MacLeish, then the librarian of Congress, to leave his post and to head the effort as assistant secretary of state for public and cultural relations.[3]

Throughout the fall, the State Department printed thousands of copies of the Dumbarton Oaks proposal and an eight-page question-and-answer sheet on the draft U.N. Charter, and through January began to distribute over 200,000 of them to interested parties. Summaries and clips reached some 9,000 weeklies and 1,000 small-town dailies. Clark Eichelberger wrote a thirty-two-page pamphlet on Dumbarton Oaks that, via his affiliate organizations, reached over 21,000 people. The National League of Women Voters sent out a discussion guide and text to six hundred local chapters around the land. The Woodrow Wilson Foundation mailed free of charge 318,000 copies of the Dumbarton Oaks text to individuals—nearly going bankrupt in the gesture. And the national commander of the American Legion dispatched letters to his 12,000 posts urging the adoption of the U.N. Charter.[4]

By year's end, the State Department had substantially broadened its efforts. For two months, beginning in mid-October, the department briefed over 115 individuals from dozens of professional associations; and during the first weeks of December, it formed teams of speakers to address meetings across the country. Some forty-five off-the-record sessions were held in sixteen cities. More speakers were roving around the nation on behalf of the department in this thirty-one-day span than had circulated nationwide for the department in the entire year. The total of in-house and in-city briefings would reach nearly five hundred by the time of the San Francisco Conference. MacLeish also launched lectures on the U.N. for NBC radio and persuaded Hollywood to underwrite a documentary on the salient importance of the global assembly. There was undoubtedly an element of overkill in these endeavors, but, given that League's past problems haunted Roosevelt officials, it seemed justifiable at the time.[5]

In late November, Secretary Hull resigned due to persistent ill health. Stettinius became the new secretary of state at month's end. Meanwhile, four times in November, Stettinius, along with Leo Pasvolsky, chaired an in-house working group, called the "Superior Committee," to consider the voting question and several other unresolved U.N. issues. Stettinius and Pasvolsky and their team reviewed the bidding of the Dumbarton Oaks powers on the vote formula and subsequently, on November 15, took a set of recommendations to the White House. They told FDR that the "compromise" approach on the veto Pasvolsky had advanced earlier in the fall was the only workable solution.[6]

The Pasvolsky submission had the advantage, in their minds, of being fairly straightforward in theory and equitable in principle, though admittedly not as easy to define in practice. Pasvolsky had argued that the five permanent members should be able to veto substantive political matters, including, among others, expulsion from the United Nations, membership questions, determinations of threats to peace, and, even if one of them were party to a dispute, enforcement actions—such as sanctions or military operations—because of the precept strenuously pushed by Stalin and Roosevelt to avoid divisions among the wartime allies. And, as the Big Powers would bear most of the enforcement burden, for that reason alone they should be the final arbiters on U.N. interventions. But where it was a matter of the council's simply discussing a question, this would be considered a procedural matter to be decided by a simple majority of six votes out of eleven with no veto allowed. (Here the Soviets objected, calling discussion of any sort a substantive matter since it represented the first in a progression of steps leading to more serious action.) Finally, in instances where peaceful outcome of a dispute by voluntary or investigatory means was possible, then the council would take jurisdiction under its conciliatory or quasijudicial capacity, and here no permanent member would have the right to bar consideration of such matters if it were a party to the controversy. Instead, it would have to abstain, though Big Powers, not parties to the dispute, could veto such action. This was a recognition that, if the council were not allowed to retain at least such limited authority, the smaller nations might withdraw their support of the United Nations entirely and the organization would be unable to deliver on its promises to keep the peace.[7]

Subsequently, Roosevelt on December 5 sent a telegram via Ambassador Harriman to Stalin urging his acceptance of the U.S. formula, and the next day a similar cable to Churchill asking his concurrence. Roosevelt emphasized in both communications that "we must move forward as rapidly as possible" in convening the U.N. Conference. But Stalin tarried until December 26 and then flatly turned down the proposal; he asserted that the formula, in possibly breaching the unity of the Great Powers, could have "dire consequences for the preservation of international security." Churchill waited until January 13, 1945, but he eventually changed his mind and accepted the U.S. proposal. Nonetheless he wavered once again at Yalta.[8]

Roosevelt was puzzled about how to proceed with Stalin. In his Annual Message to Congress, on January 6, 1945, he seemed to be, in part, heaving a cautionary flare in the direction of the Russian leader by stating that "in our disillusionment after the last war, we gave up the hope of achieving a better peace because we had not the courage to fulfill our responsibilities in an admittedly imperfect world. We must not let that happen again, or we shall follow the same tragic road again—the road to a third world war." Stettinius promptly sent Pasvolsky back to work. Convening a group informally titled "Mr. Pasvolsky's Committee" within his Office of Special Political Affairs, he held eighteen meetings between January 1 and February 10 to probe further how to approach Stalin on the U.S. vote proposal and to delve into various other disputed matters concerning the U.N. On January 8, Roosevelt invited Stettinius and Pasvolsky to the White House to thrash out alternatives. Pasvolsky warned the president that the State Department had conducted talks with American citizens, professional bodies, and other nations, and it now believed that the "unanimity rule needs to be modified at least to this extent" or else the U.N. could be in serious trouble. Pasvolsky, who conferred regularly with the Russian ambassador, Andrei Gromyko, contended that the Soviet position was "extremely weak" since, but for the one exception concerning peaceful settlements, the veto would remain all-potent. Roosevelt agreed.[9]

Stettinius set about to keep Congress informed about what was going on. Hull had adeptly kept the U.N. issue out of the 1944 presidential race by consulting with Roosevelt's Republican opponent, Thomas Dewey, the governor of New York, and his foreign policy advisor, John Foster Dulles, about the Dumbarton Oaks negotiations. In addition, he had dispatched copies of the Dumbarton accord to crucial members of both parties in Congress. At Hull's urging, Stettinius set up a unit within the State Department to deal with Congress. Stettinius personally saw several key senators on November 24 and December 6, and influential House representatives on December 4. On January 11, Roosevelt himself had several senators over to the White House for a briefing.[10]

In the meantime, as the meeting among the three major powers drew nearer, there began to be misgivings on the U.S. and British sides over the choice of Yalta for the conference. Stalin had begged off Roosevelt's suggestion of meeting in the Mediterranean, preferably Sicily, because, as he wrote, "I still have to pay heed to my doctors' warning of the risk involved in long journeys." He preferred instead the Soviet Black Sea coast. In retrospect, this choice seems singularly ironic; it was clearly Roosevelt, crippled and sickly, who would have to forgo the cautions of his doctors and make a journey that was far more arduous, Yalta being thousands of miles from the United States. Roosevelt was, in this tiring foray, taking a heavy risk with his health. *New York Times* columnist Anne O'Hare McCormick, an intimate of Roosevelt's who interviewed him days before he died, wrote that it was primarily because of the United Nations that he made "the hard, perhaps fatal, trip to Yalta. . . . [T]his was the thing he was straining his strength to accomplish."[11]

Of course, there were other critical issues that Roosevelt was going to deal with at Yalta, but at the forefront of his mind was Stalin's cooperation on the U.N. That was the theme of all his subsequent political, strategic, tactical, and public acts before he died. Yalta began on February 4 and lasted until February 11. To get there, Roosevelt took ten days to cross the Atlantic on the cruiser USS *Quincy* and landed at Malta, where Ambassador Harriman found him "worn, wasted" in appearance. There he was joined by his closest aide, Harry Hopkins, himself in dire health, and Winston Churchill. After a short night's rest, the U.S. team, followed ten minutes later by the British party, flew in a C-54 plane across the Mediterranean, Greece, the Macedonian peninsula, and the Black Sea to the Crimea, circumventing the German-held island of Crete—a seven-hour excursion altogether, and alighted at Sevastopol. There the principals regrouped and, with their staffs, drove another ninety miles for hours over rough roads to Yalta. The Russians housed Roosevelt, along with the U.S. delegation, in the Livadia Palace, an old Czarist residence, on a bluff overlooking the Black Sea. Though a magnificent fifty-room edifice, it was devoid of furnishings save those imported hastily from Moscow. Bedbugs plagued the Americans and British alike. The president was given the only private bathroom.[12]

By the time the Yalta talks began, Roosevelt's spirits had revived and, to other observers at the sessions, he appeared in full command of the issues at hand. Harry Hopkins, sick in bed most of the time with a chronically ailing stomach, made only occasional appearances, but tracked the talks closely. The leaders haggled over military strategy in the first few days. On the third day, February 6, they began to focus on the United Nations. That afternoon, Secretary of State Stettinius presented the U.S. position on the voting formula to Stalin and Churchill. Roosevelt discussed the proposed U.S. formula at some length. At one point, Stalin referred back to the USSR's ouster from the League of Nations in 1939, after it had invaded Finland, and wanted to know whether the veto would now protect his nation against such action in the future. Anthony Eden, the British foreign secretary, assured him it would. Eventually, Stalin suggested that the U.S. proposal be put under study, to which Roosevelt and Churchill consented. There was some foreboding that the issue might now linger past Yalta, placing the U.N. Conference in jeopardy; but Foreign Minister Molotov appeared the next afternoon and said that, because the Soviet side now had a clearer understanding of the Roosevelt plan and that his country felt it would keep the unity of the Major Powers, Moscow now found it "acceptable." Such a rapid turnaround in the Russian position came as a welcome surprise to the Americans, especially to Stettinius, who grinned broadly.[13]

But then Molotov announced another modification in a Russian position. Whereas at Dumbarton Oaks the Soviets had asked for sixteen seats in the General Assembly, now, he said, they would settle for three, "or at least two" of the Soviet Republics, preferably Belarus (White Russia), Ukraine, and Lithuania. Churchill immediately supported the Soviet request, undoubtedly squeamish about the numerous dominions within the British Empire. Roosevelt, uncertain about what he wished to do, asked that the issue be referred to the foreign ministers for discussion. By the next day, February 8, he decided to accept Molotov's suggestion for Ukraine and Belarus. He privately told Stettinius his reasons for his decision: that both states had suffered grievously in the war, that the British had extra votes anyway through their dominions, that the General Assembly was not where power lay but in the Security Council and, finally—most important—he wanted to guarantee Stalin's participation in the U.N. However, he did insist, over Stalin's objections, that the membership for both these states be decided by majority vote at the U.N. conference itself, not by the Big Powers. Later, under some pressure from his own delegation concerned about a possible U.S. public backlash over Moscow's extra votes, Roosevelt awkwardly asked for two additional votes for the United States, which Stalin and Churchill agreed to support.[14]

The three countries also agreed, after much back and forth, to limit attendance at the U.N. Conference to nations that had declared war on at least one of the Axis powers by March 1. This meant immediate membership for all the nations that had signed the original U.N. Declaration in 1942; it also opened the door to the so-called associated states, countries that, although they had broken diplomatic relations with the Axis and now worked with the Allies, had not yet declared war on the enemy, although they would do so by the deadline. Six were Latin nations. Stalin objected, however, to certain nations that stood outside those two groupings, especially Argentina, which had maintained a pro-Nazi neutrality during the war. Stalin said sharply, "I am not for the Argentines. I do not like them." Though Roosevelt quickly passed over the remark, Stalin's animosity toward Argentina soon reverberated in San Francisco.[15]

Yalta came to several other decisions affecting the San Francisco meeting. Most important, Churchill and Roosevelt attempted to convince Stalin to broaden the base of the so-called Lublin government in Poland, the Soviet-dominated regime, to include Polish democratic exiles. Roosevelt was feeling the intense heat at home from a huge Polish constituency of 3 million, and Churchill was publicly beholden to the Polish government-in-exile in London. The three men did agree on demarcating Poland's eastern border with Russia along the so-called Curzon Line. But untying the Lublin knot proved immensely difficult. Eventually, Churchill and Roosevelt persuaded a reluctant Soviet dictator to accept that the "provisional government" in Poland be "reorganized" with "the inclusion of democratic leaders from Poland itself and from Poles abroad" and that elections be held as soon as possible. A commission was established with Foreign Minister Molotov; the U.S. envoy, Averell Harriman; and the British ambassador to Moscow, Sir Archibald Clark Kerr, to negotiate the details. The wording of the declaration, however, was rather opaque—there were no enforcement provisions and no accord on supervising the elections—and it did not bring about the immediate coalition the two Western chiefs had sought. Along with the Declaration on Poland, a Declaration on Liberated Europe put Stalin on notice that he had to adhere to fair electoral standards in the region. Still, Roosevelt almost apologized for the Polish agreement, later telling one staff member, "It's the best I can do for Poland at this time" given the Red Army's occupation of the land. Indeed, this unfocused and often elusive deal later hung like a dark and forbidding storm cloud over the entire San Francisco Conference.[16]

In addition, the three leaders decided that they—as well as the other two permanent members—would consult before the San Francisco meeting on how to handle the unresolved questions of trusteeships, though without designating which specific territories would be covered. Under intense pressure from Winston Churchill, who demanded that the U.N. keep its hands off British colonies, Roosevelt and Stalin acceded to a more limited definition of what constituted a trusteeship: namely, existing mandates from the old League of Nations; territories seized from the World War II Axis powers; and any territory placed voluntarily under U.N. sponsorship. Behind this debate also lay a hidden American agenda: The U.S. military wanted to occupy all the Japanese islands taken during the war for security purposes, although Roosevelt was still ambivalent about how he wanted to do this. Another concealed understanding, which was not to surface until seven months later, was a secret accord reached between Roosevelt and Stalin whereby, to induce Russia into the war against Japan and recognition of Nationalist China, the United States consented to the Russian seizure of parts of Japan's islands and portions of China's soil.[17]

The leaders also reached an accord on where and when the U.N. Conference would occur. All agreed that the United States should be the host—a natural choice given Roosevelt's passion for the organization. Roosevelt, too, wanted the meeting at home to link the U.N. more directly to Americans, as well as to gain better control of the proceedings, and the British liked the notion of confounding U.S. isolationists in their own lair. The choice of an actual site came in a dream at three in the morning on February 9 to Edward Stettinius. He wrote that he awoke with a vision of San Francisco: "I saw the golden sunshine, and as I lay there on the shores of the Black Sea in the Crimea, I could almost feel the fresh and invigorating air from the Pacific." The next day, he told Roosevelt about it; at first, the president remained noncommittal, but, by the next to last session at Yalta, he warmed to the idea, thinking that it might dramatize the Pacific War. On February 11, Roosevelt, just before the closing dinner, finally announced that the venue would be the West Coast city and April 25 the date.[18]

Roosevelt's growing anxiety about the United Nations soon overrode his usually sound political instincts about how he would announce the Yalta results. He eschewed cautionary advice from aides to spell out everything that happened, claiming he wanted to brief congressional leaders privately first. He authorized a communiqué that simply gave the bare bones of the summit: the date and place of the U.N Conference; the rosters of nations invited to San Francisco; general outlines of a Polish pact; the agreement on a voting formula. But even on the last two matters, he did not disclose the details either of the Polish deal or of the veto formula; he, for example, wanted the other permanent member, China, and potential member, France, first to approve the vote plan before revealing it. He said nothing about the extra votes for Russia, nor did he hint of an agreement with Moscow over Japan; and he made scant reference to the trusteeship questions. Roosevelt was so determined to mold the U.S. response to the U.N. that he stayed silent about controversies he considered unnecessary distractions.[19]

One bold stroke he made on the last day was to confirm the composition of the seven-person U.S. delegation to San Francisco and announce it a day or so after Yalta, thereby moving the conference process forward speedily. He put considerable political calculation into his choices, relying on his own intuition as well as on the advice of Stettinius. First, he insisted on retaining ultimate authority by appointing Stettinius as chair of the group. Second, to insure crucial support for ratification in the Senate, he appointed the chairman of the Senate Foreign Relations Committee, Tom Connally—the powerful Texas Democrat—and to bring along the House, added the talkative though insubstantial House Foreign Affairs chairman, New York Democrat Sol Bloom. Third, remembering the League of Nations fiasco of a quarter of a century ago, he sought bipartisan coloration by inviting aboard Senator Arthur Vandenberg, a strong presence on the Foreign Relations Committee. Roosevelt wasn't a fan of the Michigan Republican, a one-time isolationist who had recently turned internationalist, but Stettinius prevailed on him to tap him for his seniority and influence within his party's caucus. Later, before he agreed to serve, Vandenberg demanded a pledge from the president that he be allowed to act as an independent agent on the U.S. delegation, which Roosevelt grudgingly gave him. Thereafter, Vandenberg swiftly offered his own amendments and told Leo Pasvolsky about them. Roosevelt brought in two other Republicans: Congressman Charles Eaton of New Jersey, an elderly man whose infirmities put serious limits on his participation; and the wunderkind former Minnesota governor, Harold Stassen, a thirty-seven-year-old liberal Republican and self-styled globalist, who as a naval reserve officer spoke for many of the servicemen overseas. And in one final flourish, he plucked out of Barnard College the female dean, Virginia Gildersleeve, also a U.N. activist and a representative of a newly energized women's constituency. Former Secretary of State Hull was to be the eighth member, but he was too ill to join the delegation and advised from the sidelines. And within a month, Roosevelt convened the first meeting of the delegation, on March 13.[20]

At home, the comments on Yalta based on the president's press statement were almost uniformly warm and enthusiastic. *Time* ran a picture of Roosevelt and Stalin with the caption: "Eight Great Days on the Russian Riviera." FDR's old adversary, Herbert Hoover, said, "It will offer a great hope to the world." Hopkins and Stettinius were exultant, but Senator Vandenberg had some doubts about the Polish compromise. Nonetheless, basking in this national praise, Roosevelt flew on to Egypt to meet with King Farouk, Prince Ibn Saud of Saudi Arabia, and Emperor Haile Selassie of Ethiopia. Stettinius and his party headed to Moscow. Then the president boarded the USS *Quincy* to travel to Algiers, where Harry Hopkins, once again stricken with stomach ailments, left the ship to return home by plane and make his way to the Mayo Clinic in Minnesota. The defection angered Roosevelt, who wanted Hopkins's help in preparing a Yalta report. Hopkins never saw his old friend again. On the Atlantic leg home, Roosevelt worked on a speech to Congress, which Truman urged him to give. Roosevelt arrived back in Washington on February 28, having been absent for more than a month in wartime.[21]

On March 1, when Roosevelt appeared in the well of the House of Representatives to deliver his address, he received a standing ovation. He spoke from a seated position—something he had never done before, explaining that he had just traveled 14,000 miles and "with ten pounds of steel around the bottom of my legs," it was easier to remain in a chair. His hour-long talk was informal, a departure for him, which occasioned many impromptu comments and sometimes halting and even slurred observations. He couldn't turn the pages of his speech with his trembling right hand, so he used his left hand. His frail appearance and sometimes fumbling manner shocked many observers. Nonetheless, he conveyed a powerful message.[22]

His speech was not so much a report on Yalta as it was a plea to Congress—his final plea, as it turned out—to rally around the creation of the United Nations. His thinking clearly reflected a personal determination to avoid the errors of the League of Nations battle of 1919–1920. The Yalta accords, he promised his audience, "ought" to spell the end of unilateral actions, spheres of influence, balances of power, and exclusive alliances that "have been tried for centuries—and have always failed." He wanted the U.N. established right away. As he said, "This time we shall not make the mistake of waiting until the end of the war to set up the machinery of peace. This time, as we fight together to get the war over quickly, we work together to keep it from happening again." He reminded Congress, too, of the bipartisan nature of the U.S. delegation to San Francisco and how his administration had kept the U.S. Senate "continuously advised" on the preparations for the United Nations. He promised the adoption of a charter that would permanently outlaw aggression, but also warned that the U.N. Charter, like the U.S. Constitution, would not be perfect and might have to be amended. Finally, he bluntly insisted upon a continuing U.S. commitment to internationalism. "There can be no middle ground here. We shall have to take the responsibility for world collaboration, or we shall have to bear the responsibility for another world conflict."[23]

Four days later, Great Britain, the United States, and the USSR, as well as China, acting as the sponsoring powers, issued the formal invitations to San Francisco—initially to the thirty-seven nations that had, by March 1, declared war on one or more of the Axis enemy. France, though included as one of the five permanent states on the Security Council, did not participate as a co-host. General Charles De Gaulle, angered by his exclusion from Yalta, demanded that, unless certain unspecified French amendments were listed along with the Dumbarton Oaks proposal as the basis for the conference, Paris could not be a sponsor. Russia turned down his request, but France said it would attend the meeting anyway. The invitation also contained the once-secret voting formula agreed upon at Yalta. Secretary Stettinius read the language on the veto to the assemblage of Latin nations meeting in Mexico City. Reaction around the United States to the proposed procedure in the Security Council proved generally favorable in the media and within the U.S. delegation, though there was grumbling among smaller states. When a reporter who asked Roosevelt whether he'd achieved a victory for the nation, the president replied, "I should say it was a common agreement. . . . If anybody has a better idea, we would be glad to consider it."[24]

But one new obstacle suddenly intervened. On March 23, Stalin let it be known that he would not send his foreign minister, Molotov, to San Francisco; he would replace him with Andrei Gromyko, the Soviet envoy to the United States. Stalin was apparently angry about the refusal of his two allies to grant immediate U.N. membership to the Ukraine and Belarus, as well as with their arguments over Poland. Roosevelt felt directly affronted by Stalin, viewing this maneuver as mischievous and a setback to success at San Francisco. Molotov's absence, he warned Stalin, would be construed as a "lack of comparable interest" by the Soviet government. When Stalin would not retreat from his decision, Roosevelt on March 29 reminded him that, by allowing Molotov to miss San Francisco, he was trifling with U.S. public opinion, a mistake that could very well turn against the organization.[25]

Still, Roosevelt was gaining support everywhere else. As president, he had always cultivated a warm relationship with Latin America, beginning with his Good Neighbor policy of the 1930s and, during wartime, at the meeting of foreign ministers at Rio de Janeiro in mid-1942, where most Latin countries agreed to break diplomatic ties with the Axis. After Dumbarton Oaks, he had instructed Stettinius, along with Nelson Rockefeller, the new assistant secretary of state for Latin America, to set up another session with the Hemisphere nations to formulate a common strategy on the United Nations. A meeting was arranged in Mexico City that lasted from February 21 though March 5.

Stettinius flew from Moscow to five other international cities for various diplomatic stopovers, and finally to Mexico City. He soon discovered there that, although the delegates by and large wished to endorse the Dumbarton Oaks proposals, they also wanted to establish their own Latin regional security system; this system would be separate from that of the U.N. Conservative Latin governments were fearful of communism. Some were even convinced that the Security Council's authority might somehow allow greater Soviet influence in the Hemisphere. The United States, while it liked the idea of a common security organ in the Americas as a substitute for its much-criticized, heavy-handed Monroe Doctrine, did not want to weaken the U.N. Stettinius sought a way to mediate between the two impulses, global and regional. He helped negotiate an agreement called the Act of Chapultepec (named for the castle where the talks took place). The act stated that an attack on one state in the region would be considered an attack on all and would demand immediate collective consultation—though not necessarily a military response.[26]

This regional bloc now had to be harmonized in San Francisco with the U.N. The conferees signaled in a public message that they wanted official recognition for Latin "methods and procedures" in settling local controversies and more power for smaller nations in the General Assembly. The Latin contingent consisted of nineteen nations—including six one-time "associate" U.N. members—who had declared their "nonbelligerency" during the world conflict but had become eligible to attend by declaring war on the Axis by the deadline of March 1.

One considerable problem remained—Argentina. During the war, it had announced its "neutrality," but was considered pro-Nazi. Stettinius had wanted to bypass dealing with Argentina to avoid a row with Moscow, but, as he wired Roosevelt: "On arrival here, I found the Argentine situation boiling." He finally succumbed to pressure from Latin officials who were fearful that Argentina's further radicalization could possibly put their own states at risk, and decided that Washington should recognize Argentina if it declared war on the Axis, purged itself of Fascist influences, agreed to the Chapultepec resolution, and signed the United Nations Declaration. All in all, knowing that every one of these countries were potential U.S. votes, Stettinius sidestepped fights over Argentina, as well as over Dumbarton Oaks. He decided to allow the San Francisco Conference to sort out the Hemispheric relationship with the U.N. Subsequently, on March 27, four weeks past the cut-off point, Argentina officially turned against the Axis. On April 9, under pressure from Rockefeller, Roosevelt finally approved diplomatic ties with Buenos Aires even though it had not met the Yalta deadline for war declaration.[27]

Roosevelt's public campaign for the United Nations was picking up steam. Archibald MacLeish and his new aide, Adlai Stevenson, disseminated information about the U.N. in weekly forums; speeches, radio broadcasts, and civic meetings were also on their docket. MacLeish distributed *Watchtower Over Tomorrow,* a film about the Dumbarton Oaks plan, to groups around the land. An eight-page pamphlet containing the text of the Dumbarton Oaks proposals was sent out to over 1.25 million people, a mass distribution unprecedented for the State Department, placing it on the best-seller list. In early April, four hundred letters daily poured into the department, and by month's end reached 5,000 a day. Twenty-eight governors agreed to proclaim April 16–22 "Dumbarton Oaks Week," during which dozens of cities held town meetings. In New York City, the League of Women Voters sent out sound trucks to arouse public interest. On Sunday, April 22, churches around the nation held special prayer services for San Francisco. In addition, private associations played an important role. The Union for Democratic Action released 1 million copies of a cartoon brochure, "From the Garden of Eden to Dumbarton Oaks." Groups such as the Congress of Industrial Organizations (CIO), the Congregational Church movement, even townships in New Hampshire, pitched in. Edward Bernays, the famous PR guru, made his new book, *Take Your Place at the Peace Table,* available to activists. Polls reflected a change in perception: In December 1944, only 43 percent of the American people had heard of Dumbarton Oaks; 52 percent by February 1945; and 60 percent by March 1945. On the San Francisco Conference, 60 percent supported it after Roosevelt's January State of the Union message; 80 percent after Yalta; and the number who had heard of it jumped to 94 percent in April, on the eve of the meeting.[28]

There were some dissenting voices. On April 15, the National Catholic Welfare Conference expressed its fear that, in permitting the veto power, the plan for the world body could allow the Big Powers to use their military muscle against smaller nations without fear of reprisal. On April 23, a group of eminent Protestant ministers issued a declaration chiding the organizers for setting up an inequitable system. It called the U.N. proposals "a mere camouflage for the continuation of imperialistic policies and the exercise of arbitrary power by the Big Three for the domination of other nations." Even the editors of *Time* felt the charter should be liberalized, giving more authority to the General Assembly. But realists, among them the theologian Reinhold Niebuhr, while admitting there were risks in relying on the Great Powers, asked what the alternative was. Wrote Niebuhr: "Nations cannot create a new universal sovereignty above themselves by a pure fiat of will and then turn around and subject themselves to this sovereignty."[29]

Many private organizations backing the U.N. now clamored to send their own representatives to San Francisco. At the second full meeting of the U.S. delegation on March 23, the members approved the idea of "observers" and recommended opening the conference to everybody. But the president preferred inviting selected groups to send consultants and giving them semiofficial status. The delegation deferred to Roosevelt and, on March 29, Stettinius designated forty-two groups, balanced by various political and regional considerations. Clark Eichelberger advised on the choices, and an official list was released on April 10. The roster included business, labor, law, veterans, farmers, women, the three major faiths, peace societies, service clubs, and education. In addition, almost four times as many other private associations said they would attend as "observers." Some newspapers expressed dissatisfaction with the official choices. The left-wing newspaper *PM* claimed that labor, industry, agriculture, and the Zionist movement were omitted. But many observers regarded the presence of these outside interests at a major global assembly as a development that could only help bolster public opinion on behalf of the world organization.[30]

Roosevelt now began to make consultations with the U.S. delegation a more regular feature of his schedule. Initially, he approved a variety of new advisors to the delegation, both from within and from outside the government. At Stettinius's insistence, and with considerable reluctance, he acquiesced in the appointment of John Foster Dulles, who had served as foreign policy advisor to Governor Thomas Dewey in the 1944 presidential election. Stettinius persuaded Dulles to issue a public promise to adhere to "the practice of bipartisan action" and also to resign as chairman of his church group, the Commission on a Just and Durable Peace. Some of the others were Leo Pasvolsky as a "principal" advisor and senior negotiator; Alger Hiss as the secretary-general of the San Francisco Conference; John McCloy from the War Department; Abe Fortas, undersecretary of the interior; Harry Dexter White, assistant secretary of the treasury; Charles Bohlen and Ralph Bunche of the State Department, as well as assistant secretaries Nelson Rockefeller and Archibald MacLeish, and the special assistant to Stettinius, Adlai Stevenson.[31]

Still Roosevelt had not yet performed his most delicate task with the U.S. delegation, namely, informing them about his promise to Stalin to grant the USSR two extra votes in the General Assembly. He failed to bring up the subject at their first get-together on March 13, instead relating a few indiscreet stories about his dealings with Stalin and Churchill at Yalta. He finally confessed to his venture at the next session on March 23, ten days later. The delegates were stunned, according to Senator Vandenberg. Roosevelt quickly reminded them that, in exchange for the extra votes, Stalin would back a similar U.S. bid for three votes. He also glibly noted that the delegates were not bound by his action since he had told Stalin only that, if he were a delegate, he would vote for the Ukraine and Belarus. Thus, it was up to the U.S. participants to make the final decision.[32]

Vandenberg was distraught, writing in his diary, "This will raise hell," and later tried to reverse the decision internally. His concern seemed merited—at least at first. Just a week later, somebody with access to the information spilled the entire story to the *New York Herald Tribune,* which printed it as a front-page exposé on March 29. A furor ensued. Reporters jumped all over the spokesmen at the State Department and at the White House. Roosevelt, trying to calm the storm, confirmed the plan, but stated that the U.N. membership would make the ultimate determination. Vandenberg was incensed that Roosevelt did not reveal that the delegates had the right to ignore his promise to

Stalin, and he issued a denunciation of the accord. The day after the revelation, Stettinius tried to calm the waters by blandly telling reporters he had "complete confidence" that all these problems would be dealt with successfully in San Francisco.[33]

By Monday, April 2, however, Stettinius had become convinced that the United States was in an untenable position and must drop its request for two extra votes—first, because of the disgruntlement among its own delegates; second, because of the beating it was suffering in the press; and, third, because the extra votes were not necessary for U.S. national interests. He telephoned Roosevelt in Warm Springs and persuaded him to forgo the votes, while, at the same time, agreeing that he should uphold the Soviet's request. The next day, he told a press conference that, although the U.S. did not need the votes, Russia deserved the two extra seats because the two Soviet Republics concerned had "borne great suffering in the prosecution of the war." He also assured reporters that there were no other hidden agreements. But the *New York Times* columnist Arthur Krock was not mollified, intoning, "What will be the date-line on the leak of the next Yalta secret?" And even Roosevelt's own speechwriter, Robert Sherwood, called the matter one of FDR's "worst all-around botches." But the public did not evince much outrage. At Warm Springs, Roosevelt airily dismissed the votes in the General Assembly as "not really of any great importance. It is an investigatory body only." The matter died, proving that Roosevelt was right in waiting six weeks after Yalta because, as he surmised, the creation of the U.N. was more important than a minor side agreement.[34]

But there was one still confidential issue simmering that Roosevelt could not finesse before San Francisco: Poland. Ambassador Averell Harriman had been attending meetings starting on February 23 in Moscow of the so-called Tripartite Commission established at Yalta. From the onset, Foreign Minister Molotov had stalled about reorganizing the government in Warsaw. At the first session, he suggested that the Lublin regime must be the "nucleus" of any government and should have the right to veto outside Poles invited to a Moscow parley. He backed down when Harriman and the British envoy, Clark Kerr, noted that the Yalta protocol called the provisional state a "new" one, not an expanded version of the present one, and thus the commission was free to invite whomever it chose. Molotov kept advancing new excuses for inaction throughout the following weeks. As the days passed, Harriman wired the president that Lublin was becoming more and more "the ruler of Poland."[35]

Frustrated by the Russian stonewalling, the British and U.S. governments in a joint statement on March 19, and in personal letters from Churchill and Roosevelt on March 29, informed Stalin that the Yalta accord on Poland was being misinterpreted. Yalta, they argued, did not permit a veto by Lublin or the Big Three of outside Poles. Further, the Poles should be able to resolve the composition of the provisional state themselves. Finally, Allied observers should be admitted to Poland. Roosevelt flatly stated in his missive that "a thinly disguised continuance of the present Warsaw regime would be unacceptable" to Washington and make Yalta a failure in the eyes of Americans. Molotov refused even to discuss the Roosevelt or Churchill cables at the sixth meeting of the commission on April 2 because, he said, they had been addressed to Marshal Stalin. And on April 7, Stalin sent a personal note to Roosevelt reiterating Molotov's contentions, saying the talks had reached a "dead end" because of the intransigence of Harriman and Kerr in departing from the Yalta "principles." He even accused them of trying to exclude Lublin officials. Only Poles who accepted the Yalta decisions, including the Curzon Line, and were "friendly" to the Soviet Union should be invited to a Moscow meeting.[36]

Amidst the increasing rancor, Roosevelt now looked upon the San Francisco Conference increasingly as the answer to all the conundrums crowding in on him. In a final interview in late March with his closest confidante among the press, Anne O'Hare McCormick, who was writing a piece for the *New York Times Magazine,* Roosevelt envisaged a different kind of world order. Though on the verge of winning the war, McCormick noted, Roosevelt's thoughts were fixed on the meeting at the Golden Gate: "He was looking to the inauguration of the San Francisco Conference as the crowning act of his career. This was his project. He prepared it, set the time and place of the meeting, speeded up the preparations in the belief that it was supremely urgent."

She observed that Roosevelt was terribly conscious that the U.N. was his most important legacy. "He dreamed," she wrote, "of going down in history as the President who had succeeded where Woodrow Wilson failed in making the United States the great bastion" of an armed security system "while the forge of war was still hot enough to fuse nations together." He persuaded her that "all his hopes of success in life and immortality in history were set on getting an international security organization in motion." He had two concerns: insuring Soviet involvement in the U.N., and U.S. participation. To win Stalin's allegiance, "he was ready to make all the advances, to ignore rebuffs, to take long journeys, to offer concessions and accept compromises." To secure U.S. support, he wanted to take advantage of an American public opinion that was as "nearly unanimous in favor of participation as it ever would be. . . . [D]elay and differences over war settlements might cause a recession of popular sentiment."[37]

Roosevelt informed McCormick that he planned to attend the opening of the San Francisco Conference. Around the same time, he also advised Robert Sherwood, "I'm going to be there are the start and at the finish, too." He told the secretary of treasury, Henry Morganthau Jr.: "I will appear on the stage in my wheelchair, and will make a speech." And he confided to members of his inner circle that he would consider resigning from the presidency when the war was over and becoming the secretary-general of the United Nations. From March 29 on, while resting in Warm Springs to recover his strength, he reviewed plans for some of the logistics of the United Nations Conference, including the seating of the delegates, and requested the railroad itinerary to the West Coast city. He received regular updates from Secretary Stettinius. On April 6, he asked Archibald MacLeish to prepare a draft of the speech he wanted to deliver on the first day of the U.N. meeting. He thought he would compare the conference to the struggles for the American Union. Just thirteen days before his rendezvous with San Francisco, he died.[38]

CHAPTER 5

TRUMAN AND STETTINIUS
The Awkward Alliance

In the days following his formal address to Congress, the new president was caught up in a whirlwind of activity. But, despite a dramatic assumption of the responsibilities and burdens of the presidency, Truman kept his eyes fixed on the conference in San Francisco. He relied heavily on the secretary of state, Edward Stettinius, whom he had inherited from his predecessor, to provide him with initial guidance. However, his relationship with Roosevelt's man quickly became strained. Rumors about Truman's imminent decision to replace Stettinius with James Byrnes were swirling around Washington, and Stettinius was painfully aware of them.

Three days after Truman's swearing in, on April 16, Stettinius confronted the new president. Tom Connally, one of the U.S. delegates, he said, had informed him that morning of a report that Byrnes was flying to San Francisco to lead the U.S. team. An indignant Stettinius offered his resignation on the spot. Truman denied the rumor and said that, quite to the contrary, Brynes was not going to the conference, and that he, Truman, reposed the greatest respect and trust in Stettinius as delegation leader. Stettinius then requested a letter or statement from the president declaring that he wanted to keep Stettinius as the mission's head and attesting publicly to his backing. Truman promised, "I'll do that." (And, keeping his vow, nine days later, in his address to the U.N. conference opening day, Truman told the worldwide audience that Edward Stettinius had his "complete confidence" as the chairman of the U.S. delegation.)[1]

Privately, though, Truman had little use for Stettinius. His offer to Byrnes to become secretary of state was a real one, and, although it reflected his concern that the man next in line for the succession be an elected official, it also revealed his intense disdain for Stettinius. Indeed, even the indiscreet way he made the overture to Byrnes, whether through impulsiveness or calculation, just days before Stettinius was to depart for San Francisco, seemed a signal act of cruelty. In a later crack at the secretary of state some years after he left office, Truman told one interviewer: "Stettinius was as dumb as they come." He observed to a biographer: "There was Stettinius, Secretary of State—a fine man, good-looking, amiable, cooperative, but never an idea new or old." There was also a feeling that Truman, as a partisan political leader, did not like Stettinius because he was not a real Democrat.[2]

Stettinius's standing among his contemporaries was not much better. Within the State Department, several top officials harbored deep reservations. Archibald MacLeish, assistant secretary of state for public affairs, called Stettinius "Snow White" for his ineffectual affability; MacLeish later said the secretary's performance in San Francisco was "beyond belief"—this, in a letter to another assistant secretary, Dean Acheson, who himself observed about Stettinius in his memoirs that he had "gone far with comparatively modest equipment." Henry Stimson, the secretary of war, considered Stettinius to be kind, pleasant, inexperienced, uninformed, and well-intentioned, but without firmness of decision or character. John McCloy, assistant secretary of war, dismissed him as possessing "no real leadership and no real ideas. He tries to keep everybody happy by jollying them and inviting them to cocktails." The treasury secretary, Henry Morganthau, wrote Stettinius off as a "lifelong Republican," and said that Roosevelt clearly wanted a "good clerk" at the State Department; and Charles Bohlen observed that he was a "decent man of considerable innocence." Within the U.S. delegation, there were also doubts. Senator Vandenberg regarded Stettinius, at least initially, as a "presidential messenger" who, although a "grand person with every good intention and high honesty of purpose," did not have the experience for the job. "He rarely contributes to our policy decisions," observed Vandenberg. "We improvise as we go along."

Delegate Virginia Gildersleeve complimented Stettinius for being "a friendly, affable 'mixer,' attractive, good-tempered" who created an "excellent team spirit"; but she also suggested that he was a "superficial person on the intellectual side" who knew little "about other countries or international relations."[3]

Or, as one outside advisor to the delegation, Ralph Bunche, flatly wrote his wife: "Stettinius is a complete dud. . . . [H]e is simply in a job for which he has utterly no qualifications and about which he knows nothing. He can't make a move without asking someone what to do." Another observer, *New York Times* correspondent James Reston, expressed his dissatisfaction with Stettinius in a letter to Arthur Krock, then Washington bureau chief of the *Times*: "I don't believe he has been able to overcome his lack of knowledge or experience in the foreign field. I do not believe he has acquired the admiration or in some cases even the respect of his own unofficial family or of the men at his own level who lead the other delegations."[4]

Stettinius, however, had his odd, if uneasy, defenders. James Forrestal, the secretary of the navy, taking exception to a May 1 editorial attack by the *Washington Post* on Stettinius, told *Time* magazine publisher Henry Luce at a dinner party that "Mr. Stettinius was the pitcher for our team and . . . he was entitled to support and cheers rather than brickbats and pop bottles from the American grandstand. I remarked it was clear that Mr. Stettinius was not a Disraeli, a Metternich, or a Machiavelli, but I remarked that neither had I seen anyone else on the horizon who has such abilities." The U.S. ambassador to the Soviet Union, Averell Harriman, briefly present in San Francisco, admired the way Stettinius as chairman judiciously conducted his daily sessions with the delegation; despite a lack of diplomatic training, he maintained a bipartisan spirit and gave all the delegates a chance to express their views fully. A Pasvolsky aide, James Green, observed that Stettinius was a "great manager" who "brought the State Department into the 20th century. He updated it. . . . A really marvelous Undersecretary, but not a first-rate Secretary." So, too, even Arthur Krock, who, like his colleague James Reston, privately regarded Stettinius as uninformed on foreign issues, praised him for being a "passive referee of disputes within the U.S. delegation" and allowing such luminaries as Dulles and Vandenberg to speak out at will, thereby preserving the unity of group and keeping rivalries "to a minimum" in negotiations with other missions. One of the few officials who openly admired Stettinius was the relatively lackluster New York congressman, Sol Bloom, who recalled with gratitude "the strong, confident leadership of young Ed Stettinius" in his memoirs. More sober scholars, looking back at what San Francisco eventually wrought, pondered where the conclave would have been had Stettinius been "more arbitrary, more self-assured, and less willing to smother his own ego and his own preconceptions in the interests of advancing the new world organization."[5]

In any event, it was difficult to square all these characterizations, whether adverse or merely circumspect, with the record Stettinius had compiled in his career in private industry and during wartime. Though from a moneyed background (his father was a partner in J. P. Morgan), and though not an especially accomplished student at the University of Virginia (he never graduated), Stettinius evinced early on a sense of social responsibility, working in the rural slums in the nearby Blue Ridge Mountains, reorganizing the campus YMCA, and helping students find local jobs. Then, in the business world, demonstrating previously concealed talents, he emerged as a hard-driving, take-charge executive with a savvy diplomatic style. In 1938, when he was chairman of the board for the U.S. Steel Company, he made an immediate impression on Franklin Roosevelt when he opposed a suggestion that his firm's wages be reduced in proportion to the declining price of steel. The next year, Roosevelt invited him to become chairman of the War Resources Board.[6]

Upon tasting government service, Stettinius plunged in full-time, resigning in May 1940 from U.S. Steel to join the National Defense Advisory Commission. Soon thereafter, Harry Hopkins, whose friendship he had cultivated, helped him obtain the directorship of priorities at the Office of Production Management, and in September, 1941, through Hopkins's lobbying with Roosevelt, the stewardship of the Lend-Lease Program. Two years later, in the fall of 1943, he went to the State Department as undersecretary, where he was immediately assigned to reorganize the department, a task he handled adeptly. His meteoric rise, especially as a nonparty representative of big business, dismayed many New Dealers. But he demonstrated skill in tapping the talents of others more experienced than he was. At Dumbarton Oaks, he continually deferred to experts such as Pasvolsky when he did not know the subject matter well. And, at Yalta, with the help of State Department aides, he delivered Churchill and Stalin a masterful briefing on the U.S. voting formula in the U.N. Security Council. Stalin remarked the following afternoon that, "as a result of the clear explanation given the previous day," he was now accepting the U.S. proposal.[7]

Part of his problem was that Stettinius did not relate well to the press corps. In one notable occasion at the Dumbarton Oaks conference, he stumbled at a press conference in trying to calm the uproar triggered by James Reston's exclusive account about the confidential U.S. proposals on the United Nations. He appeared patronizing when he tried to address the journalists by their first names and refused to answer, or deflected, most questions. His fumbling appearance left a lasting negative impression. He had also undoubtedly suffered from the "pretty boy" syndrome. He was an attractive silver-haired man, younger than most of his colleagues as well as all of the U.S. delegates. Author Patricia Bosworth, recalling the opening day of San Francisco, recounted watching "an improbably handsome man with silver hair and thick black eyebrows." Her mother, she related, whispered to her: "'My God, he's divine.'" Stettinius's matinee-idol glamour indubitably contributed to the sense of superficiality people felt about him.[8]

Nonetheless, in the furious rush of meetings and decisions and public events in Washington before the conference, Stettinius and Truman began to work out a modus operandi for San Francisco. Truman set the ground rules, telling Stettinius from the onset that he must consult with Senators Connally and Vandenberg "on every move in order to get full agreement" in San Francisco to avoid another League "tragedy" in the Senate. He warned: "If he could not get those men to go along, he was to call me, and I would try to resolve the issues by telephoning them personally." Further, he wanted Stettinius to "telephone me at the conclusion of each day and night session. He was not to hesitate to call me at any hour, and because of this arrangement, all important matters were referred to me either for my suggestions or approval." Stettinius, still struggling to fashion a relationship with Truman, embraced rather than resented the president's close oversight. Truman's marching orders provided Stettinius a direct daily line of communication to the White House, gave him an input into the major presidential deliberations on the U.N., reaffirmed his central role as the leader of the U.S. delegation, and offered him possible political cover should egregious mistakes occur in California.[9]

Stettinius made certain that Truman was kept abreast of developments within the delegation. He informed the president immediately about the consultations that occurred before Truman's takeover, whereby the U.S. team approved changes in the Dumbarton Oaks document, mainly stylistic adjustments and clarifications, many championed by the Republican advisor, John Foster Dulles. It endorsed eight amendments that Vandenberg had presented for consideration. Several related to international law and human rights, and five of the eight were designed to incorporate a principle Vandenberg sought allowing the United Nations to recommend revisions in treaties that were found unjust or threatening to peace. This was the most controversial of his proposals. Some observers suspected that Vandenberg's motivation for these changes was to rectify what he viewed as Roosevelt's infamous deal with Stalin over Poland at Yalta. Whatever the reason, Stettinius submitted that the Vandenberg emendations as well as one from Harold Stassen calling for a periodic review of the U.N. Charter should be reviewed by Truman.[10]

Truman and Stettinius met on April 19 to make the final decisions. Truman quickly okayed the Vandenberg and Stassen proposals. There was also some wording enabling the General Assembly to discuss questions bearing on peace and security, even though the Security Council hitherto had exclusive say over those matters. Stettinius favored the latter provision to make it possible for nations to circumvent the Security Council if a Big Power prevented action by use of the veto. Truman agreed, even imagining the Security Council and the General Assembly as playing the roles of the U.S. Senate and the House of Representatives—

though he soon realized that few countries were ready to accept an actual world parliament. The two men backed off and determined that, for the moment, they should reserve their position on the General Assembly until they heard from other nations. Truman was especially anxious to receive the support of the Western Hemisphere and the British Commonwealth states. As he wrote candidly in his memoirs: "We felt if we had that sort of backing, we would get almost anything we wanted." At the same time, Truman seemed to revel in his keen attention to the details about the U.N. "I went over these proposed changes," he recalled. "They were accepted and, with my approval, constituted a directive and working guide for the conference."[11]

One other issue of contention was the dispute over trusteeships. The war and navy departments had persisted in holding to a position that the United States for security purposes should control all the Japanese islands it seized during the war—and wanted to postpone discussion of the matter at San Francisco. Stettinius and the interior department were adamantly opposed to a public "annexation" policy, and regarded a resolution of the issues at the conference as essential. Only a firm U.S. stance for U.N. ministration, they argued, would prevent other Big Powers from grabbing conquered land for themselves. So divisive was this matter that, over the course of months, it roiled the Roosevelt administration and was threatening now to do the same to Truman's fledgling government. It would have damaged Stettinius's standing if he had allowed it to get out of control.

Bumping into James Forrestal, as well as Admiral Ernest King and General George Marshall, while waiting to board Roosevelt's funeral train in Washington's Union Station on the morning of April 14, Stettinius offered to talk compromise with the defense establishment. Over the next few days, with Forrestal and Stimson in attendance, Stettinius devised a plan to designate certain areas of trust territories held by administering nations as "strategic," which meant they would be used solely for military bases and be exempt from oversight by the General Assembly and its Trusteeship Council (though the Security Council, where the United States had the veto, could exercise some supervision over them). The rest of the territories would go to the Trusteeship Council.

When he had the agreement of all the parties, on April 17 he presented
the proposal to the U.S. delegation, which, with minor changes, agreed
to it, and then to Truman at a session the next day. Forrestal and Stimson
were present at both meetings. To Stettinius's relief, Truman approved
the approach—a week before the opening of San Francisco.[12]

Stettinius also arranged for Truman to hold a private meeting with
the U.S. delegation on Tuesday, April 17, his first official encounter
with the group, just before the seven members left for the West Coast.
Truman made a favorable impression. Vandenberg found him to be
"modest, unassuming and cordial." Truman set out his agenda to the
delegates, saying that "we ought to strive for an organization to which
all nations would delegate enough powers to prevent another world
war"—a candid acceptance on his part of a somewhat lessened U.S.
sovereignty within the global community. At the same time, though, he
cautioned the delegates that they still had to adopt a charter that was
acceptable to the U.S. Senate. "I emphasized," he later recalled, "that I
wanted them to write a document that would pass the U.S. Senate and
that would not arouse such opposition as confronted Woodrow Wilson." Later that morning, he told his first press conference that since he
had a "competent" delegation traveling to the Golden Gate city, there
was no need for him to go himself. Three days later, on April 20, Truman met with Senator Connally just before the latter's departure for
California and, in a brief chat, gave him an enthusiastic and forceful
send-off. That afternoon, he attended a reception at Blair House for the
heads of all of the U.N. delegations on their way to San Francisco.[13]

Whether deliberately or not, the breadth of Truman's involvement
with the U.N. so soon into his administration sent an unambiguous
message to the public—that he placed great value on this historic
event. His close public identification with the world conference soon
helped to generate among Americans a wave of excitement and anticipation about an assembly to end all wars—a mood arising in spite of
the prevailing sadness and profound dismay felt over the loss of the nation's leader, Franklin Roosevelt, days earlier. This swelling tide of ex-
hilaration and tension came to a climax of sorts on Friday, April 20,
when Senators Connally and Vandenberg took their formal leave from

the Senate to fly to San Francisco. Both men delivered brief talks on the floor to a crowded and hushed chamber. In an eloquent and simple oration, Connally promised that the delegation would operate on a nonpartisan basis, seek to liberalize the Dumbarton Oaks text, and try to restore durable peace to the world. At the same time, he warned that he could not be expected to "bring back perfection." He added, with a note of missionary pride, "The United States has a peculiar responsibility. It has a lofty duty to perform in leading the peoples of the earth away from the concepts of rule by the sword." Connally had tears in his eyes as he sat down. Vandenberg complimented Connally and, after cautioning in short remarks of his own that "I have no illusions that the San Francisco Conference can chart the Millennium," nonetheless vowed that he was setting forth "with a sense of the deepest dedication to a supreme cause." The presentations by the two senators from different parties stirred deep emotions in a normally placid arena. Legislators on both sides of the aisles clambered to their feet, clapping in violation of the Senate rules and surging forward to shake their hands, to hug the two delegates, and to wish them well. The Senate adjourned promptly for the day in their honor.[14]

The next day, April 21, Stettinius had yet another private session with Truman in which the men grappled again with two additional matters facing the conference. The first was the simmering controversy over the two extra votes Roosevelt had promised the Soviet Union at Yalta. Truman had, along with the U.S. delegation, and with some reluctance, agreed to support the Roosevelt position. Now, as a way of reinforcing Stettinius's authority in San Francisco in dealing with Molotov, Truman handed him a formal letter affirming U.S. backing for the Soviet proposal—though, at the same time, pointing out that it was ultimately a matter for the conference itself to determine.

The other burning question was Argentina. Stettinius told Truman that "there were commitments involved" in permitting Buenos Aires to attend the U.N. meeting in San Francisco. Truman's answer was that he didn't like it at all and that it was wrong. Argentina, he said, reminded him of a guy who gets on the political bandwagon "in the last five minutes" to qualify for an ambassadorship.[15]

But Stettinius reminded the president of the recent history of U.S.-Argentine relations. For over a year since March 14, 1944, he noted, Washington had refused to recognize the pro-fascist regime of General Edelmiro Farrell and his swashbuckling deputy, Colonel Juan Peron—the regime that had ousted another military government which, under U.S. pressure, had broken with the Axis. Now, at the recent conference in Mexico City, he recalled, Washington had acquiesced in a Latin proposal to recognize Argentina once it agreed to declare war on the Axis powers and adhere to the conference's declaration that, among other things, obligated that nation to relax censorship and revise right-wing textbooks. In a meeting with Nelson Rockefeller, the assistant secretary of state, Roosevelt had given his personal blessing to a deal for diplomatic recognition of Argentina. Subsequently, on March 27, Buenos Aires declared war, and on April 4, signed the so-called Chapultepec document. The country then began to seize pro-Axis properties, though there was some ambiguity about whether Argentina was really cracking down on Nazi sympathizers. Finally, on April 9, the United States extended formal relations to Argentina. Truman now said he would stand by any Roosevelt commitment but he did not want to take the lead on the proposal—meaning that he'd reluctantly approve Argentina's eventual admission to the U.N., but not necessarily its signing of the U.N. Declaration or its participation in the conference itself.[16]

The one formidable challenge still facing Truman and Stettinius was the continuing quarrel with the Soviets over Poland. The U.S. ambassador to the USSR, Averell Harriman, played the major role here. He had twice pleaded with Stettinius for permission to return to Washington in early April before Roosevelt's demise so that he could personally explain to the president why, in his judgment, Stalin was reneging on the Yalta agreement over Poland and how he should handle it. After Roosevelt died, Harriman redoubled his efforts to fly home, but Stettinius kept turning him down, telling him on April 13 that Truman felt it "essential that we have you in Moscow." Then Harriman, a force on his own, persuaded Stalin to send Molotov to San Francisco. This compelled Stettinius to give in to Harriman and permit him to accompany Molotov to Washington.[17]

The role of Harriman suddenly took center stage. Indeed, Harriman's initial outmaneuvering of Stettinius and landing in Washington with a strategy on Poland was no surprise to most observers, given his imposing personality. The son of Edward H. Harriman, president of the Union Pacific Railroad, one of the notable "robber barons" of the nineteenth century, Harriman was accustomed to handling wealth and exercising power and to getting his own way. A venturesome character, he had developed the Sun Valley resort in his youth, was a renowned polo player, had won a manganese concession in Russia in 1924, had conferred frequently with Leon Trotsky and other Communist sachems in the 1920s, and had become acquainted with Winston Churchill and Benito Mussolini, among many foreign leaders. Originally a Republican, he turned Democratic upon voting for Alfred Smith, the governor of New York, for president in 1928. A friend of both Roosevelt and Hopkins, he joined the New Deal as an official of the National Recovery Administration. Because of Harriman's reputation as a hard-nosed negotiator, Roosevelt sent him to London in 1941 to gauge British war needs, and later to visit Moscow to see Stalin. There, eventually, he became the U.S. ambassador. During his two-and-one-half-year stint in Moscow from 1943 to 1945, Harriman carried on a lonely and effective, if often contentious, relationship with the Soviet dictator.[18]

But before the ambassador's departure from Moscow, Stettinius asked Harriman to caution Stalin that President Roosevelt's "greatest concern" before his death was the failure of the Polish negotiations. Stettinius wanted Harriman to gain Stalin's consent for Molotov to speak about Poland with Truman—apparently a last-minute endeavor by the secretary of state to settle a stubborn problem before San Francisco, for which he might also earn credit with his boss. At their Kremlin talks on April 15, Harriman did win the iron man's assent to such an arrangement. But subsequently, Harriman learned that Moscow was preparing to sign a treaty of mutual assistance with the pro-Soviet government in Warsaw, violating the Yalta Declaration. He wired Stettinius and the State Department promptly asked Stalin that the pact be deferred. Meanwhile, Harriman dispatched his own confidential assessment of the Polish situation to Stettinius who, in turn, conveyed it to

Truman on the morning of April 16, at a White House meeting. Harriman, according to his toughly worded memo, appraised Stalin's April 7 replies to Roosevelt and Churchill as "contributing little of a concrete nature toward a solution of the impasse now existing." He added that Washington should again urge that the Polish state "be reorganized on a broad democratic basis" and that the United States not "accept a whitewash of the Warsaw regime."[19]

Later that same morning in Washington, in a meeting with Anthony Eden, the British foreign minister, Truman ironed out the final text of the message he and Churchill were sending to Stalin designed "to correct the completely erroneous impression" regarding the stance of the Western allies toward Warsaw. Their message faithfully reaffirmed Roosevelt's position arguing for the inclusion of the Lublin leadership in any Moscow parley, but disagreed with the contention that Warsaw should have a veto over opposition members in any coalition. The two leaders forcefully defended their right to recommend outside participants as part of the original Yalta bargain, and they even forwarded eight names of underground Poles and those in the government-in-exile in London to be considered for a part in the consultations.[20]

Impetuous and headstrong as ever, little daunted by all the issues at stake, Harriman left Moscow for Washington at 5:00 A.M. on April 17, setting out before Molotov boarded his plane so that he could beat him to Washington and brief Truman first. Harriman took a private craft, a B-24 named "Becky," and flew a direct route over the Balkans to Italy, refueling in Casablanca, crossing the Atlantic, making another refueling stop in the Azores, then on to on Prince Edward Island for more fuel, and thence to Washington, arriving at 11:30 P.M. local time on April 18. His flight of forty-nine hours and eighteen minutes established a new record for air travel between Moscow and Washington, shaving seven hours off the previous mark. Molotov, for whom the United States had placed a C-54 at his disposal, arrived almost four days later, on April 22, following a more traditional—and longer—itinerary over Soviet territory, via the Bering Strait, and down over Alaska.[21]

While Harriman was in the air, the Kremlin radio reported a Soviet statement insisting that Poland's Warsaw regime be seated at San Francisco—a position contrary to Roosevelt's express injunction at Yalta. The next day, the State Department received a formal note from the Soviet Union asking for the admission of the Polish "provisional government" as a U.N. member. On April 19, Stettinius rejected the request, pointing out that such an invitation could only be issued "in accordance with the Crimea agreement," which meant a coalition government had first to be constructed. It was now becoming clear that the Soviets had no intention of moderating or dropping their increasingly inflexible position over Poland, no matter that the San Francisco conference was about to begin. Harriman reinforced a hawkish response of the Americans. On the morning of April 20, at a seminar Harriman held at the State Department for some top officials, he argued that there was a "basic and irreconcilable difference of objectives between the Soviet Union and the United States." Stalin's insistence on "friendly" governments near his borders was really a demand for regimes under Moscow's domination. Harriman regarded concessions to Stalin on Eastern Europe as an encouragement to his country's further encroachment into Europe proper.[22]

Following his State Department stopover, around noontime, Stettinius took Harriman, Undersecretary Joseph Grew, and Charles Bohlen across the street for Harriman's first meeting with Truman. About to face Molotov, Truman was eager to obtain a reading on the Polish situation from the most important U.S. official at the front line. While Stettinius sat silently, Harriman gave a candid, if grim, rundown on the Soviet problem as he saw it after two years of dealings with Stalin. Moscow, he said, was pursuing two contradictory approaches—cooperating with the West while seizing control in the East. Yet, even with such behavior, Harriman felt Stalin would not risk damaging his ties with the United States because he desperately needed U.S. postwar reconstruction aid; and, besides, Stalin thought the United States badly wanted access to the Soviet market. The United States had nothing to lose, then, by showing some obstinacy. Truman jumped in to say that he personally was not afraid of the Russians. He planned to be firm but fair with them. "Anyway," he told Harriman, "the Russians need us more than we need them."[23]

Harriman then reiterated the argument he had presented earlier at the State Department: that Russia sought total subservience of all of its neighboring countries and would use the secret police and other totalitarian methods to tighten its grip. It was a new "barbarian invasion of Europe," devoid of lawful basis. Still, he argued, the United States could establish a working relationship with Moscow. Truman answered that he could never expect 100 percent cooperation with U.S. proposals, but, he added with the naïveté of an eager pupil, maybe 85 percent. Harriman reviewed the Polish situation, stating his opinion that Stalin didn't want to comply with the Yalta accord because the Lublin regime would lose control. Harriman wondered what Truman would do if Stalin rejected the joint proposal on Poland that he and Churchill had just sent to the Kremlin. Truman's emphatic answer was that, if Russia did not do its duty on Poland, the Senate would not approve a U.N. treaty. "I intended to tell Molotov just that in words of one syllable," he proclaimed. When Harriman pressed him on how he would respond if the USSR walked out of the U.N. conference, Truman, still unsure of his footing on that matter, replied truthfully that there would be no organization without Russia. Harriman, who personally believed that Washington should hold the conference even if the Soviets dropped out, was nonplussed, as he later confessed.[24]

Still, because Truman had read the Yalta agreements and the Stalin-Roosevelt correspondence, he impressed Harriman—even though the president seemed overly humble about foreign policy. Harriman confided to Truman at the conclusion of the session that he had rushed back to Washington because he was concerned that Truman "did not understand, as I had seen Roosevelt understand, that Stalin is breaking his agreements. My fear was inspired by the fact that you could not have had time to catch up with all the recent cables. But I must say that I am greatly relieved to discover that you have read them all and that we see eye to eye on the situation." Truman replied: "I am glad that you are going to be available to our delegation in San Francisco."[25]

The following day, Stettinius saw Truman at the White House at a morning meeting—the same session in which the two had found common cause on how to proceed on Argentina and the two extra votes for the USSR. Truman spoke about Poland and confessed to Stettinius that, despite his close reading of the Yalta minutes regarding the Lublin regime, he found the agreement "very hazy." Nonetheless, he told Stettinius, as he had told Harriman, that a failure to reach agreement on Poland would "jeopardize" the U.N. conference and endanger its chances for ratification in the Senate. Shortly afterward, and unbeknownst to Stettinius, Truman met with Harriman for another briefing. The next day, upon learning of Truman's confidential tryst, Stettinius betrayed his insecurity in a bitter memorandum: "I am burned up with the way in which Harriman has been acting. He went to see the president without any of us knowing about it and has not reported to anyone yet what took place."[26]

On April 22, Molotov arrived in Washington at 5:46 in the evening aboard a giant four-motored U.S. plane, waving a gray fedora as he disembarked. He was quickly escorted to Blair-Lee House, next door to Blair House, where the Trumans were in temporary residence. Earlier the same day, the Soviet Union in a surprise announcement accorded diplomatic recognition to the Lublin faction, placing Molotov's visit in a new and ominous light. Stalin himself attended the formal ceremony of Soviet and Polish officials, personally signing the treaty of mutual assistance and even making a speech calling the occasion one of "historical significance"—an unusual departure for the normally taciturn dictator. It was a move apparently designed to let the West know that Moscow would follow its own path on Poland. Truman learned about Stalin's maneuver as he was prepping for his Molotov encounter with his inner circle of advisors—Stettinius, Harriman, Bohlen, Assistant Secretary of State James Dunn, and visiting Foreign Minister Eden. On hearing the news, Truman reacted calmly and told his aides that the Soviet action was not "helpful," but he would not raise the matter with Molotov unless the latter did so first.[27]

At 8:30 in the evening, Truman finally met Molotov for thirty minutes. It was in the nature of a courtesy visit before the more extended discussions the next day. Truman reassured Molotov that he would abide by all the commitments that Franklin Roosevelt had made as president; he also referred briefly to his concern over Poland, saying that it was a matter of "great importance" to American public opinion. Molotov, in turn, reminded the president of Poland's proximity to Russia and its historical significance in the nation's security, but said he was sure a deal could be worked out "provided the views of the Soviet Union were taken into consideration." Truman then turned to Stettinius and expressed his hope that he, Eden, and Molotov might resolve the matter in a series of meetings they were starting that night at the State Department.[28]

The next afternoon at 2:00 P.M., several hours before his formal session at 5:30 P.M. with Molotov, Truman convened a council of his advisors to assess how to deal with the Soviet visitor. Truman called in Stettinius, Secretary of War Stimson, Secretary of the Navy Forrestal, Admiral Leahy, General Marshall, Admiral King, Assistant Secretary of State Dunn, Ambassador Harriman, General Deane, and Charles Bohlen. First, Stettinius reported back to Truman that, sadly, after a three-hour session with Molotov the night before and another that morning, the principals had reached a "complete deadlock" on Poland. Stettinius had even warned Molotov that, without progress on Poland, the San Francisco conference was in serious trouble—an admonition to no avail. Molotov clung tenaciously to the predetermined Soviet position. Warsaw, he said, should have the final say about participants in any coalition government because it was the only regime now in Poland and it alone was mentioned in the Yalta Declaration. The allies, he insisted, should follow the model of Yugoslavia in composing the new government, giving the Lublinites three to four members for every non-Communist Pole. Lastly he reiterated the Russian demand that Poland be admitted forthwith to the United Nations conference in San Francisco.[29]

Whether it was his several talks with Harriman, the news the day before of Stalin's precipitous diplomatic embrace of Poland, or Stettinius's report, Truman seemed now no longer in any mood for charity toward the Soviet foreign minister. Truman told his aides in no uncertain terms that, so far as he was concerned, U.S. agreements with the USSR had so far been a "one-way street" and this could not continue. As he later recalled in his memoirs: "I told my advisors that we intended to go on with the plans for San Francisco and if the Russians did not wish to join us, that would be too bad." Others at the preparatory talks remember that Truman used saltier language and said at one point that the Russians could "go to hell," and that "it was now or never."[30]

The reaction among his coterie was, for the most part, supportive. Secretary Forrestal, a crusty but thoughtful conservative, felt that the United States had better have a showdown with the Russians over Eastern Europe "now rather than later." Harriman believed the government should make a stand over Soviet "domination" of Poland, and that it could do so without severing ties with Moscow. Admiral Leahy, who had attended Yalta, felt the Soviets had "no intention" of freeing Poland but that, given Yalta's ambiguous prose, he was still concerned over breaking off relations with Russia. Among the more cautious voices were Secretary Stimson and General Marshall, both of whom believed the Soviets had kept to their military commitments to the West and were now about to enter the war against Japan. Hence they cautioned that the United States should avoid estrangement if possible over Poland, especially since, in any event, it was a country critical to Russia's security. Stimson contended that few nations anyway really "understood free elections" and that the United States should at least first find out Stalin's "motives." Truman reassured the group that he had no intention of delivering an ultimatum; he was only making the U.S. position clear to Molotov. Still, as Stimson later noted in his diary, the president was "evidently disappointed at my caution." Significantly, Truman asked only Stettinius, Harriman, Leahy, and Bohlen to stay behind for his Molotov encounter.[31]

Truman's demeanor when Molotov arrived for the meeting, accompanied by the Russian envoy to the United States, Andrei Gromyko, and an interpreter, Vladimir Pavlov, was a mix of deliberate skepticism and controlled fury. As Truman related, "There was little protocol," and then he went straight to the point: "I was sorry to learn . . . there was no progress" on Poland. Molotov, in turn, expressed his regrets. Truman reiterated that his joint four-point proposal with Churchill dispatched to Moscow on April 16 was "eminently fair and reasonable." The Polish government had to have representative "democratic elements" within it, and it was "deeply" disappointing to him that Warsaw had not held consultations with the other parties. Truman stated that he was now prepared to go forward with the U.N. meeting "no matter what difficulties or differences might arise with regard to other matters"—an obvious hint to Molotov that the United States was ready to go it alone if the Russians bowed out of San Francisco over the Polish matter. He also suggested that Congress would enact no foreign economic assistance "unless there was public support" for legislation—another signal to Moscow that it should not necessarily expect U.S. help. Then he handed a note to Molotov to give to Stalin that restated all his points on Poland and warned that without an agreement the unity of the wartime Allies would be "seriously" shaken.[32]

Molotov held unswervingly to his script. He was a cold and obdurate figure, a survivor of civil war, deathly political intrigues, bloody purges, and the banishment of his wife by Stalin, a man whom Alexsandr Solzhenitsyn had once described as "saturated in blood." He replied that Russia objected to any one of the Allies imposing its will on any of the others. Truman answered that he was just asking for the USSR to uphold Yalta. Molotov said it was a "matter of honor" for his country and that all difficulties could be overcome. Truman retorted sharply that Stalin must keep to his word. Molotov noted Stalin's April 7 message calling for a Yugoslav-type settlement. Truman cuttingly repeated that the Yalta accord must be carried out. Molotov accused others of abrogating the Yalta agreement, not the Soviets, and said that, as Poland was a neighbor, she was within the Russian "interest." In Truman's eyes, Molotov seemed to be "avoiding the main issue." He finally rejoined in exasperation that the United States was prepared to adhere to Yalta, but that it was not a "one-way street" and Russia must do the same.[33]

At this point, Molotov "turned a little ashy" and tried to begin a discussion of the Japanese war. Truman cut him off. "That will be all, Mr. Molotov. I would appreciate if you could transmit my views to Marshall Stalin." "I have never been talked to like that in my life," Molotov responded. Truman spoke bluntly: "Carry out your agreements and you won't get talked to like that." Truman abruptly got up and waved the meeting to an end. Molotov, according to Gromyko, had been prepared to promise Truman that Russia would work together with the United States at San Francisco on a variety of issues, but he never got the chance. He walked out instead. From that day on, he expressed a lifelong dislike of the president—a feeling that Truman cordially reciprocated.[34]

Averell Harriman was taken aback at Truman's unyielding performance and wondered whether Molotov would now tell Stalin that Truman was abandoning Roosevelt's policies. Charles Bohlen was pleased, however, later recalling "how I enjoyed translating Truman's sentences." In his opinion, Truman was only reaffirming Roosevelt's course, albeit with a Missourian's rough-edged approach. Later, Stettinius recounted the tale of the showdown in San Francisco to members of the U.S. delegation. Vandenberg, still seething over what he conceived as the unfairness of Roosevelt's Polish deal, was euphoric, writing in his diary, "FDR's appeasement of Russia is over. . . . [I]t is no longer going to be all 'give' and no 'take.'"[35]

By the next evening, Stalin, after hearing from Molotov, sent his reply to the joint Truman-Churchill missive on Poland. Truman called it "one of the most revealing and disquieting messages to reach me during my first days in the White House." In it, Stalin asserted that the Yalta agreement had made the Warsaw regime the "core" of any future Polish government, not just one among several Polish factions. Further, he wrote, his nation's desire for security vis-à-vis Poland was no different from Great Britain's insistence on having sympathetic governments in Belgium and Greece. Russia could not, in any event, permit a "hostile" state next door on whose fields "the blood of the Soviet people [was] abundantly shed." The settlement had to be in accordance with Soviet interests. He once again cited the Yugoslav precedent as the model for Poland. He concluded his prickly message: "You demand too much of me." Still, Stalin did not use Truman's dressing down of Molotov as an excuse to withdraw from the U.N. conference. Truman won this round.[36]

Sobered by his exchange with the Russian leader, twenty-four hours later President Truman delivered an opening speech to the San Francisco Conference by radio at 7:30 in the evening Eastern time from the White House. He was introduced by Stettinius, who had just arrived in the California city and was serving as chairman of the first session in the city's opera house. Truman's address to the quietly attentive delegates from forty-six nations by and large maintained a positive note. Ever conscious of the shadow cast by the League of Nations, he reminded his listeners that the conference was not going to be a peace negotiation as at Versailles. "It is not the purpose of this conference to draft a treaty of peace in the old sense of that term. It is not our assignment to settle specific questions of territories, boundaries, citizenship and reparations." Rather, this was a meeting devoted "exclusively to the single problem of setting up the essential organization to keep the peace. You are to write the fundamental charter."

Toward the end, he said: "The essence of our problem here is to provide sensible machinery for the settlement of disputes among nations," and he reminded the participants: "We were not isolated during the wars, we dare not become isolated in peace." And he reiterated: "If we do not want to die together in war, we must learn to live together in peace." Finally, Truman called for "building a permanent monument to those who gave their lives that this moment might come." He paid singular tribute to President Roosevelt: "Franklin Roosevelt gave his life while trying to perpetuate these high ideals. This Conference owes its existence, in a large part, to the vision and foresight and determination of Franklin Roosevelt."

New York Times correspondent Anne O'Hare McCormick observed that "President Truman's was not the magic voice of Franklin Roosevelt, but it was the voice of a man bent on the same end." Secretary Stettinius followed Truman, comparing the job ahead of the delegates to the task facing the pioneers who conquered the West by believing that all things were possible. He concluded: "We must and we shall fulfill the purpose for which we have come together." For all the apprehensions of the hour, the theme of hope still ran through the words of the Americans.[37]

CHAPTER 6

SECRET AGENTS,
BIG POWERS

Stettinius had considerable reason to be optimistic about San Francisco. Through the help of the U.S. Army Signal Security Agency (SSA), forerunner of the National Security Agency, and the Federal Bureau of Investigation, he was regularly given information about the foreign governments and domestic lobbying groups that came to the Golden Gate city. Via the SSA, he had an advanced peek at most of the diplomatic cable traffic on the United Nations emanating from at least forty-three of the forty-five nations (excluding Great Britain and the USSR) attending the meeting—as well as a continuing update on delegates' activities via a military listening post at the Presidio army base in San Francisco. So useful were these intercepts that, just days after the conference ended, he wrote a confidential letter to General Bissell, head of the SSA, telling him that the data he had received "has been of the greatest value to the State Department officials on the U.S. delegation" and expressed his "appreciation for their efforts." The FBI's own contribution, including backdoor snooping on the foreign emissaries, and even some freelance spying on the U.S. delegates themselves—as well as an investigation nationwide of San Francisco–bound pressure groups—also proved to be highly informative.[1]

There was a curious interlude, or bureaucratic squabble, that preceded the U.S. espionage operations in San Francisco. In mid-March 1945, the chief of the Office of Strategic Services (OSS), William Donovan, wrote to Stettinius to offer the services of his organization in collecting intelligence on the conference. He suggested that the OSS could conduct studies on critical questions facing the meeting, prepare dossiers on the delegates, and gather "a group of foreign experts" to do research on the organization. Stettinius discussed the proposal with his advisors, among them Alger Hiss. Hiss vociferously opposed the Donovan proposal, supporting the view of another Stettinius advisor who feared such undercover derring-do might "seriously embarrass us as host to the conference." Whether it was because he already had sufficient intelligence or because he was truly concerned about the public exposure, Stettinius turned down the OSS. But there may have been another reason—the struggle between J. Edgar Hoover, the FBI director, and Donovan over international intelligence operations had soured the State Department's attitude towards the OSS. Hoover's own Special Intelligence Service (SIS), which watched for subversion in the Hemisphere, aided by a State Department ally, Adolf Berle, the assistant secretary of state, had once tried unsuccessfully to take over some of the functions of the OSS. Stettinius had also in another instance forced the OSS to return the Soviet diplomatic codes it had seized to Moscow. These incidents probably steered Stettinius away from Donovan.[2]

In due course, Stettinius and his staff received some 635 pages of diplomatic messages from the SSA. The U.S. Army agency had access to most embassy cables through Western Union and other commercial telegraph companies that, under wartime censorship laws, had to pass on to the U.S. government coded and uncoded telegrams. The U.S. Army Communications Service also made the intercepts easier by inviting those delegations not using the private cable companies, mostly from smaller countries, to use its radio and wire facilities. The army agency, which had a dual function—one division broke codes and solved intercepts, and the Special Branch evaluated, edited, and distributed them as "Magic" Diplomatic Summaries—reported information to Stettinius obtained from all sorts of foreign diplomatic cryptograms. One method it employed to crack a nation's code was to examine how a foreign mission would translate documents issued by the U.N. Secretariat in its messages home. The U.N. papers in other words served as cribs for code breakers. Reproduced in purple ink by the Ditto process and issued daily to Stettinius, the memos averaged fifteen pages each. All were divided into three categories—military, political, and economic—and, where needed, into two others: psychological, and subversive and miscellaneous. Sometimes annexes amplified different items or gave the full text of significant papers; occasionally maps were included. The scope was enormous; it ranged from German military plans as reported by the Japanese ambassador to attitudes of Afghan officials to Japanese intelligence activities. Stettinius received all the data relevant to the questions facing San Francisco.[3]

Stettinius's relationship with the FBI remained more ambiguous, in spite of the State Department's tilt toward the bureau. Although the FBI furnished a bodyguard for him in San Francisco, it had friendlier and more intimate ties with one of his assistant secretaries of state, Nelson Rockefeller. Rockefeller had the Latin American portfolio in the State Department, and it was in the Hemisphere that the FBI had its most intrusive foreign operations. During the Mexico City meeting, Rockefeller relied on the FBI to advise him what Latin diplomats were saying behind his back. Rockefeller had built other ties between himself and the FBI. In his earlier government posts, Rockefeller had asked Hoover, as a favor to him, from 1943 on to check his home phone for wiretaps. At the San Francisco Conference, Rockefeller now told the FBI's chief agent for the U.N. meeting, Edward Tamm, without informing Stettinius, that he would be the chief conduit for all the bureau's intelligence to the secretary. Tamm agreed to cooperate, but, knowing that Rockefeller and Stettinius had disagreed about how to handle the Mexico Conference a few months earlier (Stettinius thought Rockefeller too soft on Argentina and refused to give him a formal invitation to San Francisco), dreaded another blowup between the two because the FBI would be left without a contact. Still, Rockefeller's mini-coup worked. Stettinius never noticed the FBI's dealings with Rockefeller.[4]

It was chiefly the issue of Poland, which had preoccupied Roosevelt and was now sorely trying the patience of Truman, that soon came under the most intense scrutiny by both the SSA and the FBI. The tidings from both organizations began to reinforce many of the concerns harbored by Stettinius about Moscow. In early 1945, the army group conveyed to Stettinius the contents of a cable intercepted from the French envoy to the Lublin regime in which the ambassador observed to the Quai d'Orsay that the Polish government was turning into a "quasi-protectorate" of the Soviet Union. In early March, France's Moscow ambassador reported that the Yalta Commission, designed to settle the Polish dispute, was "running into great difficulties" because, according to information from the Ambassador Harriman, the Soviets didn't like "the choice of Polish leaders to be consulted." By mid-March, the same French diplomat, army signals operators revealed, was having conversations with Poland's pro-Soviet delegate to the Kremlin and had learned that the Soviets would probably impose their own regime on Poland.[5]

At home, the FBI attempted to detail the activities of groups trying to support the Lublin regime and isolate the London exiles. A University of Chicago economist, Oskar Lange, the FBI taps disclosed, was traveling around the United States to meet with such bodies as the American Polish Labor Council, the Chicago Council of American Soviet Friendship, and the Czechoslovak National Council, to urge them to press Washington at the San Francisco Conference for recognition of the Polish provisional government. Lange told them that "the wisdom of the Lublin government in staking Poland's future on friendship with Russia" would be proved. It is not clear from the FBI documents whether the bureau hampered Lange's mission but, other realities outside the San Francisco Conference eventually dictated the course of U.S. strategy toward the Lublin regime.[6]

On the equally compelling matter of Latin America, Stettinius learned of the vigorous debate in Latin capitals over the admission of Argentina, something that the USSR adamantly opposed. As described earlier, the crypto-Nazi regime in Argentina had sought to end its pariah status within the Hemisphere almost a year earlier in 1944. Buenos Aires asked for a meeting of the Pan American Union to win the backing of Latin America for renewed Argentine ties with the United States. But Stettinius had finessed the Argentine proposal by instead convening an inter-American conference in Mexico City in February 1945 to discuss "hemispheric postwar problems," relegating the Argentine issue to a minor item on the agenda. U.S. code breakers enabled the United States to track Latin American reaction to the Stettinius strategic countermove.

The Chilean envoy in Washington, for example, telegraphed Santiago in mid-January 1945 to report on a luncheon Nelson Rockefeller had given at the Cuban embassy. Rockefeller and seven other ambassadors agreed there that Argentina had to be told to "adopt concrete and effective measures to eradicate the conviction of all the American peoples that she has been antagonistic toward the democracies of the continent." In mid-February 1945, shortly before the assemblage in Mexico City, a flurry of messages scanned by the army eavesdroppers indicated that Paraguay was now proposing to Colombia, Ecuador, and Venezuela that pressure be put on Buenos Aires to join the Allied war cause directly in exchange for diplomatic recognition. At about this time, the Argentine chargé in Washington informed his government that, although the Mexico Conference would cover the "misunderstanding" over his nation, his country still might have to think soon about a compromise with the United States. The information Stettinius received contributed to the deal he eventually forged whereby Buenos Aires agreed to declare war on the Axis and the United States renewed diplomatic ties.[7]

But the accompanying matter of how to bring Argentina into the U.N. over the objections of Russia remained in abeyance. That was of keen interest to Stettinius, who would have to handle the delicate situation himself in San Francisco. On April 7, Colombia's foreign minister, according to Ultra intercepts, instructed his envoy in Moscow to tell the Soviet regime that if it were now to oppose Buenos Aires, "we fear it would be a bad beginning for her relations with the American countries, which, for the most part, have established relations with Russia without much conviction and against considerable internal opposition." In addition, Ecuador was now enlisting Peru, Mexico, Cuba, Panama, Venezuela, and Brazil in a campaign to change the mind of the Kremlin about Argentina. The U.S. intercepts were beginning to alert Stettinius that the Latin nations were ready to do hand-to-hand combat with the Soviets over the admission of this Latin state in San Francisco, and, if they did not get their way, they might turn against Moscow or desert the world assembly altogether. This information began to influence the way Stettinius would deal with the Russians over Argentina at the conference.[8]

Another nagging problem, growing more difficult by the day, was the matter of trusteeships. At the Yalta summit, the British had expressed their deep opposition to any U.N. control of their territories. From Ultra, Stettinius learned that other colonial powers in Europe were equally aggrieved and openly resistant. The United States, for example, became aware of French apprehensions as early as mid-January, 1945. France's provisional foreign minister, Georges Bidault, telegraphed his ambassador in Washington about reports from a preliminary U.N. Conference saying that the Americans were pressing for an international U.N. committee for colonies modeled on the controversial Mandates Commission of the League of Nations. A French diplomat went to great lengths to reassure Bidault that he and others had forced the United States to drop their approach: "The American tendency of hastening the normal evolution of colonies toward autonomy, dominion status, or independence was met by objections—and even the protests—of qualified delegates . . . including ours." But the issue was not dead.[9]

After the Yalta meeting in early February (from which the French had been excluded), the French representative in Moscow sought out Molotov to obtain additional assurances that the U.N. would take no action against Paris's colonial possessions. Molotov responded that Paris should take the matter up with the White House, which, he said, was now assuming primary responsibility over the matter of colonialism. In any event, he informed the French that a system of "trusteeship" for the mandated territories had been "defined only in principle" at Yalta. The French later shared their concerns with the British. After meeting with Anthony Eden in London, Bidault, according to Ultra, cited his satisfaction with the results: "Mr. Eden explained to me," the French ambassador to the Court of St. James reported, "that the idea [of the trusteeship] was an American one and would permit the United States to lay hands chastely on the Japanese islands in the Pacific. The system is not to be applied to any region in Europe nor to any colonies belonging to the Allied countries. The English are determined that no misunderstanding arise in this regard." In their talks, Eden and Churchill also approved a continuation of France's "privileged position" in Syria and Lebanon.[10]

The French, not entirely reassured by the British promises, undertook a broader offensive to protect their colonies. For example, they convened talks in Paris between General Charles de Gaulle and the foreign minister of the Netherlands, which also had overseas territories. Both men agreed, according to Bidault, on "the impossibility of surrendering to an international authority any of their colonies." By early April, Bidault wired all his envoys that France would flatly reject all plans of international control "over all or part of her colonial empire or of the countries placed under her protection." France would, however, uphold U.N. trusteeships for former Japanese or Italian territories. Bidault told the Greek ambassador that the United States was promoting trusteeships simply because it "wants to exercise influence on other people's colonies for selfish political and economic reasons." The coded information had an impact on the views of the Americans regarding the colonial issue. Stettinius began to reconsider whether the United States should maintain a hard line on the issue in view of the fact that it was antagonizing its allies, even as the French, too, were gradually reconsidering their strident campaign to hold on to their possessions. Midway through the conference, a French official in the United States advised his home office that Paris should "not turn down a text in which independence is set as the eventual goal for trusteeship, for we would be approximately the only ones to do so."[11]

At the same time, at home the FBI was gathering background information on the preparatory labors of other lobbying groups opposed to colonialism—especially the Council on African Affairs in New York City, which was one of several such organizations planning to go to San Francisco. The bureau tracked the movements of its executive director, Max Yergan, whom it labeled a "Negro Communist" who had met with luminaries such as W. E. B. Dubois, the National Association for the Advancement of Colored People (NAACP) director of special research, and

Ben Davis, a New York City black councilman who, according to the FBI, was another "Negro Communist," to discuss matters such as distributing 50,000 pamphlets in San Francisco stating their anticolonial viewpoints. According to FBI intercepts, the Council on African Affairs intended to contact black delegates from Ethiopia, Liberia, India, Panama, Cuba, France, Britain, and Belgium and "influence them considerably" toward decolonization. In addition, the CAA head told Davis that he had had a meeting with Archibald MacLeish, the assistant secretary of state, who agreed to receive the organization's proposals on the International Mandates Commission. The FBI report noted that it now planned to "cover the activities" of the CAA in San Francisco using "technical informants" and tailing the local office.[12]

At one point, the FBI also transcribed a ten-page record of a conversation between Yergen and Councilman Davis as a demonstration of how the black radicals were intending to exploit San Francisco. An excerpt follows:

> YERGEN: One of the reasons why that we've gone ahead with regard to [establishing] some sort of bureau out at San Francisco. You see the whole negro press will be there and we'll have a chance to not only confer with them but to arrange conferences between them and delegates who will be there.
>
> DAVIS: You know, because the negroes, all of them more or less disconnected and scattered and confused attitudes and expressions with regard to the future of the Colonial people, these things have got to be channeled now along constructive lines within the framework of the world security organization.[13]

One of the most vexing problems for Stettinius, though, was the billowing controversy over the veto. The smaller nations coming to the conference sent signals through heated cable traffic implying that they would not necessarily accept as a fait accompli the special powers bestowed upon the five nations. U.S. intelligence obtained a message in mid-March 1945 from the Chilean foreign minister offering his "personal opinion" that "the procedure devised at the Crimea Conference for voting in the Security Council is not in accord with the sovereign equality of all peace-loving states and, in operation, would put the permanent members of the Council above the law which will govern all nations." The minister requested his diplomats abroad to find out how other countries regarded the special status of the Big Powers at the U.N. He received at least five replies—from Costa Rica, Cuba, Italy, Switzerland, and the Vatican—all agreeing with Chile's reservations. This group was representative of the forty or so states that were convening at San Francisco, and their reservations suggested the growing opposition to the Big Powers' position.[14]

In a dispatch in late March, Turkish officials also expressed doubts about the voting procedures. They told French diplomats in Ankara that the setup "seemed destined to make lawful the projects of the large powers against the small—with the system of voting in the Security Council ensuring them impunity." The Turks warned that "the small states are inevitably going to be reduced to the status of satellites of the great." They also feared that bilateral alliances, as, for instance, their 1939 mutual-assistance pact with England, could be overridden during a crisis, say, with the USSR, by the veto. But they also conceded the "futility" of modifying the U.N. Charter. Instead, they hoped to increase "the number of non-permanent members on the Security Council from six to nine in order to give the Great Powers a less preponderant majority."[15]

France's worries with respect to Security Council procedures increased as the conference neared, though with a growing sense of realism. In early March, Bidault instructed his ambassador in Moscow to advise the Soviets of his concern that, under the veto arrangement, regional and bilateral treaties could be "subordinated to the previous agreement of the Security Council." This was dangerous, he added, because the "automatic nature of regional pacts is . . . the essential element of collective security." The French enlisted the Belgians and sounded out the British on an amendment to "clarify" the section on regional agreements in the U.N. Charter.[16]

Alerted to France's hesitancy by reading French diplomatic transmissions, Washington soon decided it had influence Paris, which had now made itself the leader of the recalcitrant member states. As the San Francisco Conference drew closer, Stettinius intensified his overtures to France to reconsider its decision to forgo its role as the fifth permanent member of the Security Council. This approach, coming at a time when France was finding it increasingly difficult to act as the champion of the smaller nations, as well as flattering France's pretensions to being a great power (thereby salving its hurt over Yalta), reignited the Quai d'Orsay's interest. The French soon decided to accept their earlier assigned spot on the Security Council. France's decision brought about a gradual collapse of the campaign to thwart the veto.[17]

While ostensibly staying above the battle, Ultra showed, the French were experiencing a change of heart. The French U.N. delegate cabled Paris: "However far apart we [the Five Powers and small and medium powers] still are, a conciliatory solution is not impossible, for everyone is beginning to realize that the veto is a necessity and that its limits could not be further defined without risks for which no one wishes seriously to assume responsibility." Later, in summing up his country's achievements at San Francisco, the French delegate reflected: "Although it may in some case seem an annoyance—and a very grave annoyance— it [the veto] may also in others be a means of preventing the Council from meddling unduly in affairs which are our own or which we intend to settle through other channels."[18]

Meantime, the other great power, the Soviet Union, was also operating an espionage campaign of sorts in San Francisco. It had dispatched a large ship to be used as an "entertainment" vessel at the conference; purportedly it was loaded with a cargo of caviar and vodka and anchored in San Francisco Bay. The boat, called the *Smolnle,* was a 2,153-ton craft that could hold 138 passengers, including twenty-eight first class ticket holders (the Soviet delegation consisted of 122 officials). But it was soon learned that the vessel was also designed for other uses, namely, to convey diplomatic messages from the Soviet delegation back to the Kremlin. The *Smolnle* received the dispatches in secrecy via a secure telephone line connected to a soundproof room in the Russian suite at the St. Francis Hotel, and, in turn, relayed them to Moscow via radio. Although there was no direct evidence of other spying apparatus aboard the ship, the implications of a sophisticated technology sitting on a foreign craft anchored in a West Coast harbor suggests that the Soviets might also have had listening devices or tapping equipment of their own to overhear the conversations of U.S. officials or intercept the cable traffic of State Department diplomats in the city conveying messages to Washinton during U.N. sessions.[19]

There were also other claims that the Soviets may have had operatives in San Francisco. The evidence remains highly suspect and is scanty, but, in 1996, when the United States published the so-called Venona papers, it became possible to imagine a few possible connections, some entirely innocent, of Roosevelt officials to the Russian intelligence service. The term "Venona" was a code word arbitrarily stamped on a small cache of documents, some 2,900 Soviet diplomatic telegrams, sent between 1940 and 1948 between Washington and Moscow; the documents had certain common encryption flaws that enabled U.S. cryptanalysts to decipher parts of them by taking advantage of the recurring vulnerabilities in the texts. But, because of the fragmentary nature of the solutions found, the code breakers were able to retrieve only tantalizing clues and hints of what the telegrams may have really meant—and, meantime, the translations themselves, which the FBI only became involved with in 1948, occurred long after the events had transpired.[20]

The first person of any importance noted was Alger Hiss, the acting secretary general of the United Nations, originally appointed to that post on the recommendation of President Roosevelt and Secretary Stettinius. Hiss, who had attended Yalta, was a highly visible figure at San Francisco in his administrative role. He had accountability for all the "nuts and bolts" of the conference. As he recalls in his memoirs: "We were responsible for the daily operations of the conference, for providing secretaries and interpreters for the various committee meetings . . . and for housing, communications, transportation, and general comfort of the delegates and their staffs, numbering more than a thousand. In addition, my aides and I saw to the needs of more than a thousand press representatives from all over the world." Hiss also attended many of the private meetings held by Secretary Stettinius in his penthouse suite at the Fairmont Hotel.[21]

Hiss's upbringing had been somber and often mournful. He was born in 1904 into a shabby-genteel family in Baltimore, Maryland. When Hiss was two, his father, a wholesale grocer and importer, committed suicide; an older brother, an alcoholic, died of kidney failure in 1926; a sister, Mary, killed herself three years later. By dint of hard work and perseverance, Hiss surmounted his family troubles and made Phi Beta Kappa at Johns Hopkins in his junior year; in 1929, he graduated cum laude from Harvard Law School, where he served on the Harvard Law Review; thereafter, on the recommendation of his professor, Felix Frankfurter, he clerked for Supreme Court Justice Oliver Wendell Holmes. He soon joined the New Deal, working in rapid succession in three cabinet departments—agriculture, justice, and state.

In September 1939, a journalist named Whittaker Chambers, who had served as a courier for the Communist underground in the United States from 1932 until 1938, defected from the party and recounted a secret history to the then assistant secretary of state, Adolf Berle, naming Communists in the Roosevelt administration, among them Alger Hiss. Nothing ensued as a result of Chambers's story. Then, in 1942, the FBI interrogated Chambers and Hiss. Chambers repeated his tale; Hiss denied it. Interest again faded. In 1944, Hiss was promoted to become Leo Pasvolsky's assistant on U.N. matters. By May 1945, the FBI had reopened the investigation into espionage, after Hiss was chosen to head the U.N. Conference. This time, the bureau twice interviewed Chambers, once for eight hours; again, he fingered Hiss. Given a mounting scandal, including leaks to Congress about Hiss, Secretary of State Byrnes finally forced Hiss out of the State Department in 1946. Hiss then took over the largely ceremonial presidency of the Carnegie Endowment for International Peace on the recommendation of Republican stalwart John Foster Dulles.[22]

In July 1948, the House Un-American Activities Committee (HUAC) called Elizabeth Bentley, who had succeeded Chambers in his role as Soviet agent in Washington, D.C., but had broken with the party in the mid-1940s. She corroborated Chambers on Hiss's Communist past. The HUAC then asked Chambers to testify. Chambers repeated his accusation against Hiss, though he did not claim any knowledge of espionage.

Next, Hiss testified; he denied all charges, first disputing that he knew Chambers, but later said that he knew him under another name. Subsequently, Hiss sued Chambers for slander when, on a radio program and outside the legal protection afforded by a House hearing, Chambers reiterated his accusations of Communist membership by Hiss. Compelled to show evidence of Hiss's complicity, Chambers produced for the HUAC sixty-five pages of retyped State Department confidential documents and four memorandums in Hiss's handwriting. A few weeks later, Chambers produced microfilms—the entire lot dating from the 1930s and, he asserted, given to him by Hiss—that he had hidden in a hollowed-out pumpkin on his farm. The HUAC passed the material on to a grand jury; on December 15, 1948, Hiss was indicted, not for espionage because the statute of limitations had passed, but for two counts of perjury for denying under oath that he had seen Chambers in early 1938 and for claiming, also under oath, that he had never given secret files to Chambers. A first trial ended with a hung jury; in a second trial, in early 1950, Hiss was found guilty of perjury and subsequently served forty-four months in prison.

Still, in 1945, at the beginning of the San Francisco Conference, there was no hint of wrongdoing by Hiss. Chambers at the time did privately whisper to people about Hiss's Communist background, though never proffering proof that he was a Communist. He informed Raymond Murphy, a special assistant in the State Department's Office of European Affairs, who had long studied Soviet intelligence methods, and warned that if Hiss were named permanent secretary of the U.N., he would publicly denounce him. Henry Grunwald, a writer at *Time* magazine, where Chambers was then an editor, recalled that in the spring of 1945 he was reading a news story in Chambers's presence referring to Hiss's role as acting secretary general of the U.N. Conference, when Chambers said: "'He is a communist, you know.'" "'Oh really?'" I asked. "'Yes,'" replied Chambers, "'and he keeps getting these important jobs. But that's a long story.'" Grunwald failed to pursue the matter—"the name Alger Hiss meant nothing to me, and I let it pass." Ironically, the founder of *Time*, Henry Luce, bedazzled by Hiss's performance at San Francisco, ordered his writers to praise Hiss profusely in the pages of the same magazine. One story began: "In a class by himself was young, handsome Alger Hiss [who] was master of the incredibly complicated conference machinery."[23]

Later, at Hiss's perjury trial in 1949, Chambers admitted that he was probably the author of that *Time* piece. Asked by Hiss's defense attorney why he did not immediately "wire the Secretary of State, the President of the United States or the Department of Justice or the Attorney General and say, 'Watch out! This man should not be trusted with that important post. He was in a conspiracy with me to get papers from the State Department and turn them over to some Russian fellow by the name of Bykov in Prospect Park.' Did you communicate any such thing to your government then? Yes or no?" Chambers answered: "I did not." Almost shouting now, the lawyer inquired whether the witness thought it important to "protect your government." Chambers replied weakly, "I didn't think it was possible to interest anyone in the subject."[24]

Meantime, the Venona records suggested there might have been another avenue of conspiracy, though unproved, that involved Hiss. A cable from the Russian embassy in Washington to Moscow dated March 30, 1945, describes the work of a State Department official known as "ALES." The FBI agent assigned to interpret the telegram labeled ALES as "probably Alger Hiss." The explanation for denoting ALES as Hiss was that the transmission mentioned that ALES had relatives working with him (Hiss had a brother in the State Department) and that the initials bore a relationship to the man's name. But what made the case particularly damning was that part of the message had ALES traveling to Moscow after the Yalta Conference ostensibly to receive congratulations from the Soviet deputy foreign minister, Andre Vyshinskii. Knowing that Hiss had participated in Yalta and thereafter had accompanied Stettinius to Moscow as part of a U.S. delegation, the FBI analyst attempted to confirm Hiss's identity conclusively.[25]

Still, for all the speculation by the FBI, unless Hiss was playing a double game at Yalta, he seems an unlikely candidate for Soviet honors. At the Crimea Conference, he had opposed the addition of other Soviet states to the U.N., even authoring a paper titled "Arguments Against the Inclusion of Any of the Soviet Republics Among the Initial Members." Furthermore, viewing the Soviet cable from a purely linguistic viewpoint, Vyshinskii, who was also at Yalta, could actually have been the person who took the trip to Moscow, not Hiss. The text reads: "After the Yalta conference, when he had gone on to Moscow, a Soviet personage in a very responsible position (ALES gave us to understand that it was Comrade Vyshinskii) allegedly got in touch with ALES and at the behest of the Military Neighbors [GRU, Soviet military intelligence] passed on to him their gratitude." Moreover, the cable also has ALES working "on obtaining military information only." But Hiss, in the State Department, was not in a position to provide much in the way of military information—though there were some indications that, before Yalta, he did request secret data on the "internal security" of major nations to prepare for the meeting. Further, no additional Venona telegrams, including any from San Francisco, ever indicated other potential Hiss involvement. And Secretary of State Stettinius himself stated in an affidavit in Hiss's first trial that "at no time during my service in the Department was I advised, from inside or outside the Department, of any question relative to Mr. Hiss' loyalty." (Incidentally, the Soviet ambassador, Andrei Gromyko, later told Stettinius—on September 7, 1945—that he had "high regard" for Hiss and that Hiss could make a good permanent U.N. secretary general).[26]

There was, however, one other U.S. official singled out in San Francisco by the Venona documents—the then assistant secretary of the treasury, Harry Dexter White—as possibly passing information to the Soviets. Chambers had confided to Adolf Berle in September 1939, and to Raymond Murphy of the State Department in March 1945, that White was "a member at large but rather timid" in the 1930s. On July 31, 1948, Elizabeth Bentley informed the HUAC of White's alleged complicity with the Soviets, and subsequently Chambers himself provided the committee a handwritten memorandum by White said to be supplied to him by Hiss. Yet none of these testimonies or files necessarily proved that White was a part of the Communist underground or that he was handing over confidential data to Moscow.[27]

There has always been great historical controversy about the intensity of White's leftist sympathies. White, born in Boston in 1892, had served with the U.S. Army in France during World War I, later earned a doctorate at Stanford University, and then joined the U.S. Treasury Department in 1934. Over the years, he had climbed the ranks and, by late 1941, received the authority (but without the title) as assistant secretary of the treasury from his boss, Henry Morgenthau, Jr., the treasury secretary. Eventually, at the Bretton Woods Conference in July 1944, he led the U.S. effort to create a postwar international financial order that established both the World Bank and the International Monetary Fund. White, a man of less than medium height, stocky in appearance, with a moustache and rimless glasses on a round face, was an exceptionally hard worker with a rasping voice who could be, on occasion, gratuitously blunt and sarcastic in his conversations with others.[28]

It is undoubtedly clear from an overview of his friends and from the roster of the people he surrounded himself with in the Treasury Department—all of them left-wingers of various sorts—that White believed devoutly that cooperation between the United States and the Soviet Union was essential to forge a peaceful and progressive world. He admired Soviet planning and its passionate anti-Nazism. Whether that actually made him a spy, however, is another matter. Chambers suggested that White handed over documents voluntarily to him to strengthen his idea of the global antifascist alliance. Later, Elizabeth Bentley claimed that White and some of the aides he had brought into the Treasury Department conveyed confidential memos to Soviet contacts knowing full well what they were doing. Truman eventually forced White out of the department, but the U.S. government never prosecuted White because the evidence needed to convict him, if it did exist, was itself classified. Among historians, the verdict about White is still unresolved, but many incline toward the view that he wanted to help the Russians but did not regard the actions he took as constituting espionage.[29]

The two memos in the Venona collection that are most suggestive of White's role in passing information to the Soviets during the U.N. Conference both concern a man code-named "Richard." The FBI, in its reading of the cables, determined that "Richard" was Harry Dexter White, though it is not clear how the bureau arrived at its finding. The first transmission, dated May 4, 1945, states that "Richard" had a "prolonged conversation" with a Soviet operative in San Francisco over the Polish question and the veto. The FBI never was able to glean anything further from the telegram beyond these brief shards of information. The second transmission, dated May 5, proved more substantial. Here "Richard" told the Soviet agent that "Truman and Stettinius want to achieve the success of the conference at any price." Then there are various cryptic references to members of the U.S. State Department and the U.S. delegation, including a suggestion that Senator Vandenberg would blame the Democratic Party for the failure if the conference collapsed. Finally, "Richard" conducted a wide-ranging discussion of the veto controversy, suggesting ways the Soviet Union might counteract "the attempts of the USA to put the USSR in a disadvantageous position," presumably over its fierce advocacy of the absolute veto. One idea was to propose allowing economic sanctions to be applied by a simple majority of the Security Council with no veto permitted, a proposition which "Richard" opines the U.S. "will oppose," thereby weakening its prestige.[30]

It is not certain how White might have gained access to the U.S. negotiators concerning the veto issue. First, he was never part of the State Department's United Nations task forces, particularly those dealing with the Security Council. Second, the individual to whom "Richard" was talking was identified by the FBI as "SergeJ," probably Vladimir Pravden, the *Tass* correspondent in San Francisco. From "Richard's" point of view, he could well have believed he was speaking with a reporter and was merely giving his views as a professional. Third, there was still an active alliance between the United States and Russia in May 1945, so gossip or exchanges of views between allies at these sorts of meetings was not regarded as unusual or necessarily dubious. Still, if the FBI was right, and "Richard" was White, and if Chambers was correct that White was long part of the Communist apparatus in the United States, the details divulged in the Venona cable seem rather inconsequential.

It is undoubted, though, that the Russians did seek, like all the other Great Powers in San Francisco, to ferret out as much information surreptitiously as possible from their friends as well as their adversaries during the conference. It is equally certain, too, that the Soviets had agents, or "fellow travelers," working for their cause. But from the spying data uncovered thus far, it appears that Washington was far ahead of Moscow in gaining the most "inside" knowledge. Further, the Soviets seemingly apprehended more from their own private talks with the Americans over issues such as the veto than they might have learned from intelligence gathering, intercepts, or taps about U.S. strategy. Even the information the Americans themselves gathered comprehensively through the Army Signal Corps and the FBI was for the most part already in the public domain—either via the daily press, in statements by participating officials, or as part of the debate at the conference itself. The U.S. espionage operations may have been set up merely to "insure" success at San Francisco, as Alger Hiss once observed, but the steps Washington took looked a little like overreach. In any event, with over 1,000 delegates and staff in attendance, some 2,000 journalists wandering around the town hunting for news, and hundreds of spectators on the loose, it seems almost impossible for either Moscow or Washington or any other power to have controlled, sequestered, or secreted the kernels of knowledge that were traded, collected, or overheard among all the delegates in residence in the city on the bay.[31]

CHAPTER 7

AMERICANIZING
THE CONFERENCE

With due allowance for mishap, the strategists behind the U.N. Conference in the State Department sought to make certain that the meeting was choreographed, if not meticulously directed, within the boundaries of the possible, by the experts in Washington. Following the controversial demise of the League of Nations, nothing was left to chance. Quite apart from the surreptitious use of electronic intercepts, the organizers spent months before the event anticipating all the possible moves and shifts that might occur among the delegates, the press, and the public, acting akin to lawyers preparing for possibly unruly courtroom cross-examinations. The administration tacticians scrutinized a whole compass of issues, from the grand to the mundane, that could conceivably affect the outcome of the conference, and designed an approach that narrowed as much as possible the range of calamity or misadventure. Questions as to who should exercise the real authority in the meetings to the design of the security badges and the distribution of tickets were closely considered. The War Department and the OSS abetted the operations. Nobody, however, could control everything.

Washington as host agreed to pay all the costs of the conference— except for the personal expenses of the delegates. Initially, $1.4 million was allotted from the State Department's budget—an amount that eventually rose to almost $2 million by the end of the proceedings (U.S. expectations had been a four-week session; the conference lasted nine weeks). There were other, uncounted, funds spent by the armed forces, Federal investigatory bodies, and government bureaucracies. The investment by the United States was considerable for a nation already underwriting wars in Europe and Asia, manufacturing massive amounts of planes and tanks and rifles, constructing an atomic bomb, supplying the Allies with large shipments of armaments, and expending capital on other wartime projects. It was the modern equivalent of around $25 million. Still the United States, at war's end, was the only nation with the resources to finance this sort of major gathering. Now, with San Francisco selected as the site, the planners had two months' notice to allocate their monies where they would count the most and meticulously erect a grand scaffolding for the conference. The conferees chose two major edifices in San Francisco, which stood next to each other in the city's downtown area—the stately opera house for the more lofty Plenary Sessions of the delegates, and the four-story War Memorial Veterans Building constructed in memory of World War 1 soldiers, for smaller meetings.[1]

In addition, the United States designed all the public presentations at the conference. Although Stettinius may have differed with General Donovan of the Office of Strategic Services (OSS) on some aspects of his operation, the secretary wanted to use every method at hand to influence American public opinion. Long an admirer of the talent the OSS had assembled, on January 10, 1945, Stettinius formally requested from Donovan a loan of specialists to superintend pictorial projects. OSS draftsmen had already been informally helping out Assistant Secretary Archibald Macleish on the promotional work for Dumbarton Oaks— preparing, for example, graphs and slide shows for his speaker's bureau. Now Stettinius moved these artisans into the San Francisco site. The craftsmen began to attend to such details as exactly where the largest assembly would be held, the contours of meeting rooms, the housing for delegates, a press room, media passes, photographic brochures of all the delegations, tickets, invitations, programs, special visual props for various events, the Order of the Day postings, the motifs for the documents to be used at the commissions, city maps and guides, and the displays of various U.N. organizational charts.[2]

The artists and decorators soon created credentials, buttons, lapel pins, flags, and badges, and stamped on all conference insignia a U.N. emblem that they devised. The emblem was a world map set against a blue backdrop. This logo of the globe was, in many respects, the same as that which today is on all U.N. identification. Oliver Lundquist, one of the principal stylists, recounted that he and his fellow fashioners patterned their design on "an azimuthal north polar projection of the world," in which all the land masses were spun around a concentric circle with the United States, as the host nation, in the center; at first, Argentina was deliberately cut off, since it was at that time excluded from the organization. The diagram was then encircled by crossed branches of olive. Later on, soon after the San Francisco Conference had ended and the U.N. was set up, the map was slightly tilted so that the international dateline became its centerpiece, symbolizing the East-West world, and the entire Southern Hemisphere was now included, bringing Argentina back into view. Lunquist's group also recommended the color blue as the backdrop, representing peace—in opposition to red, for war.[3]

The OSS, with Stettinius's consent, also brought in its own production people, photographers, and recording technicians. As the secret outfit was exempt from governmental rules requiring that official papers be printed at governmental printing offices, it was able to set up its own facility at the headquarters and churn out conference documents to be distributed within hours of a request. The average output of printed or mimeographed materials was 500,000 pages a day. Meantime, OSS lensmen also circulated through the meeting halls, snapping over 3,000 photos for public consumption—and for posterity. The OSS established a recording studio run by a young army officer who employed magnetic wire recorders captured from the Germans (similar to today's magnetic tape recorders) to memorialize the statements of the participants. The studio also made 78-RPM records of the main speeches at the conference.[4]

The titular authority at San Francisco was the Steering Committee, composed of the forty-six delegation chieftains and designated to handle all major policy issues. But, as host of the event, the United States retained the power to recommend the precise day-to-day organizational structure for U.N. sessions. Following the opening day of the assembly, having earlier gotten approval from other nations, Stettinius presented a U.S. blueprint to the Steering Committee, which gave it quick approval. Stettinius set up an Executive Committee consisting of fourteen delegation heads, including the five permanent members of the Security Council, with twenty-four-hour responsibility for all decisions. Next he created four general commissions controlling twelve technical committees; each commission was responsible for drafting a particular section of the U.N. Charter. One tracked the preamble, the trusteeships, and the economic and social council; another, the General Assembly; a third, the Security Council and regional bodies; and a fourth, the World Court. There was also a Coordinating Committee to prepare a final text. All recommendations from the commissions ultimately went to the Steering Committee for approval and finally to the conference in Plenary Session for ratification.[5]

As sponsors of the U.N. Conference, the United States and the other Big Four (including France) had the responsibility to keep everything on course—an authority tacitly recognized by the Steering Committee. This special entitlement had grown out of the Dumbarton Oaks Conference and was reinforced by the sessions held at Yalta and later gatherings of the four foreign ministers in Washington and elsewhere concerning U.N. preparations. In San Francisco, the Big Five began to meet nightly to review strategy, assess possible amendments, consider requests from other countries, and resolve internal disputes. Stettinius's central position among the five was maintained because all the meetings were convened in the penthouse apartment he occupied atop the Fairmont Hotel. Although operational authority in the end resided with the Big Five, all delegates had a public voice, the Executive Committee could make interim decisions, and the commissions afforded direct policy participation for every nation.[6]

Stettinius had, in addition, made the U.S. presence even more notable by installing his close associate, Alger Hiss, as the acting secretary-general of the U.N. Hiss presided over the administrative side of the conference, helping to devise the rules for the commissions, even sitting next to the chairmen when they ran the Steering Committee meetings. He supervised over 1,000 people, including the many U.S. Army and Navy officers detailed to the event, personnel from fourteen federal agencies (five hundred of whom were recruited locally), and fifty-one technical experts from sixteen countries. He looked after the welfare of the forty-six delegations and watched out for the press corps. He stayed in constant touch with Stettinius.[7]

The delegates, the press, and the staffers flooded into San Francisco between April 22–25. The United States handed much of the transportation to San Francisco for most delegations. The government even provided direct air travel to San Francisco for several impoverished and war-torn nations. For example, it flew in the Chinese and Philippines missions across the Pacific in U.S. Army Transport Command aircraft. It also paid for fifteen-hour flights from Washington for delegates. Its biggest outlays were for trains: up to eighteen coaches each to bring some 2,300 delegates, State Department officials, and press from the East Coast to California. The trains, the first ever to travel nonstop from East to West coasts, took four days and four nights following a zigzag route through Chicago, south to Texas, west to New Mexico and Arizona, and then on to San Diego and San Francisco. Among the first group was one dubbed the "Pre-Con" train, which conveyed the U.N. Secretariat, U.S. military and naval representatives, and some elected officials. A few days later came the "Correspondent" with newspaper and radio reporters, and the "Mora-Press" for additional media folk. Last came the "Delegate," for those participants not arriving by air, and the "Del-Bar," for State Department staff and lawyers. In San Francisco, the U.S. Army and Navy supplied a fleet of 215 sedans, 25 jeeps, 50 gray naval buses, and 48 private limousines to carry delegates and Secretariat officials about the town. There were also some 800 taxicabs in reserve. Shuttle buses ran between the meeting sites and hotels every ten minutes.[8]

The trains themselves seemingly had a purpose, though perhaps unintended, as an exercise in diplomacy for Washington. Anne O'Hare McCormick, the *New York Times* columnist, who accompanied the foreign press on one of these cross-country jaunts, remarked on how "the transcontinental trip has the effect of giving the delegates a view of the size and power of the United States. They exclaim at the bigness, the emptiness of the great prairies, the still untapped resources of a land that surprises them when they see it, because so much of it is primeval still." Claiborne Pell, later the Democratic senator from Rhode Island, then a junior enlisted man who escorted several delegations, vividly re-called that the guests "were given a powerful picture of the United States. They could not miss the contrast with their ravaged countries, as they saw mile after mile of our extraordinarily productive pastures and seemingly endless fields, punctuated by mighty industrial cities and prospering towns."[9]

Participants also found their destination, San Francisco, as com-pelling. McCormick, in her own mind, knew why. "San Francisco," she wrote, "is a lusty city, with youth in every line of its uplifted profile and vigor in every breath of its brisk trade winds. It must be a sight for the sore eyes of delegates who come to the world security conference from London and The Hague, Belgrade, Chungking, and all the shat-tered cities of the war zones. More than any other city, it is a sign of the promise of resurrection." A U.S. official wrote to his wife that "we are in an atmosphere of dazzling splendor" where there are "rich hotels teeming with diplomatic corps of the world—food beyond descrip-tion—wines—liquors—provide cars for one's beck and call—free movies." Francis Williams, controller of press and censorship for Britain, remembered: "I had flown straight from blacked-out London into a fantastic world of glitter and light and extravagant parties and food and drink and constantly spiraling talk."[10]

In fact, for a ration-starved world, the plentiful stock of food in San Francisco alone, available due to a relaxation in the rationing rules, was noted by everybody. The owner of the Omar Khayam Restaurant catered daily spreads that celebrated the ethnic foods and decor of the visiting nations. The American Women's Volunteers Service staffed a cafeteria in the basement of the opera house that served a lunch buffet at a dollar a meal for 1,200 participants morning until late at night. Nonetheless, delegates complained about the shoddy food in their ho-tels, and some hoteliers groused, in turn, about the wartime shortages of beef and pork. Still, special efforts were made to provide scotch, bourbon, champagne, rum, and brandies, as well as cigarettes—all commodities that had utterly vanished during the war.[11]

There was some grumbling about hotel rooms. One of the U.S. delegates, Virginia Gildersleeve, conceded that the United States "got too much of the best hotel accommodations for their own delegation," namely, a series of suites on the fourth floor of the Fairmont Hotel, just ten minutes away from the opera house by car. She was chagrined, too, to discover that some of the foreigners had been overlooked by U.S. organizers. When the Norway delegation arrived, it found to its dismay that there was no housing for its members. Eventually, the State Department was able to "scatter" the group to different hotels. But such indifferent treatment, together with the lengthy distances many had to traverse within San Francisco, and finally the knowledge that small countries basically didn't count for much, left many delegates feeling isolated and neglected. Gildersleeve spent a considerable amount of her own time trying to entertain individuals she considered bereft or friendless, especially delegates from the Middle East with whom she had ties. As the United States made little effort to cultivate the newly formed Arab League, she decided on her own to host a luncheon for the Muslim visitors. She was the only American delegate present.[12]

Washington's security was considerable. The Pacific War was still being fought, and sentries were placed on roofs and antiaircraft guns on the top of tall buildings to ward off paper balloon attacks by the Japanese. Washington had plans to black out the Veterans Building so the meetings could proceed even during an air raid. When a sudden shortage of typewriters was discovered, the State Department resupplied the city with dozens of them. It even constructed a reference library on the second floor of the Veteran's Building for the various countries to consult—a knowledge bank consisting of daily newspapers, a microfilm cache of the *New York Times* back to 1916, all records of the League of Nations, and 3,000 volumes contributed by the Library of Congress, the University of California, Stanford, Mills College, Hoover War Library, and the San Francisco Public Library. Besides, the U.S. Postal Service issued 1 million commemorative five-cent blue stamps. Finally, local officials hosted symphony concerts in the Civic Auditorium for the delegations.[13]

Many San Franciscans helped out as volunteers. As one reporter put it, "The city has the hum, stir and expectancy of a national convention." Natives placed "World Peace Conference" stickers on their shop windows and windshields. A Citizens' Shopping Service offered to do purchasing for busy delegates and staff and arranged for Boy Scout messengers to deliver the goods. A special U.N. theater showed Hollywood's latest fare daily, free to participants with conference badges. One enterprising company promised to mend glasses within two hours and clean suits speedily. The city sponsored blimp rides from Moffett Field and jaunts around the bay aboard Coast Guard cutters. As a portside town already bursting its seams with soldiers readying to go to the Pacific—San Francisco's population had by now increased by 200,000 to 800,000 people—the citizens maintained an unusual enthusiasm for the historic meeting and did what they could to contribute car service, furnish the odd delegate or reporter a bed in their homes, throw welcoming parties, bring nutriment to the panels, and accord the overseas guests all due consideration and courtesies.[14]

The most theatrical flourish of the U.S. arrangements came with the opening ceremony on April 25. Thousands had thronged on the streets outside in light rainfall to watch the delegates arrive. Oliver Lundquist and Jo Mielziner—the latter famous as a Broadway designer of musicals—had transformed the $5 million San Francisco Opera House into a glittering hall. Escorts guided the 3,000 or so delegates, onlookers, and media—by and large a silent and solemn audience still recovering from wartime trauma—to red plush seats in a classic auditorium and be observed by movie cameramen and still photographers (Soviet Foreign Minister Molotov, seated in the ninth row of the orchestra, attracted many cheers when he arrived). Lundquist and Mielziner adorned the stage with four golden pillars tied together with olive branch wreaths symbolizing the four freedoms that President Roosevelt had proclaimed in 1941: freedom of speech and worship, freedom from want and fear. Forming a semicircular row among the columns was an array of flags affixed to pikes from all the nations attending the conference, floodlit against a backdrop of gray-blue drapes. The two men garlanded the stairs to the stage with flowers, lit the stage like a sunburst, and tinted twenty-four big spotlights with blue filters for cosmetic impact. Finally, they had an off-stage band playing martial music as a silhouette-like line of U.S. armed services personnel marched to the platform followed by Secretary Stettinius, Earl Warren, the governor of California, Alger Hiss, and the city's mayor, Roger Lapham. Stettinius, silver-haired and distinguished, convened the meeting at the podium and called for a minute of silent meditation; he then introduced President Truman, who delivered his ten-minute radio address.[15]

The United States delegation and other foreign missions quickly began to settle in. But a conflict that had been simmering burst into the open on the second day of the conference as the participants were getting organized in the Steering Committee. A grim-faced Molotov rose to object to a motion naming Stettinius president of the conference and demanded instead that a Russian proposal presented to President Roosevelt in early April now be adopted to elevate the four sponsoring powers to be rotating co-presidents of the conference based on what Molotov termed "a principle of equality." Molotov, in a foul mood since his encounter with President Truman in Washington, openly hinted that he might downgrade Soviet participation or even leave for home if he did not achieve his goal. Already, he irritated the press corps in the city by walking in public protected by dozens of husky and imperious bodyguards, refusing to answer reporters' questions. Alger Hiss privately regarded Molotov as "aggressive to the point of combativeness, quick to disagree, voluble, and inflexible"; Stettinius wrote that Molotov reminded him of a "Buddhist idol" and a "greengrocer"; Walter Lippmann, who was sympathetic to the foreign minister, observed that he had "the physical toughness of a peasant and the manner of a French academic"; and the columnist Anne O'Hare McCormick observed that Molotov "is prickly and difficult to deal with, at once blunt and secretive, cavalier toward small nations and assertive toward the big powers."[16]

Molotov's initiative violated the precept that the host nation of an international conference always serve as presiding officer. Stettinius feared that Molotov's move would necessitate unanimous votes among the Big Four, might result in the appointment of four chairmen of the Security Council, and could diminish U.S. control of the proceedings. That evening, Stettinius phoned Truman about his concerns. Truman's response was: "Stay with your guns." The following day, Truman told Henry Wallace, the secretary of commerce, that he had instructed Stettinius to tell Molotov "to go to hell" if the foreign minister was displeased. Anthony Eden sought a resolution of the dispute by suggesting that the five Big Powers serve as rotating presidents of the Plenary meetings and that Stettinius preside over private gatherings of the four chairmen, as well as over the Steering Committee and the Executive Committee. Although this was not exactly what he wanted, Stettinius reluctantly backed the proposal. Realizing that he was outnumbered and his bluff called, Molotov backed down and accepted the deal twenty-four hours later.[17]

This U.S. triumph in the chairmanship, however partial, was Stettinius's first success at the conference. It was to prove prophetic in several ways. It hinted early on of Washington's domination of San Francisco by suggesting that the United States could rally most convention members behind objectives it sought. This included the Latin American bloc, which in this case voted solidly for the United States (the Hemispheric community had been offended by Molotov's rude insinuation that the Mexican foreign minister, Ezequiel Padilla, was subservient to the United States). It also foreshadowed the continuing civil, if gradually more contentious, rivalry between Moscow and Washington that was to bedevil the entire San Francisco conference. One young Hearst journalist, a naval veteran named John F. Kennedy, observed shrewdly that Molotov's readiness to pick a fight over the "comparatively small question" of chairman was "the tip-off that the Russians are going to make a fight on all of the little issues in the hope they can write their own terms on the big ones." Finally, it foresaw that, in the end, the Big Powers would determine the outcome of most contested matters at the conference. For, in this instance, it was Britain that brokered an accord between the USSR and the United States over the chairman's post.[18]

Meanwhile, Stettinius began to blossom in his element. He was accompanied by an enormous mission. There were four other members of Congress present, as well as seventeen advisors from various U.S. agencies, including the agricultural secretary, the undersecretary of the interior, and the assistant secretaries of treasury and war. In addition, there were three assistant secretaries from the State Department, fourteen political and liaison officers, and five delegation advisors. In his seemingly casual manner, from the start, Stettinius exercised tight control over the assemblage, beginning with his own delegation. He had the group convene every morning at 9 A.M. in the Fairmont Hotel's penthouse. He made clear to the seven members from the outset that they did not have "very much elbow room" to effect changes in the basic Dumbarton Oaks text lest they upset the Soviets—except to deal with issues relating to the legal foundations and broad definitions of the charter. He assigned Leo Pasvolsky to supply background summaries of possible U.S. positions on still unsettled issues, along with the viewpoints of outside bodies, but Pasvolsky marked the stances that Stettinius "preferred." The secretary's most obstreperous colleague was Senator Vandenberg, a self-important man, who, according to Senator Connally, "saw dark plots everywhere" and kept the delegation "in a state of ferment." Stettinius, heeding Truman's instructions, though, gave special deference to the Republican Vandenberg (and, for that matter, to Senator Tom Connally). As a result, the vain Vandenberg went along with most of Stettinius's decisions. Stettinius, in addition, held regular press conferences to highlight U.S. themes and ideas and help shape public opinion, though his wooden manner often impeded his message.[19]

Ultimately, a fluctuating populace of some 5,000 people participated in the conference. There were some 850 delegates and advisors; 2,600 media; over 1,000 workers at the U.N. Secretariat; 300 or so security people; 120 interpreters translating the five main languages—English, French, Spanish, Russian, and Chinese; 37 foreign ministers; and 5 prime ministers. Untold numbers of local San Franciscans also attended sessions. Forty-six nations began the proceedings on the official roster, but, by the end, the U.N. had added four more nations to that list. U.S.

statisticians calculated that the participants consumed 78 tons of paper and averaged 500,000 sheets of papers per day over the course of the extended parley.[20]

There was also a vast unofficial U.S. presence blanketing the conference—the consultants, lobbyists, and special pleaders who crowded into San Francisco. At the sign-up desk, these outsiders had amounted to a mere hundred or so, but, in fact, at least 1,500 actually showed up, often operating under the guise of reporter or correspondent for their special interest or crusade. Most were statesiders, the only people who could afford to visit San Francisco. They played various roles. Some sought to alter the outcome of the debates; others merely paraded their credos before the delegates to gain public recognition. A delegation of Iroquois Indians, for example, appeared at one point to protest against the nonobservance of treaties with Washington. The voices of the tribe, however, could not be gainsaid in the tumult and cacophony of the Golden Gate.[21]

The forty-two consultants recognized officially by the U.S. government played the most public role. They ranged from Philip Murray, the head of the Congress of Industrial Organizations (CIO) to Thomas Finletter, representing the Council on Foreign Relations, to James Shotwell, the Columbia professor who was the maestro of globalism, to the American Jewish Committee; the American Bar Association; the League of Women Voters; the Catholic Welfare Conference; the Foreign Policy Association; the NAACP; the Kiwanis International; the Lions International; the Rotary International; the National Education Association; the American Legion; the National Lawyers' Guild; and twenty-seven other organizations. Many brought along fellow members and staff to San Francisco. The Commission to Study the Organization of Peace assembled forty-seven of their brethren; the Rotary summoned twenty-seven from their ranks.[22]

The State Department oversaw the participation of the consultants and some 160 other observers. It gave special recognition to the role of the consultants, arranging transportation and hotel reservations for all forty-two of them (though requiring that they pay their own travel and living expenses). It also bestowed on each a U.N. ID pin, which allowed them to enter areas restricted to delegates and to sit in on commission meetings. The department provided most of the consultants with their own working facilities, including the use of typewriters, press rooms, and U.N. documentation, and access to the public health building nearby for meetings. The department, too, accorded an unprecedented status to the observers, allocating tickets to many conference meetings, briefings, and forums, and it also offered work space.[23]

The consultants, nonetheless, were on the sidelines of the momentous decisions reached at San Francisco; indeed, the State Department and the U.S. delegation were not even sure at first what to do with them. But, as the conference evolved, the consultants pressed members of the U.S. delegation into holding regular sessions with them. These occurred twenty-five times—often in the mornings—over the two-month period, almost every other day. Usually, the delegates would make presentations on their work to the consultants and then answer questions from the floor. During this period, there were at least three critical, if modest, instances when the consultants did make a difference in the U.N. Charter: in education, in human rights, and in the formal recognition of the consultative role of nongovernmental organizations at the U.N. None of these ideas had garnered reference in the original Dumbarton Oaks draft.[24]

The first two matters came to the fore only after Virginia Gildersleeve, who had her own concerns over education and human rights, tipped off Clark Eichelberger that her efforts to convince the U.S. mission to embrace these positions had failed. Eichelberger then mounted a spirited campaign to reverse the views of the U.S. representatives. On education, Eichelberger was helping to ride a wave that was already cresting. Before the conference began, the presidents and chancellors of five hundred U.S. colleges and universities, backed by educators from thirty-five other countries, had issued a statement urging the inclusion of the word "education" in the U.N. Charter. U.S. delegates such as Senator Vandenberg feared that placing that word into the charter might open the floodgates to Soviet indoctrination in U.S. public schools. He and some of his cohorts equated education with propaganda. However, on May 17, at a meeting with the U.S. delegates, many of the consultants, led by an unusual coalition of the American Federation of Labor, the U.S. Chamber of Commerce, and the National Association of Manufacturers, forcefully argued for sewing the word "education" into the fabric of the charter. Five days later, the U.S. delegation changed its mind and adopted the idea.[25]

On human rights, Eichelberger, roused urgently by Gildersleeve's warning, called together key consultants for a meeting at the opera house. There, his quick-reaction band came up with four amendments for the charter. On May 2, Eichelberger and others then drafted a supporting letter, which James Shotwell and twenty other consultants signed on short notice, asking that the phrase "human rights" be inserted in relevant chapters of the document, including making a provision for the establishment of a human rights commission. At 5:00 P.M. that afternoon, they handed their letter to Stettinius and presented their individual statements. The secretary explained that he had no idea of the "intensity of feeling on this subject." Two days later, he announced that he would incorporate the suggestions; the following morning, he showed the changes to the consultants, remarking with a broad grin that they "could justly claim credit for getting a consideration of human rights into the Charter."[26]

Consultants were also successful in pushing for one other amendment, namely, a new article, Number 71, which would permit the Economic and Social Council of the United Nations to "make suitable arrangements for consultations with nongovernmental organizations [NGOs] which are concerned with matters within its competence." This article had its champions in the so-called ABLE group representing U.S. agriculture, business, labor, and education. On May 15, the ABLE participants sent a request to Stettinius urging a role for NGOs at the U.N. Stettinius quickly embraced the idea, hailing the development as an "unprecedented example of cooperation and unanimity" between the delegates and these independent groups. This provision marked a major departure from the stuffy old formalities of the League of Nations that had failed to provide a hearing to outside affiliates. Article 71 led to the ongoing collaborative relationship between the U.N. and NGOs that endures to this day.[27]

The consultants performed one other service for the State Department. They helped to corral the 160 or so "observers" who restlessly roamed the convention halls, many still seething over not being named consultants. Some might have made public protests, but Stettinius helped to finess the situation by urging the consultants to convey to the observers what they were doing, inform them of important hearings, brief them on special developments, and give them a sense of participation. As Dorothy Robins noted in her book, *Experiment in Democracy,* "The consultants functioned tirelessly, virtually around the clock, to fulfill their own responsibilities and to share with the other organizers, in so far as they could, the privileges they had."[28]

Some critics were alarmed that Stettinius might be opening a Pandora's box by inviting consultants and observers to San Francisco in the first place. But Stettinius needed broad-based national backing for the U.N., and these groups could guarantee continent-wide support. He may have also guessed that the din created by them in San Francisco could also aid him in pressuring his U.N. colleagues over issues he cared about. It could be argued, though, that Stettinius was buying off the consultants with relatively innocuous concessions on education, human rights, and NGOs that enabled him to appear more inclusive and beneficent than he really was. Stettinius, after all, did not listen to the NGOs on security matters or on the issue of the veto or trusteeship questions except in so far as they already supported U.S. positions. Furthermore, he had preselected all the consultants, deliberately not choosing those who advocated global government, for example, the World Federalists, the World Government Association, and the Federal Union, as well as those who scorned global institutions, such as the Daughters of the American Revolution (though many of these groups came to San Francisco anyway as observers). Yet, in the end, without the simple, if obvious, emendations of the charter persuasively advocated by the consultants, the U.N. might not have shone quite so humanely in the world as it subsequently did.[29]

Given the enormous stress of hosting the worldwide meeting, with the League of Nations fiasco haunting the background, Stettinius and his aides relied heavily on their ability to overcome various obstacles by imbuing the conference with U.S. values and goals. The sheer scope of this operation helped to limit the areas of maneuver for other nations, stave off deadlock and collapse, and enhance the likelihood that the Roosevelt and Truman administrations would achieve the aims they sought. Nonetheless, the United States insistently communicated a public impression that it was just one among many participants engaged in an arduous intellectual process that it did not intend to dominate.

CHAPTER 8

THE BITTER TRADE-OFF

The warnings had sounded for some time on the growing Soviet demands that the two states, Belarus and Ukraine, be enrolled in the first days in San Francisco. At Yalta, Stalin had originally expressed his uneasiness that the USSR might be outvoted in the United Nations. Great Britain, he thought, could control the Commonwealth votes. The United States could control the Latin American votes. But what votes would the Soviets bring to the U.N. table?

Even though Roosevelt and Churchill had both promised to support the entry of Belarus and Ukraine in exchange for Stalin's consent to the limited veto, they still had left the final determination of U.N. membership up to the San Francisco Conference. The Anglo-American position on this and on Poland increasingly vexed Stalin as the weeks passed. In late March, he had cancelled Molotov as his representative to the California meeting—though changing his mind after Roosevelt's death. In the days leading up to the conference, Stalin's preoccupation with these nations and with Poland overrode all his other concerns about the U.N.

Stalin's two emissaries, Ambassador Andrei Gromyko and Foreign Minister Molotov, repeatedly brought up questions of the three countries with Stettinius in Washington and then in San Francisco. On April 13, at talks between the four sponsoring powers, colloquially known as the Informal Organizing Group, Gromyko pressed the issue of the admission and the immediate seating of the two of the Soviet satellites, threatening that the USSR would not agree to the appointment of any commission heads or committee chairs at San Francisco until the business of Belarus and Ukraine was resolved. Stettinius tried to remind Gromyko of the accord reached at Yalta on handling these two countries, but he couldn't overcome Gromyko's intransigence. The Soviets, he wrote to President Truman that day, were so "insistent" on garnering the two votes that they might jeopardize the entire conference if they weren't given their way. Again, at a meeting on April 18, Gromyko informed Stettinius that Moscow would not agree to appoint the various charter review teams at San Francisco until he was assured the two states would achieve membership. At yet another talk in San Francisco on April 24, Molotov told Stettinius flatly that he would "go home" if the situation of all three states was not clarified by the opening date of the conference. Molotov's threat may have applied only to himself, not to the entire Russian delegation. Still, his tone was menacing.[1]

On the morning of April 25, the day the conference opened, Stettinius informed the U.S. delegation at a meeting in his penthouse apartment atop the Fairmont Hotel about the crisis with the Soviets. He read the letter Truman had given him in which the United States endorsed entry for the two Russian states and allowed them to be listed in the conference annex—though Washington did not take a position on their immediate seating. Without instant attention to Stalin's demand, Stettinius told the group, the Russians might walk out of the conference. He asked for judgments on what to do. The responses of the members varied. Ambassador Averell Harriman, attending the meeting at Stettinius's invitation (and staying in the Fairmont Hotel suite reserved for Cordell Hull), argued for complying with the Yalta agreement and thus demonstrating U.S. allegiance to global accords as opposed to a pattern of Soviet violations of the pact. Senator Vandenberg, on the other hand, wanted to postpone taking any step, at least until later in the conference, out of concern that Washington would be seen as capitulating to Stalin. Most other members conceded the ultimate admission of the two states, but were uncertain about supporting the involvement of the pair in the conference itself.[2]

One unexpected drop-in to the U.S. assemblage—not invited, he had come on his own to San Francisco—was Nelson Rockefeller, the assistant secretary of state for Latin America, who introduced a surprising and, in many ways, unsettling note of warning. Through his contacts in Latin America, he reported that the Western Hemisphere bloc objected to the admission and seating of Belarus and Ukraine without assurance first of Argentina's enrollment in the U.N. He reminded the delegates that Buenos Aires had complied with the Mexico City treaty (though it had missed the Yalta deadline of March 1 for its declaration of war by a month) and now wanted to sign the U.N. Declaration and gain membership. "We should not forget," he advised the delegation, "that we have to carry this out with the American republics, and if we want to put the proposal through, we will have to have their votes. And I think the only way we could get their votes is to give in to their desires on Argentina."[3]

Most delegates expressed abhorrence about any dealings with Argentina—especially Leo Pasvolsky and Senator Connally. Rockefeller retorted: "I cannot be held responsible for delivering the vote if nothing is done on Argentina." After the meeting, Averell Harriman said harshly to Rockefeller: "Nelson, are you the ambassador to the Argentine or the ambassador of the Argentine?" The Rockefeller dispute jarred Stettinius, reminding him that, in order to insure the admission of Belarus and Ukraine, he needed the nineteen Latin votes and thus he might have to permit Argentina's membership, at the distinct risk of infuriating Molotov.[4]

That Rockefeller was even in San Francisco was another shock for Stettinius. Stettinius had not asked Rockefeller to be part of the U.S. delegation because he regarded him as a lone ranger more interested in Latin concerns than U.S. ones. But Stettinius also had never instructed him to remain in Washington. So Rockefeller, taking advantage of Stettinius's lack of orders, had proceeded westward, unbidden and uncredentialed, to the conference. He had apparently decided that, as the U.S. agent on the Hemisphere at Mexico City, he had to be present in San Francisco to supervise any Latin strategy. On April 21, he flew with twelve Latin envoys from Washington to the Golden Gate City, traveling serenely as if he were a participant. He swiftly took over the St. Francis Hotel and placed his own staff there, and took personal charge of the Hemispheric officials, arranging breakfasts for them, even ordering the U.S. Navy to take care of their laundry. By his second day in town, April 22, he was conferring with most of the nineteen Latin governments over many U.N. issues. One of his meeting reportedly lasted some two and one-half hours. His decision to come to San Francisco, his high-handed appropriation of the Latin delegates, and his brash pronouncement on Argentina, as one of his biographers later observed, "bordered on rank insubordination."[5]

Those who knew him well were not surprised by his bold, if impetuous, ways. Born into a family of remarkable wealth, Nelson Rockefeller was accustomed to cutting his own pathway, regardless of others. Only thirty-seven years old at the time of the conference, he had lived a tempestuous life. In his teenage years, he overcame crippling dyslexia and hyperactivity by relentless determination and bull-like willpower. An ebullient, exuberant personality, he had seized control when only in his twenties of the Rockefeller Center project from his father's hirelings and revamped the Museum of Modern Art, turning it into a world-class institution. In March 1933, he had an infamous clash with the painter Diego Rivera over a mural Rivera had done for the RCA Building celebrating May Day in Red Square and exalting Lenin, leading Rockefeller to destroy the mural later, and precipitating in him a lifelong mistrust of communism.

By the late 1930s, though a Republican, Rockefeller solicited Harry Hopkins about a possible job in the Roosevelt administration as regards Latin America. In July 1940, Roosevelt appointed Rockefeller to be the coordinator of Inter-American Affairs—a nebulous position that Rockefeller soon built into a powerful post that dispatched food, economic aid, and anti-Nazi propaganda throughout the Americas. Rockefeller grew so popular among the Latins that Roosevelt, who appreciated Rockefeller's talent and bravado, made him assistant secretary for Latin America by the end of 1944. At San Francisco, he was the only person in the delegation in a position, one biographer noted, able "to tame the fractious elements of the [Latin] coalition, to build a consensus, to see to it that the votes were really there." Unabashed and indifferent to State Department protocol, he thrust himself into the critical decisions of the conference.[6]

That afternoon, April 25, following the opening speeches in the opera house, Stettinius telephoned Truman. He told the president bluntly that "Molotov would go home if [he] did not get the two republics admitted as initial members." The U.S. delegation just that morning, he reported, had agreed to back the entry of Belarus and Ukraine. Stettinius did not mention the Argentine impasse to Truman at that time. Impressed with Stettinius's concerns, Truman instructed him to make public his letter endorsing the Yalta agreement and to "go down and put it across" for the two republics. But, meanwhile, Stettinius brooded more and more over the sharp warnings he had received from Rockefeller. As he later wrote irritably in his diary: "Nelson Rockefeller undoubtedly had been responsible for bringing the situation to the point where the nineteen Latin American republics probably would not vote for the two new Soviet republics being seated until Argentina was also admitted to the conference."[7]

That night, he convened the U.S. team and consulted them a second time on strategy. He now wondered whether he should simply accept Argentina's candidacy. He was aware of President Truman's serious reservations about Argentina's behavior during the war. However, he had to consider the likelihood that the Hemisphere might vote in unison against the USSR on its two states if Argentina didn't achieve membership. He was now contemplating a proposal that all three nations be admitted as initial members and then made full participants a few weeks later. He asked whether the delegates would support such a proposition. Each one of them, in turn, cautiously assented to the idea—except for Vandenberg who, unwilling to placate the Soviets in any fashion, reserved his position. Stettinius announced he would call Truman the next morning and tell him that a "majority" of the delegation now supported a three-country entry.[8]

Early on Thursday morning, April 26, Stettinius spoke by phone to Truman. Aware of the president's antipathy toward Buenos Aires, he gingerly told Truman about the consensus within the delegation to accept the enrollment not only of the two Soviet republics but also of Argentina. The United States needed Argentina, he explained, to guarantee acceptance of the two republics and to fulfill Roosevelt's understanding with

Stalin. Truman growled in his Missouri twang that Argentina "doesn't deserve to be elected a member of the United Nations. . . . While most of the United Nations were suffering for the common cause, she was standing aside, if not helping the enemy." But he finally conceded Stettinius's point. He insisted, however, that all three nations be seated at a later date, and that Argentina not be permitted to sign the original United Nations Declaration. Such an act would, in his view, be an insult to those countries that had shed blood to defeat the Axis.[9]

Armed with Truman's reluctant consent, Stettinius strode to the morning meeting in the penthouse and informed the delegates of his conversation. He had, meantime, learned that Argentina had withdrawn its request to place its name on the U.N. Declaration. The delegation reaffirmed its backing for the Secretary's approach. Stettinius left to see Molotov to reassure him again about U.S. support for the two Soviet states—though confiding to the delegates that he was not going to inform Molotov about Argentina. He did tell the Latin emissaries that he would support Argentina in exchange for their votes on the Russian states.[10]

That afternoon, Molotov, following his meeting with Stettinius, attended a twenty-four-minute press conference held in a St. Francis Hotel conference room, accompanied, as usual, by his flying wedge of bodyguards. Whether because he had received firm assurances from Stettinius earlier about Belarus and Ukraine, or for some other reason, he seemed in a more benign frame of mind. He brushed aside discussion of any difficulties at San Francisco and told the several hundred journalists that he felt the Polish question would be settled soon. Later in the day, addressing the Plenary Session, he conveyed an even rosier message. He expressed "deep" gratitude "personally" to Stettinius for his work in organizing the conference, paid tribute to Franklin Roosevelt, and noted that the Soviet Union attached "great importance" to the outcome of the U.N. meeting. While assailing the League of Nations as being a "tool" of "reactionary forces," he envisaged the United Nations by contrast as a "joint effort of peace-loving nations," and a "great coalition of·democratic powers," all of whom were forged "in the fire of struggle."[11]

When the Steering Committee convened the next day, April 27, Molotov was now ready to make his move. Accompanied by the two senators, Connally and Vandenberg, Stettinius arrived at the meeting armed with the Truman letter. Molotov had earlier accepted the Eden compromise on the chairmanships. Then, as the U.N. committee heads were about to be chosen, Molotov offered his motion to admit Belarus and Ukraine to "original membership." He reminded the delegates that the three Big Powers had united behind this proposal at the Crimea Conference. He also pointed out that the two republics had "borne the major burden" of the German invasion of Russia, each contributing up to 1 million of their citizens to the Red Army. At a prearranged signal, Stettinius stood up and read the contents of Truman's letter supporting the accession of the two nations. Subsequently, the British and Chinese foreign ministers rose to express their approval. A vote was taken. The Steering Committee gave its unanimous consent. All nineteen Latin states, relying on U.S. assurances that Argentina's turn would come next and agreeing not to mention Buenos Aires to avoid disrupting the event, voted for the motion. But Molotov could not let well enough alone. He requested that both states be immediately invited to participate in the San Francisco meeting. At this point, the Columbian foreign minister, Alberto Lleras Camargo, asked that Molotov's proposal be referred to the Executive Committee for review. He wanted to preserve this issue as a bargaining chip for the Latin bloc. Molotov reluctantly assented, but made clear that he had no plans to drop the matter.[12]

The Czechoslovakian foreign minister, Jan Masaryk, asked for the floor. He abruptly proposed, "as a neighbor of Poland," that Warsaw be forthwith seated at San Francisco. The assembly was startled, not anticipating that the Soviet bloc would raise so controversial a subject at this session. Molotov had apparently, in secrecy, devised this gambit. The Czech minister, one of his country's leading progressives, had introduced the proposition under intense Soviet pressure. Masaryk later that afternoon confided to U.S. envoy Charles Bohlen, at the Fairmont Hotel bar: "What can one do with these Russians? Out of the clear blue sky I got a note from Molotov saying Czechoslovakia must vote for the Soviet proposition in regard to Poland, or else forfeit the friendship of the Soviet government. . . . You can be on your knees and this is not enough for the Russians." Since Soviet troops occupied his homeland, Masaryk had little choice in the matter. (Three years later, he committed suicide under Soviet duress.)[13]

The oft volatile Senator Vandenberg took umbrage at what he considered this "direct violation of Yalta" over Poland. Sitting directly behind Stettinius, he hurriedly scribbled a statement for him to use. Stettinius took one glance at it, and, realizing it made sense, quoted Vandenberg's remarks directly. "He never hesitated an instant," Vandenberg confided glowingly to his diary. Stettinius told the delegates: "I remind the Conference that we have just honored our Yalta engagements in behalf of Russia. I also remind the Conference that there are other Yalta obligations which equally require allegiance. One of them calls for a new and representative Polish Provisional Government. Until that happens, the Conference cannot, in good conscience, recognize the Lublin government. It would be a sordid exhibition of bad faith." Vandenberg later told others that Stettinius had made him "proud to be an American." Foreign Minister Eden of Great Britain now seconded the Stettinius statement, saying that his government had no means of knowing whether Poles supported the provisional regime because the Soviets would not permit any British observers to enter the country. The sentiment of the Steering Committee suddenly shifted against Molotov. The Belgian foreign minister, Paul Henri Spaak, rescued Molotov from an embarrassing defeat by offering a motion—quickly adopted—expressing the hope that the new Polish government might be organized in time to be represented in San Francisco. Much to Stettinius's relief, Molotov did not use this occasion to walk out of the conference.[14]

Stettinius telephoned Truman again. He related the news of the Steering Committee's balloting on Belarus and Ukraine. He explained that Argentina's admission had not yet come up. To let the newly enrolled states participate in the sessions themselves, he told Truman, "we are going to have to make a deal" now on Argentina. Argentina, in addition, had decided not to pursue signing the U.N. Declaration and wouldn't be allowed to reconsider that decision. Truman gave his consent: "You have to get that thing going." Stettinius also told Truman: "I was very tough on Poland today." He had brought along the two Senators, Vandenberg and Connally, he informed him, and "they went along every step of the road and are in complete accord." All this pleased the president. "I am going to take a drink and really sleep tonight." Stettinius also telephoned his old boss, Cordell Hull, still in the hospital and, with some trepidation, informed him that the United States was likely to support Argentina's admission to the U.N. Hull, who couldn't abide the regime, reacted coolly. Later in the day, at a press conference, Stettinius downplayed the Argentina controversy, saying correctly, though somewhat disingenuously, that nobody had raised the issue at the Steering Committee.[15]

Stettinius was now hard at work trying to figure out a dignified exit from the Argentine imbroglio and head off a public spat with the Soviets. At the urging of Nelson Rockefeller, he decided to invite four representatives of the Latin American nations—the foreign ministers of Venezuela, Brazil, Chile, and Mexico—to meet with the Big Four foreign ministers the next day, Saturday, to thrash out a possible settlement. On April 28, at 6:45 P.M., fifteen people assembled in Stettinius's penthouse apartment, including Anthony Eden, Molotov, T. V. Soong, the Chinese foreign minister, Stettinius, Rockefeller, and assorted staffers, as well as the four Latin representatives. The urbane Mexican, Ezequiel Padilla, whom Molotov had rudely upbraided days earlier as a U.S. lackey, opened the session by reminding Molotov that all his Latin brethren had voted "gladly" for the two Soviet republics just twenty-four hours earlier. Now the Latin representatives and the United States were concerned about redeeming a "commitment" they had made to Argentina at the Mexico City meeting in March to include her in San Francisco once she had signed the Act of Chapultepec and launched war on the Axis. Buenos Aires had made the moves. Now he hoped that Molotov would consent to her membership.[16]

Molotov said flatly no—unless Poland were admitted, too. After all, how could Poland be excluded and Argentina be included, he reasoned, when Poland "had suffered so much in this war and had been the first country to be invaded whereas Argentina had, in effect, helped the enemy"? Padilla rejoined that Poland was a separate matter for the

Big Powers to decide. But Molotov insisted that the linkage was between Argentina and Poland, not between Argentina and Belarus/Ukraine. However, if Molotov thought his ultimatum might intimidate the Latin emissaries, he was mistaken. Instead, the Latins saw a man trying to collect twice on the same proposition. Pedro Leão Velloso, the Brazilian foreign minister, cautioned Molotov that, should Argentina not be admitted, the Latin nations would vote against Belarus and Ukraine. Molotov replied that the Executive Committee should decide on Monday. That night, Stettinius phoned Truman to bring him up-to-date on what had happened. Truman crisply rejected Molotov's position, saying that he would not agree to seating the two Soviet states if Poland were admitted.[17]

Monday morning, April 30, Stettinius was still trying to find ways to accommodate Molotov for fear of driving him out of the conference—though, by now, he knew that Molotov was planning to return to Moscow in a few days anyway due to prior commitments. James Reston, in a Sunday, April 29, *New York Times* story, wrote that U.S. officials were concerned they might be seen as "ganging up on the Russians." In any event, just before the 9:00 A.M. Executive Committee meeting in the Veterans Building, Stettinius attempted to finesse the situation by agreeing to back the immediate seating of the two Soviet republics—the first item on the agenda—and said he would urge his allies to do the same. On Molotov's motion, the fourteen member group unanimously ratified participation by the two states in the conference. This strategy to placate Molotov, however, did not work. Molotov stuck by his anti-Argentine position.[18]

When Padilla stood up, along with Chile's foreign minister, and asked that Argentina be admitted forthwith, Molotov took the floor. He claimed he did not know that the issue was to come before the committee (though Stettinius interjected to remind him of the Saturday briefing). In any event, Argentina, Molotov argued, was an entirely different situation from that of Belarus and Ukraine. Argentina had helped the enemy throughout the war. He could agree to Argentina's membership only if Poland, which had fought the Nazis, was also admitted. Further, he maintained, if the Argentine government was considered unrepresentative of the people but was admitted, then, by the same logic, so should the Lublin regime be admitted. To give Argentina a seat without giving one to Poland would be a "blow to the prestige of the conference." Poland, Padilla replied, was a problem to be solved by the Big Three. As for Argentina, its people were democratic even if its government was not, and it, in any event, should be encouraged to move in the direction of freedom. Stettinius read a statement from his black-ringed binder notebook in support of Padilla. He called for a vote. Argentina's admission won 9 to 3 (with two abstentions). A motion by Molotov to refer the matter to the Big Four went down to defeat 8 to 3. The meeting concluded at 11:00 A.M.[19]

Thirty minutes later, Molotov brought the matter now to the forty-six-member Steering Committee convening in another room in the Veterans Building. The committee did its part and admitted Belarus and Ukraine. But once the Argentina request came before them, a repeat of the morning arguments ensued. This time, Molotov, marshaling new arguments against Buenos Aires, slyly quoted statements uttered in late 1944 by President Roosevelt and former Secretary of State Cordell Hull identifying Argentina as "the headquarters of the Fascist movement in the Hemisphere." Still, a large number of the Latin delegates answered passionately for Argentina's admission on the grounds of Hemispheric "unity." Molotov now introduced a new strategy asking for further study of the Argentina question, but this motion lost 25 to 7. Subsequently, the Steering Committee approved Argentina's enrollment 29 to 5, eleven states abstaining. Russia, Czechoslovakia, Yugoslavia, Bulgaria, and Greece made up the opposition. Molotov immediately asked for a Plenary Session that afternoon to reconsider the question.[20]

Before the Plenary Session, Molotov called a press conference. Five hundred reporters assembled in the ballroom of the St. Francis Hotel at 2:45 P.M. to hear Molotov speak for forty-five minutes. In front of the international media, he made his case publicly against Argentina and for Poland. His intensifying campaign was so out of proportion to the importance of the matter that suspicions grew among some in the media that perhaps Josef Stalin himself was behind Molotov's fierce counterattack. Whatever his motives, Molotov raised legitimate concerns about Argentina's government. Many Americans who already abhorred the military junta run by General Farrell because of its pro-Nazi sympathies supported Molotov's intransigent stand. Molotov's proposal that, at the very least, the admission of the Latin country be postponed for "a few days" so that more "documentation" could be found to determine whether the country was truly democratic appeared reasonable on its face. His proposition helped to turn public opinion against Washington even while Molotov was privately aware that the only reason for U.S. advocacy for Argentina was to assure the Latin votes for enrollment of the two Soviet states in the U.N.[21]

At 3:30 P.M., the Plenary Session of the U.N. Conference commenced in the opera house, next door to the Veterans Building. This time, with the media again heavily in attendance and thousands sitting in the galleries, the Plenary decided to give unanimous backing to Belarus and Ukraine. Next came the Argentine case. Molotov walked rapidly to the podium and delivered a blistering indictment of the Argentine regime as well as making his broadest plea for Poland's membership. Speaking extemporaneously and casting sardonic asides, he restated his outrage over Argentina's pro-Nazi past, quoted again the Hull-FDR condemnations of Buenos Aires, and pointed out once more that, if Poland's regime was unrepresentative, so was Argentina's. He added one new twist: If other countries asserted that Poland was not independent of the Soviet Union, then by the same token, India and the Philippines should not be admitted to the United Nations because they were not independent of Great Britain or the United States.

James Reston wrote in the *New York Times* that, among the delegates, "there was considerable admiration for the skill and persistence with which Molotov put his case." But the weight of the Latin nations and the United States proved too much for the Soviets. On his proposition to defer an invitation to Buenos Aires, Molotov failed 28 to 7, and on the invitation to Argentina to join the U.N., Molotov was on the losing side 31 to 4, with 10 abstentions. Three new nations were now added to the San Francisco roster with a tacit agreement that they would join the meeting right away—making forty-nine at the U.N. conference. Poland remained the outsider.[22]

While Molotov lost in San Francisco, it was soon apparent he had won the public relations contest around the globe. Even in the United States, many political figures rallied to his banner. Adlai Stevenson, then a special assistant to Stettinius, told Commerce Secretary Henry Wallace in Washington that "the Russians were right with regard to Argentina and that many people in the State Department realized this to be the case." Stettinius's power play, he contended, would only disillusion the Soviets about the fairness of the U.N. Wallace himself confessed to feeling "very much depressed." Cordell Hull, resting in his bed in the Naval Hospital at Bethesda, blamed Stettinius's incompetence for allowing the fascist government in Buenos Aires to get a seat in the U.N. and "dangerously" alienate the Russians. Two staunch U.N. supporters in the U.S. Senate, Carl Hatch and Joseph Ball, wired Stettinius that what occurred was a "cynical repudiation of the whole cause of democracy and freedom for which we are fighting this war against the Nazis." Only a telegram a few days later from Vandenberg explaining that the decision was "unavoidable" and "save[d] the conference," and later a personal visit from Nelson Rockefeller, persuaded both men to withdraw their complaints.[23]

The press meanwhile was furious. *Time* intoned that the Truman administration was using the conference to humiliate the Russians, playing a "straight power" game in the Hemisphere "as amoral as Russia's game in eastern Europe." In an especially strident editorial in its May 1 edition, the *Washington Post* pontificated: "The moral sense of onlookers has been affronted [by] the bush league diplomacy of the State Department headed by Secretary Stettinius." All Molotov can conclude, the paper continued, "is that incompetence has taken hold of our foreign relations. However, Molotov is not averse to playing poker with men who, compared with him, don't even know the rudiments of the game." Finally, it said: "At the hands of amateurs of the State Department, this kind of blundering is worse than criminal for the consequences may be grievous."

Columnist Walter Lippmann, writing a few days afterward, regarded Stettinius's use of bloc politics as "dangerous" with the potential to "diminish" the U.N. He reflected later, "I saw Stettinius and Nelson

Rockefeller marshal the twenty Latin American republics in one solid bloc and steam-roll that through the United Nations," even though, in Lippmann's view, the Soviets had "a good case on Argentina and we wouldn't listen to it." In response to these efforts to "dominate things," he warned: "We were going to run into iron resistance to anything else from the Russians." Yet not all correspondents were so sure that the United States had acted wrongly. Some months later, E. B. White of the *New Yorker* observed: "You don't necessarily get rid of a smell by the simple act of refusing to sit in the same room with it. And you do not achieve security by suspending, from a security league, an enemy of security."[24]

Three Americans, however, were greatly pleased by the turn of events. The implacable anti-Communist Senator Vandenberg joyfully confided to his diary that Molotov had "done more in four days to solidify Pan America against Russia than anything that ever happened." Suddenly, the Hemisphere nations were, in the Senator's words, "our only friends," "the one group of states we could count on." Nelson Rockefeller jubilantly telephoned his mother the next day with the news of his triumph. "We had a great tussle," he said, "but things have come through successfully." He thought Stettinius had done a "magnificent" job, though he was concerned that "certain groups" were trying to push him around. But he was "backing up" the secretary and now trying to "convince him to meet with the press."[25]

Stettinius himself called Truman that evening to tell him proudly about the day's proceedings. "We had another tough day—got by some more hurdles," he told Truman. "We had a public showdown with [Molotov]. There was nothing else to do." But now he reassured Truman, "I believe we will have clear sailing from here on." Truman replied: "I am glad to hear that." (The next day, Truman, in the wake of the acerbic *Washington Post* editorial, spoke with Stettinius again and buoyed up the secretary's spirits by telling him that he "was doing the best possible job out there.") Minutes later, Stettinius called Hull and told him about Molotov: "We gave him a good licking, a good public licking." That evening, he spoke with the U.S. delegation and recounted the "great resentment" among the delegates over Molotov's tactics on Poland and Argentina and affirmed that the United States had "stood its ground."

But, disregarding Rockefeller's advice, Stettinius failed to talk to the media and elucidate at length the reasons why the U.S. government acted as it did. Stettinius could have explained that the administration supported Argentina to guarantee the seating of two Soviet lands—information already in most newspapers—but he avoided any comment at all and, in effect, gave Molotov free rein to say what he wanted. Stettinius even blocked Rockefeller, who had briefed Truman on a May 3 visit to Washington, from issuing a statement of explanation. He may have wished to avoid further aggravating Moscow. On May 4, for example, Stettinius spoke at the University of California at Berkeley and stressed the "steady rock of unity" among the Big Four. The State Department eventually did approve a form reply to critics. Stettinius's silence, though, only added to the overall impression of his ineffectuality. Almost a month later, on May 28, Stettinius finally delivered a speech defending his actions on Argentina, but by then no one was listening.[26]

The irony of the Molotov performance was that he had deftly deflected public attention from the real issues at hand while managing to keep the spotlight focused on Stettinius's deficiencies and U.S. complicity with Buenos Aires. Molotov never owned up to, for example, the issue of Soviet domination of Belarus or Ukraine or the subservience of the Warsaw government to Moscow. Nor did his promise to vote for Argentina if Poland got in—a posture that undermined his moral standing on the Nazi issue—ever receive much attention in the press. But his meticulous attention to the matter of voting numbers did indicate how much fear the Russian regime had that its authority with the Big Four might be eroded by being outvoted in the United Nations General Assembly. At a dinner party hosted by Anthony Eden the day following the Argentine vote, Molotov still complained about the "enormous influence" of the Latin bloc, "out of all proportion to their power and resources."[27]

That evening, on April 30, after the Argentine showdown, Stettinius convened a meeting of the sponsoring powers in his penthouse to work out exactly who would run the four commissions and various committees at the San Francisco Conference. There was still some trepidation about whether Molotov might boycott the Big Four session. But he showed up in a conciliatory mood: "Molotov's spirits were much better," Stettinius informed Truman. "He thinks everything is clear." Privately, Molotov confided to Stettinius that "he felt from now on matters should go smoothly." The four foreign ministers unanimously approved a list of officerships. Out of deference to Russian sensibilities, a line was left blank for an Argentine to be one of the rapporteurs. James Reston wrote in the next morning's *New York Times* that the Stettinius meeting was "the most friendly" of the conference and that Molotov had let it be known that he "wanted the conference to succeed."[28]

How to account for this sudden change of tactics by Moscow? The series of rejections suffered by the Russians in the opening skirmishes may have impressed the Soviet delegation with Washington's determination to employ her voting prowess to obtain her aims. Molotov, on the instruction of Stalin, may also have decided that the prestige of being a permanent member of the United Nations with veto power outweighed any failure—albeit a temporary one—to secure Poland's berth in the organization. Besides, being the wary leader he was, Stalin may have wished to stay in the U.N. to keep tabs on his foes and assure that the U.N. did not turn into an alliance against the Soviet Union. Molotov and Stalin, in addition, probably figured they had reaped a public relations bonanza from the Argentine contretemps by putting the West on the defensive. At this point there was nothing more to be gained. Finally, Molotov could well have been influenced by Stettinius's earnest behind-the-scenes efforts to reassure him that the United States wanted to work with the USSR on all U.N. matters outside the issue of Poland. The confrontation over Argentina probably, in that sense, may have cleared the air for the moment.[29]

CHAPTER 9

FULL-COURT PRESS

The Argentine victory, although clear-cut, left Stettinius somewhat shaken and harried. He had but a few hours to savor his success before the press assault began on his handiwork. The harshest critic was the *Washington Post*. The morning following the stinging editorial in the newspaper, Stettinius ran into the publisher of the newspaper, Eugene Meyer, in the lobby of the Fairmont Hotel. Barely containing his anger, Stettinius motioned Meyer over. "What the heck are you trying to do—completely destroy me?" he demanded. Meyer replied, "No, you are my friend." Stettinius went on: "I have always liked and admired you, so what causes you to do this? It isn't fair." Meyer answered defensively: "Have you heard all the nice things they have been saying about you on the air?" Stettinius, unmollified, retorted: "I am not referring to the radio. I am referring to what you have just published in your God-darned bloody sheet." Meyer responded: "I would like to talk to you again when you have calmed down." Stettinius backed off and agreed to see him later. A few days afterwards, however, he told Archibald MacLeish, the assistant secretary of state, that the *Post* "was out to destroy him and [was] building up Sumner Welles for his job."[1]

Stettinius was keenly aware that U.S. press coverage was indispensable to public support for ratification of the U.N. Treaty in the U.S. Senate—as well as for his own efforts to solidify his standing with President Truman. His State Department advisors were also acutely sensitive to protecting Stettinius's reputation. At a morning meeting that same day, Averell Harriman, Nelson Rockefeller, Harold Stassen, and several others, considered ways to contain or soften the adverse fallout from the *Post* editorial. A few brushed aside the criticism of Walter Lippmann and other columnists, insisting they were simply "out to get" the secretary of state. Though, Stassen, a young but seasoned media pro as an ex-governor, shrugged off most of the negative commentary, reminding everyone that the best thing they could do now was to "stay on the main track." Nonetheless, all decided that Senator Vandenberg should send President Truman a telegram stating that the entire delegation backed Stettinius, which he agreed to do. Vandenberg also sent reassuring notes to restive senators, but it rapidly became evident that all of these measures were neither adequate to the task, nor were they helped by Stettinius's unwillingness to meet with the press. The uproar was not going to subside. The State Department received over five hundred letters and wires protesting U.S. action on Argentina. An aide wrote: "Very few of these letters appear to be inspired, and a large number of them are violent." Stettinius's form reply did nothing to quell the critics.[2]

The lack of a coherent media policy allowed the United States to stumble. Stettinius had not really thought through how he wished to brief newsmen about what was going on at the conference. He figured he had honed the right strategy at the Mexico City Conference earlier in the year. In Mexico he had pursued, by his own lights, a "liberal and progressive policy," which meant that he alone spoke for the delegation after consultation with its members. He had also allowed the press to attend all Plenary Sessions and commission meetings while closing the media to the meetings of the delegation itself, the Executive and Steering Committees, and all subcommittees. But, by relying on the Mexico model, Stettinius failed to take into account that the gathering south of the border was far less important in journalists' views than the meeting in San Francisco. Mexico City was a sideshow by international press standards. The foreign correspondents who attended scanted controversies that occurred at the daily sessions because they regarded the stakes to be so low. By contrast, in San Francisco, the eyes of the world were on the conference. Indeed, as Arthur Krock wrote, it was the "most over-reported of all international conferences (where the observers outnumber the principals manifold)."[3]

Thousands of reporters, indeed, arrived from all over the world, most of them from the United States, and displayed an insatiable appetite for stories. The *New York Times* published a daily wire-photo edition, and the *New York Post* printed a morning San Francisco issue. The media filed over 150,000 words a day. This created an arena for hyperbolic press excess. As Anne O'Hare McCormick observed: "Finding it hard at best to drum up daily interest in a drafting job, especially in competition with a crashing drama of action in the war theaters, the reporters [here] tend to exaggerate the tugs and pulls that are bound to develop in such meetings and to describe them in terms of real warfare as 'victories' and 'retreats.' The delegates, too, lack perspective and assurance. The result is a distorted picture of what goes on." Isolationist newspapers such as the *Chicago Tribune* were especially intent on inflating every nuance or small dispute into cataclysmic events to validate their own ideological predilections against the U.N. Newsmen everywhere listened to rumor mills and overstated flare-ups at the Veterans Hall meetings; indeed, they sought out whatever sources they could find, usually other delegations, seldom the reticent Americans.[4]

Stettinius had, though, in March and April, even before the conference began, started to take cognizance of press angst and agreed to a few steps to mend frayed media relations. One concession he made early on for the U.S. delegation, at its initial meeting in March, was to allow the delegates to speak to reporters; at the same time, though, he made an agreement that, after the conference commenced, no public statements would be permitted without approval from the entire delegation. However, when word leaked out in March about President Roosevelt's secret pledge to support Stalin's request for three Russian votes at the U.N., Stettinius changed his tune. Then he instructed the members that there should be no public statements in the pre–San Francisco period without the full sanction of the delegation. But strains over this strategy soon developed. Senator Vandenberg, as the former editor of Michigan's *Grand Rapids Herald* for over twenty years, wanted to inform the media about the progress of the delegation's work on the U.N. Charter. Senator Connally, on the contrary, wished to exclude the press altogether to maintain delegation "unity." Stettinius wavered between the views of the two men. On several occasions, he did approve the release of generalized notices about the group's labors. But for the most part he maintained silence. By and large, the press left the delegation alone.[5]

Once the conference went forward, however, the media in San Francisco reconsidered their quiescent position and turned on Stettinius with a vengeance. Two events, in particular, became emblematic of a new aggressiveness by reporters. The United States had set up a press room on the fourth floor of the Fairmont Hotel. On the first day of the conference, April 25, several American newsmen tried to gain access to the floor above the press room where the delegates were holding a morning meeting. Benjamin Gerig, the deputy secretary-general to Alger Hiss, attempted to block the journalists from the session, but they brushed by him and, once there, would not leave. Gerig finally gave up. The story of the scuffle got into the next day's newspapers. The newsmen explained that they had behaved as they did because they felt the procedures for procuring information at the conference were "largely of a patchwork nature with each delegation working in its own way and on its own behalf." They were plying Soviet, French, and British sources for data, facts, and schedules that the United States would not give them. In response, Vandenberg now insisted that the U.S. delegation devise a plan to make more information available.

A few days later, a press officer for the Americans, Homer Byington, proposed some revised rules: The U.S. delegation would assign members to do background briefings daily on an "experimental" basis, and delegates would be free to converse with reporters in a personal vein; Stettinius would still make all the official public pronouncements. These new guidelines, however, didn't solve the problem. Instead, there were now so many discordant voices representing the U.S. delegation that further confusion spread about exactly what message Stettinius was trying to convey to the U.S. public. As Stettinius ruefully told Joseph Grew, the undersecretary of state, a few days later: There are "2,300 newspaper people here and it is hard to keep an account of such a large unprecedented group."[6]

The disarray continued into early May, culminating finally in a public fracas with James Reston, the chief correspondent of the *New York*

Times. On May 10, Reston wrote a piece suggesting that, in direct contradiction to the promises made by Secretary Stettinius that committee deliberations would be open to the media as had been true at the Mexico City Conference, the discussions at the U.N. Conference had so far been kept secret. Stettinius complained bitterly about Reston's charge and called him in for a talk. Subsequently, his arm twisted by Stettinius, Reston in the May 13 edition of the *Times* retracted his accusation as "not accurate" and reported that Stettinius had promised access only to Plenary and principal commission sessions, and that the commitment actually "has been carried out." But he also noted that commission sessions at San Francisco, unlike the daily committee meetings, were seldom convened. However, he said, Stettinius was broadening media coverage and planning to open committee meetings for "special reporters to attend" and to give a brief outline of what went on to the press.[7]

A further complication involved Averell Harriman. In San Francisco to keep an eye on Molotov and to advise Stettinius on how to handle all U.N. negotiations with the Soviets, Harriman warned the secretary that many U.S. journalists seemed overly euphoric about Soviet intentions. He felt strongly that the media needed a talking to about Stalin from somebody like himself who worked on the frontlines in Moscow. He persuaded Stettinius to let him hold three off-the-record talks—one for working reporters in the Palace Hotel and two for editors, publishers, and commentators in the Fairmont Hotel. Harriman's discourse was, indeed, tough. He sounded the warnings he had given earlier to the State Department, namely, that Stalin was violating the Yalta accords over Poland and was intent on subverting Eastern Europe. At one session, Harriman cautioned the gatherings: "We must recognize that our objectives and the Kremlin's objectives are irreconcilable. The Kremlin wants to promote Communist dictatorships controlled from Moscow, whereas we want, as far as possible, to see a world of governments responsive to the will of the people. We will have to find ways of composing our differences in the United Nations and elsewhere in order to live without war on this small planet."[8]

At one of these meetings, two journalists in the audience, Walter Lippmann and the radio broadcaster Raymond Gram Swing, were so outraged by what they heard that they got up and left the room (Swing later apologized to Harriman but Lippmann refused to do so). Lippmann had had his own personal association with the U.S. delegation— he had helped Senator Vandenberg (along with James Reston) write his famous Senate speech delivered four months earlier in which he had repudiated his long-standing isolationist tenets and embraced internationalism. But Vandenberg, soon after encountering intense opposition from the Polish-American community in Detroit, retreated from many convictions that Lippmann, in particular, had put forward, including a call for a greater understanding of Soviet security interests in Eastern Europe; he had started to listen more attentively to Harriman's wary counsel about the USSR.

Lippmann, upon hearing Harriman, now feared that he and Vandenberg would exert pressure on Stettinius to use the U.N. meeting as a club to bash the Soviets. That same day, he wrote a column excoriating those who "are thinking of the international organization as a means of policing the Soviet Union." Swing, in his turn, told his radio audience that policymakers who no longer believed in diplomacy with Moscow should step aside. Harriman was astonished by the intemperate behavior of the two men: "I said that in dealing with the Russians we have to have our guard up, but at the same time, to have a friendly hand outstretched. Some of the journalists appeared to accept my analysis, but others were not prepared to listen. Their faith in the future was great and they could not believe at the time that the Russians who had suffered so deeply in the war, would not want to live amicably with their neighbors and with ourselves."[9]

The Harriman press conference led to a series of rancorous articles in the media on the theme that the United States was now following an anti-Soviet line in San Francisco. Some left-wing observers simply dismissed Harriman's admonitions. Author Patricia Bosworth's father, California attorney Bartley Crum, remembered the "volatile meeting" at which Harriman expressed his concerns about Soviet expansionism and said the United States must retain its formidable military establishment; Crum did not take Harriman's words seriously. But, on the other hand, an angry correspondent of the liberal New York newspaper, *PM,*

Alexander Uhl, violating the no-attribution rule, blamed Harriman directly for stirring up anti-Soviet sentiment. On May 28, he wrote, "A good deal of the wave of 'get tough with Russia' talk that went through the Conference circles during the Polish dispute got a lot of its inspiration from Harriman, who was here at the time." Journalist I. F. Stone, in his turn, wrote that Washington was organizing an anti-Soviet bloc in San Francisco, plainly referring to the Harriman remarks. Thomas Reynolds of the *New Republic* claimed that the U.S. delegation had missed no opportunity "to throw rocks in private at the Soviet hobgoblin"; the magazine's editors demanded that Truman dismiss anti-Soviet officials in the State Department. *Nation* editor Freda Kirchwey entreated the United States to preserve the unity of the Big Three. "Without it, there is nothing," she noted on May 5. "With it there is hope and a machine." She later reconsidered, suggesting that Russia, like the United States, was in some respects pursuing an unilateralist policy as a hedge against the possible collapse of the U.N. Mainstream publications, such as *Newsweek,* picked up on Harriman's caveat. Columnist Ernest K. Lindley observed in the May 21 issue: "The Yalta agreements has hardly been proclaimed before the Russians began to back away from them." *Time,* in its edition of the same week, noted: "Harriman, usually a mild fellow, was ready to go to the mat." But *Time* also presented a sober assessment of the United Nations: San Francisco could at best, it suggested, draft "a charter for a world divided into power spheres" that would set peaceful limits to the rivalry. Only those who naïvely rested their hopes on a system of genuine collective security were going to be disappointed, the editors claimed.[10]

With all the press ruminations, with the mixed messages emanating from the U.S. delegation, with the passionate second-guessing over the Argentine vote, with Stettinius's stony silence and with Molotov's formidable press presence, seasoned reporters were becoming increasingly dismayed by American mismanagement of media relations. Finally, the dean of the *New York Times,* Arthur Krock, along with his chief correspondent, James Reston, visited Stettinius in exasperation in early May and urged him to appoint somebody to brief newsmen on U.S. views—even if it was only an unofficial spokesman whom Stettinius could later repudiate. Krock recommended Adlai Stevenson, who was known to reporters as trustworthy, and Thomas Finletter, representing the Council on Foreign Relations, who could cover for him until Stevenson came from Washington. Stettinius, who had appointed Stevenson as his special assistant on February 23, 1945, to work with Archibald MacLeish, agreed and quickly summoned Stevenson on May 10, 1945. When Stevenson arrived in San Francisco, he told a friend, "I'm the official leak."[11]

Stevenson was an urbane, warm, and friendly personage who was blessed with a sparkling wit and keen native intelligence. Born on February 5, 1900, he inherited a notable political tradition—his grandfather had served as Grover Cleveland's vice president in 1892. As an idealistic young lawyer from Illinois, he joined the New Deal briefly in 1933–1934 in the Agricultural Adjustment Administration and later in the Federal Alcohol Control Administration. He returned to Chicago to practice law, but soon became deeply involved with the Chicago Council on Foreign Relations, where he served two terms as president in the mid-1930s. In 1940, he led a courageous battle against isolationism in the citadel of the *Chicago Tribune*. In 1941, he joined the Navy Department as special assistant to Secretary Knox. Two years later, he took a leave of absence to lead a special Foreign Economic Administration mission to survey Italy's economic situation, and a year after that he was part of a Strategic Bombing Survey team. These experiences soon brought him to the attention of Stettinius, who asked him to join the State Department in early 1945.

Stevenson called his secret work "Operation Titanic." He began all his sub-rosa briefings in Room 576 of the Fairmont Hotel. He was amused by the irony of his situation: "It was all a little ridiculous—me interpreting developments play by play in a secret room in the Fairmont Hotel, whose number was known to not less than 50–75 U.S. correspondents, when I had only a primary education in the charter." But in time, the U.S. position was reported more accurately. In a letter on May 16 to Archibald MacLeish, Stevenson noted that "we've really put in some effective lids on the press"—though he conceded that Stettinius was at one point disturbed by a *New York Times* story giving Truman credit for some triumph he himself had achieved. So, as

Stevenson explained, "I've corrected that here and there." Eight days later, on May 24, an article appeared in the *Times* that hailed Stettinius for his role at the parley, stating that "it is generally agreed that he has made important contributions to the success of the conference" and further saying that he had preserved unity among the wartime allies, including the Russians, made the U.N. more effective, helped to liberalize the charter, and protected U.S. security interests. "His approach is that of the practical businessman," summarized the *Times,* "and he has a genuinely friendly way of dealing with people." Stevenson's fine hand could be seen in the wording. Also, just a few days after that, a *New York Times* editorial citing "all our reports from San Francisco" lauded the secretary for handling himself "with the skill of a veteran."[12]

Occasionally, Stevenson slipped up. Once he leaked a U.S. position to the *New York Times* before the delegation had even acted on the issue. On those occasions, he notes, "the Secretary and the senators would get apoplectic with rage and make speeches about the flannel-mouthed staff or look at one another suspiciously or threaten to call the President, while I cowered in my corner in abject terror, timidly proclaiming my innocence. But as they filed out of the room after the meeting, I always had an approving wink from Vandenberg and Stassen." Soon, Stevenson added, it became standard operating procedure for Stettinius once a week in front of certain unsuspecting U.S. delegates "to read me a burning lecture on the essential importance of absolute secrecy about delegation and Big Five meetings in the famous penthouse on top of the Fairmont." Stettinius would later take him into his bedroom for a private drink and review future press tactics and spinning stratagems.[13]

The Big Five delegates were particularly sympathetic to Stevenson. At one Big Five meeting, Lord Halifax realized that Stevenson would have to reconcile so many differing opinions for the media that he observed, "We are asking Mr. Stevenson to make bricks without straw, you know." On June 3, for example, Stevenson had to contend with varying viewpoints on how to deal with amendments to the charter pressed by some of the smaller states. At a private afternoon meeting of the Big Five powers in Secretary Stettinius's penthouse apartment, Stettinius informed the group that this "was a difficult situation with re-

gard to the press." He asked Stevenson to read a draft statement that
hinted at an accord among the five powers over suggested changes
without specifying what they were. An excerpt from the transcript of
that session illuminates Stevenson's difficulties:

> Senator Vandenberg thought that any list of questions which might be
> included in the statement would be those which run against the
> smaller powers and that it would have an unhappy impact. Mr. Steven-
> son stated that there was such a general state of alarm that he thought
> we should let the world know, in some way or other, that we were con-
> tinuing to seek agreement on outstanding questions. Senator Vanden-
> berg thought that such a list was worse than nothing because it would
> confirm the impression that we were plowing under the smaller na-
> tions. Mr. Rockefeller stated that the listing of items would throw the
> small states into confusion. Mr. Stevenson hoped that it would be pos-
> sible to give some affirmative positive statement. Mr. Stettinius
> thought that we should recognize that a number of delegations are be-
> coming discouraged and that it was incumbent upon the Big Five to re-
> store confidence in the success of the Conference. This must be done
> promptly in some way or other. . . . Lord Halifax feared that the kind
> of statement prepared by Mr. Stevenson would hardly do the job. He
> agreed with the point of view expressed by Senator Vandenberg and
> Mr. Rockefeller. He found no fault with Mr. Stevenson but said that we
> were not helping ourselves in this situation. He thought that it was
> dangerous to say that all is going well when it really isn't and that we
> couldn't alter the situation until we have gotten along farther. Senator
> Vandenberg thought that the facts should be told and that the position
> of various governments on controversial issues should be stated. He
> thought it might be better if each government were to state its own po-
> sition rather than try to get an agreed statement among the Five. Mr.
> Stettinius pointed out that we were still in a negotiating stage and Mr.
> Stevenson added that a statement by each delegation would tend to
> freeze positions. Senator Vandenberg referred to the objective story
> published in The New York Times and thought that it didn't do any
> damage. . . . Lord Halifax suggested that we tell the press that the five

principal powers have held a lot of meeting, have reached agreement on a number of matters, and have also failed to reach agreement on some important matters but they are continuing their effort to find solutions to outstanding problems. Ambassador Gromyko stated that it was difficult to discuss any statement without a text before him, and that agreement on the issuance of a statement would depend on what was included in it. He added that he would want to communicate with his Government on the issuance of any statement. Lord Halifax suggested the Chairman be authorized to issue a general objective statement which was not controversial. Mr. Stettinius stated that that had been tried last night with no result. The only statement he could make was as Chairman of the United States Delegation. Representative Eaton inquired why each Delegation should not make a statement on its position. He observed that we came here as a parliament of mankind and that each Delegation should take a position before the public. He, for one, did not care for all this picayune stuff. Lord Halifax stated that he hoped that the British position had not been backward. Representative Eaten then inquired how we could develop public opinion in the world if we sat around and chattered like a bunch of magpies. Mr. Stettinius adjourned the meeting.[14]

Stevenson managed to sustain a sense of equilibrium throughout these daily gatherings. But there were those attached to the U.S. delegation over whom he could not exercise much control. The most problematical was John Foster Dulles. Dulles invariably promoted his own version of events to newsmen. Dulles would always leak "from a Republican slant, and lay emphasis on his own constructive part in the discussions," reported one delegate insider. "Whenever you had Foster in a bipartisan policy, you had to have a Democrat with a Democratic leak to counterbalance the Republican leak which Foster would already have made, otherwise you would be cheated out of the next day's headline." Nonetheless, overall, James Reston concluded: "This was one of the few conferences where the press was handled really well."[15]

Still, there was an ever-present danger of trivialization. A circuslike aura at times enveloped the conference, muddling the U.S. message.

Stettinius worriedly told his advisors on May 10 that "already too much of a carnival atmosphere [has] prevailed in San Francisco with too much flash-light photography and motion picture activity," emphasizing that "this was a most serious working Conference and a spirit of gaiety would create adverse reactions." A not untypical instance of such a show occurred on May 9, according to Arthur Krock, when Anthony Eden, the British foreign secretary, held a press conference before an audience "crowded with sight-seers, autograph-seekers and propagandists for special causes whom insatiable photographers kept under steady fire from their flashlights." Krock said that, under the circumstances, it was impossible for Eden to give any background quotations, which, in his view, "are the chief reasons for press conferences, and make them mutually advantageous to public men and the publics they serve." He concluded: "It is neither wise nor possible to talk confidentially to a heterogeneous gathering. And for the same cause, the open record has to be limited, since so many present have little acquaintance with the subjects under discussion." Indeed, among the accredited correspondents seen wandering the meeting halls were movie stars such as Lana Turner, Orson Welles, and Rita Hayworth. Such tyro journalists might well have had benign motives in attending the conference, but others saw them as celebrities seeking to promote their own careers and gain publicity; certainly they were distractions, and, in fact, none remained at the event for very long.[16]

There was also a multitude of gossip columnists. For example, society maven Elsa Maxwell wrote about how the Soviets were a "bunch of magnificent he-men." Earl Wilson exasperated Molotov at a press conference by asking him the correct pronunciation of the word "vodka." Hedda Hopper and Louella Parsons weighed in with delegate scuttlebutt and gauzy reports about socialites seen at the sessions, as did Walter Winchell. In addition, there were press parties galore all over San Francisco; these helped disseminate rumors and turn the conference, on occasion, into a series of floating cocktail receptions. Francis Williams, former editor of the *London Daily Herald,* recalled imbibing champagne with Orson Welles, among others, at a bacchanalia at the Palace Hotel: "We stood there talking by a fountain banked by a mass of vivid red flowers, and every now and then as the chain of champagne bottles moved past us, Welles would lean forward and pluck one from a waiter's hand and say, 'Ours, I think, George,' and we would deposit our empty bottle in the fountain and fill our glasses to the brim from a new one." At a soiree given by Patricia Bosworth's father, Paul Robeson, the famous African American singer, entertained notables such as I. F. Stone, Adlai Stevenson, Alger Hiss, Hollywood producer Walter Wanger, movie star Joan Bennett, screenwriter Dalton Trumbo, opera singer Lily Pons, and columnist Herb Caen. Controversial longshoreman union leader Harry Bridges, facing deportation for his alleged Communist affiliations, tossed his own party at the Palace Hotel and attracted such conservative moguls as Roy Howard of the Scripps-Howard newspaper chain. Arthur Krock recalls another festive occasion where he saw the youthful journalist John Fitzgerald Kennedy "cutting in on Anthony Eden, who was dancing with the beautiful lady who became Viscountess Harcourt—and getting promptly cut in on again by Eden himself."[17]

Still, the meeting attracted some of the world's finest journalists, including many top-flight American and English correspondents. They included luminaries Alistair Cooke, Eric Sevareid, and Wiliam Shirer, as well as the former diplomat Sumner Welles. Cooke himself sent over 40,000 short cables over the two-month period to his English newspaper, the *Manchester Guardian*. Welles gave a fifteen-minute radio commentary every night. And the young former naval officer, Kennedy, a twenty-seven-year-old correspondent representing the *Chicago Herald American* of the Hearst network, filed daily stories. The meeting was to have a noteworthy impact on Kennedy's career. In the view of one of Kennedy's biographers, "It would be no exaggeration to say that it was in San Francisco in the spring of 1945 that Jack's political career actively began." It was there that Kennedy first seriously examined national security issues, met some of the main players in U.S. foreign policy, and grappled with the implications of a looming East-West rivalry. He also got to know four men—Averell Harriman, Adlai Stevenson, Charles Bohlen, and Thomas Finletter—who would later play important roles in his own administration.[18]

Kennedy, indeed, came away from San Francisco sobered by the harsh realities of global politics. He surmised that nations would not easily surrender their sovereignty to an international organization. In a letter he wrote to a PT-boat friend who asked about the conference, Kennedy observed: "The international relinquishing of sovereignty would have to spring from the people—it would have to be so strong that the elected delegates would be turned out of office if they failed to do it. . . . We must face the truth that the people have not been horrified by war to a sufficient extent to force them to go to any extent rather than have another war. . . . War will exist until that distant day when the conscientious objector enjoys the same reputation and prestige that the warrior does today." He summarized his feelings in a notebook as "mustn't expect too much." "Admittedly world organization with common obedience to law would be solution," he continued. "Not that easy . . . things can't be forced from the top." But, overall, when assessing the conference in San Francisco, "you must measure its accomplishments against its possibilities. What [the] Conference accomplished is that it made war more difficult."[19]

Not all the writers who observed the conference came away similarly enthralled. E. B. White of the *New Yorker,* a passionate advocate of world government, was bitterly disappointed by San Francisco. "The first misconception," he wrote "is the assumption that nation-states are capable of, or even desirous of, applying law and justice to each other." He complained: "It would be deluding the people to imply that controversies, from now on, will be settled in accordance with 'principles of justice.'. . . [J]ustice and law do not now operate and will never operate until there is international government." The key issue is that "under all is the steady throbbing of the engines: sovereignty, sovereignty, sovereignty." That was the heart of his despair, he concluded: "They ducked it at Yalta, they ducked it at Dumbarton Oaks, they ducked it at San Francisco, and now it dogs them relentlessly, and will continue to dog them until they turn and face it."[20]

With the exception of ideologues of the left and the right, the team of Stettinius and Stevenson slowly turned around the negative impressions made by the U.S. delegation in the early days of the conference and gradually presented to the world the image of a united delegation hewing firmly to a set of principles and fighting for American values. And this was despite, as Arthur Krock pointed out, having "been obliged to work every minute under a blistering spotlight and to discuss the most complex questions at what are press conferences in name only." Indeed, just two weeks into the conference, Krock believed that Stettinius and his crew had "already achieved much more by way of difficult agreement than the drafters of Philadelphia, year 1787, would have thought possible." But, even as Krock concluded that the "fanned flames of dispute . . . were being brought under control," little was he aware that the conference was ready to drag on for another six and one-half weeks.[21]

CHAPTER 10

THE AMENDMENT MARATHON

The forty-nine nations at the conference faced a self-imposed deadline of midnight on Friday, May 4, to propose final amendments to
the Dumbarton Oaks Charter. This was the core business for San Francisco—collecting proposed changes from the national delegations and
spending the rest of the sessions via the four commissions and numerous
committees deciding on what to accept, amplify, augment, abridge, or
reject. Secretary Stettinius had already presided over the labors of the
U.S. delegation to complete its own series of emendations approved by
President Truman on April 19, and another set on May 1. Now in this
latest phase, known as the "Little Dumbarton Oaks" period, Stettinius
and the foreign ministers of the Big Four privately linked up to devise
joint amendments incorporating proposals from all four nations, before
the final hour tolled. At the same time, the smaller countries were ea-
gerly advancing their own revisions before the twelfth stroke on the
night of May 4, a tonnage of ideas amounting to over 1,000 pages.[1]

The Dumbarton Oaks Charter gave the Big Four a formidable edge in
the competition over amendments, for the sponsors had the right to veto
all amendments from lesser countries. The reasoning behind such a
grant of authority was that otherwise less important nations could pass
an amendment to eliminate the veto and end the special status of the Big
Four. Consequently, all changes in the charter at San Francisco were
made at the sufferance of the Big Powers. Armed with this immense
weapon, theoretically the Big Four could have unsheathed their swords
and, in a few short swift strokes, wiped out all obstreperous opposition

from the smaller countries. Politically, though, such an action would have created a furor and shattered any consensus. Stettinius, with the assent of his fellow Big Four foreign ministers, instead decided to give the smaller nations the chairmanships of most committees and make it known to them that the Big Four would listen carefully to the small nations' concerns and deliberate judiciously over their amendments. As for their own suggested changes, which, as noted, were not subject to veto, they agreed to abide by the rules of the conference stating that any substantive alterations, including ostensibly most proposals by the Four Powers, would require a two-thirds vote of the U.N. Assembly; procedural modifications would necessitate only a simple majority.[2]

Still, as sponsors, the Four Powers made the most important of the amendments in the proceedings, and hence, their internal negotiations drew the most attention. Serious talks among the Big Four commenced once Molotov rejoined the group on April 30 and promised, despite his intent to depart for Moscow, to stay until he had signed off on the joint amendments. During a rush from Wednesday, May 2, to Friday, May 4, he, Stettinius, Anthony Eden, and T. V. Soong, the Chinese foreign minister, were "practically in continuous session in the 'Penthouse' for forty-eight hours," according to Senator Vandenberg. Six formal gatherings were held, many lasting hours. Between those sessions, the U.S. delegation convened its own half-dozen strategy meetings. Eventually, twenty-four amendments were approved. Of the Big Four amendments, a smattering had come from the Soviet Union, including one favoring self-determination and another, more controversial, exempting Russia's bilateral security treaties with five nations from Security Council veto; several from Great Britain on the Security Council's powers and on strengthening the International Labor Organization; and three from China urging, among other matters, that the charter mention international law, education, and cultural affairs. Most were from the United States, which had, as indicated earlier, sent forth two successive packages of changes, primarily covering revisions in the U.N.'s mission statement; enhancing the powers of the General Assembly, especially on security issues, the revision of treaties, and the expansion of the Economic and Social Council; redefining the Security Council's authority; more fully explaining the responsibilities of the Secretariat; and establishing a U.N. Charter review.[3]

The U.S. offerings were mainly the result of Senator Arthur Vandenberg's relentless campaign to place his personal stamp on the U.N. Charter. Vandenberg, as the newcomer to the U.S. delegation, the most prestigious Republican on board and a long-time antagonist of FDR's, sought to prove that his party would not be a patsy for the Democrats. He had enlisted his party's rising Republican foreign policy advisor, the prickly John Foster Dulles, to be his consigliere. Stettinius, who initially proposed Vandenberg's appointment despite Roosevelt's qualms and, in turn, acquiesced in the senator's choice of Dulles, showed deference to Vandenberg throughout the conference to guarantee Republican support for the U.N. Treaty. Vandenberg's demands, eight in all, centered primarily on relatively innocuous measures such as listing "international law" and the word "justice" in the charter's text, and one controversial proposal to permit the General Assembly to overturn old treaties if they threatened world peace. Another well-known Republican on the delegation, former Minnesota governor Harold Stassen, favored an idea of holding a constitutional convention every so often to review the U.N. Charter.

Stettinius paid special heed to these two men—as well as to Tom Connally, the leading Democrat on the delegation and chairman of the Senate Foreign Relations Committee, which would ultimately decide the U.N. Treaty's fate. As part of his recognition of the main U.S. players on the charter, he always placed Vandenberg and Connally regularly on each side of him at the long delegate table in the penthouse. He was also attentive as well to two other men, Leo Pasvolsky and John Foster Dulles, both advisors attached to the delegation who had gained singular influence by dint of their intellectual prowess and personal aplomb. On the consultative level, these two had, at times, seemed to dominate the daily conferences.

There was no real surprise in Pasvolsky's rise to prominence. From the beginning, he was the acknowledged head priest alone able to interpret the holy book to the brethren. At the beginning of every session, Secretary Stettinius instructed Pasvolsky to read a new section of the charter and explain it to the delegates. Pasvolsky knew every term, word, and syllable of it. He could construe a passage with an understanding of its verb usage, noun choice, and precise nuance. He could quote paragraphs and subsections without notes, cite passages and clauses from memory, and jump on errant locutions like a cat pouncing on a mouse. He knew why the framers had placed the comma here and the period there, which phrase was deliberately ambiguous, and what arguments led to a particular outcome and conclusion. He was also pursuing his own agenda; that is, to see that a strong, centralized world body was created in San Francisco.[4]

At the first drafting session on April 9, 1945, Pasvolsky, pipe in hand, spoke confidently to the delegates about what was expected of them: "We shall concern ourselves only with the basic ideas and not bother about the language" of the draft charter, he explained. The delegation, he reminded them, was being relied on to turn a rough set of rules into a legal document. The delegates may make "some additions," he added, but only "to more fully define the criteria of action of members of the Organization and to clarify the operation of the machinery." Many of the delegates later mentioned Pasvolsky with awe in their memoirs. Virginia Gildersleeve, the dean of Barnard College, for example, observed in her recollections: "Mr. Pasvolsky was a kind of focus of responsibility for the actual drafting. He sat in the middle directly opposite Mr. Stettinius and recorded and formulated our ideas." The more formidable Senator Connally, no bashful backbencher himself, paid special tribute in his book to Pasvolsky. "He was extremely capable," Connally reflected, "and the one person we all turned to for explanation of details. Certainly, he had more to do with writing the framework of the charter than anyone else." Stettinius himself, according to one of his aides, two weeks into the conference turned to Pasvolsky, who was sitting behind him at a meeting, and said: "If I say anything wrong, kick me in the ass."[5]

The surprise of the pack, though, turned out to be Dulles. There were other strong-minded men in attendance at these parleys who expressed their views candidly over the two months of conclaves: Isaiah Bowman, a special advisor to Stettinius and president of Johns Hopkins University; Hamilton Fish Armstrong, editor of *Foreign Affairs* magazine; James Dunn, an assistant secretary of state who had worked with Pasvolsky on the U.N. Charter; Green Hackworth, the State Department's legal advisor; and Harley Notter, one of Pasvolsky's officials. But Dulles stood out. He had the aura of having attended the Versailles Conference ending World War I. Vandenberg once said, in admiration, that Dulles seemed to know more people at the San Francisco Conference than anyone else in the U.S. delegation. Congressman Sol Bloom called him "our brains." Dulles swiftly took over the role of de facto legal analyst and most reliable wordsmith for the delegation. He was sanctimonious on occasion, and he could become rigid in his views. He always looked for ways to publicize himself. He even reserved a small dining room at the St. Francis Hotel, where he privately lunched with foreign leaders such as the British diplomat Lord Halifax and the French foreign minister, Georges Bidault. As one biographer noted: "His role was very much like the one he had played at the Paris Peace Conference of 1919. It involved first, last, and always extensive participation in American delegation discussion of issues and strategy."[6]

There should have been no surprise here. Dulles came from a formidable lineage. Born in 1888, he was the grandson and namesake of one secretary of state, John Foster, who served under President Benjamin Harrison, and the nephew of President Woodrow Wilson's secretary of state, Robert Lansing. He attended Princeton University and George Washington Law School. In 1907, at age nineteen, he accompanied his grandfather, John Foster, to the second international peace conference in the Hague. At thirty, Wilson named Dulles legal counsel to the U.S. delegation to the Versailles Conference. In between public service stints, Dulles joined the law firm of Sullivan and Cromwell in New York. By 1920, he had become a senior partner; by 1927, head of the firm. Before World War II, he developed a lay interest in the Presbyterian Church, for which his father served as a minister. By the late 1930s, he was organizing a campaign for the Federal Council of Churches as chairman of the Commission on a Just and Durable Peace, though as late as 1939 he wrote a book, *War, Peace and Change*, in which he endorsed a program of isolationism for the United States. In San Francisco, Dulles was ready to launch a crusade for a reformed world order, which he felt would shift the United States from the pursuit of selfish national interest to Christian cooperation. But his views evolved sharply during the conference.[7]

Pasvolsky, though, as the guide for the talks, took the paramount role from the onset. The State Department's summaries of discussions, published twenty-two years after the event, contain dozens of Pasvolsky's not-so-subtle pointers to an often confused delegation, summed up by sentences beginning: "Mr. Pasvolsky explained," "Mr. Pasvolsky stated," "Mr. Pasvolsky took the view," "Mr. Pasvolsky suggested the following formula," "Mr. Pasvolsky made the further point," "Mr. Pasvolsky called attention to," and so forth. The effect of Pasvolsky's unremitting attentiveness to every exchange as well as his unsurpassed comprehension of the charter was such that, eventually, the delegates automatically turned to him for counsel. At an April 12 meeting, for example, Pasvolsky mentioned a request conveyed to him by the so-called Middle Powers to have regular representation on the Security Council. Pasvolsky advised the delegates that any U.S. measuring stick for assessing the selection of nonpermanent members should be kept confidential and "should not be incorporated in the Charter itself" to allow the United States maximum flexibility in determining the composition of that body. As often proved to be true, the delegates consented to his recommendation without a question.[8]

Dulles was not hesitant about sharing his views, though. He dove in at the delegation's first drafting session on April 9. Responsive to Vandenberg's ardent desire to include the word "justice" in the text, he asked that the "Purposes" section be reworded to incorporate the term. Nobody demurred. He then rejected a statement about guaranteeing the "independence of states" in the same section because, he said, that would sanctify "the possession by nations of their colonies for all time." There was no dissent. Over Pasvolsky's polite protests, he also managed to insist on a redrafting of a separate "Principles" section of the charter. "The looseness of the commitments" expressed in the draft, Dulles said, bothered him. For example, what did it mean when the charter said that "all members undertake to give every assistance or they undertake not to give any assistance"? Such generalized commitments within the chapter "might jeopardize getting the charter through the Senate," he warned. He said he did not even know what the term "Principle" meant. He was especially bewildered about the "obligation" to settle disputes by "peaceful means." Pasvolsky replied dryly that "this meant that states would use peaceful means in the settlement of their disputes." Dulles did not relent. The next day, April 10, he again addressed the "Principles" chapter, asserting that it was "too broad in scope [and] gave the illusion of security through sweeping commitments." Pasvolsky and the delegates wearily agreed to modify much of its phraseology.[9]

The following morning, on April 11, Dulles and Pasvolsky clashed over what the standards should be to admit a representative of a nation to the United Nations. Dulles contended that there should be a committee on credentials, arguing that it was important to have some procedure for vetting a delegate "because of changing conditions" or a "fluctuating situation." Pasvolsky replied that the General Assembly already had such power or, if necessary, could create an agency to discharge such a function. He did not feel it had to be spelled out. After much back and forth, in which other members joined, Pasvolsky eventually backed away from his position, noting, nonetheless, that the Security Council should still have some oversight over the matter for "security considerations." He scribbled out a new amendment stating: "The General Assembly should be empowered to determine the qualifications of membership and admit new members unless the Security Council interposes objections on security grounds." Dulles and the others agreed to it.[10]

These debates continued on and off for the ensuing dozen or so weeks as the delegation rewrote the Dumbarton Oaks text line by line. Pasvolsky and Dulles sometimes joined forces together. In one long evening session on April 27 stretching from 8:30 P.M. until almost 11:00 P.M., Pasvolsky, Dulles, and the delegation reviewed various charter changes, including a paragraph that Dulles had helped to rewrite permitting the Security Council to make recommendations on how to maintain or restore peace. Pasvolsky and Dulles discussed together ways they could refine the Dulles statement. Pasvolsky thought Dulles had reconfigured the council's duty differently from the Dumbarton Oaks text where, he claimed, it was considered an affirmative or mandatory obligation rather than a permissive one. Dulles impatiently complained that "they could sit around in the meeting all night discussing language." But eventually they compromised agreeably on a few word changes, Pasvolsky accepting the general gist of a new Dulles formula.[11]

Despite their roles, both Pasvolsky and Dulles, as advisors rather than delegates, often found their positions overruled. At one point, Pasvolsky, for example, reflecting a long-standing stance of Cordell Hull, had passionately opposed the seating of Argentina. He gave way quickly when Stettinius championed Buenos Aires's position. Pasvolsky also fought a larger role for regional organizations. However, once Stettinius, under the pressure of events, conceded a higher status to such bodies, Pasvolsky reluctantly backed off. Finally, Pasvolsky didn't like Stassen's suggestion for charter review on the grounds that it would "detract from the prestige of the Organization," but he lost that battle. Meantime, Dulles had deep reservations about granting regional bodies any authority on the grounds that their presence would deprive the Security Council of its power. He also considered the notion of "domestic sovereignty" as overrated in the U.N. Charter, arguing that, when any so-called domestic issue imperils global security, "the Security Council should have authority to consider any matter which threatened the peace of the world." And on the trusteeship issue, he disagreed with the U.S. military, seeing no reason why the right of the U.N. to "look into the conditions of colonial peoples" could conceivably hamper U.S. security requirements.[12]

Dulles eventually abandoned his positions on all three issues and opted for the practical considerations of U.S. national self-interest. Whether it was for reasons of realpolitik, to curry favor with his mentor, Senator Vandenberg, out of consideration for his own political future, or a genuine change of mind, he embraced regional organizations, domestic jurisdiction, and the exclusivity of U.S. security areas. Accused after the conference of forsaking the moral goals of his Commission on a Just and Durable Peace, Dulles answered one critic: "On the contrary, at San Francisco and at London, I stood strongly for the principles which the Commission had advocated and to a considerable extent those principles became the official American position. Of course, one who has official responsibility must conduct himself somewhat differently from one who, as a private citizen, stands on the side-lines giving advice. I am sure you realize that." Yet for all his inconsistencies, Dulles was later commended by James Reston for helping to "bring the parties together under Truman," "a greater contribution," in Reston's view, than his service as secretary of state under President Dwight Eisenhower.[13]

In any event, Stettinius and the U.S. delegation entered the "Little Dumbarton Oaks" phase in a harmonious frame of mind. On May 2, Stettinius telephoned President Truman at 6:45 P.M. to tell him delightedly that both Vandenberg and Connally were fully supportive of the U.S. approach and the rest of the delegation was "absolutely solid." Meanwhile, talks continued day and night among the Big Four on the twenty-four amendments they submitted. Earlier, the group had adopted several unobjectionable Chinese amendments. By May 3, the parties had reached full agreement, with minor word changes, on almost all the amendments. "It was an amazing achievement," reflected Vandenberg. Though none altered the fundamental nature of the U.N. structure, some were significant: provisions for charter review and a human rights commission, which had been requested by the United States; the Soviet proposal for adding self-determination, allowing countries to become independent states; a British proposition to guarantee representation on the Security Council of so-called Middle Powers. Even Senator Vandenberg's crusade to include the word "justice" in the charter also proved to be relatively easy. Senator Connally had a more mordant view of Vandenberg's long march: The senator, he wrote, "acted as if there were a great deal of opposition to his proposal. Actually, I didn't meet anyone at the Conference who objected to the inclusion of the word. . . . When the Conference adopted the word, the senator beamed like a knight who had just shattered the stout lance of a fierce opponent."[14]

On Friday night, May 4, two issues were still not resolved; a third issue, namely, trusteeships, the Big Four put aside altogether for the time being. The most contentious of the unresolved issues was Senator Vandenberg's pet idea to give the General Assembly the right to "recommend measures" to revise or even terminate treaties that would "impair the general welfare" or violate U.N. principles. On May 2, Vandenberg warned a morning meeting of the Big Four that critics of the U.N. were already claiming that the charter "will freeze the post war world in a rigid pattern created by expedient decisions made during the war" and hence the world organization could be defeated. Vandenberg insisted that new flexibility was needed "to win adequate Senate support." Soviet Foreign Minister Molotov objected to the inclusion of the term "treaty" because, he said, it would weaken compacts among nations; a revived Germany might even later demand a change in any peace settlement with the Allies following World War II, as it had attempted to do after World War I. In his colloquial English, he told Vandenberg: "Not OK."

The second unresolved issue was the Soviet proposal to exempt its bilateral treaties with five European states designed to promote coordinated action against new hostilities by Axis countries from a charter provision allowing the Security Council to veto enforcement action by regional authorities. On this proposal, Stettinius assured Molotov that he would consider it without making any final promises—but he grew more heedful of it after the Russian hinted that he could not make any commitment about the Vandenberg plan until the Big Four had acted on his submission.[15]

Stettinius, indeed, faced a delicate situation on both amendments. He had to satisfy Vandenberg to insure that this Republican heavyweight would return to the Senate and rally his brethren behind the U.N. Treaty. On the other hand, he could not afford to disappoint Molotov because his OK was a prerequisite to winning approval for the senator's petition. So, in short, he felt compelled to amend the Vandenberg amendment if he could do so without upsetting its author to please Moscow.

Complicating the Molotov story, on the evening of May 3, the Soviet foreign minister informed Stettinius that sixteen Polish government-in-exile officials who had recently visited Poland and disappeared, and about whom both London and Washington had been making inquiries for weeks, had been arrested in late March by the Red Army for committing "diversionist acts" against Red soldiers. The detention of the exiled Poles caused an immediate sensation, eliciting a banner headline in the *New York Times* on May 6 and suddenly overshadowing all the work at the U.N. In his diary, Vandenberg labeled the revelations "bad business" and "a serious shadow" on San Francisco. Anne O'Hare Mc-Cormick wrote later that "the temperature dropped like a plummet" on the news. Further confusing the situation, too, the Latin American nations, having learned about the Molotov ploy to exempt Russian treaties, were now arguing that their inter-American regional organization should also get a pass from the Security Council veto. They suggested they might vote against Molotov's plan unless the conference gave them similar treatment.[16]

Within a few days, though, Stettinius began to thread his way through most of the obstacles and reach accords on both amendments. On May 4, the British foreign minister, Anthony Eden, the Chinese foreign minister, T. V. Soong, and Stettinius came up with a substitute formulation for the Vandenberg proposal that now permitted the assembly to consider the adjustment of "any situation regardless of origin" that imperiled peace—striking out the word "treaties" altogether, although not excluding them from the category of "situations." Vandenberg quickly professed himself pleased by the revision. Molotov, in his turn, approved the change "in principle." Stettinius reported to Truman proudly that "we won out on Vandenberg's point of the right to review treaties," at least implicitly, and that the senator was "extremely happy." The next day, Molotov accepted the revision officially. As for the Molotov effort to retain Russia's bilateral pacts, despite the abrupt atmospheric change over the Polish arrests and growing Latin discontent, Stettinius and the rest of the Big Four reached agreement on May 6. A slightly revised "regional arrangements" clause was now introduced that would allow bilateral treaties directed against Axis powers to operate without Security Council interference (though encouraging eventual U.N. intervention), but not any other treaties. The newspapers in the ensuing days now expressed praise about Soviet "moderation" on the proposed Big Four agreements. Arthur Krock, in fact, published an entire column praising Molotov's cooperative spirit.[17]

On the morning of May 5, Stettinius appeared at a press conference to announce the joint amendments. They already appeared to be popular. Journalists saw them as further evidence of a "liberalization" of

Dumbarton Oaks for they appeared to spread power more widely among member states. Stettinius praised the role of the other three foreign ministers, but still the issue of Poland intruded into the celebration. Stettinius delivered a short statement on the Polish arrests at the close of the event. He announced that Washington had asked the Kremlin for a list of the Poles who had been incarcerated: "We told Mr. Molotov of our great concern in learning, after such a long delay, of this disturbing development which has a direct bearing on the working out of the Polish problem." Still, Stettinius was not going to let the arrests impede his ongoing work. That afternoon, he even took Molotov to visit the Kaiser shipyards outside San Francisco to see the five-mile-long factory where ships were being manufactured at the rate of two or three a week. As Anne O'Hare McCormick aptly noted a few days later: "The Polish issue cannot be downed and will overshadow the peace as surely as it overshadows San Francisco if it is not settled, but it will not break up the conference." Stettinius later cabled President Truman that his press conference was "large and successful."[18]

Molotov, on the eve of his departure for Moscow, held his own farewell press conference on May 8. In a packed hotel banquet hall, which he entered seven minutes late accompanied by fellow delegates and Russian army officers, Molotov strode immediately to the front of the room and, standing, read a prepared statement lauding the "unanimity" of the Big Four in creating a new blueprint for the U.N. His reference on unity drew strong applause from the audience. At one point, in his nimble way, he managed to reinterpret one of the joint accords—the Vandenberg compromise—as the defeat of an effort to give the U.N. unprecedented powers to revise treaties. Though that was not how the U.S. delegation saw it, Senator Vandenberg publicly acquiesced in Molotov's explanation. Molotov took questions, briefly speaking about the Polish affair and then dismissing further mention of it, and hastily departed after twenty-six minutes. One reporter observed that "the short stocky man from Moscow with the Teddy Roosevelt smile handles himself with adroitness and humor that, despite the barrier of language, would do credit to the late Franklin Roosevelt himself, the master of the press conference art." That evening, Molotov visited Stettinius before parting. The secretary of state gave him a salad bowl made of redwood as a going-away gift.[19]

These two reassuring press briefings by the two leading figures at the conference did go far toward heartening the world in general about the proceedings in San Francisco, but did not go far in calming the fears of the smaller nations. Much frustration and apprehension had grown among these states because none of them had the ability to appeal to the Big Powers for genuine changes in the text in their favor. France had, at one point, seemed a likely ally, but on May 3, the French foreign minister, Georges Bidault, privately approached Stettinius and demanded that his country be admitted as one of the Big Powers, as promised in the Yalta accords, threatening to leave the conference if this didn't happen. France, Bidault insisted to Stettinius, didn't want to be "pushed into playing the games of the little nations." In response, Stettinius pledged to enlist France into the permanent five as soon as possible. That ended the French role as agent for the less powerful lands.

The USSR also had appeared, at first, to be a champion of the smaller states. But as, the Philippines representative, Carlos Romulo, later remarked, even while the Soviets preached the rhetoric of liberation from oppression, they behaved "toward all of us representatives of smaller countries as though we scarcely existed. They acted as if they owned the world, strutting around like conquerors in their ill-cut suits with bell-bottom trousers." The Chinese were themselves too preoccupied with the conflicts and turmoil at home to help out. Great Britain was still a diehard colonial power and unmoved by the concerns of lesser nations. And the United States, consumed with assuring Senate ratification of the U.N. Treaty, was unwilling to relinquish any of its views on the San Francisco Charter. Indeed, in one moment of exasperation, Senator Connally exclaimed: "These little countries are going to bellyache and raise hell no matter what you do about it. We're doing all this for them. We could make an alliance with Great Britain and Russia and be done with it."[20]

Consequently, the left-out states together and separately pushed ahead and advanced dozens of last-minute amendments designed to forestall at least five aspects of the charter they disliked: the "permanent" presence of the Big Five (counting France) in the Security Council; the Big Five veto over amendments; the Big Five control over U.N. military ventures that excluded smaller states from participating in the decisionmaking even if they were asked to contribute troops; the limitation on the Security Council that constricted its authority to "recommending" inquiries into disputes rather than having the broader right to "investigate" them; and, finally, the circumscribed authority of the Economic and Social Council. Although their own ability to affect events was finite, as one analyst in the *New York Times* observed, "if it came to a showdown the small countries could wreck the conference and sabotage world peace by refusing to accept the substance of the Dumbarton Oaks plan."[21]

But that tack was extremely unlikely. Indeed, just the opposite response was more likely. As the same observer noted: "The smaller nations have reluctantly accepted the idea of virtual world dictatorship by the great powers, for the time at least, because they know that they cannot have a world organization, in view of war conditions and the present state of the world in general, without letting the big powers run it. And the little countries want a world organization very badly." Most nations seemed resigned to whittling down the dominance of the big nations, but not driving them out of the organization. They also felt caught in their own peculiar dilemma. If they criticized the charter too strongly, their reservations might actually be used against them when they returned to their countries to seek ratification of the treaty. In other words, their complaints in San Francisco might be thrown back at them in their own parliaments; for this reason, they had to walk a fine line between studious disagreement and a more generous public acceptance.[22]

A few grew so despondent in this marginalized backwater that they, in effect, took a walk. Thirty-nine-year-old Charles Malik, Lebanon's representative, recorded in his diary: "Intrigue, lobbying, secret arrangements, blocs, etc. It's terrible. Power politics and bargaining nauseate me. There is so much unreality and play and sham that I can't swing myself into this atmosphere and act." Others were too preoccupied by problems in their homelands to focus on the sessions, for example, Norway's foreign minister, Trygve Lie, who left San Francisco early to attend to his just-liberated land. Correspondent Anne O'Hare McCormick reported that "many came from countries laid waste by war." The views of these delegates, she wrote, "are colored and their minds are distracted by their immediate anxieties. For many the cessation of hostilities is the beginning of another struggle, as stark as war, for mere survival."[23]

The amendments phase signaled the conclusion of the conference's most serious task—that of setting the terms of the debate. Now the next phase was about to begin; the delegates had to shape the final charter in such a way that it would be acceptable to all forty-nine nations. There was a general feeling that this could be done quickly. On May 9, Stettinius optimistically told a meeting of the U.S. consultants that the conference would be over "in perhaps three weeks." Coincidentally, combat in Europe was winding down and officially ended on May 8. Despite the momentous nature of the war's end in Europe, it occasioned no special celebration in San Francisco. As one reporter wrote: "Neither marching bands nor revelry signalized the end of the second World War in Europe for the United Nations: not a single torn telephone directory nor impromptu street dance marked the news in this temporary world capital." But the demise of the Nazi reign prompted foreign ministers from many of the major nations to depart for their homelands. From V-E Day on over the next ten days or so, indeed, four of the Big Five—Eden from Great Britain, Bidault from France, Molotov from the Soviet Union, and Soong from China—as well as foreign ministers from lesser nations such as Belgium and Norway, exited California, leaving Stettinius as the sole remaining high-level figure among the original founding band.[24]

Whether this exodus was a good sign—that the major questions had been settled among the top leaders and that deputies could now handle the fine details—or a bad sign, namely, that with the war's demise foreign officials no longer thought it was important to occupy themselves with the U.N., was an issue still to be determined. Nonetheless, there were some suggestions that the U.N. Conference might now pause, collect its breath, and take time to reflect before continuing on its way. But the ubiquitous commentator Arthur Krock reported in early May that he had "yet to find a leader of an influential delegation who believes the main business of the conference—the composition of a chart—should be postponed." He warned, indeed, that any time-out might lead to a loss of interest in the U.N. and make the world organization "seem more illusory in the presence of post-war facts" and that, further, "arguments will have arisen among governments now cooperating that will set public opinion against this enterprise." There was, in short, no good coming from any delay at all. Even though the meeting might bring only half a loaf, Krock wrote, "the non-Axis world must have this much of the spiritual bread for which it has been hungering and which has been the pledge of its statesmen, or it may get none at all."[25]

Certainly, the departures placed a heavier burden on the shoulders of Secretary Stettinius. For the first time, he had to be the charter's main advocate without the backing of such names as Eden, Molotov, Soong, and Bidault. Nor could he necessarily depend on their capable deputies—Lord Halifax, Andrei Gromyko, Dr. Wellington Koo, the Chinese ambassador to England, and Henri Bonnet, the French ambassador to the United States, to fill their seats with the same sense of public gravity and mastery of issues. As he remarked to the Norwegian foreign minister, Trygve Lie, who was departing: "We have to finish the drafting of the Charter. We cannot have all the Foreign Ministers go home and leave second string men behind in San Francisco who will not have the authority or prestige to conclude the drafting of the Charter in the quickest possible time."[26]

On the other hand, Stettinius was well aware that the U.N. meeting was, from the beginning, a project of the United States, devised by the State Department, expertly guided by two hands-on presidents, Roosevelt and Truman, and propelled by U.S. power. So Stettinius was presiding over an enterprise his nation was already dominating and molding. Thus, he had the ability to move the meeting in any direction he desired. His prime concern, then, was to bring the conference to an end as expeditiously as possible before things might get out of control. On the day the war ended in Europe, Stettinius issued a statement saying that the German surrender had now created an urgency for those in San Francisco to complete their labors. The countdown, in his view, should begin now. What Stettinius couldn't know at the time, however, was that new, unforeseen complications were about to disrupt the process and keep it going for another forty-nine excruciating days.[27]

CHAPTER 11

ROCKEFELLER'S BOUNTY
The Regional Option

The evening following Stettinius's proud announcement of the joint amendments of the Big Four, May 5, Leo Pasvolsky brought disquieting news. The Latin bloc, he reported via telephone, was suddenly stepping up its pressure on the United States—albeit behind the scenes—to challenge the clause in the U.N. Charter giving the Security Council the right to veto any action by a regional body. What especially triggered the group's anger were tidings that the USSR had just won a bye from the regional veto for its own bilateral treaties with European nations designed to repel an Axis revival. During a three-hour talk with the foreign ministers of Brazil, Colombia, and Cuba, Pasvolsky told Stettinius, all three had expressed apprehensions that a predatory foreign nation might attack the Americas by colluding with one of the Big Five to secure a veto against a collective Hemisphere response and, according to Colombia's foreign minister, Lleras Camargo, thereafter could "proceed with impunity."[1]

The unspoken concern was apparently communism. The regional clause, one foreign minister declared to Pasvolsky, could permit "political infiltration from abroad," implying Soviet machinations, and might even lead to an assault on the United States, provoking a World War III. The trio wondered whether President Truman was now, in effect, abandoning the Mexico City agreement and ending FDR's Good Neighbor policy. They were even dismayed that the Monroe Doctrine, long resented by Latin Americans as an instrument for unilateral U.S. intervention, might be discarded. They insisted in the end that the inter-American security pact should be "completely free of the world arrangement." Pasvolsky disagreed, arguing that, from his perspective, the real danger for the U.N. were regional alliances because they could subvert, if not destroy, the world organization. Regional groupings of any sort for Pasvolsky, as was true for his old boss Cordell Hull, were reprehensible "spheres of influence." As for the Security Council veto, he said the Latins would just have to take it on faith that the Big Five would act honorably and forestall outside invasion. The participants departed, both sides unmollified.[2]

Nelson Rockefeller, who had just flown back from Washington, D.C., that day, learned of Pasvolsky's contentious encounter. He sought a meeting with Stettinius to discuss the dispute, but the secretary sent back word that he was too tired and wanted to rest over the weekend. He suggested that Rockefeller see Pasvolsky. The ever resourceful Rockefeller balked at attempting to persuade the implacable Pasvolsky to reconsider his views. Instead, Rockefeller phoned Senator Vandenberg, his ally on the delegation, and invited him to his St. Francis Hotel suite for supper to talk about the Latin situation. At that moment, Vandenberg happened to be preoccupied about the regional proviso. The day before, he had told the U.S. delegation that he feared the Security Council's stipulation "spelled the end of the Monroe Doctrine" and wondered whether the Hemisphere would now have to forfeit its right to self-defense.[3]

At the dinner, Vandenberg wrote later in his diary, Nelson Rockefeller "disclosed these same fears and said the South American Republics are up in arms." Indeed, Rockefeller echoed exactly the Latin anxieties, especially those concerning the Marxist threat. In his view, it was more than coincidence that the Soviets endorsed Pasvolsky's critiques of the regional pacts since they would be unaffected in Europe but still allowed to meddle in Latin America. Nonetheless, even as Vandenberg agreed with Rockefeller and retained an overarching concern about preserving "legitimate regional arrangements" such as Chapultepec, he did not wish to derail the United Nations or sanction local "balance of power" enclaves. Vandenberg's solution was to give the Latins the same exemption from the regional provision that the Soviets had—

an idea Rockefeller enthusiastically embraced. Rockefeller called in two of the envoys who had met with Pasvolsky earlier in the day, the Cuban and Colombian foreign ministers, to obtain their views on Vandenberg's new proposal. Both championed it, and not surprisingly since they and others had leaked a similar proposition to the newspapers some days earlier calling for the same thing. With Rockefeller's help, Vandenberg that night began to write Stettinius a letter detailing his plan.[4]

Seated on the sofa in Rockefeller's hotel room, clenching a cigar between his teeth, Vandenberg dictated the letter to Rockefeller's secretary. The letter, completed near midnight, was simple and straightforward. Vandenberg wrote that he was "greatly disturbed" that Washington was, in effect, tossing out both the Monroe Doctrine and the Act of Chapultepec by allowing the Security Council to continue its unfettered regional oversight. Such a stance was sure to imperil "Pan-American solidarity" and risk Senate rejection of the U.N. Treaty. Instead, he argued, the administration should give the security pact of the Latin Americans the same immunity from the veto as the Soviets had received for their bilateral treaties. This would not necessarily lead to a U.N. break-up into regional entities because the Monroe Doctrine, as he said, was recognized as "an existing implement which is the expression of a continuous inter-American policy for more than a century." He warned that if the United States did not take the initiative in reining in the veto, the Hemisphere surely would, putting the United States in the position of having to follow after its Latin neighbors.[5]

After Vandenberg had his letter delivered on Sunday morning, May 6, to Stettinius, the secretary of state agreed to circulate it right away to all the delegates. Stettinius was highly sensitive to Vandenberg's political influence in the U.S. Senate and fully aware that Truman wanted good relations with the Republicans over the U.N. But privately he was irritated by Vandenberg's peremptory intrusion in what he thought was a settled matter. Now he was would have to reopen his discussions with Molotov. That night around 7:45 P.M., in a state of some indignation, he asked Rockefeller point-blank whether he had written Vandenberg's letter. Rockefeller answered "No"—which was technically true, though he had helped inspire the missive. Stettinius was not appeased by Rockefeller's reply. Later in the evening, he told his aide, James Dunn, in reference to the Vandenberg epistle that "Rockefeller had stirred up things since he came back." Even John Foster Dulles later got into the act, angrily upbraiding Rockefeller. "That letter," he growled to the young scion, "could wreck the conference." "Well," Rockefeller responded lamely, "I didn't write it. Van wrote it." But Dulles had heard enough. "You've hoodwinked the Senator," he snapped. "You've taken a man I was sent out here to keep from doing some goddamn fool thing, and you've gotten us into a real pickle."[6]

But Rockefeller was unshaken. That evening he convened a group of U.S. military advisors in the bedroom of one of the U.S. advisors, Isaiah Bowman, the president of Johns Hopkins University. Present were John McCloy, the assistant secretary of war, General Embrick of the Joint Chiefs of Staff, Hamilton Fish Armstrong, one of the delegation advisors, and Bowman. Rockefeller reiterated his argument for demanding a Latin exemption from the veto, this time mainly on the grounds of potential Communist subversion in the Americas, rather than on U.S. moral obligations to the Hemisphere. He spoke about how "a new era, with new forces, is upon us," noting recent Communist riots in Montevideo and rumors from fellow Latins about a possible Soviet invasion of "fascist" Argentina designed to put it in its place. McCloy assented to Rockefeller's views and reported that his own boss, Henry Stimson, too, was "heartily in favor of alliances."[7]

The next day, according to Vandenberg, all "hell broke loose" at a series of U.S. delegation meetings. At the opening parley, Vandenberg presented his proposal, blaming a "brain fag" for not having raised it the week before. Stassen immediately assailed it as a "tragic mistake." He insisted that it could fatally weaken the Security Council by taking away its jurisdiction. He preferred instead that the Council's veto power be "softened." Leo Pasvolsky, whom Vandenberg tabbed as "bitter" about regional caucuses, joined forces with Stassen. He fiercely opposed Vandenberg's amendment. "If we open up the Dumbarton Oaks proposals to allow for regional enforcement action on a collective basis," he warned, "the world organization is finished." He drew a dire picture: "We then move into a system in which we rely for our security on regional groups, large states with their spheres of influence surrounded by groups of smaller states. We will convert the world into armed camps and end up with a world war unlike any we have yet seen." Finally, he reminded the delegation, self-defense on a regional basis was still extant under the present charter if the Security Council did not act. John Foster Dulles, breaking with Vandenberg, also challenged the idea of a Latin exception, maintaining that the Soviet Union was likely to agree to it simply to justify excluding the U.N.—and the United States—from influence in Europe. He asserted, like Pasvolsky, that self-defense was still possible under the current U.N. arrangements and could encompass both the Act of Chapultepec and the Monroe Doctrine.[8]

Vandenberg's main allies were Rockefeller, McCloy, Congressmen Eaton and Bloom, and, to a lesser degree, Senator Connally. When his turn came to speak on the matter, Rockefeller chose to dwell not on the Communist menace but on the "word of honor" the U.S. government had given in February to abide by the Act of Chapultepec. A possible alternative, Connally suggested, was a protocol whereby the Big Five would agree in advance to allow the inter-American system to take enforcement measures in any local dispute. Vandenberg said he might insist on a Senate reservation on the right of self-defense if the Latin exemption were not granted. Stettinius, trying to play his role as arbiter, was beleaguered. At one point, "he did not see how he could go to Molotov and make an about face" by asking the Russian for a reconsideration of the regional provision. When Rockefeller pressed him about raising the matter at that afternoon's Big Five session, Stettinius brushed him off, saying that he had to wait at least until the following day because it was "psychologically impossible for him to discuss the revision of an amendment that was still warm." Finally, at the suggestion of one of the delegates, Stettinius did agree to meet with a group of Latin officials in his Fairmont suite the next morning to hear their complaints.[9]

An unrepentant Rockefeller took full advantage of this last-minute opening. He corralled eight ministers and shepherded them at 9:00 A.M. on a foggy and drizzly day to Stettinius's penthouse. When the host casually joked about the inclement weather, Ezequiel Padilla, the Mexican foreign minister, replied, to much laughter, that the "sunshine is in our hearts." But the tone of the meeting was stormy. The Bolivian ambassador to the United States, Victor Andrade, expressed Latin dissatisfaction over the possible abandonment of "solid inter-American cohesion," concerned that "the solidarity of the republics will be broken." Cuba's ambassador, Ramariz Belt, drew attention once again to the Red peril: "An international party exists in Latin America. It takes its orders from Moscow. Why put such an advantage in the hands of this party?" Colombia's foreign minister, Alberto Lleras Camargo, bluntly seconded the Belt thesis: "Russia's purpose is to intervene in Latin America via domestic action." Finally, the Chilean foreign minister, Joaquin Fernandez y Fernandez, twisted the knife into the old Roosevelt hand by asking Stettinius whether he was prepared to throw out the whole inter-American system thirty days after the death of his boss. Stettinius, for his part, pleaded unavailingly with the Latins that he did not intend to weaken the U.N. at the expense of regional interests, but, at the same time, he was intent on seeking "a formula satisfactory to the American countries and to the Soviets also." He departed, seething privately over the intemperate comments of some of the participants.[10]

That evening, he reported to the U. S. delegation that, at his 4:00 P.M. press briefing, the media had pounded him with questions about the Latin grievances. The story about the Latin uprising, he said, was now "out in the open." At one point, he gazed at Nelson Rockefeller and asked: "What has happened to the Latin Americans during the past two weeks to destroy their faith in the international organization?" Rockefeller cited the unfriendly Soviet maneuvers against the Latin bloc in the opening days that had led to fears about the Soviet role on the Security Council. Stettinius did not appear persuaded. Later that evening, in a phone call, Stettinius told Rockefeller that "the tragedy of the matter was Vandenberg's letter"—an issue still vexing him. Another burden he carried was a rumor that the Arab League was trying to form a coalition with the Latins to broaden the fight against the regional veto. "These were low points during the conference," he scribbled in his diary, a notable confession for a man who allowed little time for self-reflection and who showed virtually no despondency.[11]

Stettinius remained uncertain now about how he wanted to placate the Latins. His own delegation was divided and unhelpful. John Foster Dulles in one memo warned Stettinius that he faced a "Hobson's choice." A rejection of the Latin proposals "would seriously impair his Latin American relations," but accession to them could gravely undermine the authority of the Security Council and "invite Russian domination of all Europe." At the evening delegation meeting of May 8, Dulles circulated another memo, restating his and Pasvolsky's position that there was really no need for a Latin exemption because the right of self-defense already existed in the charter. Vandenberg, for his turn, thought Dulles's commentary on self-defense gave the United States an unlimited right to "do anything we please" and was a misreading of the charter. The legalistic Vandenberg wanted the protection for the Latin states spelled out clearly either as an exception, a protocol, or a Senate reservation, but not left implicit. In a similar, more calculated fashion, John McCloy, the assistant secretary of war, wanted full regional flexibility for U.S. decisionmakers with or without Russia's assent. This reflected, he told the delegates, the position of his boss, Secretary of War Henry Stimson, and the U.S. military. In a recorded transcript of a talk he held with Stimson earlier in the day, McCloy said he was lobbying hard at San Francisco for their goal: "I've been taking the position that we ought to have our cake and eat it too; that we ought to be free to operate under this regional amendment in South America, at the same time intervene promptly in Europe; that we oughtn't to give away either asset."[12]

Even as he was still trying to figure out how to accommodate the Latins, Stettinius had not yet found time to talk with Molotov about a revamping of the regional amendment. For him, Molotov was the crucial player in a final resolution of this problem. Stettinius was aware that Molotov still possessed a white-hot rage over Argentina's admission, and that he was alarmed, too, by the voting strength of the Latin bloc at the United Nations. For Stettinius now to approach him for yet another concession on behalf of the Hemisphere seemed a formidable, if not hopeless, task. But time was pressing and Stettinius knew that even now the Latins were prowling the corridors of the War Memorial Veterans Building trying to sway member nations to their cause. Furthermore, it was imperative to see Molotov forthwith because he was due to depart the next day for Moscow. Finally, after much back and forth at the delegation powwow, Stettinius told his team that he would raise the matter with Molotov that evening at a farewell ceremony at the penthouse. Around 8:30 P.M., Stettinius finally broached the subject to Molotov, placing the Latin question last on a list of three items. He gingerly alluded to the ferment over the regional veto. Molotov was noncommittal, suggesting he'd have to hear the arguments about the changes first. Then he exited. Although this encounter appeared to settle nothing, Stettinius at least had given due warning to Molotov about a possible struggle ahead.[13]

On the next day, Wednesday morning, May 9, the matter blossomed into a major public embarrassment for Stettinius. The *New York Times* emblazoned on the top left-side of its front page a lead story on how the United States was, in effect, retreating before the rising Latin demands by making revisions in the regional clause. The following day, Walter Lippmann in his column criticized the Latins for disrupting San Francisco's so far successful labors. And the day after, the *Washington Post* weighed in with a stinging editorial assailing Latin chutzpah for sending a "flying wedge into the very soul of the world organization" and fingered Nelson Rockefeller as one of the ringleaders behind the campaign. Given the deteriorating state of affairs, Stettinius took matters into his own hands. In a step to head off any further Rockefeller maneuvers, Stettinius immediately sent Harold Stassen to see his assistant secretary—on the day the *Times* ran its scoop. Stassen, reluctant to become entangled with this master of intrigue, had earlier turned Rockefeller down for dinner that night. But Stettinius, knowing of the Rockefeller supper invitation, appealed to Stassen to find out what Rockefeller was doing. Stassen agreed. For self-protection, though, he brought along a proposal he had been considering on the Latin question that involved self-defense rather than regionalism. That evening, he told Rockefeller of his proposition, which was to have the charter enshrine self-defense as a right, thereby immunizing the Chapultepec Act and the Monroe Doctrine from veto. Rockefeller was astonished that the former governor on his own had delivered a solution to the

Leo Pasvolsky, seated, conferring with left, Charles Bohlen, and right, Secretary of State Edward Stettinius, at the Dumbarton Oaks Conference in the summer of 1944 (Edward R. Stettinius Papers (#2723), Special Collections Department, University of Virginia Library)

Secretary of State Edward Stettinius greets Soviet Foreign Minister Vyacheslav Molotov at Washington airport with Russian Ambassador to the U.S. Andrei Gromyko and State Department official Charles Bohlen (left) (Bettmann/Corbis — No. U1016132INP)

U.S. envoy to the Soviet Union Averell Harriman arrives with British Ambassador to the USSR Sir Archibald Clark Kerr in Washington, April 18, 1945 (UN/DPI — No. 14)

American delegation at Fairmont Hotel including at table, left to right: Dean Virginia Gildersleeve, Congressman Sol Bloom, Senator Thomas Connally, Secretary of State Edward Stettinius, Senator Arthur Vandenberg, Congressman Charles Eaton, Harold Stassen, Nelson Rockefeller, Adlai Stevenson, John Foster Dulles (UN/DPI — No. 1734)

Key members of U.S. delegation, including left to right: Congressman Sol
Bloom, Senator Thomas Connally, Secretary of State Edward Stettinius,
Senator Arthur Vandenberg, Congressman Charles Eaton, Harold Stassen,
Adlai Stevenson (UN/DPI — No. 1534)

Senator Thomas Connally, center, walking with friend in front of Veterans Building
(Peter Stackpole/Timepix: No. 636619)

Left to right: Soviet Foreign Minister Vyacheslav Molotov, Secretary of State
Edward Stettinius, and British Foreign Secretary Anthony Eden conferring at a
May 1, 1945, Plenary Session (UN/DPI — No. 245)

Assistant Secretary of State Nelson Rockefeller, center, at radio broadcast on June 6,
1945 (UN/DPI — No. 1837)

Australian Foreign Minister
Herbert Evatt (left) confers
with delegate (Thomas D.
McAvoy/Timepix: No. 636222)

Meeting of Big Five delegations in Fairmont Hotel penthouse on May 29, 1945
(UN/DPI —No. 7)

Big Four confer at Fairmont Hotel penthouse left to right: British Foreign Secretary Anthony Eden, Secretary of State Edward Stettinius, Soviet Foreign Minister Vyacheslav Molotov, and Chinese Foreign Minister T. V. Soong (UN/DPI — No. 982)

Secretary of State Edward Stettinius greets President Harry Truman with Senator Thomas Connally at San Francisco airport on June 25, 1945 (UN/DPI — No. 2505)

President Harry Truman and Secretary of State Edward Stettinius shake hands with delegation heads at airport on June 25, 1945 (UN/DPI — No. 2179)

Secretary of State Edward Stettinius signs U.N. Charter next to President Harry Truman with Harold Stassen looking on, June 26, 1945 (UN/DPI — No. 2463)

President Harry Truman delivers address at U.N. Conference on April 26, 1945 with Secretary of State Edward Stettinius and acting U.N. Secretary-General Alger Hiss (UN/DPI — No. 2906)

Alger Hiss disembarks from special Army plane in Washington on June 28th to deliver U.N. Charter, wrapped in parachute, to President Harry Truman (National Archives)

whole Latin conundrum. "My God, Harold," Rockefeller exulted, "You've got it!" The two men refined the language and, by the next day, Stassen submitted it to the delegation.[14]

By now, the outlines of a refashioned amendment consistent with the Stassen approach were, to Stettinius's astonishment and relief, beginning to emerge. At the U.S. delegation session on Thursday, May 10, the Stassen/Rockefeller memo and one from Dulles—itself suggesting five ways of resolving the knotty quandary—were placed on the table. From these and other briefs, a team of advisors, including Dulles, Pasvolsky, Dunn, and Bowman, began to fashion a new proposal. They rearranged words, rewrote sentences, cut and pasted phrases, and trimmed and revised the text until they had sketched out a new article that seemed to cover practically all the important bases. The newly configured passage discarded all mention of regionalism, but it gave clear voice to the "inherent" right of self-defense, which could be invoked when there was an "armed attack"—though it required that a state report its act of self-defense to the Security Council immediately and gave the council authority to supersede such self-defense if it desired; finally, it named the Act of Chapultepec as the signature treaty for the provision. The new provision, in short, offered the Latins the right to act if the Security Council ducked its own responsibilities in settling conflicts. Still Stettinius was not happy with the state of play. Even now infuriated over the poor press coverage of the past few days, he erupted at Friday morning's delegation council (May 11) against the Latins. "The time has arrived," he sternly cautioned his compatriots, "when we must not be pushed around by a lot of small American republics who are dependent on us in many ways—economically, politically, militarily. We must provide leadership." The Latins, he added, say they have lost faith in the conference and want to "build a fence around the Hemisphere." Well, enough. "We have come to this conference," his tone hardened, "to create an international organization, and we will not be deviated from that course."[15]

Once his emotions had subsided, however, Stettinius turned rapidly to the matter of pulling together support for a U.S. formula. Over the weekend, he had a telephone consultation with John McCloy, the assistant secretary of war, who was then in Washington, about the military views on the draft amendment. McCloy reported that they approved of it, but some felt it "placed too much emphasis on regionalism at the expense of the world system." Next, Stettinius gathered together his delegation on Saturday morning, May 12, and won their unanimous backing for the proposal—though some of the delegates, anxious to head off future revisions, were emphatic in their desire to retain mention of the Chapultepec Act in the amendment for its "sales value" within the Hispanic community. Finally, at midday, Stettinius spoke with Truman by phone. Stettinius told the president about the new provision, which now included the reference to Chapultepec, explaining that it would allow the United States to "act immediately if the Security Council doesn't act and we have the inherent right of self-defense." Truman replied, "That's what we want."[16]

Next Stettinius took it to the Big Five. Here Stettinius hit an unexpected obstacle in the unlikely personage of Anthony Eden, the British foreign minister, who was leaving San Francisco for England the next day. At the Great Powers session at 2:30 P.M. in the afternoon, Eden expressed his "intense dislike" for the draft and cited its Latin American "origin," insisting it would "result in regionalism of the worst kind." Stettinius knew that Eden had gained some foreknowledge of the proposal, though he had not seen the final wording. Nonetheless, Eden's disapproval still came as a shock to him. Senators Vandenberg and Connally and former Governor Stassen instantly leapt to Stettinius's defense, asserting, among other things, that the Latin exemption was no different from the Soviet one. Finally, Eden requested a private tête-à-tête with Stettinius. There, Stettinius tried to explain that he believed the main reason the United States was pushing this change was that otherwise the Latins might walk out and, more ominously, the U.S. Senate might reject the treaty altogether.[17]

Eden was sympathetic, but soon betrayed the true reason for his own irritable opposition. He wanted to eliminate all references to Chapultepec, and he also disapproved of the stipulation that the right of self-defense became operative only when there was an "armed attack." He argued, first, that the mention of the pact would only encourage the Arab League and such groups to insist on a similar inclusion, and, in any event, a notation about one official regional body would delimit the range of the article. Second, as the British wanted to be able to act under the proviso, if necessary, against such contingencies as the USSR's possible expansionist aims in Europe and the Mediterranean, the clause, he felt, needed a more expansive triggering mechanism than "armed attack," one that permitted action against every sort of aggression, direct or indirect. Twenty-seven hours later, on Monday morning, May 14, Stettinius capitulated to the first of Eden's pleas, on Chapultepec. Instead of mentioning that pact, the British and U.S. negotiators agreed to use the phrase "inherent right of individual or collective self-defense." Vandenberg, in his turn, promised to get the Senate to insert a reservation construing the word "collective" to refer to Chapultepec. On the second request, Stettinius refused to budge, contending that a broader phraseology would allow states too great a leeway, including the right of preventative actions, which could legally wreck the organization. World Wars I and II, after all, had both begun with preventative attacks. The British finally backed down.[18]

Now the problem was shifted to the Latins. Stettinius arranged a meeting that same Monday at 2:30 P.M. in his penthouse headquarters in the Fairmont Hotel. Seven Latin ministers showed up. With his delegation sitting next to him, Stettinius presented several alternative revisions of the amendment, two of which omitted the appellation of Chapultepec. He and Vandenberg told the assemblage that they favored the versions that didn't name the Mexican accord. They reiterated the old arguments against Chapultepec's inclusion: Other regional actors would demand to be included; the other Great Powers would probably reject any such formulation; and Vandenberg himself had promised the U.S. Senate would enact a reservation on Chapultepec. On that latter point, Vandenberg vowed: "The Senate of the United States will nail this down so nobody on earth can misunderstand it," later proudly telling Stettinius that, for an "old isolationist" like himself, that was something for him to say.

The Latins responded with their concern that the omission of the inter-American accord's name from the amendment would upset the Hemispheric community with the United Nations. Whatever was decided about Chapultepec, they also wanted clearer language, so that the clause would enjoin the Security Council to *support* rather than simply *encourage* settlement of local disputes through regional arrangements. Stettinius sharply reminded the ministers that "the primary goal was world organization and that the success of the San Francisco Conference must not be impaired by any exaggerated emphasis on regionalism." Stettinius pressed his point that the Latins must decide whether they were seeking a world body or a regional body. He warned, too, that "rumors of the desire of American Republics to build a fence around the Hemisphere were causing a great deal of damage. We cannot let the policy of hemispheric solidarity interfere with a world system of security." Eventually, the Latins at the meeting started to backtrack, still insisting, though, that they needed a publicly announced commitment of some sort by the United States. Stettinius finally asked the group to take a break and get back to him that evening.[19]

That night, the participants assembled once again in the penthouse at 9:00 P.M. Now the arguments began anew—this time lasting until 3:40 A.M. During the lengthy and often acrimonious discussions, State Department aide James Dunn advanced an idea that, he thought, might help reassure the Latins. He pointed out that Chapultepec was simply a set of principles and did not go into operation as a treaty until it was signed by all the nations in the Americas. Why could the Latins not agree to drop all references to the Mexican accord in the charter in exchange for a Washington promise to hold a conference on inter-American security later in the fall and elevate Chapultepec into a formal Hemispheric-wide pact? That would give the Latin ministers something tangible to take back to their constituents. The idea stirred some interest among the Latins present because it provided a public reassurance of a U.S. commitment to their security, but still they reserved their views. Stettinius, by his own account, resisted the idea, believing that Vandenberg's Senate reservation was sufficient and that announcing an imminent Latin conclave during the San Francisco meeting might look to the outside world like a vote of no-confidence by the United States in the U.N.[20]

By the time the delegation met the next morning, the pressure was beginning to mount for some sort of deal. Still, Stettinius held out against a fall conference. He may have been somewhat shaken, though, by the account in that morning's *New York Times,* which related the entire tale of the tortuous U.S. negotiations with the Latins over the past days. It even hinted that a settlement was imminent through the very sort of fall parley that Stettinius opposed. Stettinius himself reported he only heard "defeatist talk" at the meeting. Nobody was confident that there was a clear plan to extricate Washington from this crisis; indeed, negotiations had dragged on for days without resolution.

Critics were now asking why Stettinius had not anticipated the Latin demands. Stettinius, in his turn, was furious over the behavior both of the Latins and his own aide, Nelson Rockefeller. Once again, he confronted Rockefeller, this time grousing that "it was most embarrassing to have the Latin Americans speak out the way they did." Rockefeller replied with a hint of impertinence: "The difficulty is that they feel that our promises might be carried out or they might not be carried out. They are concerned whether the Secretary is speaking for the President and whether he is voicing the foreign policy of this government." At another point, Stettinius fumed to Rockefeller: "In spite of the obvious hazards to the world organization, you keep tenaciously and exclusively advocating the limited Latin American viewpoint." "I personally have stood for nothing but what was in the interest of the United States," Rockefeller stammered in response. "I favor only what is in our interests." "Well then," Stettinius replied, intent on trapping him, "are you willing to say that the world organization is a matter of primary interest to us?" "Yes, I do," Rockefeller replied. "It is essential for our interests." "Then," Stettinius persisted, "could you get our Southern friends to say this?" "Yes, I can," Rockefeller answered. A frustrated Stettinius had scored a point.[21]

However, Vandenberg, concerned about extraneous conversations and a drifting session, jerked Stettinius back to the issue at hand. He admonished the secretary that he must personally "take charge of this whole matter as the first advisor to the President on foreign policy and to make plain our policy regarding the Act of Chapultepec." It is time, he said, "to stop quibbling and to make a decision." Stettinius, as the representative of the Truman administration in San Francisco, he said, must formulate a position on the Latins and aim to achieve that outcome. Stettinius was just at that moment in the process of making up his mind, prodded especially by the *Times* article. The idea of a fall conference, he recalled, began to appear at that moment "to advantage in my mind and I realized that this would mean we would not have to go so far in keeping satisfaction of Latin American demands." He finally seized on the notion and asked the delegation to support a grand bargain. The U.S. would remove Chapultepec from the article but confirm a formal treaty get-together that fall. Such a promise, he told the delegation, he could persuade the president to approve, and thereafter he'd go to the Latins and Great Powers for their support. The delegation gave him its immediate backing.[22]

Later that morning, Stettinius called Truman at the White House and informed him of the new development. The delegation, he explained, now believed it would be a "mistake" to mention the Act of Chapultepec in the regional amendment and that it was more appropriate to employ general language on "inherent self-defense." However, "to get it by" the Latins, he needed to "assure" them that the president would consent to a conference in the fall to ratify the Act of Chapultepec and demonstrate to the Hemisphere that his administration was loyal to Roosevelt's Good Neighbor policy and to James Monroe's doctrine. Truman was agreeable on all points. Stettinius now prepared for the afternoon showdown with the restive Latin chiefs.[23]

At 2:45 P.M., Stettinius, accompanied by his aides, called eight Latin delegation heads to his penthouse living room. At the opening, Stettinius cautioned the leaders that what he had to say was to remain private, though he authorized them to communicate his remarks to their governments. He placed a card squarely on the table, stating that the Act of Chapultepec had to be dropped from the proposed article. At the same time, however, he laid down a trump card, saying that President Truman had agreed, hours earlier, to convene a conference of Hemisphere nations to turn Chapultepec into a binding treaty. The Latins initially seemed interested, but also suspicious. They did not want such an agreement to be kept secret. Instead, they wanted a public statement by the secretary of state acknowledging the new development. Such an announcement would enable them to explain to their citizenry why

Chapultepec had been dropped from the charter. As Ambassador Belt from Cuba noted, "the Latin American group had taken a definite position and must justify an apparent retreat from it."[24]

In the midst of this debate, an exasperated Senator Connally abruptly rose and proceeded to deliver a stem-winder of a speech that visibly stunned his audience. Connally, a tall, distinguished-looking man wearing a dark gray suit, black bow tie, gold shirt studs, and a pair of tortoiseshell glasses, reminded the Latins how much they all depended on each other. He added: "You know the United States is not going to allow interference by any outside power in the hemisphere." Further, he declaimed, President Truman was committed to negotiating a treaty over Chapultepec and "it was a question of their confidence and trust in the intention of the government to give complete fulfillment to its word." Finally, he recalled that "the United States had not failed them before." Then, reaching rhetorical heights, he pleaded with them, his face reddened, his arms flailing: "I appeal to you, 'Trust us!' We are in the Western Hemisphere just as much as you are. We can't do it alone—you've got to help us—to harmonize this with the international system." Stettinius watched in fascination. It seemed to him as if Connally were speaking "on the Senate floor or perhaps at a political rally." Stettinius observed, "He made an unforgettable picture of a senator in action against the background of its huge Gobelin tapestry."[25]

As Connally sat down, Colombia's foreign minister, Lleras Camargo, got up and agreed that the words uttered by Connally, and earlier Stettinius, were good enough for him; he had "no need of any additional assurances or documents" and was quite willing to leave it to Stettinius now to decide on how he wished to inform the continent about how the U.S. planned to safeguard the inter-American system. Several other Latin ministers also stood up to praise Connally and Stettinius and to agree with Lleras. The meeting was over. Vandenberg, sitting for the most part on the sidelines, was greatly impressed. "The Latins took it," he exclaimed in his diary. "This has been a great piece of work." As for Stettinius, whom he had alternately derided and praised during the first three weeks of the conference, Vandenberg was now a fan: "Stettinius is entitled to immense credit for having made a job of it and having driven it through. It shows what he can do. I hope he continues to be Secretary of State."[26]

There was still much work to be done. Stettinius took the agreement back to the Big Five at 5:00 that afternoon. All the main players were present except Gromyko. The secretary presented the new U.S. formula to them. Lord Halifax, the British representative, said his government would support it and thanked the "ingenuity and industry of the United States delegation" for arriving at the solution. The Chinese delegate, Ambassador Koo, approved it. Mr. Bidault, the French foreign minister, indicated that he wished to study it first and then give an answer; but, by the next day, he had okayed it. Meantime, Stettinius decried the press misinformation and speculation on the U.S. position and, eager to respond to the Latin American importuning (and aware that the *New York Times* unofficially had the story anyway), asked whether it would be acceptable to "make the United States position known promptly." Nobody objected. As the ministers left, Stettinius phoned Gromyko about the formula as well as about his decision to publicize it. Gromyko begged off from making a decision until he had spoken to his government. Adlai Stevenson later remarked that Gromyko couldn't "spit without permission from Moscow."[27]

Stettinius consulted with the U.S. delegation at 6:00 P.M. about whether to release a statement in light of Gromyko's irresolution. Dulles pressed him to go ahead with the announcement without Soviet approval. Stettinius decided that was the right move. As Dulles recalled: "We felt that only in this way could the Soviet hand be forced." Armed with the delegation's backing, Stettinius called Truman at 7:00 P.M. and Truman gave him a green light to issue a press release outlining the amendment and confirming a fall conference. The statement appeared in the next morning's *New York Times,* May 16. As a result of this action, Walter Lippmann composed a highly flattering column about Stettinius, calling him "a leader instead of an arbitrator between nations." The Soviets never registered any public objections.[28]

But privately they did. Indeed, over the next few days, the Big Five continued to hold negotiating sessions with the Soviets, trying to work out various compromises over the proposed amendment. "The Soviet delegation," as Dulles observed, "at first refused to accept the text we had publicly sponsored." Among other issues, the Soviets were concerned that the word "collective" was too unclear. Leo Pasvolsky noted that they were "afraid that it would make possible a coalition against them." Ultimately, however, acting on instructions from Moscow, Gromyko on May 19 and May 20, after some minor revisions, placed his official imprimatur on all the changes. Dulles believed that the decision to make public the U.S. formula helped bring about the Soviet turnaround. "The tactic succeeded," he crowed. "Eventually they gave in." Subsequently, the Big Five and the various committees in San Francisco decided to divide the proposals on regionalism into three separate articles within the United Nations Charter. The most consequential was Article 51, which enshrined the collective self-defense concept; Article 52 legitimized the right of states to form regional associations to settle disputes; Article 53 allowed nations in regional configurations to act against former Axis powers without Security Council clearance (the Soviet amendment). All the alterations recognized the final authority of the Security Council to oversee world enforcement and to hear complaints from any state.[29]

Curiously enough, Pasvolsky's foreboding about the possible Balkanization of the United Nations through regional agencies—shared by other writers about the San Francisco Conference, including Evan Luard (Article 51, in his view, substantially lessened the U.N.'s "revolutionary significance" as a world enforcement agency), Gabriel Kolko (Article 51 gave "spheres of influence and competing blocs a formal legal structure"), and Carey Reich (Article 51 hobbled U.N. peacekeeping and turned the organization into a "helpless bystander to bloody conflicts to come")—over the years did not come to pass as he (or they) foresaw. On the contrary, most regional groupings usually proved ineffectual. One scholar of the United Nations, Benjamin Rivlin, wrote in 1991 that after forty-six years in operation, "regional authorities generally lack the credibility, the capacity and, hence, the clout to act effectively as agents for collective security and peaceful settlement." The U.N., in retrospect, would have welcomed more regional participation since it would have relieved its overburdened officials of some of their responsibilities. When the Big Five occasionally did allow local control by vetoing Security Council involvement in regional disputes, success came infrequently, for ill—such as during the CIA coup in Guatemala in 1954—or for good—the NATO (North American Treaty Organization) intervention in Kosovo in 1998–1999. But more often than not, regional agencies fumbled the ball.[30]

Still, the singular accomplishment of Article 51, in retrospect, was to lay the legal groundwork for the creation of a series of security pacts around the world, ranging from the North American Treaty Organization to the South East Treaty Organization (SEATO) to the Warsaw Pact. Hence John Foster Dulles called Article 51 "of incalculable value." Without it, he observed, "the Soviet Union would have had an unlimited right to prevent organization of effective defense agreements against its own possible aggression." During the 1950s, Dulles, then secretary of state, once found himself seated next to Nelson Rockefeller at a dinner. "I owe you an apology," Dulles said. "If you fellows hadn't done it, we might never have had NATO."[31]

Now, with the contretemps over regionalism settled, Secretary Stettinius wanted more than ever to wind up the conference. Yet, just as he was ready to put the finishing touches on the charter, without warning another eruption spewed on San Francisco. This time, it was an issue that had lain just below the surface in the early sessions, but had been threatening to flare up for weeks from the camp of the smaller states: the move to restrict the veto. Simultaneously, the Soviet Union was starting its own campaign to enlarge the veto. Stettinius had anticipated a controversy of only minimal consequence over the issue. But now, suddenly, he had a battle on two fronts over the matter: his most important wartime ally and a group of small upstart states. Each held a viewpoint that could possibly tear the United Nations asunder. This imbroglio now threatened the U.N. and delayed the conference for several more harrowing weeks.

CHAPTER 12

THE TWENTY-THREE
QUESTIONS

The operative principle among the Big Three in San Francisco was that the Great Power veto had to be preserved at all costs (China and France shared this view). Otherwise, they believed, the wartime alliance would collapse, and the United Nations could not survive. According to the formula agreed upon at Yalta four months earlier, the five permanent members of the Security Council had an absolute veto over "substantive" matters—enforcement measures, investigations, the imposition of settlements, and related questions. However, they could not cast a veto over "procedural" issues, especially the right to discuss a dispute at the council level; a majority of the eleven-member Security Council would decide any such controversy. When a dispute arose to which one of the Big Five was a party, the permanent member had to abstain, though the remaining Big Powers could wield their veto.

Consequently, Secretary Stettinius's mantra to the U.S. delegation was that the Yalta formula was untouchable: It formed the basis of the United Nations and must be upheld without change. There was no dissent among the U.S. delegates. Both Senators Connally and Vandenberg, who were crucial to a ratification fight in the Senate, felt the veto was essential because it provided a shield against encroachments on national sovereignty, something that had not been available to the United States under the League of Nations covenant. Without such protection, Connally argued, a majority of U.N. states, all Lilliputian in size, could vote the United States into a war that Washington did not want: "Since we would have to furnish most of the resources and manpower, I believed the U.S. should retain the right to say 'no.'" The Soviets and the British agreed. The British permanent undersecretary for foreign affairs, Sir Alexander Cadogan, emphasized that the Big Five represented more than half the world's population and constituted much more than half its military might; thus, it had to have the veto. In any event, he said, no armed action could take place under Security Council auspices without Big Power unity. Disunity rendered any council resolution worthless.[1]

But the actual Yalta text defining the veto lacked precision. Stettinius was well aware that there was ambiguity about the breadth and limits of the veto. It was an uncertainty that so pervaded the conference that in due course it was to prompt the smaller nations to demand answers to almost two dozen questions about the scope of the veto. Shortly after the Yalta meeting, Stettinius on March 5, and later Undersecretary of State Grew on March 24, tried to clear up the fuzzy language in public statements. They were, in part, reacting to Army Signal Corps intercepts showing dissatisfaction over the veto among many delegations. Grew reminded the smaller nations of the distinction made at Yalta between voting on "substantive" and on "procedural" matters. Under this prescription, Grew explained, states that feared they might never be able to bring a dispute to the Security Council should recognize that discussion in the council was considered inherently "procedural" and thus exempt from "nay" votes. "There is nothing in these provisions," he emphasized, "which could prevent any party to a dispute or situation from receiving a hearing before the Council and having the case discussed."[2]

But this did not calm the worries. Although, as the *New York Times* observed in early May, many countries so pined for a global security organization that they had "reluctantly accepted the idea of virtual world dictatorship by the great powers," nonetheless they planned on "seeking through amendments to whittle down the dominance of the big nations as much as possible." In particular, they aimed at cutting back the veto on amendments, investigations, regional actions, recommendations for or impositions of settlements, the right of states to participate in Security Council decisions on troop deployments involving their own forces, and peaceful resolutions of disputes to which members of the Big Five were not a party. This campaign, at first scattered and confused, was gradually gaining headway under the articulate and passionate leadership of Herbert Vere Evatt, the Australian minister for external affairs.[3]

Evatt was a formidable presence at San Francisco. Born in 1894, he was fifty-one at the time of the conference. He already had a reputation in his homeland as a fearless advocate of civil liberties, having fought successfully against a ban on the Australian Communist Party. In the 1930s, he wrote several books about the British colonial system. During the war, he served in the Labour government as attorney general and then as minister for external affairs. For one year, in 1942, he was a member of the British war cabinet. The *Encyclopedia Britannica* wrote about him: "In all fields his contribution was substantial, although—as in his politics—an occasional false note obtruded. Historians may long debate whether, all in all, Evatt was faintly ridiculous or nearly sublime." In San Francisco, Evatt riveted the conference with defiant gestures, laying down a road map for the smaller states to follow.[4]

On May 9, at the height of the controversy over the right of the Big Five to veto military interventions by regional authorities, Evatt weighed in with his own radical proposal. The Security Council, he said, should have the first right to stop regional policing, but it should do so only on a combination of three vetoes instead of one and, if the council refused to do anything at all, then the local bodies would be authorized to take over the dispute. On May 14, he directly assailed "special immunity" for "American regionalism" as potentially destabilizing the Security Council as well as fostering an "isolationism" that could kill the U.N. "at its birth."

A few days later, Evatt introduced an amendment requiring that the Security Council not merely oppose aggression but also enforce agreements on the warring parties. This notable modification challenged the very notion of the Security Council as a political instrument. "One theory had been followed" in drafting the proposal on the council, as Harley Notter, one of the State Department advisors, observed: "The International Organization is being created because the nations want peace. It is not basically concerned with just settlements." The charter itself was supposed to lend guidance on how jousting nations could negotiate their differences, but it did not view the Security Council as the justice of the peace who brings conflicts to a fair end; rather, it was merely the instrument to gain a break in the fighting.[5]

Then, on May 18, Evatt delivered a powerful speech before the Committee on Structures and Procedures calling attention to the illogic in the Yalta formula that allowed the Big Five to veto pacific resolutions of disputes to which they were not a party but obliged a Big Power that was a principal in a conflict to abstain. Why not abolish the veto for all the Great Powers when settling a controversy peacefully? Evatt's analysis drew enthusiastic backing from Mexico, Belgium, El Salvador, Chile, Colombia, Peru, and New Zealand. On that same day, Evatt pushed to increase the importance of the General Assembly by permitting it to make recommendations on matters affecting international relations, except where the Security Council was already engaged in the issue. In face of Evatt's campaigns—eventually he was to offer some thirty-eight amendments, of which twenty-six later adopted or reflected in the final charter—Stettinius remained wary, but stoic. In due course, he informed Truman that he had spoken with a "responsible career member" of the Australian delegation who explained to him that Evatt was trying to curry favor with smaller countries to please his left-wing constituency at home, but he did not intend to wreck the conference.[6]

Nonetheless, the U.S. delegation was starting to waver a bit under his relentless pressure. Senator Vandenberg ruminated in his diary: "This 'veto' bizness is making it very difficult to maintain any semblance of a fiction of 'sovereign equality' among the nations here in Frisco." At a lengthy meeting on the morning of Thursday, May 17, some delegates even began to wonder whether it might be prudent to consider ending the veto altogether on peaceful pacts. Harold Stassen noted that fifteen amendments had already been introduced to that effect. He himself thought a revamping might be "highly desirable." At an evening session that same day, after hearing further grumbling from foreign delegations, Leo Pasvolsky proposed that "if it appears that the line cannot be held, it may be necessary to confer on the possible modification of the position to be taken." By May 19, indeed, the United States did bend one rule a bit by agreeing to a Canadian idea that would allow nonmember states contributing troops to a U.N. operation to vote as ad hoc participants in the Security Council on strategic decisions. But over the next few days, despite the few cracks in the ranks and the small concession to the Canadians, and despite reports surfacing in newspapers suggesting that the Americans, British, and Chinese were reconsidering the veto on pacific deals if the USSR agreed, the United States hardened its line on the Yalta accord.[7]

By now the crusade by the smaller nations was reaching a climax of sorts. On the night of May 18 at a meeting of Committee 1 of Commission III, which dealt with the Security Council, delegates from the smaller sovereignties, led by Colombia, tried to set up a subcommittee specifically to redraft or amend the veto, focusing initially on eliminating the veto over pacific compacts. Delegates were apparently willing to concede the veto on enforcement actions, but they wanted to pare it down in other areas. Then Connally and the British minister, Sir Alexander Cadogan, as representatives of the sponsoring powers on the committee and fearful that this could become a runaway committee, intervened by appealing to the Latins for help. They brokered a vote of 23 to 3 to redirect the subcommittee simply to "clarify" the language of the veto as a task force rather than to offer alternatives to it. The newly anointed panel, though, took its duties seriously and began over the next four days to develop a series of questions to be sent to the Big Powers to help define the entire Yalta equation. They ultimately compiled twenty-three sharply delineated interrogatories on the veto.[8]

In the meantime, Stettinius pondered how he could contain this incipient uprising. The Big Five each had the power to thwart restrictions placed on the veto by dint of its right to block amendments. But such a move was not really an option. The Big Powers had already tacitly agreed that they would not forbid amendments passed by a two-thirds vote in San Francisco; nor did Stettinius wish to provoke a walkout by irritating the smaller states any more than he already had. He had to be cognizant that global public opinion was not likely to look favorably on efforts by the Big Five to steamroll smaller nations able to garner at least 33 (out of 49) votes for change.

Privately, Stettinius was exasperated by the behavior of his Latin "friends," who appeared to take all sides of the veto issue, even though, at the same time, he was telling the press that the Hemispheric bloc could vote as it wished. At a delegation meeting on May 22, he complained to Rockfeller that "we had to sweat blood to satisfy" the Latins. Senator Connally, in his turn, rattled by his experiences quashing the rogue antiveto subcommittee, which was full of Latins, observed that "our bloc is a road block." He warned the assistant secretary that "we're up against a buzz saw here and unless Mr. Rockefeller can gather up four or five Latinos, we're going to get the hide licked off of us." Rockefeller reassured both men that "any time we wanted something, we asked them to come along with us," and the Latins always did. However, later Rockefeller sent Stettinius a memo pleading for modifications in the veto power. In his heart he was uncertain of his troops' reliability. Stettinius did not stop his needling of Rockefeller; a few days later, he taxed his deputy again on whether the Latin Americans would "unanimously support Yalta." Rockefeller now said only that he *thought* they would.[9]

With this continuing unrest and tumult, the twenty-three questions unexpectedly assumed much importance. James Reston in the *New York Times* reported that the "small nations have the will and the votes" to alter the veto. Stettinius was now genuinely concerned that things could unravel. On May 21, Stettinius warned Truman, "It is becoming increasingly clear that it will be extremely difficult, if not impossible, to obtain a two-thirds vote in the conference in favor of the Yalta formula exactly as it stands"—especially in relation to peaceful settlements and amendments. Truman immediately understood the gravity of Stettinius's alert, recalling in his memoirs "the question of the veto power in the Council was emerging as the single outstanding issue of the conference." When Truman asked Stettinius to return to Washington to review what the United States should do, Setttinius flew to the capital the next day.[10]

Stettinius met with Truman at 10:15 A.M. on the morning of May 23. Truman greeted him "with great warmth," told him "the delegation was doing an excellent job," and got down to business. He instructed Stettinius that "we would stand by the Yalta formula in the Security

Council. We were committed to this formula, and we would abide by it." He let the secretary know that he personally opposed the veto on pacific accords but didn't want to break with President Roosevelt's agreement at Yalta "if the Russians insist," so he was going to leave the matter to the delegation to handle. The two men reviewed other pending issues at the conference, including the status of the World Court, trusteeship details, a provision for states to withdraw from the U.N., Truman's opposition to postponing the conference, his appearance at the closing ceremonies (tentatively set for June 5), and the appropriate date to send the U.N. Treaty to the Senate ("We should do it immediately and dramatically," he told Stettinius). Then Truman brought the secretary up-to-date about the diplomatic trip he had just asked Harry Hopkins that very day to take to Moscow to meet with Stalin about the Polish crisis and other global wrangles. The president was confident that Hopkins would "be able to straighten things out with Stalin."[11]

Bolstered by his encounter with Truman, Stettinius rushed back to San Francisco. He found his delegation in considerable disarray. It was trying with much effort but no real strategy to figure out how to answer the twenty-three questions of the smaller nations, and to coordinate its replies with the other Big Five. By raising such issues as whether the veto applied to investigations and whether the veto determined the selection of the secretary-general or his assistants, the lesser states were, in effect, forcing the major powers to confront precisely what their understanding of Yalta was. But the Big Five were starting to realize they did not always agree on every detail of Yalta among themselves. Their staffs tried several times to produce draft replies, but these never proved quite acceptable among the major powers. One draft, for example, seemed to allow for the veto on discussion. Washington and London were also reexamining whether investigating a dispute might be properly considered procedural rather than substantive in opposition to the views of the Chinese and Soviets.[12]

Eventually, the parties papered over their differences. A draft written with the assistance of John Foster Dulles and Pasvolsky, brought general agreement among the Big Five. The statement eliminated the Anglo-American effort to exempt investigations from the veto, but otherwise faithfully reflected the U.S. position on discussion. Still, all was not harmonious. Reports of clashes within the U.S. delegation, as well of disputes among the Big Five, found their way into the *New York Times,* embarrassing Stettinius and prompting him to scold his own delegation for leaks. Reston of the *Times* evidently had his own private channel into the delegation, for each day he reported accurately what had happened at the previous day's meetings.[13]

On the evening of May 26, the Big Four gathered at the penthouse to complete a review of their overall statement to the smaller countries. Midway through the session, however, without warning, Ambassador Gromyko broached the hitherto unremarked—and still somewhat esoteric—question concerning the Big Five's right to veto the decision as to whether issues brought before the council were of a procedural character. This was Question 19 on the small nations' list. Gromyko thought that such a determination could be vetoed. Stettinius, noting wanly that the parties had "after all not reached complete agreement," saw the Gromyko riposte as striking at the heart of the question of free and open discussion. If Gromyko's interpretation carried, then any Big Power could block discussion simply by deciding that a dispute was not procedural in nature and therefore was subject to the veto.

Pasvolsky jumped in and tried to steer a way around Gromyko's point. The charter, he said, would necessarily list questions purely procedural in character and thus not subject to the veto, hence making irrelevant the matter of deciding whether a dispute was procedural—at least concerning the enumerated items. The charter would also specify what issues were substantive in nature and therefore vulnerable to a veto. "In the third category," he continued, "would be the unforseen questions." Here is where Gromyko's formula might apply. But the Soviet envoy said he could not respond to Pasvolsky's exegesis until he got his instructions from Moscow. Meanwhile, he held to his original conviction. In a front-page story in the *Times* the following day, Reston cited Gromyko's stance as possibly snarling the talks, though he suggested optimistically that "expectations are that the controversy will be reconciled after further discussion."[14]

Just at this moment, an event outside the conference further roiled the waters. The French government under General de Gaulle had sent troops into Syria and Lebanon, two states it had previously occupied under League of Nations mandates. During World War II, the Allies had recognized both lands as independent nations, and both now had representatives in San Francisco. But the French, intent on restoring colonial privileges, attempted to strong-arm their way back, provoking riots and causing bloodshed along the way. France's behavior alarmed the little nations, who suddenly saw the affair as a preview of what might happen under the rule of the five permanent members of the Security Council. France, after all, could potentially veto investigations or enforcement measures in the region against its own actions. Truman perceived the dangers at once, and he encouraged Churchill to deploy British troops to end the fighting, restore order, and persuade the French to withdraw. Churchill's intervention proved successful, but the episode nonetheless further agitated the U.N. meeting.[15]

To shore up support for Yalta, Stettinius now delivered a worldwide radio address on the evening of May 28 and vigorously defended the Crimean formula against critics such as Evatt. "It is not a question of privilege," he contended, "but of using the present distribution of military and industrial power in the world for the maintenance of peace." The permanent members were "essential," he added, "for without their strength and their unanimous will to peace the Council would be helpless to enforce its decisions." That same night, Gromyko spoke to five hundred people at a dinner sponsored by the American-Russian Institute in San Francisco and also expressed his undying support for the Yalta arrangement. He assailed all amendments designed to diminish the power of the Security Council. In defense of the veto, he argued: "If the problem of the peace is to be solved, there must be mutual trust and harmony among the greatest world powers, and they must act in harmony."[16]

However, days soon passed without word from Gromyko on the procedural versus substantive veto issue. Stettinius grew singularly impatient. Vandenberg bitterly complained about the lengthy delay, which had now lasted four days. Alger Hiss reported that committees dealing with the Security Council could not complete their work because of the impasse. Emissaries from Truman were pressing Stettinius to wind up the conference. Finally, Stettinius requested an afternoon tête-à-tête with Gromyko at the penthouse on the last day in May. After thanking the Russian envoy for coming, Stettinius cited the "growing feeling" that the state of play at the conference was "drifting away and they would have to act quickly" to retrieve it. The unresolved veto was the "bottleneck." Stettinius asked Pasvolsky to present his formula for solving the discussion dispute. Pasvolsky rattled off again his proposal and wondered, at the end, whether future Security Councils were going to be forced to decide from month to month and from year to year what was substantive and what was procedural—an effort, that, in his view, would surely immobilize the body. In response, Gromyko repeated his stance, and, in answer to Pasvolsky's final point, stated flatly that the council was responsible for all political issues.[17]

The next evening, on June 1, the Big Five reconvened. Gromyko said he had finally received instructions from Moscow, and the answer was *nyet*. The Soviet government did not agree with the viewpoint about discussion held by the Americans, British, and French. The Soviet regime, Gromyko said, believed that discussion was the first step in the chain of events that would inevitably lead to enforcement action or war. Therefore, it was a political issue and must be subject to the veto. He promised that the Soviets would use the veto rarely, but his government would not retreat from this position, which, in its opinion, was the only proper interpretation of the Yalta accord.

Senator Vandenberg described the shocked reaction of the Americans: "When Gromyko made his report to us in the Penthouse, we all knew that we had reached the 'zero hour' of this great adventure. . . . Did it mean the immediate break-up of the Conference? Did it mean going on to a Charter without Russia?" The Soviet decision "collides with the grim conviction of almost every other power at Frisco. It is 'Yalta' carried to the final, absurd extreme." Stettinius wrapped up the meeting quickly without saying anything in reply. He wanted time to figure out his response. The resourceful Reston soon got wind of the drama, probably through Vandenberg and Dulles, who were both fiercely anti-Soviet. On the following two days, June 2 and June 3, he penned front-page stories with successive headlines that attested to the growing crisis: "Moscow Rejects US-British View of Yalta Formula" and, twenty-four hours later, "Russia Asks Global Veto for Big Five, Parley Split Wide."[18]

Stettinius phoned Truman the next morning. The conversation was brief and to the point. He informed the president about the stalemate, and Truman reiterated his position that "this interpretation was completely unacceptable to the United States." Stettinius then broached an idea borrowed from Lord Halifax, which was to make a private approach to Stalin about the veto and use the coincidence of Harry Hopkins's visit to Moscow as the means of transmitting the U.S. concern. Stettinius reminded Truman that, on previous occasions, Stettinius had found "that Stalin had not always been informed of the instructions that had been issued by the Kremlin, and that on occasion, it had been Molotov himself who had failed to inform his superior." Truman, who detested Molotov, gave him the go-ahead, but told him to do it secretly. Thereafter, Stettinius began to draft an urgent cable to Hopkins and Averell Harriman, the U.S. ambassador, without notifying the U.S. delegation, asking their help on this matter.[19]

At a gathering of the Big Four just hours after his Truman chat, Stettinius sternly gave the U.S. position: "It would be utterly impossible for us," he told Gromyko, to join an organization holding veto power over discussion. "Tension in the room," recalled Stettinius, "was extreme." He continued, "I did not mince matters at all," for it was vital that "the importance of our stand could not be misunderstood." When Gromyko began to read from the Dumbarton Oaks text, Stettinius cut him off coldly; the United States had, he said, "stated [its] position and our efforts would result in no Charter at all if the Soviet view should prevail." Gromyko responded harshly by calling the U.S. position a "retreat" and a "unilateral" interpretation of Yalta unsupported by the language of the accord. Senators Vandenberg and Connally chimed to say in that the U.N. Charter would not pass the Senate without a guarantee of free discussion. Connally drawled sarcastically in his Texas twang that if members applied to the Security Council for help, it would be better to "send 'em to the deaf and dumb asylum instead." The British, Chinese, and French also threw their support behind the administration's views.[20]

That same day, June 2, Stettinius sent his telegram to Hopkins and Harriman. "We have reached a very serious crisis in the Conference in San Francisco," Stettinius wired the two men. "We feel that [the Soviet position] would make a farce of the whole proposed world organization." Until now, Stettinius observed, the Soviets had never publicly disagreed with or contradicted the U.S. understanding of Yalta, even after the State Department released its gloss, including Roosevelt's own words published just after the conference. Stalin might not know, Stettinius suggested, what was taking place in his name: "Please tell him in no uncertain words that this country would not possibly join an organization based on so unreasonable an interpretation of the provision of the great powers in the Security Council." The United States would not accept, Stettinius concluded, this "wholly new and impossible interpretation" of the Soviets.[21]

By the next day, Stettinius was depressed over Reston's second front-page article on the Gromyko rebuff. He feared that the piece, by appearing to place all the blame on the Russians, might derail any behind-the-scenes endeavors to settle the disagreements through Hopkins. He discussed with Pasvolsky how to handle the leak. Pasvolsky remarked: "This article has done us more harm than anything else." The main reason was that "we have taken a position from which we cannot withdraw and we have put them in exactly the same position." Pasvolsky's concern was that now, even if Hopkins did convince Moscow to adopt the U.S. viewpoint, it would be at the cost of publicly humiliating the Soviet government. Rather than face such an embarrassing situation, the Kremlin was not likely to budge at all. Pasvolsky's pessimism coincided with the general gloom spreading among the delegates.[22]

Given a lack of progress, Stettinius decided once more to call in Gromyko for a talk. The next day, June 4, in another penthouse session, Stettinius went out of his way to reassure Gromyko that to his knowledge none of his delegates had spoken with the press. He now suggested that Moscow and Washington issue a joint statement outlining subjects on which they did agree to give the conference and the U.S. public confidence that the U.N. meeting was making progress. Gromyko sourly replied that the idea was "unnecessary" since the media already had all the information it needed. Pasvolsky, in attendance at Stettinius's invitation, made one last futile plea, asking Gromyko how the Security Council was supposed to vote on an issue if the facts weren't first presented to it. Gromyko gave a nonanswer, assuring him that free discussion was not, after all, prevented once a matter was placed on the agenda.[23]

As this discouraging encounter was taking place, an increasingly distraught Senator Vandenberg was conferring privately with his two fellow Republicans, Stassen and Dulles. "We all agreed that we could not possibly sanction any surrender to Russia on this matter," he confided to his diary. "We could no longer go along if there is any surrender to the Soviets upon this score." Dulles tossed in a memo of his own detailing the horrors that would flow from a U.S. back-down. Stettinius, who had not yet tipped off Vandenberg about his message to Hopkins and Harriman, learned that day of the Republican uneasiness. He saw Vandenberg at once. Vandenberg said that he wanted the U.S. delegation to issue a clear-cut statement setting forth the U.S. opposition to the Soviet position. If Washington did not do so, he added, "the Republicans are certainly going to do it."

Alarmed about a revival of partisanship, Stettinius called Truman and sought permission to tell Vandenberg about the Hopkins mission. With reluctance, Truman agreed. Stettinius called in Senators Connally and Vandenberg and promptly read his telegram aloud to them. "I was amazed," Vandenberg recalled. "It was magnificent in its unqualified assertion of our position. It would not have been stronger if I had written it myself. . . . I was proud of my country when I heard the Stettinius message. It is in the best American tradition."[24]

The next morning, Reston broke the story of the American approach to Stalin with a headline reading: "U.S., Britain to Ask Stalin End Veto Row." Whether Vandenberg or Dulles was responsible for the disclosure, it was clear that somebody on the U.S. team was intent on increasing the pressure on Moscow. A public showdown with Stalin was a potentially dangerous game. The gist of the Reston account was that the Western Allies felt ratification of the entire U.N. Charter would be "imperiled" without the right to discussion. But the article also divulged a new Western concern, namely, an apprehension that the Soviet stance could weaken the Security Council by shifting most discussion in the future to the General Assembly. Stettinius told his delegation that Reston's story had "put him in an embarrassing situation." In a follow-up piece the next day, Reston indicated that the U.S. position had hardened. Now, he stated authoritatively, Washington was of the view that its position on discussion was "as basic a principle as the freedom of speech principle in the First Amendment, and, if the issue is forced, there can be no doubt the United States will not retreat."[25]

Meanwhile, the smaller countries, who had forced the debate over the veto in the first place, were growing increasingly frustrated. Given the hostile Russian response to their questionnaire over the veto, they realized they might have pushed the Big Powers too far. One commentator felt they had committed a major blunder by sending their questionnaire to the Big Five. "The sole result of the attack of the smaller powers," the historian Sir Charles Webster observed, "was to make more hard and definite everything which they most disliked" about the veto. "When forced to define future actions," he continued, "states, like individuals, try to safeguard themselves against unforeseen contingencies. The Soviet Union, indeed, in such circumstances, pressed its point of view so far that the failure of the whole Conference was threatened." Now the little states began to consider backing off altogether on their demands and settling simply for the right to discussion without a veto.[26]

By now, the conference was on the edge of collapse. Everything was at a standstill. Stettinius told several foreign ministers on June 4 that "the hope of the ages should not be permitted to go on the rocks over the question of discussion and consideration." The U.S. delegation, while waiting for the Hopkins meeting with Stalin, privately considered what to do in the event of a defeat. Ironically, the Hopkins trip had been primarily organized to rekindle the embers of the old FDR-Stalin friendship. Now the entire U.N. Charter appeared to hinge on whether Hopkins could persuade Stalin to change his mind on this issue. Hopkins was also seeking a date for a summer summit with Truman, Churchill, and Stalin so that the major powers could settle the peace in the aftermath of the most destructive war in the history of humankind; not only that, he was trying to break the deadlock between the United States and the Soviet Union over Poland, the other unresolved issue still shadowing the U.N. Conference.[27]

Hopkins had only intended to deal with Poland—not the other controversies at San Francisco. Whatever diplomatic and political strengths he possessed—and they were considerable—Hopkins was a very ill man and could sustain only so many burdens. There was no guarantee that, at this very last minute, for all his past plenipotentiary achievements, he might be able to suture a wound as deep as this one apparently had become.

CHAPTER 13

THE MISSION TO MOSCOW

Harry Hopkins had first seen Truman two days after Roosevelt's death, on the morning of April 14. Only fifty-five years old, he was undoubtedly a sickly man. A tall, formidable figure, he had shrunk in physical stature, having lost seventeen pounds since his return from Yalta. He was suffering from stomach cancer, and a sojourn at the Mayo Clinic had not improved his health. His biographer, Robert Emmet Sherwood, wrote that he looked "like death." After preliminary talks, Truman asked Hopkins to stay for lunch. Toward the end of the meal, the new president inquired whether Hopkins might be willing to go on a "personal mission" for him to Stalin and reassure the Russian leader that Truman was not going to alter Roosevelt's policies. Hopkins begged off because of his ailments and suggested that Harriman go instead.[1]

Truman's appeal to Hopkins just a few days into his administration was understandable. Hopkins was a symbol of the successful wartime alliance. He had met the Soviet dictator three times—in July 1941 on a mission for FDR, at the Teheran Conference in 1943, and at Yalta—and had helped resolve some of the problems that inevitably cropped up in Soviet-American relations. In view of Hopkins's original interest in social work, his involvement in international affairs was unexpected. Hopkins served as Governor Franklin Roosevelt's director of the New York State emergency relief administration; on becoming president, Roosevelt recruited him to run the federal relief agency as well as launch the famous Works Progress Administration (WPA). By 1938, Hopkins had become FDR's secretary of commerce. When war broke out, Roosevelt asked him to head up the Lend-Lease Program. In the 1940s, Hopkins grew so close to the president that he eventually lived in the White House and Roosevelt made him his personal emissary to the wartime Allies.

Following the arguments in San Francisco over Poland and other matters that had so soured Soviet-American relations, Truman saw Hopkins again on May 4 and May 5, three weeks after their first encounter. By now, the president was preoccupied with what to do with the Soviets, especially by the lack of progress in resolving the fate of the Lublin regime. That sore seemed to infect every aspect of his communications with Stalin and threatened failure at San Francisco. Yalta had clearly not brought an end to the Poland problem, as had been hoped; instead, the three officials designated by the Crimean leaders to reorganize the regime—Averell Harriman, British envoy to the USSR Sir Archibald Clark Kerr, and Foreign Minister Molotov—bickered regularly over the meaning of the Big Three accord. Later, Truman's angry tangle with Molotov at the White House and his subsequent messages to the Kremlin had led nowhere. Finally, Molotov's precipitous attempt to seat the Warsaw regime at the U.N. meeting had proven to be an embarrassing flop. From whatever angle one viewed these incidents, as E. B. White observed in San Francisco, "over the city the Polish question hovered like a foul bird."[2]

Now a more ominous controversy over Poland was brewing. Less than twenty-four hours before Truman's two days of talks with Hopkins, Stettinius had learned from Molotov that sixteen Poles, missing since late March and subject to numerous unanswered inquiries by the U.S. and British governments, had been arrested by Soviet soldiers for "diversionist acts against the Red Army." The Soviets accused the underground fighters (and one above-ground official) of causing the deaths of more than one hundred Russian soldiers and using "illegal radio transmitters" within the territory controlled by the Soviet Army in order to talk with the exile command in London. But the displaced Poles stationed in England told a different tale: namely, that the Russians on March 27 had lured the fifteen men, all distinguished resistance leaders or prewar political chiefs, into a trap by promising them a meeting with top Soviet generals to discuss a new Polish state, then convincing them to shed their covers by guaranteeing their safety and imprisoning them the moment they revealed themselves. Nothing had been known of their whereabouts until Molotov's revelation to Stettinius.[3]

As a consequence of this unsettling news, British Foreign Minister Anthony Eden and Stettinius met with Molotov on the evening of May 4, in the midst of their intensive work on the Big Five amendments, to discuss the matter of the jailed Poles. When they pressed Molotov for details, he gave unsatisfactory answers. Both decided that, under the circumstances, they could not discuss the Polish question any longer. The next day, Stettinius issued a public statement, along with one from Eden, in which he elaborated his reasons for breaking off talks: "We told Mr. Molotov of our great concern on learning, after such a long delay, of this disturbing development which has a direct bearing on the working out of the Polish problem. . . . We have asked Mr. Molotov for a complete list of names of these Polish leaders who have been arrested and a full explanation of this action. Further discussions must await a reply." Vandenberg called the whole episode "bad business." As Anne O'Hare McCormick aptly noted, the power of the Polish issue was such that it "beclouded other questions, became the touchstone of cooperation among the great powers."[4]

Against this backdrop, Hopkins and Truman now discussed what might be done to improve relations with the Russians. Measuring Hopkins as a "man of courage" despite his health, Truman "presumed again," he wrote, "to raise the subject of [Hopkins's] undertaking a mission to Stalin." Hopkins this time expressed a willingness to go. But Truman then hedged on the proposal; before making a decision, he wanted first to consult with, among others, Cordell Hull, James Byrnes, Averell Harriman, officials at the State Department (though not Stettinius) and, of course, Stalin himself. Byrnes and some in the State Department, he soon learned, opposed the trip, feeling that Hopkins was overly trusting of Stalin. Harriman, on the other hand, despite his duties as U.S. envoy to the USSR, vigorously urged Truman to send Hopkins—an idea he had gotten from Charles Bohlen on the flight back to Washington from San Francisco. "Stalin had told me of his respect for

Hopkins' courage and determination," Harriman later recalled. "He had been particularly impressed that Hopkins should have made the long trip to Russia in July 1941 in spite of his ill health." Harriman and Bohlen now called on Hopkins at his home in Georgetown to plead with him to make the trip. Hopkins, recalled Harriman, did not have to be persuaded; he was ready to hit the trail like an "old war horse." But he feared Truman might pass him over because of his illness. Two other advisors finally clinched it for Hopkins: Hull, his longtime foe, and Stalin himself, both opted for the old FDR hand. With their endorsements, Truman felt confident enough to dispatch Hopkins.[5]

In the interim, the Polish situation had worsened. On May 10, Stalin, in reply to a cable from Truman, who had once again urged Stalin's compliance with the Yalta agreement on Poland, delivered a rude response. He insisted that since "you are unwilling to consider" the Lublin team "as a basis" for a new government, "I am obliged to say that this attitude rules out an agreed decision on the Polish question." Later, on May 19, in replies to a series of written questions from an English correspondent based in Moscow, Stalin laid down three "elementary" conditions for settlement of the crisis: that the Warsaw government be the "core" of any coalition regime; that the new state shall "pursue a policy of friendship with the Soviet Union and not the policy of *cordon sanitaire*"; and that the reorganization of the government be "resolved with the Poles who at present have ties with the Polish nation and not without them"—apparently ruling out exiles and underground resistance. Anne O'Hara McCormick noted that, in the enumeration of Stalin's stipulations, the fact that Molotov on his return from San Francisco had made no apparent effort to convey the views of U.N. delegates to the marshal about Poland— or, if he had, that the information had made no impact on Stalin, "dispels the hope that democratic opinion as plainly expressed in San Francisco might influence Soviet policy on this issue." Crowning these events was Truman's abrupt decision in mid-May to terminate Lend-Lease to the Soviet Union with the war in Europe over—a decision that jarred Stalin deeply (Truman quickly reversed it under heavy criticism).[6]

On the day that the Stalin interview was released, Hopkins returned to the White House to receive his parting instructions. Truman charged

Hopkins at this meeting to tell Stalin that the United States expected him "to carry out his agreements," and added, "I made it plain to Hopkins that in talking to Stalin, he was free to use diplomatic language or a baseball bat if he thought that was the proper approach." In addition, though, he wanted Hopkins to convey the message that he was willing to meet with Stalin "personally" at any time. And, as he scribbled later in his diary, "I want peace and I am willing to work hard for it," emphasizing that, "to have a reasonably lasting peace, the three great powers must be able to trust each other." He told Stettinius in a meeting a few days later, "Harry will be able to straighten things out with Stalin." He is going to "make it clear to Uncle Joe Stalin that I knew what I wanted—and that I intended to get—peace for the world for at least 90 years." But, unacknowledged, Truman gave the special envoy far more running room to deal with Stalin than might have been evident at the time. In private notes he wrote to himself, Truman had also instructed Hopkins to tell Stalin that, for the sake of peace, "Poland, Romania, Bulgaria, Czechoslovakia, Austria, Yugoslavia, Latvia, Lithuania, Estonia, et al make no difference to U.S. interests"—that, indeed, an election in Poland could be as free as Tom Pendergast's in Kansas or Boss Hague's in Chicago. It was a clear concession to a Soviet sphere of influence in Eastern Europe, representing an abrupt about-face from the tougher sentiments Truman had expressed about Poland to Molotov in the early days of his administration.[7]

On May 23, Hopkins departed for Moscow, accompanied by his wife and Charles Bohlen. The trio first flew to Paris, where they met up with Harriman, who had just visited Churchill—and then all took a plane across conquered Germany. Peering out of a window, Hopkins looked down at the ruins of Berlin and remarked: "It's another Carthage." The foursome arrived in Moscow on the evening of May 25. Hopkins expected at most to stay four or five days, but his visit lasted two weeks. The next evening, on May 26, at 8:00 P.M., Hopkins met with Stalin, Harriman, Bohlen, and Motolov; a Soviet interpreter was also present. Hopkins began the meeting on a note of levity, asking Molotov whether "he had recovered from the battle of San Francisco." Molotov replied with a smile that he did not recall any battles, merely "arguments" at the U.N. Conference.[8]

Hopkins then spent some time explaining to Stalin why Truman had requested that he make this trip. Hopkins himself "had not been well and would not be in Moscow unless he had felt the situation was serious." He said that he had to be honest and say there had been a "deterioration of public opinion" in the United States toward the Soviet Union in the last six weeks that was "adversely" affecting relations between the two countries. "[I]f present trends continued unchecked," he continued, "the entire structure of world cooperation and relations with the Soviet Union . . . would be destroyed." The problem, he said, centered on Poland. Stalin interrupted Hopkins at that point and said that all the USSR desired at this time was a "friendly Poland," but that British conservatives were intent on stirring up trouble by reviving a system of cordon sanitaire along Soviet borders. Hopkins, who had little sympathy for the British imperialists, answered that the U.S. "would desire a Poland friendly to the Soviet Union and in fact desired to see friendly countries all along the Soviet borders"—an echo of Truman's note a few days earlier. Stalin's reply was a notable one: "[I]f that be so, we can easily come to terms in regard to Poland." This short exchange apparently set the accommodating tone for the remainder of Hopkins's discussions with the Soviet leader over Poland.[9]

By next evening, Hopkins and Stalin began to move further along in their Polish discussions. But the Soviet leader raised the ante a bit by asking Hopkins to explain more fully why Washington had endorsed Argentina's admission to the United Nations and why it, too, had suspended Lend-Lease aid to the USSR. Stalin pointed out that Buenos Aires had not, as required by Yalta, declared war on Germany by March 1 and, in the instance of Lend-Lease, Washington's manner of cancellation was an "unfortunate and even brutal" one. Stalin advised that if the U.S. was planning to use Lend-Lease to put pressure on the Soviets "to soften them up, then it was a fundamental mistake." In his answers, Hopkins cited pressure from Latin America on Washington for Argentina's membership and a "mistaken order" for causing the Lend-Lease mishap. He promised that no such miscues would happen again and asserted that neither episode should impair U.S. ties with the USSR. Stalin, in his turn, conceded that the Argentina question now "belonged to the past" and accepted Hopkins's explanation for the Lend-Lease misadventure—though he did say that, until its cutoff, he had once considered making "a suitable expression of gratitude to the United States" for the aid.[10]

Returning to the subject of Poland, Hopkins now reiterated that the U.S. had "no special desire to see any particular kind of government," but simply wanted one chosen by the Polish people in free elections and "at the same time friendly to the Soviet government." But Washington did not wish to be excluded from the process of creating the new state. Stalin said that his nation was concerned that Germany had twice invaded Russia through Poland, so, of course, Moscow did not plan to allow that to happen again. It must have a cooperative neighbor. At the same time, he could not understand why the Yalta agreement had been subject to so much confusion since it quite plainly called for the new government to be formed "on the basis" of the existing regime in Lublin. Still, he recognized that U.S. was a world power and had a right to participate in Polish affairs. Consequently, he was willing to offer four cabinet posts out of twenty in a newly organized "provisional government of national unity" to individuals chosen by the British and U.S. administrations—with the proviso that the Poles selected be well-disposed toward the Soviet Union. He said he would accept, for example, the leader of the large prewar Peasants Party, Stanislaw Mikolajczyk, whom he felt had shown a cordial attitude toward the Soviet Union. Hopkins promised to consider the marshal's suggestion.[11]

Three days later, at their fourth meeting, Hopkins delivered his response to Stalin's proposal. He said that all he had been trying to do for the Poles was give them the opportunity to have a democracy—something the United States valued deeply. Stalin replied that democracy was a luxury only for peacetime and that, even then, it was not for Fascist-type parties. Hopkins said he "thoroughly understood the Marshal's opinions," but, nonetheless, he had to report that a "strong feeling" existed in the United States "that the Soviet Union wished to dominate Poland." He did not share that view, he said, but it was a sentiment that had to be acknowledged. Meanwhile, though, if Stalin was worried that the exile government in London would exert undue influence on a new Warsaw regime, he wanted to explain that "we had no interest" in its participation. Furthermore, Washington "had always anticipated that the members of the present Polish government would constitute a majority" of the members of a new state. Hopkins's views might have surprised Secretary Stettinius, who had vociferously insisted to Molotov in San Francisco on the necessity for the involvement of the London Poles in any regime, and for a tripartite sharing of power among the exiles, the underground, and the Lublin faction in the final make-up of an administration.[12]

But Hopkins was apparently following the Truman script as closely as he thought was reasonable under the circumstances, conceding Stalin's formidable strength on the matter. In any event, Stalin replied that he was agreeable to inviting eight Poles outside of the Lublin regime for consultations—three from London and five from Poland. After his session, Hopkins sent an upbeat cable to Truman saying that Stalin was prepared "to permit a representative group of Poles to come to Moscow" to join a new government. The next day, Stalin and Hopkins at their fifth session actually began to exchange the names of possible candidates for the Polish cabinet, discarding any officials out of favor with the Russians. Hopkins then briefly also brought up the plight of the Polish prisoners. At a dinner given in Hopkins's honor that same night, on Truman's instructions, Hopkins openly pleaded for the lives of the sixteen imprisoned Poles. Stalin said he could not delay or adjourn the trials, but he promised that the individuals "would be treated leniently." Having done his duty, Hopkins returned to the talks on a Polish settlement. It appeared now that, not wishing to jeopardize any deal, he had decided to separate the issue of the detainees from the issue of forming a provisional government. On the evening of June 1, he called Truman to get his OK for this strategy. The president approved it and the consultations continued.[13]

Suddenly, Hopkins received the urgent telegram from Stettinius asking for his help on the veto dispute. At that time, Hopkins had taken several days off from his sessions with Stalin to use his free hours to review the Polish bidding and do some sight-seeing while Harriman worked with the Soviets on the final details of the list of Poles for the

Warsaw ministries. Now, with this alert from Stettinius, Hopkins turned to educate himself on the particulars of the U.N. veto controversy before his next and final meeting with Stalin. On the evening of June 6, he went to Stalin's office and moved directly to the issue of the veto. Harriman, who had been at San Francisco, explained the rationale for veto-free discussions. Molotov interjected that the Soviet disagreement with the United States "was based squarely on the Crimea decision." Stalin impatiently interrupted Molotov, asking him in Russian what this dispute was all about. Stalin had appeared not to understand—or at least pretend not to know—what was involved. Molotov explained the situation to him, whereupon he remarked that he thought "it was an insignificant matter and that they should accept the American position." Stalin turned to Hopkins and said that he agreed with the U.S. position. He blamed the small states for stirring up all this trouble—implying that great power unity required disregarding the interests of lesser nations. In this sudden stroke, Stalin had cut the rope that had threatened to strangle the U.N. at its birth. As Stettinius later wrote, "If Stalin had adamantly supported Molotov, there would have been no United Nations formed at San Francisco."[14]

The puzzle is why, after almost two weeks of tension at San Francisco, Stalin abruptly surrendered the Soviet position on the absolute veto without so much as an argument, dismissing it as a sideshow of no great import. Surely he had to be aware of what was happening at the U.N., especially regarding the Allies' disgruntlement. He was receiving regular reports from Molotov, who kept tight rein on the Soviet delegation. Furthermore, Gromyko was going around the conference championing the cause of the full veto in Stalin's name. Perhaps Hopkins's presence in Moscow quieted some of Stalin's concerns on this matter since Hopkins was known to be sympathetic to Stalin for the sacrifices his country had incurred during the war. In addition, Stalin probably knew, too, that, if he could work out some sort of deal with Truman's special emissary on Poland, he might assure U.S. economic help to Russia in the future—including a possible continuation of Lend-Lease.

But there may have been a deeper calculation behind his change of mind. He had won the struggle with the West over the primacy of the

Lublin regime. Why not now let the Allies have their way at the U.N.?
If the West was now, in effect, going to tolerate his occupation of Eastern Europe, and, in particular, Poland, and thereby protect his borders,
he could certainly afford to show magnanimity on an issue less than
vital to the USSR's security. The Soviet Union would, of course, still retain the veto on enforcement, which was all that really mattered to
Stalin. The Russian leader had made a similar compromise at Yalta,
when, in exchange for accepting Roosevelt's veto plan, Stalin had won
FDR's consent to the Soviet formula on Poland; and, now, as Hopkins
acquiesced in Russia's latest Polish arrangements, Moscow was undoubtedly less anxious about the Allies' request for the limited veto.[15]

Was Hopkins—and by extension Truman—right to give in to Stalin
over Poland? They really had no choice. Russia occupied Poland and
was determined to keep it at all costs. Furthermore, the USSR still had 1
million men whom it could put into the fight against Japan in a war the
United States had not yet won. In addition, a peaceful settlement between Moscow and Washington promised the benefits of long-term cooperation. The Soviet Union could cripple, if not entirely scuttle, the
United Nations if it did not get its way over Poland. In any event, the
United States was not prepared to go to war over that country. The nation was weary from fighting; indisputably, it would have opposed further combat in Europe—and the Pacific War still had to be won. As
Stettinius himself noted, "It was not a question of what Great Britain
and the United States would permit Russia to do in Poland, but what
the two countries could persuade the Soviet Union to accept." Or as
Robert Donovan ventured from a different perspective: "Whatever
diplomatic chips may once have been on the American side of the table
had long ago been spent. They had been used to shore up the military
alliance with Stalin, to win his promise to enter the Japanese war, and
to bring him into the United Nations."[16]

Indeed, given the realities throughout Eastern Europe, the most that
the United States might have aspired to at this time was the hope that
global public opinion—perhaps expressed through the U.N.—might
eventually force the Soviets to allow democratic elections in Poland. So,
in the end, Truman felt that the Hopkins trade-off was a deal he could

live with. As his biographer, Alonzo Hamby, observed, "On substance, the pact was a defeat for American policy, but it wore fig leaves that were vital to [Truman]. Stalin had conceded on U.N.-related matters of no importance to him; Truman had caved on Poland, but few Americans cared." Truman had made a virtue out of necessity. Still, as Charles Bohlen astutely reflected, the truth in the last instance was that Stalin "held all the cards and played them well. Eventually we had to throw in the hand."[17]

In San Francisco, all the behind-the-scenes maneuvering was unknown and, for most of the diplomats, irrelevant. The only thing that mattered was settling the veto dispute. Stettinius received the welcome news from Harriman midday on June 6 via Undersecretary Joseph Grew, who received a telegram from Moscow. Stettinius was elated. He invited Gromyko to the penthouse and related what he had heard: "I feel I owe it to you in all friendliness," he said, "to tell you immediately of this word." He reported that "Ambassador Gromyko's expression was rather strained and he had a ruddy complexion." The Kremlin, it turned out, had not yet divulged its decision to him. Gromyko begged off talking any further about the veto until he had received his instructions from Stalin. The next day, his marching orders arrived. Stettinius now persuaded Gromyko that the two of them should sit down and prepare a joint statement to dampen any speculation that this turn of events might "appear as a defeat for the Soviet Union and a victory for the U.S." Rather, said Stettinius, it should be seen as a common accord among the five permanent members to agree on the meaning of Yalta.[18]

Gromyko reluctantly acceded to Stettinius's plan. By the time of the Big Five meeting at 3:00 P.M. on the afternoon of June 7, Stettinius was able to open the session by saying, "Ambassador Gromyko has a statement to make." Gromyko delivered his remarks in a slow cadence. He grudgingly edged away from his original position and now stated: "The Soviet Government continues to consider that Yalta prevents deviation from unanimity. But in the interest of unanimity of [the] four sponsoring powers," the Soviets, he said, would permit the change as laid out in the interpretive document of May 26—the unpublished statement drafted by the Big Five, which endorsed the original U.S. position on discussion—as an "exception." However, he insisted that any "further" items not squarely listed as procedural in the charter should be treated as substantive questions and therefore subject to the veto. All parties agreed on this. A later, more formal statement issued by the Soviets elaborated a bit defensively on Gromyko's remarks: "Our policy has never been inflexible; we know this to be a favorite opinion but it is completely without foundation. If a point is proved to us with which we disagree and we see and feel that it is based on good will and justified desires, we agree to it. Exactly that has happened now. You have convinced us and we agreed."[19]

Vandenberg's response in his notebook, though, was: "America Wins! The 'veto' crisis broke today—and it broke our way. . . . It is a complete and total surrender. No attempt at any weasel-worded compromise." He lauded the secretary of state: "I think everyone is convinced that the blunt, unconditional message which Stettinius sent to Moscow turned the trick." At the same meeting, Vandenberg and the rest of the U.S. delegation agreed on a joint press release with the Big Five that they planned to offer to the U.N. that states an agreed-upon interpretation of the veto, and, more broadly, was their formal reply to the twenty-three questions submitted by the smaller nations. Amidst the collective euphoria, Stettinius watched as his two chief word-smiths, Pasvolsky and Dulles, labored on this new pronouncement. Pasvolsky, he wrote, "was perched high on one of the little gold chairs with red plush seats, pressed between Lord Halifax and myself. He indeed was the picture of a little wizard sitting against the background view of San Francisco and the treeless tow-colored hills in the far distance." Dulles "wandered about the open center of the floor across the elaborately figured oriental rug, with his hands jammed into his pockets, his head bowed a little, especially as he bent over to consult with me or someone else among the U.S. delegates or advisors. As he listened during these little interchanges of consultation, he blinked slightly through his dark thick glasses."[20]

As the statement was being drafted, Stettinius attended a meeting of the Steering Committee and delivered the news about the veto breakthrough. There was immediate "resounding applause," he reported, including "pounding on the tables"—but, on the sidelines, Evatt sat unimpressed. Stettinius attended a press conference, which drew a huge throng of newsmen, and disclosed for the first time the outcome of the controversy. The assembled reporters clapped spontaneously. Indeed, a half-dozen or so correspondents sought Stettinius out at the podium and shook his hand, offering their congratulations.

Minutes later, Stettinius was on the phone to Truman. "It's all done," he told him, "and it had the most electrifying effect you can possibly imagine." Truman was delighted. "It gives me a mighty good feeling, too." Stettinius told the president that he was "playing down" the triumph in deference to the Soviets. Truman agreed: "Yes, indeed. We have got a lot of other things to settle with them, you know." Stettinius told Truman that now, as a result of these recent delays, the closing of the U.N. meeting would still be several weeks off, meaning that the president's much-postponed trip to the West Coast had to be put off yet again. Truman gamely okayed the delay. That night, Stettinius dined at a local spaghetti restaurant, Amelio's, where, in celebration, the proprietor opened a magnum of Three-Star Hennessey for everyone at the Stettinius table.[21]

The next day's *New York Times* (June 8) heralded in a large headline, "Veto Row Is Ended as Russia Yields, Permitting Discussion of Disputes." This news overshadowed even the report that Hopkins had also secured both a date and a site for the Big Three summit at Potsdam. In his account, James Reston cautioned that, other than on discussions, the veto power still held intact. It applied, for example, to all military actions, investigations, and recommendations for settlements. Furthermore, the smaller nations, which had cranked up a considerable momentum in their campaign to limit the veto, saw their crusade now lurch to a halt. "The truth is," wrote Reston, "that the Russians have, by their tactics, produced the votes, if not the whole-hearted support, of the small powers for a Big Five veto over virtually every decision in the Security Council, except a decision on the right of the Council to take up a case and hear discussion on it."[22]

An editorial in the following day's *New York Times* hailed the veto settlement as a "victory for Secretary Stettinius and his colleagues on the

American delegation" and, for the Soviets, a "highly abstract and theoretical loss compared with what they gain in immediate and practical
good will." For Anne O'Hare McCormick, the lesson was that "the weak
have one weapon by which they can influence the powerful—the
weapon of persuasion—and it has worked at San Francisco." The *Times*
now carried the entire 1,400-word text of the Big Five answer to the
twenty-three questions. It contained the rationale for the veto, explicated
at length by the five permanent council members. Their central argument
was that, beyond discussion, the Big Powers, as the nations that would
supply the troops for the U.N., had to be allowed to veto "decisions and
actions by the Security Council [that] may well have major political consequences and may even initiate a chain of events" that could lead to enforcement measures. Nonetheless, this system, they argued, was far
preferable to that of the old League of Nations, which had required the
unanimous support of every member before any intervention could
occur because all states possessed the veto. Still, to be on the safe side,
each of the five permanent members also issued individual public warnings to the lesser states saying that if the formula on the veto was not
adopted at San Francisco, there was going to be no organization.[23]

Some of the smaller states took offense at the Big Five's position,
which they considered imperious. They felt that the Big Powers' declaration did not deal with all of their twenty-three questions, was too
general in its exposition, did nothing to modify the veto, and treated
all new items for the Security Council now as matters subject to the
veto. As a consequence, over the next few days, Herbert Evatt attempted last-minute efforts to derail or amend the agreement. On June
8, the day after Gromyko's concession, Evatt claimed that "at first
glance" the accord seemed to allow the Big Five to use their veto
weapon to determine whether an issue in dispute was procedural or
not. Senator Connally, Evatt's formidable adversary, pounced on his remarks and said to him sharply: "If you want to go away from San Francisco with a charter, let us deal with this promptly." On June 12, Evatt
launched a major campaign to include peaceful settlements among the
procedural items in the charter not subject to the veto. Stettinius immediately warned the White House, "Evatt is running around to every

committee and is just like a wild steer, doing everything possible he can to break this Conference up," and asked that Truman convey formal U.S. displeasure to Australian officials. Once again, though, Connally acted as the enforcer for the Big Five. Connally recalled the scene vividly: "Then standing before the assembled delegates with a copy of the charter draft in my hands, I made the final plea. 'You may go home from San Francisco—if you wish,' I cautioned the delegates, 'and report that you have defeated the veto. Yes,' I went on, 'You can say you defeated the veto. . . . But you can also say, 'We tore up the charter!' At that point, I sweepingly ripped the charter draft in my hands to shreds and flung the scraps with disgust on the table. The delegates fell silent, while I stared belligerently at one face after another."[24]

Connally's theatrical gesture may have helped save the day for Stettinius, but he also almost cost the secretary a victory. In the end, the Australian amendment lost 20 to 10, with fifteen abstentions and five absent. Though the margin looked impressive, the number of abstentions nonetheless showed a serious amount of antipathy among the smaller nations over the veto. Among those either opposing or abstaining were many of the Latin nations that Rockefeller had so assiduously cultivated. As Vandenberg wrote in his diary on June 14: "It is perfectly evident that most of the nations do not like any part of this 'veto' business. Led by Dr. Evatt of Australia, they have put up a bitter fight. But it also has been evident from the first that this kind of a League (dependent primarily upon the Big Five for its real authority) must have the Big Five veto in all matters involving force. Yesterday the other nations simply surrendered to the inevitable." This was Evatt's last grand battle. His defeat sounded the death knell for the small nations' revolt.[25]

On June 13, Harry Hopkins breakfasted with President Truman at the White House. Truman gave him profuse thanks for his accomplishments in Moscow and asked whether he might now be willing to accompany the U.S. delegation to the Potsdam Conference the following month. Hopkins politely turned him down, believing his presence might undermine the secretary of state, especially given Hopkins's track record of bypassing institutional authority at the behest of presidents. Truman granted the validity of Hopkins's argument and did not press him to reconsider. Shortly after the meeting, Truman held a press conference with some two hundred correspondents. He told the assemblage that the Hopkins agreement was "gratifying." As for U.S. relations with the USSR, he said that there had been "a very pleasant yielding on the part of the Russians in regard to Poland." "The Russians," he said, "are just as anxious to get along with us as we are to get along with them." When some journalists recalled Stettinius's stern admonition in San Francisco that Washington would not talk with Moscow about Poland until the status of the sixteen jailed Poles was "cleared up," Truman conceded that the United States had modified its position regarding the arrested men. Truman insisted now, however, that "every effort" was being made on the prisoners' behalf. Meanwhile, Washington was moving forward with the Russians to establish a new government in Warsaw. He hoped, he added, that its first act would be to hold free elections.[26]

A few days later, several exiled Poles, including Mikolajczyk and the Lublin comrades, gathered in Moscow to map out the details for a new regime. Meantime, on June 21, after a brief trial in which no witnesses for the defense were permitted because of "transport difficulties," twelve of the sixteen imprisoned Poles were found guilty as charged and sentenced. Their punishments ranged from ten years for General Okulicki to one to eight years for six of the men, the remainder receiving eight months or less. The Soviet prosecutor, a Russian general, declared: "Let the sentence be a warning to all enemies of the Soviet Union who are trying to shake the friendship of the United Nations." Hopkins remained convinced that his talks with Stalin had lessened the severity of the penalties. On June 23, the informal coalition of Poles in Moscow announced a twenty-one-member cabinet for the new government; seven seats went to democratic Poles, the rest to Communist Party members or their sympathizers. Mikolajczyk became vice premier. The *New York Times* editorialized on June 25 that the new administration was only "provisional" until elections were held. On July 5—eleven days after the United Nations Conference concluded—the U.S. and British governments granted diplomatic recognition to the new government of "national unity" and withdrew their ties to the exiles in London. Following its announcement, Poland gained admission to the U.N. Eventually, on January 19, 1947, the first Polish elections were held. They were widely seen as fraudulent. In October, 1947, Mikola-jczyk, after trying for two years to create a democratic opening in Poland, fled the country.[27]

Harry Hopkins returned to the White House for the last time on September 4, 1945, when President Truman honored him with the Distinguished Service Medal in the Rose Garden. Shortly thereafter, Hopkins moved to New York City, where he took a new job as labor arbitrator for the needles trade. Four months later, the illness that had plagued him all through the war finally consumed him; on January 29, 1946, he died.

The veto drama now subsided. The conference was back on track and the meeting was in the final leg of the race. Every indication was that the seemingly endless event would be over soon—until one final crisis.

CHAPTER 14

THE FINAL BATTLES

A s the San Francisco Conference neared its end, delegates, pressed on urgently by Secretary Stettinius and by President Truman, labored extra hours to make last-minute adjustments and forge final compromises over the language of the U.N. Charter. Truman was particularly eager to have the charter completed, signed, and ratified by the U.S. Senate in early July before his Big Three meeting in Postdam. But there was one last obstacle.

Ambassador Gromyko had a final complaint. On June 4, Gromyko objected to giving the General Assembly the broad right of discussion. At a Big Five session, he fought to retain the text in the Dumbarton Oaks draft that gave the assembly the power "to discuss any questions relating to the maintenance of peace and security" and decried newer language, adopted in San Francisco, permitting the assembly "to discuss any matter within the sphere of international relations" (though, in both instances, the assembly was precluded from reviewing issues already being heard by the Security Council). The distinction between the two passages hardly seemed to make a lot of difference. As a *New York Times* editorial noted bemusedly, the second set of words was perhaps broader "by at least a hair" than the first.[1]

But Gromyko felt the amended clause was "undesirable." Stettinius, taken aback by Gromyko's reproach, admonished him that an alteration in the amendment would be a "slap-down" to the smaller states that might upset the conference and harm the chances of the charter's adoption. He urged Gromyko to go easy on the question, saying that, if he pressed the matter, he would surely lose votes on the proposal in the committees. Instead, he suggested there might be a way of working out new phrasing. Neither Stettinius nor the U.S. delegation took Gromyko's initial umbrage very seriously. Most members were still transfixed by the struggle over the veto under discussion in the Security Council, believing that the settlement of that divisive matter would finally clear the way for adjournment. Further, it was not at all obvious why Gromyko was now raising this particular provision. In various exchanges, he hinted, though, that he did not want the General Assembly to pry into the domestic affairs of other countries, though that possibility already was foreclosed by a separate section of the charter. At one point, he vaguely alluded to the possibility that a nation disapproving an action of a neighbor on immigration or tariffs, even if that state acted legally, could subsequently raise a question in the assembly that was none of its business. At another point, he mentioned that somebody might want to discuss relations between Czechoslovakia and the USSR. In any event, he appeared to feel that the Big Powers had already made too many concessions to the smaller states.[2]

Stettinius and Vandenberg soon challenged Gromyko. Stettinius said the change in the passage had been a "small unimportant concession as a gesture to the small countries." Vandenberg, in his turn, labeled Gromyko's demand as an "attack on free speech" and an attempt to restrict open discourse in the "town meetings of the world." Vandenberg was especially puzzled by Gromyko's vexation since his own amendment, which had passed several weeks earlier, already allowed the assembly to debate and recommend on issues regarding "the peaceful adjustment of any situation, regardless of origin, which it deems likely to impair the general welfare"—as expansive a grant for talk as one could imagine. Senator Connally also pointed out that, in any event, the Big Powers still wielded the veto and could block any General Assembly action they disliked. Because of the curious nature of Gromyko's complaint, the British, French, and Chinese joined Stettinius in opposing the Soviets' request to raise the question at meetings of the Executive and Steering Committees (the latter composed of heads of all of the delegations).[3]

Gromyko remained unmoved. He told Stettinius that he had instructions from his government "to carry the question all the way through the Conference, if necessary." At a Big Five meeting on June 13, he grumbled openly again that the activities of the General Assembly should not be "unlimited." Three days after that, on the night of June 16, he informed the secretary of state flatly that the Soviets would not sign the charter unless the language was altered. Stettinius promptly notified President Truman of the growing crisis. He told Truman, according to Truman's account, that, among the majority of the delegates, "support for this proposal had grown stronger because it gave voice to the smaller nations, who felt they were being overshadowed by the dominant position of the Security Council and especially by the veto privilege of the permanent members."[4]

Vandenberg was now fearful of the outcome. "The last three days," he wrote in his diary, "has developed the latest and perhaps the worst of the Conference 'crises.'" Vandenberg was incredulous that "the whole amazing row is over these few limiting words" and further that "Gromyko's bitter objection . . . is wholly inscrutable." One member of the U.S. delegation, Harold Stassen, tried to change the U.S. position and rally support for the Soviet position, believing that the Russian request made no difference to the U.N. Charter—but to no avail. On Sunday, June 17, Gromyko finally made a private presentation at the Executive and Steering Committees arguing that the General Assembly's powers of deliberation were simply too broad. His remarks triggered an outburst by the smaller states, led by the Australian foreign minister, Herbert Evatt. Evatt contended that he and his fellow diplomats had already made many concessions on other charter provisions to guarantee the assembly's full right of consideration of all questions presented to it. Stettinius, sensing that the situation was now spinning out of control, took matters in hand. He persuaded Gromyko that day to form a subcommittee of himself, Evatt, and Stettinius to work out a solution.[5]

Stettinius's subcommittee met three times the same day, indicating the urgency Stettinius felt over the wrangle. Stettinius, after all, knew that in just nine days President Truman, after many delays, was coming to San Francisco to sign the charter. There was little time to wind things up. The secretary of state and Evatt devised compromise language. In place of the old Dumbarton Oaks clause, Evatt suggested that the right of the General Assembly on discussion now be defined to include "any matters covered by the purposes and principles of the Charter or within the sphere of action of the United Nations." Stettinius found the Evatt substitution acceptable. Gromyko rejected it. Stettinius, nonetheless, at the urging of a suddenly concerned Truman, who said he was ready to call Stalin himself, asked Gromyko to send the wording to Moscow for Molotov's review. The Soviet envoy agreed to do so. Meantime, Stettinius cabled the text on his own to Ambassador Harriman in Moscow with the request for him to "see Molotov at once" with it. "A bitter public debate on this subject in the final days of the conference," he wrote, "would in our opinion be extremely harmful." He warned that if the Senate did not get the charter by the end of June, it might be too late for that body to ratify it in July; thereafter, the Senate might cool on the entire project.[6]

To nobody's surprise, the story broke in the press. James Reston's lead story on Monday, June 18, reported the Soviet intransigence under the headline "Russians Demand Curb on Assembly or They Won't Sign." That same morning, Stettinius reproached the delegation at the daily U.S. meeting about the leak to Reston. Gromyko, he declared, "was of the impression that the United States was using the press as a means for bringing pressure to bear on the USSR." Blame immediately fell not on the U.S. delegates but on Evatt. By the next day, Stettinius received a message back from Harriman that Molotov had forwarded a new Soviet version for the charter. The draft, according to Harriman's notes, narrowed the General Assembly debate to "the scope of the functions or powers" of that section of the charter devoted to the assembly and to "the powers and functions of any of the organs provided for in the Charter." Evatt turned it down as too constricted. Vandenberg characterized the revision as "wholly unacceptable." According to Vandenberg, "Gromyko was obdurate." That same day, Truman arrived on the West Coast, landing in Washington State on a chief executive's first transcontinental flight ever in U.S. aviation history, a flight of twelve hours and sixteen minutes—before his next stop in a few days in San Francisco. Informed of Molotov's reply, Truman dismissed it as insufficient.[7]

That evening, in advance of yet another meeting of the Big Five, Stettinius went to Evatt and convinced him to modify some of his objections to Molotov's position. Next, he informed Gromyko that he had secured agreement from the smaller powers led by Evatt to accept the Soviet amendment with one "minor change." All they asked for, Stettinius reported, was a substitution for the phrase that had limited discussion to "within the scope of the functions or powers" of the assembly chapter of the charter. They proposed three alternatives: "within the sphere of the Charter"; "within the scope of the Charter"; or "within the sphere of action of the Organization." Any one of these phrases would provide the correct—and more expansive—foundation for discussion. Stettinius pointed out that "Mr. Evatt was not happy about the text, but would take it. He believed that we could not get a successful vote without this additional wording." Gromyko brushed off the Evatt idea as "indefinite," but promised to consult his government. Stettinius went behind Gromyko's back again and dispatched yet another urgent request to Harriman, pleading with him to "call on Molotov immediately" about the three alternatives proposed for the amendment. Otherwise, he warned Harriman, according to Vandenberg, the United States "would move alone" the next day. Vandenberg was thrilled by Stettinius's firm stance: "It was 'straight between the eyes.' He stood up like a concrete column." That evening, Vandenberg and the others, though, had uneasy sleep. "We all had a nervous night," he related. "There was a chance that the Soviets would kick everything over at the last minute."[8]

The next day, Wednesday, June 20, just six days before the official close of the conference, Gromyko announced at a midday meeting of the Big Five a Soviet turnabout. His country, he declared, now accepted the compromise. He had "instructions" from his government, Gromyko said, to incorporate one of the three alternatives. He would add the words "within the scope of the Charter." Vandenberg immediately reported "all smiles and sweetness." He told Gromyko that this outcome guaranteed "good will among the American people." Dulles, praising the Soviets for their concession, complimented Gromyko for engineering a "better result." Stettinius, relieved to have what appeared to be a final crisis at the conference resolved, expressed "his personal and official delight at the splendid conciliatory attitude of the Ambassador and his government, which had made it possible to solve this difficult matter." With that, the new amendment was rushed off to the U.N. committees and adopted.[9]

Why had Stalin—and Gromyko—caved in? The speculation was considerable. Some observers noted that much of the Soviet indignation during the U.N. Conference had been aimed mainly at the smaller countries. Soviet diplomats abhorred the behavior of the lesser lands, especially the Latin American states, which Molotov had considered particularly obstreperous over the issue of Argentina. Molotov was also dismayed over the collective dislike of the Latins for communism. Then there was Poland. The USSR team knew that it had aroused fear among the San Francisco conferees regarding its antics over the seating of the Warsaw delegation. But again, the Russians remembered only that the smaller nations opposed them on one of their cardinal causes. The final indignity in their minds was the attempt by the least regarded countries to circumscribe the veto. Perhaps, for the Kremlin, the most effective way to quash such obstructionism was limit the debate in the General Assembly. But the strategy pursued by Molotov and Gromyko, it was soon clear, was getting nowhere. And, facing a deadline for winding up the United Nations, Stalin apparently felt that he had to retreat and accept the cosmetic changes in the discussion passage to avoid further offending his allies.

With days to go, though, the United States and its compatriots still had several crucial gaps left in the charter provisions to fill in. One of the more fractious matters was the question of trusteeship. The Truman administration had ironed out internal differences between the War and State Departments over this issue just before the conference began. The U.S. military wanted to retain Japanese islands seized during the war, including the Marshalls, the Marianas, and the Carolines, as strategic bases under U.S. mandate, but Stettinius and his deputies wanted all such territories placed under General Assembly supervision, even while remaining in U.S. possession. Truman opted for the armed forces position, but he had no language to work with because the Big Three had not written a provision on trusteeship at the 1944 Dumbarton Oaks conference. Yalta meantime had restricted the definition of territories to a narrow list of existing mandates from the League of Nations, conquered territories, and whatever other parcels were voluntarily offered by states to the trustee command. But the Yalta participants felt the actual sorting out of what would eventually go to the U.N. should be left to the peace settlement; San Francisco should lay down only general principles on trusteeship.

On April 18, Leo Pasvolsky and a team of experts, including the trusteeship expert, Ralph Bunche, traveled on the Pre-Con Special train from Washington to San Francisco. They spent time drawing up the plans for a trusteeship system based on the compromise struck between Stettinius, Henry Stimson, secretary of war, and James Forrestal, secretary of the navy. By the time the train arrived in the Golden Gate City on the afternoon of April 22, Pasvolsky had fashioned a draft comprised of eleven guidelines. His first, and perhaps most important one, was how lands were to go into the U.N. system. Pasvolsky stated that the incorporation of properties into the trusteeship arrangement would happen only "by subsequent agreement" of a governing nation. This meant that the country holding on to a territory had the sole right to decide whether, where, and how it should be placed under U.N. authority. In short, the act of placement was to be an elective choice, not a compulsory one. John Foster Dulles recalled that the two senators on the delegation, Connally and Vandenberg, continuously wanted to make sure that the authority to assign territories to the organization remained in the hands of the states, not the U.N. Hence, according to Dulles, they "would always put to Commander Stassen this question: 'Are you sticking to the *subsequent agreement* provision?' Commander Stassen would regularly reply in the affirmative. Then the meeting would go on."[10]

Pasvolsky also carved out an exception for so-called strategic areas, as requested by the War Department. These areas were to remain under U.S. military control, and, if Washington consented to include them under the U.N., Pasvolsky insisted they would report only to the Security Council—not to the General Assembly's Trusteeship Council. The reason for designating the Security Council as the oversight chamber in these cases was that that venue would allow any one of the Big Five to veto meddling in the administration of their security outposts. Pasvolsky also proposed the idea of "self-government" for the U.N. territories, though deliberately omitting any mention of "independence" out of deference to the British and the French, the two colonial allies of the United States. He stipulated also that the trusteeship body should have the right to accept reports from the administering states, collect petitions, institute investigations, and initiate other actions in relation to trust properties. Finally, he recommended that the members of the Trusteeship Council be evenly balanced between the oversight states and noncolonial states. On the evening of April 26, Pasvolsky's brief was quickly adopted after a few emendations by the U.S. delegation.[11]

On that same day, Stettinius named Harold Stassen to lead the U.S. negotiations on trusteeships—along with John McCloy, assistant secretary of war, Abe Fortas, undersecretary of the interior, Ralph Bunche, and a few others. On April 30, the group met for the first time with the other Big Five consultative group. The U.S. plan became the centerpiece for review. Thereafter, Stassen commenced the task of sifting through drafts on the trusteeship question submitted by other nations and, most important, the French and British views against decolonization. Stassen and his assistants reviewed some four hundred pages of amendments from dozens of countries over a three-week period. Eventually, Stassen wove most of these suggestions together, discarding some, keeping others, into a comprehensive document that was accepted on May 17 by the U.N. Committee on Trusteeship as the basis for its deliberations. During this period, Stassen was regularly cajoled by the British, demanding that all strategic areas come under General Assembly, and by the Soviets wanting the Security Council alone to decide on which parcels should be taken into the U.N. Stassen, with Stettinius's help, eventually sidetracked these suggestions. The U.S. provisions, by and large, carried the day.[12]

A fight remained over the principles that would guide the handling of dependent peoples, namely, the natives dwelling in colonial possessions who, for the most part, were not self-governing and not under the U.N. trust authority. The ever-vigilant British advanced a provision obligating the administering country to help develop self-government, but not independence. The United States backed this position, with reluctance, but it was vociferously opposed by the USSR, China, and many smaller states. Indeed, some delegates, such as Carlos Romulo of the Philippines, stalked the conference seeking to make the goal of independence preeminent. Romulo became "a nuisance, a gadfly, a pest," by his own admission. "I prowled corridors, buttonholed delegates, cornered unwilling victims in hotel lobbies and men's rooms." But Stettinius was not about to allow anybody to jeopardize the outcome of his carefully designed Trusteeship Council. Despite divisions within the delegation over concern that the United States might be painted as an apologist for colonialism, the Truman administration was even more fearful that Churchill would defeat any Trusteeship Council at all if the word "independence" found its way into the chapter on dependent peoples. The United States was convinced, in any event, that "self-government" implied independence. Nonetheless, Stettinius did, in due course, forge a compromise whereby the British were able to retain the notion of self-government in the dependent peoples section; but the Americans, eager to burnish their image as anti-imperialists, were able to stick the word "independence" in the provision dealing with the principles of the trusteeship system, designated Chapter XII.[13]

Many delegates like Romulo remained disgruntled by the results. The three chapters dealing with trusteeship—Chapter XI, "Declaration Regarding Non-Self-Governing Territories"; Chapter XII, "The International Trusteeship System"; and Chapter XIII, "The Trusteeship Council"—though, proved far more potent as catalysts for change than many thought possible. Stettinius had believed that, over time, the high principles stated in the charter, as well as the combined force of public opinion in the dependent areas and around the world, would operate as a powerful influence to compel colonial overlords to relinquish control of their possessions and move toward independence. The record of the years since 1950 vindicated Stettinius's beliefs. As former U.N. official Sir Brian Urquhart noted more than five decades later, "The three chapters of the Charter on dependent peoples and trustee-ship gave a momentum and a legitimacy to decolonization which allowed the process to be completed within thirty years of the San Francisco Conference, putting an end to the long era of colonial empires, and radically changing both the geopolitical map of the world and the membership of the United Nations."[14]

Another pressing issue was the preamble. It might seem strange, in retrospect, that the delegates would pay much attention to something as inconsequential as the prelude to the U.N. Charter. But Field Marshal Smuts of South Africa, who had attended the Versailles Conference establishing the League of Nations, had elevated the question to a matter of some seriousness by telling a London audience, shortly before San Francisco, that the charter should be introduced "by a Preamble setting forth, in language which should appeal to the heart as well as the mind of men, the purposes which the United Nations were setting themselves to achieve." And, early in the San Francisco Conference, the field marshal—"a glamorous figure as he stood before the committee," according to one U.S. delegate, "still slender and straight in spite of his age, in his marshal's uniform with its decorations"—presented his version of a preamble. Due to the high emotions of the moment, his language won immediate adoption by acclamation "in principle." Unfortunately, the text was clumsily written, partly based on the old League preamble, and it went on for too long (two hundred words), lacking any soul to its words. Archibald MacLeish, then assistant secretary of state, called it a "literary and intellectual abortion." The opening words of the Smuts tract read: "The high contracting parties determined to prevent a recurrence of the fratricidal strife which twice in our generation has brought untold sorrow and loss upon mankind and . . ." and ending "agree to this Charter of the United Nations."[15]

The U.S. delegation, for the better part of the conference, seemed uninterested in working on the preamble, preferring to focus its efforts on the power arrangements in the charter. Virginia Gildersleeve, the most retiring member of the U.S. delegation, however, came afire over the preamble. As a former professor of literature and a long-time admirer of the United States Constitution, she cared deeply about the phraseology of the charter preamble, even as she confessed that nobody else took "the faintest interest" in that part of the document. Two other members of the delegation, she acknowledged, had given some thought to the preamble. Congressman Bloom, otherwise an inconsequential player at the conference, expressed a keen desire to see that the preamble was patterned after the U.S. Constitution's opening, a mere 52 words. He wanted it to start, "We, the people of the United Nations," just as the U.S. covenant begins, "We, the people of the United States." Harold Stassen also ached for an eloquent preamble. He told the delegation at one point that the preamble should be short and moving and beautiful and, according to Gildersleeve, "something simple that every school child in the world could commit to memory and that could hang, framed, in every cottage on the globe."[16]

Gildersleeve decided on her own to rewrite Smuts's prose. Eventually, she produced a competing version, which included Bloom's beginning, numbering 133 words. It started: "We, the People of the United Nations, determined to save succeeding generations from the scourge of war, which in our time has brought untold sorrow to mankind" and ended "through our representatives assembled in San Francisco agree to this charter." She presented her offering to the subcommittee handling the matter. To her great surprise, after considerable argument, the subcommittee adopted her language on May 29. A smattering of opposition did occur because, in some countries, delegates pointed out, "authority did not rise up from the people but came from above, from the throne." Others reminded Gildersleeve that sovereign governments had set up the U.N., not the global citizenry. Gildersleeve won her point, but this was to be her last victory. General Smuts and his allies counterattacked and reattached much of his lost text to the preamble. Gildersleeve's ringing peroration, nonetheless, remained.[17]

There were innumerable other obstacles. The matter of domestic jurisdiction, for example, elicited considerable dismay within the U.S. delegation. The original Dumbarton Oaks proposal had included language that would have allowed international law to determine what is "solely within the domestic jurisdiction of a member." The congressional wing of the U.S. team objected with vehemence to that phrasing as too intrusive on domestic status and wanted to broaden any prohibition against U.N. involvement in homegrown matters. The legislators demanded that the phrase "international law" be dropped from the clause on the grounds that it was always unpredictable in determining the proper allocation of responsibilities between states and the world community, and also that the word "essentially" be substituted for "solely" in order to widen the domestic oversight of the state.[18]

Ironically, John Foster Dulles, who had come to San Francisco aglow with fervor to override domestic sovereignty, now became the leading advocate for expanding homeland protection. Indeed, Stettinius anointed him as the U.S. representative in the negotiations with other nations. Though Washington already had veto power to block intrusions into its sovereign terrain, Dulles, nonetheless, treated the Dumbarton Oaks proposal with alarm, contending that "international law was subject to constant change and therefore escaped definition" and was incapable of clarifying the outer limits of domestic boundaries. He dismissed the draft language for another reason, too—that it was merely referring to questions dealing with enforcement action against an aggressor. San Francisco, he now argued, had since broadened the charter, switching its emphasis from taking repressive measures against aggressors to removing the economic and social causes of war. Thus the charter now covered a much wider field of human activity in which the national rights of the member states had to be even more carefully shielded. Dulles also fought off attempts to have the World Court decide the ambit of domestic coverage since, he claimed, many countries would not accept its jurisdiction.[19]

Eventually, Dulles achieved a result whereby each country became the sole judge of what constitutes domestic sovereignty. The final language in the charter read: "Nothing contained in the present Charter shall authorize the United Nations to intervene in matters which are essentially within the domestic jurisdiction of any states." Some delegates remained unmollified. The Norwegian representative remarked with some asperity, for example, that this outcome was "tantamount to saying that we are in favor of the Council maintaining or restoring peace, but we will have to do so only on our own conditions. . . . One is reminded," he continued, "of the caustic remark of Elihu Root: 'The people of the state of New York are in favor of prohibition, but against the application of it.'"[20]

Other states raised important additional questions about how the United Nations should handle such matters as the admission of new states, the expulsion or suspension of old states, and the right of a nation to withdraw from the organization. On the admission issue, the Big Four had earlier formulated a provision at Dumbarton Oaks giving the Security Council final say on recommending to the General Assembly which states could join the U.N., meaning its veto would still apply to all applicants. In San Francisco, the smaller states put up a fight to allow the General Assembly alone to make the decisions on admissions without any veto. But the major powers prevailed. The Big Five also got their way on the issues concerning the expulsion and suspension of nations that violated the charter. The major powers insisted that the Security Council, where they retained the veto, should have the final power to recommend to the General Assembly the correct course of action on punishing the behavior of errant governments.[21]

Some states also wanted the right to withdraw from the United Nations. Stettinius opposed this idea, fearing that if a secession was included in the charter, it could fatally undermine the body even before it began. "This would be most unfortunate for the psychology of the Conference," he said, "and even the public opinion of it." He preferred instead not to say anything about the question. Other delegates agreed, though for a different reason; namely, it would eliminate the possibility of nations flouncing out of the U.N. and issuing swaggering pronouncements, as Germany and Italy did in quitting the League of Nations in the 1930s. But the United States, nonetheless, accepted the notion that withdrawal was possible if a state, for example, did not like an amendment passed by the U.N. Still Stettinius opposed formalizing an exit route, believing that, once it was accomplished, the U.N. would then have to provide sanctions against the transgressor, forcing all the other nations to take similar enforcement actions—all of which seemed unlikely to happen. Better, Stettinius thought, not to dignify the issue at all with regulations. Stettinius's stance prevailed.[22]

The San Francisco Conference agreed, too, without much controversy, to accept a clause obligating members to make available troops and bases to the Security Council through "special agreements." No nation at the meeting objected to this provision because every state wanted to guarantee that the United Nations would protect them against future wars. A Military Staff Committee, composed only of Chiefs of Staff of the Big Five, was also created under Article 47; this committee was to be responsible for the "strategic direction of any armed forces placed at the disposal of the Security Council." It proved useless in practice. Still, in reference to the accords, the *New York Times* observed at the time: "For the first time in history, they tentatively bind a world-wide family of nations to specify in peacetime, the exact character and extent of armed forces and other facilities they will make available to a central supervising agency for use in preventing aggression." Despite additional lobbying by France, the conference refused to authorize the creation of a U.N. international police force.[23]

The secretary-general's position was also accorded the status of an independent charter office, elevating this post above the clerical/administrative status given it by the League of Nations. The secretary-general now had authority to take certain actions on behalf of the U.N. He could, for example, initiate debate and, when necessary, propose courses of action—neither of which powers the League had granted him. Article 99 formally provided the secretary-general the power "to bring to the attention of the Security Council any matter which in his opinion may threaten the maintenance of peace and security." Still, the secretary-general was not a lone actor by any means. Besides the General Assembly, he owed his position to the support of the permanent members of the Security Council since anyone of the five states could veto his selection; this set certain conditions for the post: He had, for example, to speak French to please France.

The U.N. Conference also placed a particular emphasis on setting up an Economic and Social Council. The theory was that since wars usually start over poverty or economic dissatisfaction, the U.N. should make every effort to improve living standards worldwide. As one newspaper noted, this organ might "produce a world that is economically more and more orderly, and socially more and more at ease, and therefore less and less impelled to take up arms to resolve its troubles." But the creation of the council soon led to a controversy over whether "full employment" should be listed as one of its objectives, as the Australians and Evatt desired. Washington found the expression misleading, preferring to use "high and stable levels of employment" as a more meaningful substitute. Further, some of the U.S. delegates feared that Congress would regard the term as justifying state planning, or even U.N. interference with the U.S. economy. An even more perverse thought was that nations might use the failure of the United States to reach full employment as an excuse to raise tariffs and institute trade controls. Nonetheless, the U.S. attempt to excise the term "full employment" failed, though it added language reinforcing the proposition that no international body could tamper with a country's domestic economy.[24]

In the closing days, the establishment of the World Court occasioned controversy. Almost from the beginning, nations argued over whether it was to have compulsory jurisdiction or voluntary ("optional") jurisdiction. President Truman, flaunting his proud internationalist credentials, told Stettinius that he wanted the United States to accept the compulsory jurisdiction of the Court. If "we are going to have a court," Truman explained, "it ought to be a court that would work with compulsory jurisdiction." But, mindful of an obstructionist Senate, Truman also instructed Stettinius "to strive for a formula that would make possible, at least eventually, compulsory jurisdiction of the International Court of Justice." Stettinius consulted his congressional members on the delegation and informed Truman that they felt the U.S. Senate would never ratify a World Court statute that included such a provision. Truman dropped his idea. Vandenberg later told his Senate colleagues that "we joined at San Francisco in maintaining the optional clause in order to be perfectly sure that at least this one needless hurdle would be removed from Senate consideration of the Charter." The World Court thus came into being with each nation deciding whether or not to accept its jurisdiction.[25]

Finally, the smaller states wanted the right to revise the charter at a constitutional convention in the first decade after the founding. Though the Big Five had agreed earlier that a convention could be convened at any time provided two-thirds of the General Assembly and any seven of the eleven members of the Security Council wanted it— meaning no veto could take place—they rejected proposals to call it within ten years. They felt that such a stipulation would imply to the outside world that the U.N. was only a temporary organization. The crusade by the lesser lands regarding this question also made no headway in wresting from the Big Powers the prerogative to veto amendments proposed by a convention. Both stances—opposing a convention within ten years and retaining the veto on changes—were held stubbornly by the Big Powers. Though the minor states were unhappy, they acquiesced in the Big Five views.[26]

As the committees of the U.N. now wound down their labors, the Coordinating Committee, led by Leo Pasvolsky and composed of legal specialists, translators, and wordsmiths, convened to work on the final draft. Their mission was to insure that the text read smoothly and did not contradict itself internally. "There would be over 100 articles in fifteen chapters," Pasvolsky told the U.S. delegation at one point, "which the Coordination Committee would have to examine one by one in the light of the intent of each technical committee." In addition, the committee planned to submit all legal terminology to the jurists for their review. To expedite his work, Pasvolsky placed a team of experts on the top floor of the San Francisco Opera House.[27]

One of the most able translators of Russian at the conference, brought in by the British mission in late May, was Isaiah Berlin, then in Great Britain's Washington embassy and later to become one of England's great philosophers. Berlin reacquainted himself in San Francisco with his old friend Charles Bohlen. Needing help in the final weeks to review the Russian version of the charter, Bohlen asked Berlin to join him in his office in the Veterans Building next door to the opera house. There the two men meticulously examined the Russian text line by line to see whether the Soviets had tucked in any extra phrases that could possibly change the meaning of the charter. At one point, Berlin spotted a passage dealing with the right of a member state to march its army through a second state to defend a third. He pointed out to Bohlen that the Russian term "passing through" implied a right not only to go in and out but, if need be, to stay. Berlin and Bohlen protested the wording to the Russians. The Soviet diplomats claimed that it was too late to make changes, but eventually, after some hemming and hawing, agreed. Berlin caught one other error—a Russian sentence suggesting that all British-mandated territories were to be terminated. Berlin insisted on a revision in the article's meaning. The Soviets reluctantly complied. Bohlen joshed that Berlin had saved the British Empire with the stroke of a pencil.[28]

The business of the convention was now at an end. Nelson Rockefeller threw a last-minute gala on June 18 at the St. Francis Yacht Club on San Francisco Bay; the affair was highlighted by the appearance of Carmen Miranda, the "Brazilian Bombshell," her trademark fruit-festooned hat on her head, to celebrate the wind-up. In the midst of other farewell festivities, Stettinius, with some pride, looked upon the accomplishments of this historic conference as, at least in part, due to his own management of a sometimes unruly U.S. delegation, an often surly Soviet mission, a rebellious menage of smaller states, a critical press corps, and a nervous new president in Washington. Out of a tortuous two-month deliberation, the United Nations Charter had magically emerged, like a butterfly out of a chrysalis, making all his agonies worthwhile. The next stage was the signing of the charter, which would be topped off with Truman's visit. The auguries for Stettinius in these last days were good ones.[29]

CHAPTER 15

THE FALL OF STETTINIUS

George Allen asked to see Secretary Stettinius on Thursday morning, June 21, just four days before the end of the conference. Allen was Truman's personal representative from the White House advance team sent out just a week before to prepare for the president's arrival. Already Allen had sat in on sessions with Stettinius and the delegation, and had assisted in passing messages to the White House on the secretary's behalf. Allen, a jovial old-style Democratic operative and man-about-Washington, had previously worked as a lobbyist and secretary to the party's national committee. In 1944, he had helped in the effort to place Truman on the Democratic presidential ticket and regularly played poker with him. Some observers called him a "crude self-promoter," citing *Presidents Who Have Known Me*, the book he later wrote. In the early days of Truman's presidency, however, Allen was widely viewed as an influential advisor in the White House.[1]

Allen's appearance was considered a sign of Truman's public backing of the Stettinius and inadvertently shored up the secretary's sometimes ambiguous standing in San Francisco. Stettinius had been plagued by rumors about his future throughout the conference. Conflicting signals emanating from Washington had persisted as to whether and when he was going to be replaced. On June 3, one of Stettinius's most fervent supporters in the press corps, *New York Times* columnist Arthur Krock, had felt compelled to pen a piece rebutting an unofficial campaign against the secretary. The charges, reported Krock, ranged from the fact that Stettinius did not have the "worldly experience" to advise Truman

245

on international policy, was a man of "limited mental attainments," had bungled the Argentinian affair at the conference, and that, as an individual close in line to the presidency, was unelected and not a Democrat and therefore an inappropriate person to hold the office. Krock believed that, given Stettinius's achievements, none of these criticisms could be taken seriously. He noted that Truman himself had twice denied at press conferences—indeed at one just the day before his column—that he planned any changes at the State Department. Finally, Krock observed that Stettinius had no political ambitions of his own and would "cheerfully turn back his official seals" if Truman asked him to do so.[2]

George Allen arrived at Stettinius's Fairmont penthouse on a misty San Francisco morning at 10:00 A.M. An aide led him into a pine-paneled conference room, where the secretary greeted him. Allen sat down and immediately complimented Stettinius on his accomplishments at the conference. He told the secretary that the signing of the U.N. Charter would be "the biggest day of [his] life." He even suggested that Stettinius might be a future president of the United States. Then he moved in somewhat ungainly fashion to the purpose of his visit. He did not know, he remarked, whether the president intended to make a change in the secretary of state's position, but guessed that Truman had probably made a commitment of some sort to somebody else for the job. Truman, he reported, had been flirting with Jimmy Byrnes. Stettinius, who may have started to figure at this point the significance of Allen's unmannerly musings, acknowledged that he had heard much of the same scuttlebutt. If this be so, Allen continued, then Stettinius should get "something bigger than secretary of state"—not the ambassadorship to Great Britain because that would be a "demotion and the public would say Stettinius got a kick in the tail," but another post. Stettinius interrupted: "George, what are you talking about?" Allen replied that he could be the first U.S. envoy to the United Nations.[3]

Taken aback, Stettinius abruptly stiffened. Truman, he rejoined to Allen, had to make up his mind right away about what he wanted to do: "We can't fool around any longer. I've either got to say I'm going to be secretary of state or somebody else." No matter how Truman han-

dled this, he added, for him "it will be a kick in the pants or a kick upstairs." However, he continued, if Truman wanted to replace him, then
he, Stettinius, should not accompany the president to Postdam the following month nor should he be appointed to the U.N. before the Senate had acted. Instead, he suggested, Truman should "leave [him] in
charge" of the treaty fight in the Senate. Then, reconsidering his
views, he ruminated about the possibility that Truman might instead
announce his U.N. appointment at the charter signing ceremony. Allen
grabbed at the idea as a "dramatic" one. Stettinius cautioned, however,
that the changeover had to be done "in a very careful, adroit way," for
otherwise it wouldn't hold water. Unable to hold back his curiosity,
Stettinius probed further: "Do you think the president has made a
commitment to Byrnes?" Allen answered: "I think he has." Nettled,
Stettinius pressed again: "When the president sent you out here for
this damn parade and reception, did he have in mind your talking to
me about this matter?" Allen, trying to soothe Stettinius, gave a noncommittal reply: "No. I don't think he did." Stettinius assured him at
the same time that he would not argue with the president about the
proposed switch: "I'll step aside tomorrow and still be his friend." He
merely wanted time to think about the possible U.N. posting. "I don't
like public life," he concluded.[4]

Word immediately leaked out to Stettinius's friends about his likely
departure. Senator Vandenberg wrote in his diary that he was
"shocked by the sudden presidential decapitation of Stettinius. I think
it was grossly unfair. It must have startled the foreign ministers of the
other forty-nine nations who saw Stettinius make a spectacular success
of his job." That afternoon, Arthur Krock phoned the secretary to say
that if Stettinius wished to remain at the State Department, Bernard
Baruch and Virginia Democratic senator Harry Byrd were ready to go
to Truman and have a "showdown on this thing." Stettinius told Krock
that he was grateful for the support, but that he had not focused much
on his situation while he was engaged in the San Francisco deliberations. "I just forgot about myself," he recalled. Krock sensed now that
Stettinius was deflated and was probably giving up the battle. Krock
changed his tune. In a column written a week later, Krock explained

to his *Times* readership that "it was inevitable that the President would want a Secretary of State of his own selection." He now complimented Truman on choosing the "opportune time" for replacing Stettinius after he had completed his arduous labors at the U.N. Conference amidst "universal and merited praise." Krock acknowledged that Stettinius might have felt "personal disappointment," but everybody should remember that his leave-taking was due to "no fault or failure of the Secretary of State" and that Truman had chosen "the perfect way" to honor him. "The President could not have made the change more considerately."[5]

As Stettinius pondered how he wanted to act or what route he wished to take, there was considerable back and forth for several days between the principals. George Allen had let it be known early on that Truman wished to announce Stettinius's new appointment on June 27 at a stopover in Independence, Missouri. Stettinius assigned Isaiah Bowman, one of his top aides, to negotiate the terms of any new engagement as well as a possible exchange of letters between himself and Truman. Finally, after resolving a few remaining qualms, Stettinius okayed the June 27 date for the public notification. He surmised that, if he had to give up the secretary of state job, taking the brand-new U.N. post would give him a face-saving exit, even a well-heralded one. Bowman had also persuaded Allen to allow Stettinius as U.N. envoy to keep his office in the White House. Bowman had advised his boss, too, that in revealing the change on June 27, Stettinius would be the beneficiary of excellent press coverage the next day, as Truman had agreed to postpone announcement of the Byrnes appointment in order not to detract from the media focus on Stettinius. In addition, Senators Connally and Vandenburg planned to speak on the Senate floor on June 27 and toss garlands at Stettinius for his performance in San Francisco. Finally, after the Byrnes nomination, Truman agreed to travel in person with Stettinius to the Senate Foreign Relations Committee to present the charter. All this enhanced Stettinius's standing. "Thus," according to the Bowman memo, "[Stettinius] has the limelight placed upon his achievements at the moment of retiring from the Secretaryship and again after the new man is appointed." Margaret Truman later complained that Stettinius acted "haughtily" and took too much time to send in his resignation. Stettinius, a man of vanity, clearly had tried to fish for the best exit terms; it is evident, though, in the end, contrary to Margaret Truman's charge, he never sought to derail Truman's departure schedule for him.[6]

Somewhat disingenuously, Truman later wrote in his memoirs that "Stettinius had submitted his resignation at the close of the San Francisco conference, and I had persuaded him" to stay on at the U.N. Although it is true that Stettinius had tendered his resignation at the time of President Roosevelt's death—proper protocol for all cabinet officials when a new president takes office—Truman had not acted upon it. Now, technically, Truman was able to say that he was simply accepting Stettinius's earlier offer. However one chooses to look at it, though, it was self-evident that Truman was forcing Stettinius out of the post. He undoubtedly was doing this for the reasons he had enumerated many times earlier—that he did not want the secretary of state, the next in line for the presidency after the vice president, to be an unelected official. (In fact, he was proposing legislation to change the line of succession from the secretary of state to the Speaker of the House.) But it is also clear that privately he did not much care for Stettinius. Whatever the circumstances, Truman seemed determined to accord Stettinius's leave taking with respect.[7]

Four days after the Allen conversation, on the evening of June 25, Truman arrived in San Francisco. The two men met briefly at the dinner Stettinius gave for the president at the penthouse in the Fairmont Hotel. They had a quick, if awkward, talk. In the anteroom of the apartment, Truman hailed Stettinius: "Well, you certainly have done a grand job out here. Are you satisfied with what I am planning?" Stettinius begged off replying, saying, "We can have a leisurely talk tomorrow." Truman insisted: "You have got to be satisfied—I want you to be." Stettinius reluctantly cited three "matters on my mind." First was his potential relationship with Byrnes. "He and I used to be old friends, but since I have been in the State Department, things have been different." Second was his desire to end his public service career now that the war was over. "I am making no commitment as to time." Third was his uncertainty over the power of his new office. "Unless you dress this thing up so that my prestige can be preserved, I won't be effective in the new one." Truman promised that Byrnes would be OK, that Stettinius could leave his U.N. post anytime he wished, and finally that he'd have ample authority in his U.N. position.[8]

Stettinius then pressed him on whether he was "going to make it clear I have succeeded as secretary of state." The president replied, "Yes, you have done a magnificent job and I shall say so." Beset by doubts, Stettinius sought further reassurance: "Mr. President, do you really believe that you can do this thing and put Byrnes in without its appearing publicly like a kick in the pants for me?" Truman answered: "I sincerely believe it can be done that way." The presidential announcement two days later on June 27, in fact, produced a blizzard of headlines for Stettinius, suggesting, as Truman had promised, that he had just received a well-deserved promotion. The *New York Times,* for example, despite its "insider" ties to the U.S mission, insisted in an editorial titled "Our First Delegate" that Stettinius "did a brilliant job in San Francisco. No one has worked more effectively to bring the new world organization to birth. . . . It is fitting therefore that he should be assigned to carry on the work he has so well begun." Truman had, with an instinctive politician's touch, brought off the replacement and transfer of Stettinius in a way that not only preserved Stettinius's status but also made the president look magnanimous.[9]

Even as these behind-the-scenes machinations transpired, Stettinius had to deal with last-minute mischief from Soviet representative Andrei Gromyko. On June 19, Gromyko told a morning meeting of the Big Five that, although his government had accepted that the U.N. Charter would not mention withdrawal, it objected nonetheless to the background report of the technical committee that presented grounds for this decision. The Soviets believed that language contained in the paper chastised a state improperly for quitting the U.N. even though that state might have legitimate grounds to do so; and at the same time, in a contradictory fashion, also unjustly slandered the U.N. by suggesting that it was not fulfilling its promise to bring peace. Gromyko's stance may have reflected Stalin's still irate obsession over the Soviet Union's expulsion from the League of Nations in December 1939 after its invasion of Finland. A weary Vandenberg warned Gromyko that reopening this question with the conference set to adjourn would prolong the meeting for "six weeks of debate." Eventually, Gromyko withdrew his complaint "since the four delegations did not agree," and, as he reckoned, "[I] had no other choice but to let the matter go."[10]

The next day, though—at the very session where Gromyko had previously accepted compromise language on the General Assembly's right of discussion—Gromyko pleaded for three additional days to permit his government to review the final provisions of the charter. Stettinius, relieved of his battle over the General Assembly, reluctantly granted Gromyko's request. Stettinius had to send word to Truman in Washington State now that he had to postpone his arrival for two days—until June 25. Truman seemed calm about the postponement. He went fishing from a yacht built for Herbert Hoover when he was secretary of commerce, soaked up the beautiful scenery on Puget Sound, visited Mount Rainier, and attended to his U.N. speech. Stettinius, for his part, used some of the extra days to thank his staff. At noon on June 23, for example, he convened a private gathering at the opera house of the thousands of workers, military personnel, and volunteers. He and the other Big Five delegation leaders thanked the assemblage and signed testimonial certificates, which they handed out to the participants.[11]

Meanwhile, next door, the theatrical designers, Oliver Lundquist and Jo Mielziner, prepared for the ceremonial signing on June 26 by putting last-minute touches to the site at the Herbst Theater in the Veterans War Memorial Building. On the stage they placed a large round table, eleven feet in diameter, and, continuing the color pattern of the event, draped a blue velvet cloth over it, put a single chair upholstered in blue next to it, and laid a Copenhagen-blue rug, some thirty-six feet in diameter, under it. In the background, they also hung a blue curtain. New silk flags of all the U.N. states formed a colorful semicircle behind this tableau. A twelve-inch-high rope railing cordoned off an area in front and extended outwards to a radius of twenty-five feet. A new floor was erected, too, to cover a lower portion of the sloping orchestra section and make it level with the stage. The newsreel operators, photographers, and reporters stood just behind the rope barrier on the newly constructed platform. Huge scaffolds supported an elaborate system of klieg lights that illuminated the scene for the media. Guests sat in the red plush seats behind the press corps and spectators sat in the balcony.

The choreography of the signing was extensively planned. A flow chart was prepared to track the movement of the delegates. Each delegate was asked to come to a hidden room at the rear of the stage. Delegates were then told where to stand on the stage to assure that they would be properly photographed. They were also asked to practice their signatures before the event. The charter contained their names penciled on specific lines to show them where they were to sign at the ceremonial moment. Once a delegate entered the stage between the flags, he or she was to go to the desk, and, as colleagues clustered behind and cameras rolled, sit down and sign in ink above the penciled inscription. Later, the designers erased the penciled jottings underneath.[12]

Truman arrived on the afternoon of June 25 amid a fervent air of anticipation. As Truman's huge C-54 aircraft circled Hamilton Field for its landing at 2:30 P.M., a cavalcade of delegates arrived in cars flying their national flags and waited on the nearby tarmac, led by the U.S. delegation. Truman's plane landed in a fog that still hung lightly over the city. Wearing a Western hat, a gray suit, and blue bow tie, the smiling president stepped promptly from the plane as the first gun of the twenty-one-gun salute was fired. At the bottom of the stairs, Secretary Stettinius, Governor Earl Warren of California, and the mayor of San Francisco, Roger Lapham, as well as the members of the U.S. delegation, all shook Truman's hand. As an army guard of honor of three hundred picked men stood at attention, Truman strode by, a button indicating his service in World War I noticeable in the lapel of his double-breasted suit. Then Truman stood rigidly in position as a band played the national anthem. Next, it broke into "Missouri Waltz." Stettinius introduced Truman to the chiefs of the other forty-nine delegations in alphabetical order, starting, ironically, with Argentina. Truman then rode to a nearby army hospital, amidst the cheers of hundreds of soldiers, to meet wounded veterans.[13]

From there, Truman traveled the twenty-five-mile trip to San Francisco. He and Stettinius sat side by side, along with Governor Warren and Mayor Lapham, in an open car, trailed by nearly one hundred limousines, most belonging to the delegates. A score of motorcycle police escorted the mile-long procession. Soldiers were posted along the entire route. Just as Truman passed the last hill before descending down to the Golden Gate Bridge, the fog lifted, revealing San Francisco in a blaze of bright white light. As Truman's lead car entered the Presidio on the city-side of the bridge, the crowds grew larger and more enthusiastic, people standing five or six deep. Truman's motorcade traversed six miles of the city's streets in a roundabout route to the Fairmont Hotel, allowing as much of the city's populace to see Truman as possible. The *New York Times* and the *San Francisco Chronicle* estimated the turnout to be 500,000; the *Washington Post* counted a crowd half that size. Whatever the truth of the numbers, the rising elation over the accomplishments at the U.N. Conference, as well as the chance to see the new president, seemed to capture the imagination of San Franciscans. The *Chronicle* called the turnout "the greatest demonstration in the city's history." The *New York Times* cited a "wildly enthusiastic ovation" from residents. Truman responded by standing much of the way and waving his hat. He told reporters later that he took no credit for the welcome: "Well, this wasn't for me. It was what we stand for."[14]

When Truman reached the Fairmont Hotel, he immediately went to a banquet room to host a reception for all of the 280 conference delegates. Later that evening, Stettinius gave him a formal dinner at the penthouse apartment and invited some twenty-six guests, all Americans—the delegates, a dozen or so U.S. staffers, and a group of California officials. Stettinius led his guest of honor into the living room and introduced him to the visitors. He started to tell Truman about the historic setting of the room where the U.S. delegation and the Big Five had gathered regularly for the past two months. Sol Bloom jumped in and explained "that's Eden's chair, that's Molotov's chair," at which point Stettinius himself began to describe the seating arrangements. During cocktails, Truman and Stettinius had the private talk in which Stettinius expressed his anxiety about his new posting. At one point, the U.S. delegation presented Stettinius with a parchment containing a statement of appreciation that praised his "poise and good temper, [his] tactful reconciliation of those who have differed and doubted." One U.S. delegate felt profoundly uncomfortable about the whole event—Virginia Gildersleeve. Pointing out that Stettinius had not invited any foreign delegates, much less any of the leaders of the sponsoring states, she wrote: "The whole affair seemed to me a most shocking example of international bad manners." Only she and Nelson Rockefeller, she said, had "the slightest consciousness of this scandalous breach of etiquette" in this greatest of all international conferences.[15]

If the other delegates had aggrieved feelings, though, they hid them well at 9:30 that night in the San Francisco Opera House, where the second-to-last Plenary Session was being held to adopt the charter and the World Court before an audience of 3,000. There was one last-minute complaint by Andrei Gromyko. He ascended to the podium to protest once again the technical report on "withdrawal." This time, though, he merely asked that his objections be entered into the record, and, to the relief of Stettinius, did not call for a vote. Alger Hiss, presiding at the session, called Stettinius to the rostrum and handed him a scroll of tribute signed by the forty-nine delegation chairmen. Then the vote was taken. Delegates rose in alphabetical order to register their support for the two documents. At 10:53 P.M. that Monday night, the Plenary chairman, Lord Halifax of Great Britain, declared the vote to be unanimous. A spontaneous outpouring of celebration ensued. According to Stettinius: "Everybody in the whole auditorium stood and applauded continuously for a long time—here and there people were heard to cheer and the echoes and roar of the whole acclaim came from every part of the auditorium, from the orchestra pit containing the interpreters and the stenotypists to the topmost row of the balcony high up in the shadows beyond the klieg lights—and even some of the press abandoned their activities in order to join in the general hand clapping."[16]

The next day, the signing ceremony began at noontime, after some delays. To avoid the problem of having Argentina sign the charter first, the Big Five agreed that they, as sponsors, would affix their signatures on the documents before all the other nations, and that the United States, acting as host, would be the final signatory. There were two leather-bound binders to sign—the U.N. Charter and the World Court combined in one volume, and the authority to establish a U.N. preparatory commission in the other. As there was only one signature per document, a delegate's autograph authorized all the copies in all the official languages of the conference—French, English, Russian, Chinese, and Spanish. China opened the proceedings with its own special ink and brushes. Things quickly got out of hand, however, and Argentina somehow slipped in ahead of France. The delegate chairmen, in turn, made brief remarks in their own languages on the importance of the occasion.[17]

The United States, in a last-minute switch, decided to do its signing midway through the ceremony at 3:15 P.M., thus allowing President Truman to be present. Also, this maneuver permitted the final Plenary Session, where eleven of the most influential delegates were expected to speak, to begin at 3:50 P.M., and made it possible for Truman to fly out that evening to Independence, Missouri, for a homecoming visit. The U.S. decision, however, forced twelve of the states still waiting to sign the documents to stay on until after the Plenary ended. Guatemala's representative, Guillermo Toriello, completed the signing ceremony at 7:20 P.M. that night. In the end, 153 out of the 280 delegates signed the document—a smaller figure because some countries limited the number of their signers. After that, armed guards rushed the charter upstairs and placed it in a seventy-five-pound fireproof safe to be taken to Washington a few days later.[18]

The Plenary itself, before a crowd of 3,500 people, lasted two hours. President Truman, walking on to the stage accompanied by Stettinius and the secretary-general of the conference, Alger Hiss, gave the final address. He wore appropriate colors—a navy blue double-breasted suit, blue necktie, and a blue pocket handkerchief in his lapel pocket. He opened his remarks with an interpolated remark that echoed the sentiments of the participants: "Oh, what a great day this can be in history!" He then delivered his appreciation of San Francisco's achievements. "There were many," he declaimed, "who doubted that agreement could ever be reached by fifty-three countries differing so much in race and religion, in language and culture." But what held all the delegates together, he continued, was the goal of ending all wars. "History will honor you," he said, for writing the U.N. Charter. "No one," however, "claims that it is now a final or a perfect instrument. It has not been poured into a fixed model. Changing world conditions will require readjustments of peace and not of war." What the charter means, he explained, is that "we all have to recognize—no matter how great our strength—that we must deny ourselves the license to do always as we please. . . . This is the price which each nation will have to pay for world peace." But, Truman proclaimed, "We have tested the principle of cooperation in this war and we have found it works." He reminded his listeners that "if we had had this Charter a few years ago—and, above all, the will to use it—millions now dead would be alive. If we should falter in the future in our will to use it, millions now living will surely die." He expressed his continuing marvel at the completion of the document: "That we now have this Charter at all is a great wonder."[19]

The other speakers, exhausted but exhilarated by their two months, gave impassioned addresses. The Chinese envoy, V. K. Wellington Koo, compared the document to the Magna Carta and the United States Constitution. France's delegate, Joseph Paul-Bancour, quoted the famous French writer Blaise Pascal in reference to the new powers accorded the United Nations: "Strength without justice is tyrannical, and justice without strength is mockery." Soviet representative Andrei Gromyko stressed the importance of maintaining cooperation among the Big Five to make the U.N. a workable body. The British delegate, Lord Halifax, told the story about the great church of Seville: "Long years ago in Europe men set themselves to raise a cathedral to God's glory. 'Let us,' they said, 'build a church so great that those who come after us will think us mad to have attempted it.' So they said, and wrought, and, after many years, achieved." Let us pray now, he implored, that "what we have done here in these last few weeks will be found worthy of the faith that gave it birth and the human suffering that has been its price."[20]

That night, many delegates packed their belongings and departed for their homelands. Some took specially chartered trains back to the East Coast. Most of the U.S. delegation flew to Washington that evening with Stettinius. Besides the U.S. delegates, several foreign delegates were passengers, including Lord Halifax; Pedro Leão Velloso, the Brazilian acting foreign minister; and Ezequiel Padilla, the Mexican foreign minister. At the airport, a crowd of some two hundred turned out to greet them, including the entire membership of the Senate Foreign Relations Committee and a band. Two days later, on the night of June 28, soldiers in San Francisco, accompanied by Alger Hiss, brought the newly signed U.N. Charter to a special army plane at the city's airport for a flight to Washington and its ultimate consignment to the Federal Archives until the U.N. had obtained a permanent headquarters. As a precaution in the event of airplane trouble, the charter's safe, which bore the legend "Finder! Do Not Open. Send to the Department of State, Washington," had a parachute attached to it. Hiss acted as the guardian. When he reached the capital, Hiss sped the charter to the White House for a presentation to President Truman. Truman was himself planning to give it to the Senate in person. Hiss was dismayed, however, to find that Truman was not prepared for his visit. For this solemn occasion, Hiss had expected a ceremony. Instead, Truman was in his shirtsleeves, drinking bourbon and water with an aide.[21]

The newspapers and commentators began to reflect on the enormity of what had just happened in San Francisco. Initial reviews of Stettinius's performance were perhaps the warmest. Anne O'Hare McCormick observed that "from the first day, Mr. Stettinius hammered so persistently on the theme that the conference had to succeed that in the end nobody questioned it." The *New York Times* editorialized on June 22, 1945, that "by his patience, persistence, and above all by his faith in the enterprise, the Secretary of State has done as much as any man to carry to completion the task in which the late President [Roosevelt] had set his heart." Another *Times* editorial termed Settinius's stewardship "brilliant." Averell Harriman, a shrewd scout of diplomatic talent, described Stettinius as "one of the most underrated American secretaries of state that we have." Vandenberg felt he had done a "magnificent job."[22]

Yet, in spite of all the encomiums of the time, Stettinius's reputation, never high in the first place, began to plummet. Stettinius did serve a brief term as the first U.S. envoy to the United Nations until June 2, 1946, and then authored several valuable memoirs on Lend-Lease and Yalta. He died of a heart attack at his sister's home in Greenwich, Connecticut, on October 31, 1949, at the age of fifty. Secretary-General Trygve Lie observed at the time that "he will live in history as one of the chief architects of the United Nations." Its creation, he added, owed much "to his utter devotion to the United Nations cause and to his courageous determination in the face of every obstacle to bring the United Nations into being as a world organization in which all the great nations, as well as other countries of the world, would participate." In spite of Trygve Lie's generous tribute, the United Nations never gave Stettinius—nor for that matter Leo Pasvolsky—a plaque at the U.N. for helping to bring it into existence. And, as the years passed, Stettinius's name vanished from the history books. Most modern-day commentators, taking their cue from the secretary's colleagues of the 1940s, brushed him off as a historic mediocrity, a lightweight, a failure. Stettinius remains a ghost from the Roosevelt past.[23]

Curiously enough, despite their delaying tactics, their chronic suspicions, and their persistent demands, the Soviets initially received high marks from conference observers—perhaps, in part, because expectations for them had been so low. James Reston, while conceding that other nations had made important concessions at the parley, listed nine points where he felt the Russians had given way to their Allies to assure the creation of the United Nations; he named them as: agreeing to a conference starting date with which they had originally disagreed; okaying one rather than four conference presidents; accepting regional self-defense; acknowledging a restricted veto; backing off from their own trusteeship demands; supporting the Vandenberg amendment; and acquiescing in outlawing wars, further limiting powers of the Security Council, and creating an interim U.N. body. Other analysts, however, were not so sanguine about Soviet intentions. "Insofar as Stalin attached importance to the concept of a future international organization," wrote George Kennan, "he did so in the expectation that the organization would serve as the instrument for maintenance of a U.S.-U.K.-Soviet hegemony in international affairs." Alexander Dallin noted that Moscow wished also to "avoid the stigma of non-participation and to prevent the body from becoming a hostile instrument." Stalin, in the end, appeared to have played primarily a defensive game at the U.N. Conference to protect his own security interests, especially those in Eastern Europe, and guarantee his berth on the Security Council. He did not, however, embrace the organization with much enthusiasm. Indeed, he later turned down joining both the World Bank and the International Monetary Fund.[24]

As a result of the deliberations in San Francisco, the charter's terms were greatly liberalized. The basic framework of Dumbarton Oaks was preserved, but the iron grip of the Big Five was loosened. The charter also got rid of some of the defects in the League of Nations Covenant. First, the authority of the Security Council was circumscribed to an extent by the restriction on the veto on discussion, by the new powers granted regional organizations, and by the enhanced protection for domestic sovereignty. At the same time, the power of the Security Council to deal with military emergencies was strengthened far beyond what had existed at the League of Nations, according just five nations the capacity to veto operations (a sharp departure from League rules allowing every nation the veto), setting up an agile eleven-member council able to mobilize rapidly in response to any crisis, and obliging all U.N. members to support the use of force by the council. Under the League of Nations, the only resort to action of any sort had been public opinion or economic sanctions; troop deployments were voluntary. The League was more of a mediator than a policeman. In addition, San Francisco granted the General Assembly wider dominion to review and debate and make recommendations on global issues, transforming it into a genuine "town meeting of the world." The Economic and Social Council, in turn, was elevated to equal ranking with the Security Council, the General Assembly, and the World Court, and given broader responsibility

for investigations, advisory functions, and conferences on global problems. A Trusteeship Council was also placed in the U.N. Charter. The
right to call for a constitutional convention was incorporated in the
document. The important words "human rights," "justice," "full employment," and "education" found their way into the final text. In its
newly revised form, the charter embodied a curious mixture of realism
and idealism.

The reaction of the U.S. mission was one of enthusiastic—if obviously self-interested—allegiance, primed to influence the upcoming
Senate debate over ratification. The Republicans on the delegation
swiftly issued supportive statements. On the day before Truman's address, John Foster Dulles publicly enthused: "I believe it can be a
greater Magna Carta. It is not merely a mechanistic means to prevent
wars, but rather provides a way to clear up war through the economic
sore spots." Senator Vandenberg, preparing for his speech on the Senate floor a few days hence, distributed a release that same day: "I consider collective security essential to peace with justice in a free world
of free men; and the San Francisco charter is the world's only chance
in this vital direction. Despite its infirmities, the San Francisco charter
is a sound basis for seeking organized peace. In my opinion, our intelligent American self-interest indispensably requires our loyal cooperation in this great adventure to stop World War III before it starts." Vandenberg added, "I got much more in this Charter than I came out to
get. I think that Delegate Vandenberg is in complete harmony with
Senator Vandenberg."[25]

On the Democratic side, Adlai Stevenson on June 28 told the Chicago
Bar Association: "Amid the confusion, the babel of tongues, and the
complexity of it all, a cynic would well say that the remarkable thing
was not that they wrote a better charter than anyone had a right to expect, but that they succeeded in writing a charter at all!" He continued,

As a declaration, it constitutes a binding agreement by the signatory
nations to work together for peaceful ends and to adhere to certain
standards of international morality. As a constitution, it creates four
principal social instruments by which these ends may be achieved in

practice and these standards maintained. What are these instruments? A police force continually in operation and continually vigilant; a forum in which to discuss, to let the light in, to ventilate; a court whose decisions are binding on the parties and all member states; and an institute to apply to social and economic problems the knowledge and experience of the world.

Still, he cautioned: "It is only paper and no better and no worse than the will and intentions of its five major members. Everything depends on the active participation, pacific intentions, and good faith of the Big Five."[26]

Of the major newspapers following the San Francisco Conference, the *New York Times* was probably the most enthusiastic. At the meeting's completion, the paper evinced a positive, if sometimes tempered, approach to the new U.N. Charter. One of its correspondents, Russell Porter, warned, as did Stevenson, that "the Charter can be either the soul of a brave new world or merely a scrap of paper, depending on the will and action of its creators." But, in a series of editorials, the *Times* strongly lauded the outcome. The conference, it wrote on June 22, "has accomplished all it set out to do. It has created the framework within which nations of good-will can work together. . . . The Charter written at San Francisco is an improvement on the Dumbarton Oaks proposals. It is a much more flexible and democratic document." The newspaper was pleased, too, that "power, although the ultimate, is not the only weight in the scales of decision. The new Charter bears evidence that reason counts, too, in the great sum of forces that move the world." In an editorial two days later, the *Times* observed that, unlike the League of Nations, which was merely an afterthought to the Versailles peace conference, "the new charter precedes the peace treaty or treaties and stands alone." Most important, it gives "voiceless millions" a forum to express their concerns. Nonetheless, the *Times* warned, "it does not and could not produce anything resembling a world government. It does, on paper, involve some voluntary relinquishment of sovereignty by the leading powers. Immediately it is a device to keep the peace for an indefinite term of years." Two days after that, the *Times* proclaimed "a great hope is born." Pointing out that, though "Big Power control is not new" since the charter gives the five permanent members of the Security Council absolute sovereignty through the veto, nonetheless "it is the restrictions upon such control that are new and that constitute the gains made under the Charter." These varying sentiments of the *Times* were widely echoed across the country—with the occasional opposition note in newspapers such as the *Chicago Tribune*. The charter looked in serviceable shape for ratification as the Senate hearings approached. The campaign for U.S. participation in the organization was about to begin.[27]

CHAPTER 16

THE RATIFICATION STORY

S an Francisco was only the beginning. The United Nations organization was formally established, but U.S. membership was still to be
secured. Roosevelt and Truman were haunted by the fate of the League
of Nations at the hands of the United States Senate—the nine months
of protracted, bitter debate that eroded support for U.S. membership in
the international organization.

But Roosevelt had learned from Wilson's errors. He had dispatched
influential Republicans to San Francisco as members of the U.S. delegation; his embrace of the great power veto stood as a firm wall protecting
U.S. national sovereignty. He was also determined on U.S. participation
in the United Nations while the war was still on and Americans were
still conscious of the need for collective security. Truman inherited this
view and hoped for rapid ratification by the Senate before he departed
for a mid-July summit meeting at Potsdam.

At first, observers predicted that the ratification process would not
be speedy. On June 22, under the headline "Charter Ratification Is Unlikely Before the Fall, Officials Think," the *New York Times* reported
that "the considered opinion of persons best qualified to make esti-
mates of the chances" of the charter's passage was that, though adoption was eventually assured, "there was virtually no possibility" of ratification before the fall of that year since the opposition would insist on
a Senate summer recess. But such pessimism was belied by statements
promising swift approval by Republican party chieftains. As early as
June 14, Senator Vandenberg prophesied to journalists in San Fran-

cisco: "I believe that the Senate will be quite receptive to the Charter when it is laid before it. This thing will not be the battle of the century." A poll taken by the Associated Press the day the cautionary story appeared in the *Times* revealed that fifty-two senators—and five leaning in the same direction—out of the ninety-six in the Senate, were already willing to vote for the charter. This meant that the charter was just seven votes shy of the two-thirds total of sixty-four votes needed for ratification (assuming all Senators were present and voting). The most interesting morsel of information was that, of the seventy-five Senators interviewed, not one expressed outright opposition to the pact. Indeed, many former isolationists, for example, Senator Pat McCarran of Nevada, were now backing the treaty.[1]

Leading political figures felt it imperative to convey a sense of urgency to the public about ratification—especially President Truman. "There is a time for making plans—and there is a time for action," he had declared in his closing remarks at the San Francisco Conference. "The time for action is now! Let us, therefore, each in his own nation and according to its own way, seek immediate approval of this Charter—and make it a living thing. I shall send this Charter to the United States Senate at once. I am sure that the overwhelming sentiment of the people of my country and of their representatives in the Senate is in favor of immediate ratification." A few days later, on June 28, Truman, upon receiving an honorary degree from the University of Kansas City in Missouri, repeated his message: "We are going to ratify this Charter and I want to see the United States do it first. If there is to be peace, countries must live under law just as our States and individuals do." The United States, he reminded his listeners, must shoulder responsibility in the world, and it "is absolutely necessary for the greatest republic that the sun ever shone upon to live with the world as a whole and not by itself. . . . I am anxious to bring home to you that the world is one world, just as Wendell Willkie said. It is a responsibility that this great republic ought to lead the way in—to carry out those ideas of Woodrow Wilson and Franklin D. Roosevelt."[2]

On June 27, Edward Stettinius, returning from San Francisco, put himself on record for quick action. "I hope the United States may be among the first, if not the first, to ratify the Charter," he proclaimed. "Let us get on with the work we have to do—to make victory and peace secure." Senator Connally, alighting from the same plane, told a press conference that he intended to push as promptly as possible for agreement. He still did not wish "to railroad the thing or jam it down anybody's throat," but nonetheless, he said, "I don't want the Senate dilly-dallying and honey-swoggling all through July and August just for the sake of making speeches to the people back home." He guessed, he told reporters, that no more than ten senators would now vote against the U.N. "Those Senators who believe we should tread our path alone will vote against the Charter," he opined. "But those who realize that this can't be done and that the United States cannot live in a cellophane wrapper will favor the Charter." After his press briefing, both he and Senator Vandenberg, also a passenger on the Stettinius aircraft, walked into the Senate chamber arm-in-arm to a standing ovation from their colleagues.[3]

The next day, Senator Connally took the Senate floor to deliver a 6,500-word report about the proceedings in San Francisco. An excited if tense Senate and a murmuring gallery thronging with visitors, including the British ambassador to the United States and its delegate to San Francisco, Lord Halifax, watched closely. "I do not proclaim [the Charter] as embodying perfection," Connally began. "However, the Charter marks a beginning. It will grow and develop in the light of experience. . . . The Charter must be judged not in its dissected parts—not in its dismembered and mutilated clauses and phrases, but its must be judged as an integrated body, complete in its organs and functions. Judged by that standard, it is a monumental performance." With a Texan-sized flourish, Connally vowed: "Our sons must not be sacrificed upon an altar of blood. War must be prevented before it breaks upon us in its bloody fury. Aggressors must be chained. The monster with a sword must be dethroned. The methods of peace must be enthroned. Let us," he told his fellow legislators, "be among the architects of a structure more marvelous than one built of steel and stone. Let us create a temple of law and reason and justice and peace to serve the peoples of the world." The balconies rose to their feet in applause and cheers.[4]

The next afternoon, Senator Vandenberg, with Lord Halifax again in attendance, his hands now cupped to his ears to hear better, began his plea for the charter. "The galleries were packed," Vandenberg wrote in his diary, "and there were seventy-eight senators in their seats. You could have heard a pin drop all the way through my speech; and at the finish the whole place broke out in a roar." Vandenberg made his position clear from the beginning: "I am prepared to proceed with this great adventure. I see no other way." He envisioned the charter as a major step forward for mankind's survival: "If the spirit of its authors can become the spirit of its evolution, I believe it will bless the earth. I believe it serves the intelligent self-interest of the United States which knows, by bitter experience, in the valley of the shadow of two wars alone. I believe it is our only chance to keep faith with those who have borne the heat of battle." He would support this organization, he said, "because this plan, regardless of infirmities, holds great promise that the United Nations may collaborate for peace as effectively as they have made common cause for war."[5]

People may say, he continued, that some signatories "practice the precise opposite of what they preach even as they sign." But, "I reply that the nearer right you may be in any such gloomy indictment, the greater is the need for the new pattern which promises at least to try to stem these evil tides. . . . The nearer right you are, the greater is the urgency for invoking the emancipations which the San Francisco Charter contemplates." "Mr. President," he added, "this can be a new emancipation proclamation for the world." As to the question of whether U.S. sovereignty would in any way be compromised, Vandenberg cited the veto: "It is a warrant that, though we cooperate wholeheartedly with the United Nations for peace and security, we remain the captains of our own souls." Striking a final note, he said: "America has everything to gain and nothing to lose by giving its support; everything to lose and nothing to gain by declining this continued fraternity with the United Nations in behalf of the dearest dream of humankind. I commend it to Congress and the country." On his last words, Vandenberg's Republican compatriots swarmed about him, cheering and clapping, wringing his hand, and hooting approval of his address. The next day, the *New York Times* wrote that following Vandenberg's speech there was a "snowballing of sentiment for ratification that is sweeping the Senate." In a letter to his wife, Vandenberg called it "really an amazing situation. Practically all opposition has disappeared. . . . Under such circumstances, there has been just one thing to do and that is drive ahead to ratification with the least possible delay."[6]

That same day, John Foster Dulles delivered a luncheon speech to 1,000 members of the Foreign Policy Association in Philadelphia; the address was broadcast over a countrywide hookup to FPA branches in twenty-seven other cities. "Membership in the new organization," Dulles promised, "will engage us to work with others to promote human rights and liberties; to eradicate intolerance; to clear away the obstacles to healthy trade; to insure social conditions which will breed sane and healthy men and women; to seek, for independent peoples, self-government and, meanwhile, to avoid exploitation. Such are the goals set before the members of the new organization." A few days later, the Republican presidential candidate of 1944, Governor Thomas Dewey of New York, whom Dulles had advised, endorsed the treaty. He informed newsmen: "I hope the Senate will adopt the San Francisco Charter with all possible speed," adding, "I don't think any reservations are necessary. I think they would simply delay adoption. There is a clear mandate from the American people for ratification of the Charter." Heeding the calls for rapid action, the Democratic Senate majority leader, Alben Barkley, now pledged no recess until the Senate acted on the charter.[7]

Meanwhile, outside groups lobbying for the U.N. reinforced the growing procharter sentiment in Congress. Under pressure to mount a national campaign in just a few short weeks, the leaders scrambled. The Federal Council of Churches of Christ, advised by John Foster Dulles and representing some 25 million Protestants, announced on June 26 its endorsement and issued a brochure on the virtues of the United Nations. The National Council of Jewish Women prepared a flyer on the charter for mass distribution, and the National Jewish Conference issued a study guide for Jewish associations. The Church Peace Union sponsored a conference on the U.N. in New York City. The National Catholic Welfare Council expressed its backing.[8]

Meantime, many of the consultants in San Francisco, returning to their homes and offices, organized a rump crusade on behalf of the U.N. On June 23, the American Association for the United Nations brought together over seven hundred organizations for a day meeting at the Hotel Commodore in New York titled "What Happened at San Francisco." By now, the Lions Club, with its 4,700 clubs, had enlisted; so, too, the League of Women Voters, which also published a booklet; the National Grange; the American Farm Bureau; the American Veterans Committee; the Brotherhood of Railroad Trainmen; the National Congress of Parents and Teachers; the General Federation of Women's Clubs; the National Education Association, which had more than 50,000 members; the Woodrow Wilson Foundation; the American Legion; the American Federation of Labor (AFL); the Congress of Industrial Organizations (CIO); the U.S. Chamber of Commerce; the National Association of Manufacturers; the American Bar Association; the National Maritime Union; and others.[9]

The State Department was riding this tide of support. The department had already shaped public opinion during the conference through its assistant secretary of state, Archibald MacLeish, who kept up a steady stream of reports to the public during the conference via eight weekly Saturday-night broadcasts from San Francisco. When the conference ended, the department distributed the text of the charter to pressure groups, editorial boards, and civic organizations. The department also dispatched experts around the country to explain the charter to the public, expounding on security, regionalism, and trusteeship. It reviewed and prepared interpretive documents and background data in readiness for the Senate Foreign Relations Committee hearings. The department coordinated testimony by outside individuals and organizations at the Senate hearings on the charter, beginning on July 9.[10]

On the morning of July 2, President Truman made his long-promised trip to the Capitol to present the U.N. Charter personally to the Senate. This was only the sixth time a president had done so, George Washington being the first in the summer of 1789—to discuss an Indian treaty. To underline his desire to talk directly to the Senators, Truman requested that no pictures be taken and no microphones be permitted.

With standing room only, and the galleries fully packed, it was, an observer wrote, "one of the most enthusiastic [crowds] the chamber has ever held." Wearing a gray summer suit and dotted bow-tie, tanned and smiling, Truman made his way to the Senate rostrum amidst thunderous applause; he was accompanied by an aide who held the blue-bound charter with its great gold seal. In his six-hundred-word address, Truman reminded his listeners that the Senate and the House had both passed resolutions in favor of an international security organization in 1943—the so-called Connally and Fulbright resolutions. "You," he said, "had a hand in shaping" the charter. The charter, he asserted, had the noble purposes of preventing war, settling disputes peacefully, promoting economic well-being, and eliminating poverty as a cause of social unrest. "It comes from the reality of experience in a world where one generation has failed twice to keep the peace," he stated. "The lessons of that experience have been written into the document." He closed by saying: "The choice before the Senate is now clear. The choice is not between this Charter and something else. It is between this Charter and no charter at all."[11]

For all the drama, sentiment among the U.S. public remained strangely hesitant in early July, although still holding strongly for the charter. Perhaps the actuality of a treaty after nine laborious weeks of negotiations in San Francisco had dulled the sense of excitement among the populace. Although surveys showed that three out of four Americans wanted the United States to join the United Nations, nearly 20 percent held no opinion on the issue; and in one poll, 12 percent said they had not even heard of the charter. On the question of preventing future wars, Americans were quite skeptical. One survey indicated an almost even split among respondents over the U.N.'s capacity to forestall conflicts, 39 percent stating there was a good chance the organization could stop them and 44 percent believing there was only a fair chance. A Gallup poll in late July was even more pessimistic: Only two out of five believed the body could actually preserve the peace, and an equal number thought that war would occur again.[12]

On a hot Monday morning on July 9 in Washington, Senator Connally gaveled the Foreign Relations Committee to order for the beginning of the charter hearings. Connally had attempted to gather most of the Senate membership for this opening session, but was only partially successful. For those who couldn't attend, he arranged to supply transcripts of the previous day's proceedings every morning during the week-long event. Former Secretary of State Stettinius (his successor, James Byrnes, had just taken over) was the first witness. Stettinius submitted to the committee a separate 50,000-word report, written by State Department officials, that elaborated on what had occurred in San Francisco and why the United States should now join the U.N. Expressing his final public sentiments about the conference, Stettinius told the senators that the charter, despite its imperfections, would be a "truly effective instrument for lasting peace." In response to questions from liberals about whether the veto unfairly accorded more power to the United States than to other nations, Stettinius reassured them that it did "not confer any power upon the great nations which they do not already possess." There was no need, in any event, he said, to fear the domination of the permanent members of the Security Council since "their common interest in preventing another war is fully as urgent as that of any other nation." In the final analysis, the veto was there only to protect U.S. sovereignty.[13]

Leo Pasvolsky was the next witness. In his inimitable manner, Pasvolsky spent that day and the entire next day leading the senators through the charter article by article, as he had done with the members of the U.S. delegation in San Francisco. There was only one real challenger to his nuanced explanations—Senator Eugene Millikin, a Republican from Colorado. Though not a committee member, Millikin had been invited to participate in the hearing. Adverting to the powers of the Security Council, Millikin asked Pasvolsky whether the United States would breach the charter if it reserved the right to determine in each instance whether to supply troops for council ventures. Pasvolsky reminded Millikin that Washington would first have to negotiate a special agreement with the Security Council before the United States could furnish soldiers and assets and that, in any event, it could always veto a U.N. military action if it wished. An unhappy Millikin expressed his opinion that Congress should give its approval each time the U.N. asked that forces be deployed.[14]

Sensing that the hearing had reached a point of contention, Senators Connally and Vandenberg jumped in. Both emphatically warned that any congressional intrusion advocated by Millikin would violate the spirit of the charter. Such unilateralism, said Connally, would be detrimental to the U.N. "because if every country who is a party to the Charter did that, we would be almost right where we are now, dependent upon the individual action of each nation in case a dispute arose. This is what happened in the last war and in the present war." Besides, he noted, "if we have to wait to get somebody's consent, the war will be on, and we will not be able to control it." Vandenberg, in his turn, challenged Millikin's notion that the charter would deprive Congress of its constitutional right to declare war. "But very clearly for 150 years," he observed, "the President has had the right to use our armed forces in a preliminary way for the national defense and in the interest of preventing war. That is a complete analogy to the intended use of preliminary force by the Security Council." He added: "It has been done 72 times within the last 150 years. It is as much a part of the Constitution as is the congressional right to declare war." Only when a situation reaches the point of war, he concluded, does Congress have a role in determining it. "That may be a no man's land, but it has been a no man's land for 150 years."[15]

Millikin would not abandon the issue. Toward the end of the hearing, he cross-examined John Foster Dulles about the Senate's right to define the terms under which the United States would provide troops to the Security Council. Dulles cited the provision in the charter requiring all special agreements made with the Security Council to be approved by the "constitutional processes" of member nations. This precluded any U.S. president, he said, from circumventing the Congress on the use of troops at the U.N. "It is clearly my view," Dulles remarked, "and it was the view of the entire United States delegation, that the agreement which will provide for the United States military contingent will have to be negotiated and then submitted to the Senate for ratification in the same way as a treaty." Sitting in front of him, Connally nodded his head in agreement. Millikin at last agreed to vote for the charter.[16]

Some thirty national organizations presented testimony for ratification; in addition, various organizations—two hundred local, thirty-

four national, and nine state—submitted statements backing the proposal. Some thirty-one groups appeared in opposition. The opponents
divided into two—those who abhorred the idea of the U.N. because
they saw it as a potential superstate, and those who disliked it because
it did not create a world federation. The first assailed the pact as atheis-
tic, Communist-inspired, and un-American; the second by and large
contended the body would not perform as a government, was undemocratic, upheld the myth of absolute national sovereignty, and would be
controlled by the five permanent members. Most of the representatives
for both viewpoints were marginal or unknown figures, far out of the
mainstream. To the extent their testimonies had any impact, those on
the right tended to cancel out those on the left. One of the still influential figures among this odd coterie of voices was Socialist Party leader
Norman Thomas. He proved to be somewhat of an apostate. He actually
endorsed the charter, grudgingly stating: "I agree with Senator Vandenberg that the world is even more at the mercy of the Big Three without the San Francisco Charter than with it."[17]

The hearings ended at 4:00 P.M. Friday afternoon, July 13. Senator
Connally immediately cleared the caucus room and ordered his committee into executive session. Thirty minutes later, he announced that all
twenty senators present had voted to report the charter out favorably.
Two missing senators later said they would split their vote—making
the final tally 21 to 1 in favor of ratification, Republican Senator Hiram
Johnson of California dissenting. Over the weekend, the committee
compiled a report and issued it on Monday. Its recommendations made
clear that the senators strongly approved of the treaty without amendments or reservations. All were concerned that additions might weaken
or destroy the U.N., as they had once undercut the League of Nations.
The charter already contained safeguards to protect U.S. national interest, the statement noted, including the veto, Article 51 permitting collective or individual acts of self-defense (preserving the Monroe Doctrine), and the provision broadly shielding domestic sovereignty.[18]

A week later, on July 23, the Senate began its final debate. Senator
Connally opened the proceedings with a lengthy if discursive speech
that reminded his colleagues of the bipartisan nature of the support,

listed the numerous independent groups backing the agreement, and mentioned opinion polls in favor of the U.N. Charter. Although acknowledging the pact's limitations, Connally praised it as "the greatest document of its kind that has ever been formulated." Then, in his finest grandiloquent fashion, Connally warned his brethren about the failure to enact the treaty. Other nations, he said, "know how the League of Nations was slaughtered here on the floor. Can you not see the blood on the floor? Can you not see upon the walls the marks of the conflict that raged right here in the Chamber where the League of Nations was done to death?"

Following Connally, and in his more modulated manner, Senator Vandenberg made the argument for Republican backing. Carefully playing to isolationist sensitivities concerned about the loss of U.S. sovereignty, Vandenberg denied that the U.N. could become a superstate: "The United States retains every basic attribute of its sovereignty," he stated, for the charter "gives us a veto on war and on any steps leading to war." He pleaded for all to acknowledge that two successive world wars had not brought security to the United States. A third global conflict would be too terrible to contemplate. "It clearly threatens the end of civilization," he said. "Here is our chance to stop this disaster before it starts."[19]

Over the next six days, the debate meandered in a low-key way. Most senators had by now publicly endorsed the treaty. All, however, wanted to go on record for what was an indisputably historic occasion. The Democrats generally invoked the past, citing the tragedy of the League's defeat and how war inevitably followed its demise. Republicans, possibly chagrined by their role in killing the League twenty-five years earlier, dwelt mainly on the future, repeating Vandenberg's warning about another worldwide conflagration. Only two Republican senators, life-long isolationists, indicated that they would vote against ratification. They were William Langer of North Dakota and Henrik Shipstead of Minnesota. Shipstead articulated a credo common to both men, decrying world government and disparaging reliance on force to keep the peace: "Perpetual intervention means perpetual war," he said. "We in the New World cannot and will not every twenty years redress the balance of the Old by sending our sons to war."[20]

The most dramatic moments of the debate came over the issue of "special agreements" defining the size and status of military forces that the United States would make available to the U.N. Supporters of the charter disagreed on the exact methods for enacting such Article 43 legislation. Most Democrats preferred that a joint resolution be passed by majorities in the Senate and the House. Republicans, taking their cue from earlier testimony by Dulles, contended that such an agreement should be handled as a treaty requiring ratification by a two-thirds majority of the Senate. Vandenberg, who wanted to avoid further confusion, asked Dulles for clarification on what he had meant in his Senate testimony. Dulles explained that he was simply trying to discredit the notion that a presidential executive order for U.N. troop deployments might replace a special agreement and that, although he favored the treaty route, a joint resolution would also be acceptable. To clinch the deal, Democratic senators now asked President Truman, with Stalin and Prime Minister Clement Attlee of Great Britain, in Postdam, to issue a statement addressing special agreements. On July 27, the day before the final vote was taken, Truman cabled a message saying that he intended "to ask Congress by appropriate legislation" to approve the agreements, making clear he would not send troops into U.N. combat through an executive order. When the Senate chose to interpret Truman's ambiguous pledge on legislative tactics to mean that Congress would now act by a joint resolution, the Republicans dropped their objections.[21]

On Saturday morning at 10:00 A.M. on July 28, Majority Leader Alben Barkley convened the Senate for the roll call. A final round of twenty senators spoke in support of the treaty. Then the clerk called the roster of senators. The vote was taken and the charter passed by a stunning count of 89 to 2, Senators Langer and Shipstead registering nays (five senators were absent, including at least one other negative vote, Senator Hiram Johnson, who was hospitalized). The U.S. became the third nation after Nicaragua and El Salvador to ratify the charter. Given the long days of high tension, the vote was almost an anticlimax. Though the Senate gallery remained full of spectators, there were no cheers or applause; onlookers filed out silently. The White House informed President Truman of the vote just before he retired for the night in Potsdam. Truman declared: "The action of the Senate substantially advances the cause of world peace." Senator Vandenberg himself heard the news in an elated if somewhat egomaniacal mood. "It really was an amazing action," he wrote his wife later. "Everybody now agrees that I would have beaten the Charter if I had taken the opposition tack. I must confess, now that it's all over, that I am very proud to have been one of its fathers."[22]

Still, there was some discontent among some senators, all backers of the treaty, about the lack of a more substantive and vigorous debate over the charter. The opposition had collapsed because, as one possible foe in the Senate told the *New York Times:* "There is a tide running here, and I would be a fool to risk my political future by bucking it." A hard-hitting debate might have, in retrospect, helped banish the issues of isolationism and unilateralism from the U.S. polity. Even while commending Connally and Vandenberg for their extraordinary leadership, Senator Fulbright, a Democrat from Arkansas, wryly noted that "sometimes I wish that they had not been quite so persuasive. A little more spirited debate, a little more opposition on the floor might serve to sharpen our understanding and our appreciation of the true significance of this agreement." Seasoned U.N. observers such as Edward Luck believed that, over the long run, this very "stress on unanimity and bipartisanship in 1945 created a false impression that America's commitment to the U.N. rested on far broader and deeper political foundations than was the case." Or, as Secretary of State Dean Acheson put it, the charter's "presentation to the American people as almost holy writ and with evangelical enthusiasm of a major advertising campaign seemed to me to raise popular hopes which could only lead to bitter disappointment."[23]

Some observers suggest, nonetheless, that the vote's result was due to more than just a well-orchestrated crusade for the U.N. The war had brought about a basic realignment of political forces at work in the United States in the 1940s, opening up new sectors of the nation to internationalism. In the South, once a citadel of insularity, there was an intense longing to rebuild the shattered cotton export market; in addition, the war had brought new military bases and defense industries to the region. These changes had wrought a new sympathy for foreign engagement. In the North, once the haven of the elder Henry Cabot Lodge and his allies, the war had nurtured urbanization and spawned a new trade and financial colossus that hungered for overseas customers and wider capital transfers. One still found in the Middle West that hearts and minds were encased in the provincialism of the 1920s—but even there, U.N. supporters picked up votes.[24]

Of course, there were still larger reasons for the almost unanimous support the treaty won in the Senate. There was an almost primeval sense that after two catastrophic global wars within twenty-five years—the second claiming about 67 million lives—it was imperative for humankind to bring its destructive impulses under control. In founding the United Nations, the peoples of the United States, and of the earth, could now claim to have extracted meaning out of despair and pay tribute to the millions of deaths in two calamitous struggles. The lesson of the League of Nations' defeat had also been painfully but fruitfully learned by Presidents Roosevelt and Truman, as indicated earlier. They had approached the U.N. Conference in a bipartisan spirit, sending Republicans as well as Democrats to San Francisco, appointed a conciliator in Edward Stettinius to hold the mission together, organized it before the war had ended, and embraced the veto as a key feature overcoming objections arising from feared diminution of U.S. sovereignty. The U.S. government had also engineered a public campaign for the U.N. of unprecedented proportions. As Thomas Franck, a professor at New York University Law School and a specialist on the U.N., noted, the adminstration's crusade alone was "surely one of the most dramatic examples of hard-sell huckstering in twentieth-century American politics."[25]

Now, with the triumph of the U.N., Truman faced a second goal, one perhaps more problematical: passing the remaining U.N. legislation on the agenda—the special agreements. Through the rest of the summer and well into the fall, the State Department and leaders in Congress under Truman's direction began to draft a bill, later known as the United Nations Participation Act, designed to formulate the rules under which the United States would supply troops for U.N. military actions. By its nature, it brought back into focus the constitutionality questions raised by Senator Millikin and others in the July hearings on whether Congress's right to declare war might be abridged in any way by the implementing statute required under Article 43 of the charter. Senator Connally tried from the beginning to refute suggestions that the Congress was enacting a measure departing from the U.N. Charter passed five months earlier. On November 26, 1945, at the commencement of the weeklong debate, Connally said that the "United States is undertaking no new obligations. We are but making the necessary arrangements within our own government so that we may carry out the obligations which we have already assumed under the Charter."[26]

The act did appear to fulfill the mandate laid down by Article 43. Under its most critical provision, Section 6, the president was empowered to negotiate, subject to the approval of Congress, agreements for numbers and types of U.S. forces, with the specification that the president should not be deemed "to require the authorization of Congress" to make armed forces available to the Security Council on its call pursuant to such special agreements. But the president could not dispatch troops beyond the limits set in the statute, particularly in large-scale mobilizations, without further congressional authorization. Even though this text had long been expected, some senators and outside experts wondered whether this did not represent a doubtful constitutional delegation by Congress of its war-making power. That had to be answered by whether U.S. involvement in a duly constituted U.N. security operation was seen to be the equivalent of a U.S. national war or was merely, as Senator Vandenberg had argued in July, to be treated as a small-scale police action for the purposes of preventing war or preserving the peace, thus rendering it exempt from congressional scrutiny.

Senator Burton K. Wheeler, Democrat of Montana, a prewar isolationist leader among a tiny handful of malcontent senators, did not believe that authorizing the president to dispatch small troop deployments under the U.N. umbrella would necessarily protect the congressional power to limit the numbers of fighting men. Some disputes, he said, might blossom into full-sized conflicts. Engaging in a colloquy with Senator Connally on November 26, 1945, Wheeler said that "We are then at war . . . whatever we may want to call it, and the Congress is going to have to accept that fact, and vote then for the use of more troops." Wheeler proposed an amendment that would have required the approval of Congress in each specific instance in which the president permitted U.S. troops to be used by the Security Council— notwithstanding special agreements. As an indication of how powerful were the currents now coursing through the Senate on behalf of the U.N. six months after the country had joined the organization, the Senate defeated the Wheeler amendment on December 4, 1945, by an overwhelmingly 65 to 9. The same day, the Senate passed into law the United Nations Participation Act 65 to 7. Just over two weeks later, on December 20, 1945, the House completed the bill's passage by 344 to 15. The United States had now executed all the necessary steps required under the U.N. Treaty to meet the conditions of membership, except for negotiating the actual details of the special agreement itself with the Security Council.[27]

This was not the end of the story. In practice, it was to turn out, every president who committed troops to U.N. operations, from Truman in the Korean War in 1950 to Bill Clinton in Haiti in 1994, circumvented the "Special Agreements" legislation in dispatching U.S. forces in support of U.N. operations. They did so through the simple expedient of not forwarding such agreements to the legislature. No president wanted to risk becoming embroiled in a struggle with Congress over the White House right to send forces into war. Instead, each preferred to invoke the powers of the president as commander-in-chief to post U.S. soldiers unilaterally under a U.N. resolution without Congress's prior consent. In thus circling around the special agreements, they, in effect, neutralized them, if not made them totally irrelevant.

Still, danger lurked for presidents who acted in this fashion; for without consulting Congress, a leader risked losing legitimacy for his actions with the U.S. public over the long run. As a consequence, some presidents, such as the two George Bushes, father and son, both sought at least minimal congressional authorization via joint resolutions—both in these instances for their wars against Iraq—to guarantee public backing and out of political prudence for their actions, even though both men also said publicly that they did not believe they needed to obtain such support. The senior Bush went to war after first receiving U.N. Security Council and, in turn, congressional support; the junior Bush got a congressional OK, but thereafter never received Security Council approval before he began combat.

Still, the United States, in adopting the United Nations Participation Act, crossed the final threshold of entry into an international organization, the first one it had ever joined, and the second one (including the League of Nations) it had created virtually alone. The United Nations might eventually turn out to be the most resplendent gift the United States had given the world. Still, for this country, it was taking initial footsteps on terrain on which it had never trodden before. The question of its own success or failure in that body was yet to be determined. The coming years would be the judge of that. But the first steps—the steps that many had waited for—had now been taken.

Epilogue

The San Francisco Conference proved the highlight in the careers of many of those who took part in the proceedings. Absent among the State Department representatives in the California city, Cordell Hull, who was in the U.S. delegation but hospitalized the whole time in Washington, and whose role in the U.N. was far less consequential than that of his coworkers, received the Nobel Peace Prize in 1945 for his long service as secretary of state (eleven years and nine months) and for his U.N. labors. In his memoirs, Hull recounts at length his work on the U.N. He remained in Washington until his death at age eighty-four on July 23, 1955, outliving his much younger successor, Edward Stettinius, by six years. Leo Pasvolsky retired from the State Department in 1946 and returned to the Brookings Institution, where he stayed until his death in 1953. He began an account of his experiences in San Francisco but never completed the manuscript; it was finished by his assistant, Ruth Russell, and published as her own book. The old isolationist, Senator Arthur Vandenberg, who did not survive his third term (he died on April 18, 1951, at age sixty-seven), remembered the U.N. with pride in his published diary and in his later addresses. His crusty colleague, Senator Thomas Connally, although regarding San Francisco as a notable milestone, devoted only a few pages to it in his memoirs, never bothering to quote his own eloquent and passionate speeches about the organization. Connally retired from the Senate in 1953 after six terms in office and remained in Washington until his death on October 28, 1963.

Harold Stassen, John Foster Dulles, and Nelson Rockefeller went onto distinguished careers in the Republican Party over the next half-century. Stassen served in various foreign policy advisory posts under

President Eisenhower. He is mostly remembered today, though, for his nine unsuccessful tries for the presidency—the last in 1992—which turned him into a national figure of ridicule. Memories of the U.N. Conference, however, still remained vivid in his mind, as is attested by the volume of interviews he regularly gave on the subject to all comers. Stassen managed to surpass in years all his prominent comrades from San Francisco; he survived into the new century and died on March 4, 2001, at age ninety-three. John Foster Dulles served as a U.S. representative to the U.N. from 1946 until 1948 and in 1950, and briefly as senator from New York from 1949 to 1950. President Eisenhower appointed him secretary of state in 1953. While in office, he used the U.N., among other purposes, to denounce the joint British-French seizure of the Suez Canal in the fall of 1956, seeking U.N. observers to supervise a cease-fire and withdrawal. Dulles showed respect for the organization during his tenure despite disagreements, never withholding dues or denouncing U.N. actions, as his Republican successors were later to do. Dulles died of cancer on May 24, 1959. Nelson Rockefeller's family gave the land for the U.N. building in New York City. Rockefeller himself went on to be elected to four terms as governor of New York. In his first run for office in 1958, he defeated his old San Francisco sparring partner, Averell Harriman, who had just completed a single term as New York State's chief executive. Later, President Ford chose Rockefeller as his vice president in December 1974, but dropped him from the 1976 ticket. Rockefeller died on January 26, 1979.

John Kennedy became the thirty-fifth president of the United States in 1961. He recruited for his administration several veterans of San Francisco. The most prominent was Adlai Stevenson, Democratic presidential nominee in 1952 and 1956. Kennedy appointed Stevenson as the U.S. envoy to the United Nations, where Stevenson served with great distinction until his untimely death on July 14, 1965. Kennedy also brought in Averell Harriman, whom he first made a roving ambassador, then undersecretary of state for Far Eastern affairs, and finally assistant secretary of state for political affairs, where he helped to negotiate the first Test Ban Treaty with the Soviet Union in 1963. Kennedy also chose Charles Bohlen to be the U.S. ambassador to France in 1962. And he tapped Thomas Finletter as U.S. ambassador to NATO. For Kennedy, the U.N. proved its maximum utility during the Cuban missile crisis when he used the Security Council to confront the USSR publicly with evidence that it had placed offensive missiles in Cuba. The U.N. helped to supervise the removal of the weaponry from the island nation.

Vyacheslav Molotov, the Soviet foreign minister, and the Soviet ambassador to the United States, Andrei Gromyko, among the most important foreign emissaries in San Francisco, enjoyed several second acts. Molotov continued to lead the Russian delegation to the U.N. through the late 1940s as foreign minister until 1949. In that year, he was made deputy prime minister. After Stalin's death in March 1953, the new regime reappointed him as foreign minister. In 1957, after run-ins with Nikita Khrushchev, Molotov was ousted from the government and, except for a few minor posts, including ambassador to Mongolia, never regained a significant office. He died on November 8, 1986, at the age of ninety-six—without writing his memoirs. Gromyko proved to be a wily survivor, becoming foreign minister in 1957 and remaining in that post through a succession of leaders until 1985. On retirement, he wrote his autobiography, giving only brief mention to his U.N. duty. He died on July 2, 1989, at age seventy-nine. Clement Attlee and Anthony Eden both later served as prime ministers of England, Attlee from 1945 to 1951, and Eden from 1955 to 1957. Herbert Evatt of Australia became deputy prime minister of Australia after the San Francisco Conference, from 1946 to 1949, and in 1951, leader of the opposition, but his party never gained power under his leadership. Evatt retired from politics in 1962 and died on November 2, 1965.

As for the United Nations itself, the U.N. Charter of San Francisco turned out to have several surprising consequences. First of all, many of the charter issues that so deeply divided the meeting and threatened at times to derail it proved irrelevant to the U.N.'s operations. The battles over U.N. membership for Argentina, Poland, Belarus, and Ukraine, for example, were forgotten. The cavils of the smaller states regarding the Great Powers' right to a veto in peaceful settlements (except if a party to a dispute); the convening of another conference within ten years to revise the charter; and the Big Five's power to veto amendments arising out of such meetings—all issues lost at San Francisco—faded away. The argument among delegates over making the right to withdrawal a formal clause in the U.N. Charter was not pursued; most states that didn't like Security Council resolutions simply didn't recognize or obey them. The Military Staff Committee proved a nonfunctioning body, though it still meets today. The fears of Ambassador Gromyko about a diminished veto in the Security Council or the General Assembly's too generous discussion rights were not mentioned again. And apprehensions that the Security Council would act against U.S. interests, especially during the cold war, evaporated as the United States and the Soviet Union regularly blocked each other's actions in the council.

But the veto issue did finally come to dominate the Security Council, as most small nations had predicted. Historian Gabriel Kolko insisted that the veto would make the U.N. an arena for power politics. "The new organization failed before it began," he claimed, "for Washington conceived it with exceptions and loopholes, in an atmosphere of suspicion and manipulation, not as a forum for agreement, but as an instrument in the Great Power conflict." Evan Luard observed: "For all the long discussions and bitter debates at San Francisco, the new United Nations remained an organization conceived and created by the great powers. Its form and structure clearly reflected its birth. That is, it was an organization in which the great powers of the world would have the dominant say." Yet as noted earlier, however, absent the veto, neither of the two leading nations of the time, the United States and the Soviet Union, would have ever joined the U.N. The elder Senator Henry Cabot Lodge's grandson by the same name, Eisenhower's ambassador to the United Nations, argued in a biography of the senator that his grandfather, had he lived, would have supported the U.N. because of the veto. It should also be noted that even in the Security Council, nonpermanent members could still, if united, constitute a sixth veto and, in any event, they did have to form part of a voting majority, thus making small nations far more relevant than Kolko and Luard suggest.[1]

The veto did, however, have the effect of paralyzing the Security Council for forty-five years during the cold war. After the fall of the

Berlin Wall, though, the veto actually had the paradoxical effect of turning the Security Council into one of the few countervailing powers to the United States. Because it was the only global body that could give the imprimatur of legitimacy to the use of armed force, assuring the backing of nations around the planet for such decisions, the council grew after 1989 to play a more central role in world affairs. It forced big powers like the United States planning military operations to seek its approval first or otherwise risk having to act outside of international law. This, in effect, handed power to veto-bearing nations on the council to slow down action through the threat of a "no" vote. That, in turn, sometimes compelled further debate before the council agreed to enforcement measures. On the other hand, the veto also rigidified the status quo on the council itself in so far as the five permanent members were concerned. It became evident over the years that none of them would ever consent to admit new veto-bearing states to the Council, for example, Germany or Japan—nor, for that matter, would they surrender their own vetoes.

At the same time, the charter, in the words of Sir Brian Urquhart, showed itself to be a "suprisingly practical document." At first, Winston Churchill and other leaders feared the U.N. would promise more than it could deliver. In his famous "Iron Curtain" speech on March 5, 1946, in Fulton, Missouri, Churchill warned that the organization must make sure "that its work is fruitful, that it is a reality and not a sham, that it is a force for action, and not merely a frothing of words, that it is a true temple of peace in which the shields of many nations can some day be hung, and not merely a cockpit in a tower of Babel." In fact, much of what he hoped for came true.[2]

Although the Military Staff Committee did not fulfill its anointed role, the secretary-general was nonetheless able to mount military operations of all sorts on an ad hoc basis through U.N. resolutions, especially after the end of the cold war. Under the peace and security provisions in the charter, the U.N.'s chief and the Security Council carved out a whole range of military options not foreseen in the original document, including peacekeeping, peace enforcement, cease-fires, disarmament, nuclear proliferation bans, preventive diplomacy, arms inspec-

tions, and military training. In addition, the U.N. moved gradually from
a restricted definition of aggression comprising only cross-border inva-
sions to civil wars, overcoming the previously sacrosanct presumption
in favor of national sovereignty. But the U.N. never developed a rapid-
response force of its own mainly because the Big Powers feared a loss of
control over any independent U.N. army.

The U.N. also took on a host of responsibilities that the charter had
only intermittently defined, ranging from population control to migra-
tion, famine, environment, economic development, urbanization, the
seas, the supervision of failed states, and election monitoring, among
other matters. In fact, by the collapse of the Iron Curtain, the U.N. had
become primarily a service organization—90 percent of U.N. resources
addressed these social issues as opposed to security questions. Finally
the U.N. displayed a capacity to correct its own misjudgments—for example, by repealing its resolution equating Zionism with racism; issuing an investigative report assigning blame after its failures to prevent
the Srebrenica massacres in July 1995; and belatedly creating a high
commissioner for human rights. Last, the U.N. played a useful scape-
goat. States wanting to do things opposed by their people could now
blame the U.N. for forcing them to act as they did.[3]

But there remained clear limits on the U.N.'s authority. It lived on
still totally dependent on its members for its budgets and assignments.
It was at the mercy of its five permanent members to decide what it
should do in enforcement tasks. And even if it was instructed to act in
a crisis, it could only involve itself as much as its participating states
were willing to offer soldiers and weapons. It sat on the sidelines during one of the greatest crises in the postwar era—the slaughter of
800,000 people in Rwanda in 1994—because one veto-bearing nation,
the United States, said no. In recent years, its security role has been
primarily to clean up after conflicts such as Kosovo and Iraq. In the
end, it has no independent authority and is not a world government. It
remains, in many ways, an undemocratic body.

Yet, in the sixty or so years of the U.N.'s life, there has been a remarkable change in the nature of the state structure. Whether this has
to do directly with the United Nations or not is unclear, but undoubt-

edly the presence of the U.N. reinforced such trends. First, there was the extraordinary decolonization of the world, not foreseen. Second, there has been an unprecedented spread of democracy and mixed economies around the globe. Freedom House found that, in 1950, there were twenty-two democracies accounting for 31 percent of the world's population and a further twenty-one states with restricted democratic practices accounting for 11.9 percent of the world's citizenry. In 2000, electoral democracies represented 120 of the 192 existing nations and constituted 62.5 percent of the earth's population. Third, apart from four incidents—Turkey's seizure of two-fifths of Cyprus; Morocco's incursion into Western Sahara; the invasion of Kuwait by Iraq; and Indonesia's takeover of East Timor (the latter two which have been reversed by the U.N.)—there have been almost no attempts at annexation by one state of another during the U.N.'s existence. Fourth, there have been no nuclear conflicts during the U.N.'s reign, though innumerable small wars. Fifth, the U.N. has helped to alter permanently the concept of global relations by providing a forum for states to talk to each other on a continuous basis, and has helped to assist the spread of international law through ratification of norms of behavior by all nations.[4]

It is ironic that the United States, which created the U.N., has remained wary about the assembly, if not hostile toward it. In 1945, Fareed Zakaria reminds us, "when America was even more powerful that it is today—by some measures it had fifty percent of the world output—it put into place a series of measures designed to rebuild its adversaries, institutionalize international cooperation on dozens of global issues, and alleviate poverty. No other nation would have done this." And, as President Dwight Eisenhower once said: "With all the defects, with all the failures that we can check up against it, the U.N. still represents man's best-organized hope to substitute the conference table for the battlefield." Six decades later, the United States, which showed such prescience and foresight, continues to support the U.N. only fitfully. It must now find its way back to one of its greatest creations. The process must begin anew—for the fate of our country, our world, and our future.[5]

TEXT OF PRESIDENT TRUMAN'S ADDRESS, BRINGING THE WORLD PEACE PARLEY TO AN END

Following is the text of President Truman's address to the final Plenary Session of the United Nations Conference as recorded and transcribed by the New York Times:

Mr. Chairman and delegates to the United Nations Conference on International Organization:

Oh, what a great day this can be in history.

I deeply regret that the press of circumstances when this conference opened made it impossible for me to be here to greet you in person. I have asked for the privilege of coming today, to express on behalf of the people of the United States our thanks for what you have done here, and to wish you godspeed on your journeys home.

Somewhere in this broad country, every one of you can find some of our citizens who are sons and daughters, or descendants in some degree, of your own native land. All our people are glad and proud that this historic meeting and its accomplishments have taken place in our country. And that includes the millions of loyal and patriotic Americans who stem from the countries not represented at this conference.

We are grateful for your coming. We hope you have enjoyed your stay and that you will come again.

You assembled in San Francisco almost nine weeks ago with the high hope and confidence of peace-loving people the world over.

Their confidence in you has been justified.

Their hopes for your success has been fulfilled.

Calls Charter a Victory

The charter of the United Nations which you are now signing is a solid structure upon which we can build for a better world. History will honor you for it. Between the victory in Europe and the final victory in Japan, in this most destructive of all wars, you have won a victory against war itself.

It was the hope of such a charter that helped sustain the courage of stricken peoples through the darkest days of the war. For it is a declaration of great faith by the nations of the earth—faith that war is not inevitable, faith that peace can be maintained.

If we had had this charter a few years ago—and above all, the will to use it—millions now dead would be alive. If we should falter in the future in our will to use it, millions now living will surely die.

It has already been said by many that this is only a first step to a lasting peace. That is true. The important thing is that all our thinking and all our actions be based on the realization that it is in fact only a first step. Let us all have it firmly in mind that we start today from a good beginning and, with our eye always on the final objective, let us march forward.

The Constitution of my own country came from a convention which—like this one—was made up of delegates with many different views. Like this Charter, our Constitution came from a free and sometimes bitter exchange of conflicting opinions. When it was adopted, no one regarded it as a perfect document. But it grew and developed and expanded. And upon it there was built a bigger, a better, and a more perfect union.

This charter, like our own Constitution, will be expanded and improved as time goes on. No one claims that it is now a final or a perfect instrument. It has not been poured into a fixed mold. Changing world conditions will require readjustments—but they will be the readjustments of peace and not of war.

That we now have this charter at all is a great wonder. It is also a cause for profound thanksgiving to Almighty God, who has brought us so far in our search for peace through world organization.

Differences in Views Recalled

There were many who doubted that agreement could ever be reached by these fifty countries differing so much in race and religion, in language and culture. But these differences were all forgotten in one unshakable unity of determination—to find a way to end wars.

Out of all the arguments and disputes, and different points of view, a way was found to agree. Here in the spotlight of full publicity, in the tradition of liberty-loving people, opinions were expressed openly and freely. The faith and the hope of fifty peaceful nations were laid before this world forum. Differences were overcome. This charter was not the work of any single nation or group of nations, large or small. It was the result of a spirit of give-and-take, of tolerance for the views and interests of others.

It was proof that nations, like man, can state their differences, can face them, and then can find common ground on which to stand. That is the essence of democracy; that is the essence of keeping the peace in the future. By your agreement, the way was shown toward future agreements in the years to come.

This conference owes its success largely to the fact that you have kept your minds firmly on the main objective. You had the single job of writing a constitution—a charter for peace. And you stayed on that job.

In spite of the many differences and distractions which came to you in the form of daily problems and disputes about such matters as new boundaries, control of Germany, peace settlements, reparations, war criminals, the form of Government of some of the European countries—in spite of all these, you continued in the task of framing this document.

These problems and scores of others, which will arise, are all difficult. They are complicated. They are controversial and dangerous.

Solution of Problems Is Seen

But with a united spirit we met and solved even the more difficult problems during the war. And with the same spirit, if we keep to our principles and never forsake our objectives, the problems we now face and those to come will also be solved.

We have tested the principle of cooperation in this war and have found that it works. Through the pooling of resources, through joint and combined military command, through constant staff meetings, we have shown what united strength can do in war. That united strength forced Germany to surrender. United strength will force Japan to surrender also.

The United Nations have also had experience, even while the fighting was still going on, in reaching economic agreements for times of peace. What was done on the subject of relief at Atlantic City, food at Hot Springs, finance at Bretton Woods, aviation at Chicago, was a fair test of what can be done by nations determined to live cooperatively in a world where they cannot live peacefully any other way.

What you have accomplished in San Francisco shows how well these lessons of military and economic cooperation have been learned. You have created a great instrument for peace and security and human progress in the world.

The world must now use it.

If we fail to use it, we shall betray all those who have died in order that we might meet here in freedom and safety to create it.

If we seek to use it selfishly—for the advantage of any one nation or any small group of nations—we shall be equally guilty of that betrayal.

The successful use of this instrument will require the united will and firm determination of the free peoples who have created it. The job will tax the moral strength and fiber of us all.

Special Privileges Are Opposed

We all have to recognize—no matter how great our strength—that we must deny ourselves the license to do always as we please. No one nation, no regional group, can, or should expect, any special privilege which harms any other nation. If any nation would keep security for itself, it must be ready and willing to share security with all. That is the price which each nation will have to pay for world peace. Unless we are all willing to pay that price, no organization for world peace can accomplish its purpose.

And what a reasonable price that is.

Out of this conflict have come powerful military nations, now fully trained and equipped for war. But they have no right to dominate the world. It is rather the duty of these powerful nations to assume the responsibility for leadership toward a world of peace. That is why we have here resolved that power and strength shall be used not to wage war, but keep the world at peace, and free from the fear of war.

By their own example the strong nations of the world should lead the way to international justice. That principle of justice is the foundation stone of this charter. That principle is the guiding spirit by which it must be carried out—not by words alone but by continued concrete acts of good-will.

Now there is a time for making plans—and there is a time for action. Let us, therefore, each in his own nation and according to its own way, seek immediate approval of this Charter—and make it a living thing.

Expects Speedy Senate Approval

I shall send this charter to the United States Senate at once. I am sure that the overwhelming sentiment of the people of my country and of their representatives in the Senate is in favor of immediate ratification.

A just and lasting peace cannot be attained by diplomatic agreement alone, or by military cooperation alone. Experience has shown how deeply the seeds of war are planted by economic rivalry and by social injustice. The charter recognizes this fact, for it has provided for economic and social cooperation as well. It has provided for this cooperation as a part of the very heart of the entire compact.

It has set up machinery of international cooperation which men and nations of good-will can use to help correct the economic and social causes for conflict.

Artificial and uneconomic trade barriers should be removed—to the end that the standard of living of as many people as possible throughout the world may be raised. For freedom from want is one of the basic four freedoms toward which we all strive. The large and powerful nations of the world must assume leadership in this economic field as well as in all others.

Under this document we have good reason to expect the framing of an international bill of rights, acceptable to all the nations involved. That bill of rights will be as much a part of international life as our own bill of rights is a part of our Constitution. The charter is dedicated to the achievement and observance of human rights and fundamental freedoms. Unless we can obtain those objectives for all men and women everywhere—without regard to race, language or religion—we cannot have permanent peace and security in the world.

With this charter the world can begin to look forward to the time when all worthy human beings may be permitted to live decently as free people.

The world has learned again that nations, like individuals, must know the truth if they would be free—must read and hear the truth, learn and teach the truth.

Says Ideas Still Live

We must set up an effective agency for constant and thorough interchange of thought and ideas. For there lies the road to a better and more tolerant understanding among nations and among peoples.

All fascism did not die with Mussolini, Hitler is finished—but the seeds spread by his disordered mind have firm root in too many fanatical brains. It is easier to remove tyrants and destroy concentration camps than it is to kill the ideas which gave them birth and strength. Victory on the battlefield was essential, but it was not enough. For a good peace, a lasting peace, the decent peoples of the earth must remain determined to strike down the evil spirit which has hung over the world for the last decade.

The forces of reaction and tyranny all over the world will try to keep the United Nations from remaining unified. Even while the military machine of the Axis was being destroyed in Europe—even down to its very end—they still tried to divide us.

They failed. But they will try again.

They are trying even now. To divide and conquer was—and still is—their plan. They still try to make one ally suspect the other, hate the other, desert the other.

But I know I speak for every one of you when I say that the United Nations will remain united. They will not be divided by propaganda either before the Japanese surrender or after.

This occasion shows again the continuity of history.

By this Charter you have given reality to the ideal of that great statesman of a generation ago, Woodrow Wilson.

By this charter, you have moved toward the goal for which that gallant leader in this second world struggle worked and fought and gave his life—Franklin D. Roosevelt.

By this charter you have realized the objectives of many men of vision in your own countries who have devoted their lives to the cause of world organization for peace.

Upon all of us, in all our countries, is now laid the duty of transforming into action these words which you have written. Upon our decisive action rests the hope of those who have fallen, those now living, and those yet unborn—the hope for a world of free countries—with decent standards of living—which will work and cooperate in friendly, civilized community of nations.

This new structure of peace is rising upon strong foundations.

Let us not fail to grasp this supreme chance to establish a world-wide rule of reason—to create an enduring peace under the guidance of God.

CHARTER OF THE UNITED NATIONS

WE THE PEOPLES OF THE UNITED NATIONS DETERMINED

to save succeeding generations from the scourge of war, which twice in our life-time has brought untold sorrow to mankind, and

to reaffirm faith in fundamental human rights, in the dignity and worth of the human person, and in the equal rights of men and women and of nations large and small, and

to establish conditions under which justice and respect for the obligations aris-ing from treaties and other sources of international law can be maintained, and

to promote social progress and better standards of life in larger freedom,

AND FOR THESE ENDS

to practice and live together in peace with one another as good neighbors, and

to unite our strength to maintain international peace and security, and

to ensure, by the acceptance of principles and the institution of methods, that armed force shall not be used, save in the common interest, and

to employ international machinery for the promotion of the economic and social advancement of all peoples,

HAVE RESOLVED TO COMBINE OUR EFFORTS TO ACCOMPLISH THESE AIMS.

Accordingly, our representative Governments, through representatives assem-bled in the city of San Francisco, who have exhibited their full powers found to be in good and due form, have agreed to the present Charter of the United Nations and do hereby establish an international organization known as the United Nations.

CHAPTER I. PURPOSES AND PRINCIPLES

Article 1

The Purposes of the United Nations are:

1. To maintain international peace and security, and to that end: to take effec-tive collective measures for the prevention and removal of threats to the peace, and for the suppression of acts of aggression or other breaches of the peace, and to bring about by peaceful means, and in conformity with the

principles of justice and international law, adjustment or settlement of international disputes or situations which might lead to a breach of the peace;

2. To develop friendly relations among nations based on respect for the principle of equal rights and self-determination of peoples, and to take other appropriate measures to strengthen universal peace;

3. To achieve international co-operation in solving international problems of an economic, social, cultural, or humanitarian character, and in promoting and encouraging respect for human rights and for fundamental freedoms for all without distinction as to race, sex, language, or religion; and

4. To be a centre for harmonizing the actions of nations in the attainment of these common ends.

Article 2

The Organization of its Members, in pursuit of the Purposes stated in Article 1, shall act in accordance with the following principles.

1. The Organization is based on the principle of the sovereign equality of all its Members.

2. All Members, in order to ensure to all of them the rights and benefits resulting from membership, shall fulfill in good faith the obligations assumed by them in accordance with the present Charter.

3. All Members shall settle their international disputes by peaceful means in such a manner that international peace and security, and justice, are not endangered.

4. All Members shall refrain in their international relations from the threat of use of force against the territorial integrity or political independence of any state, or in any other manner inconsistent with the Purposes of the United Nations.

5. All Members shall give the United Nations every assistance in any action it takes in accordance with the present Charter, and shall refrain from giving assistance to any state against which the United Nations is taking preventive or enforcement action.

6. The Organization shall ensure that states which are not members of the United Nations act in accordance with these Principles so far as may be necessary for the maintenance of international peace and security.

7. Nothing contained in the present Charter shall authorize the United Nations to intervene in matters which are essentially within the domestic jurisdiction of any state or shall require the Members to submit such matters to settlement under the present Charter; but this principle shall not prejudice the application of enforcement measures under Chapter VII.

CHAPTER II. MEMBERSHIP

Article 3

The original Members of the United Nations shall be the states which, having participated in the United Nations Conference on International Organization at San Francisco, or having previously signed the Declaration by United Nations of 1 January 1942, sign the present Charter and ratify it in accordance with Article 110.

Article 4

1. Membership in the United Nations is open to all other peace-loving states which accept the obligations contained in the present Charter and, in the judgement of the Organization, are able and willing to carry out these obligations.
2. The admission of any such state to membership in the United Nations will be effected by a decision of the General Assembly upon the recommendation of the Security Council.

Article 5

A Member of the United Nations against which preventative or enforcement action has been taken by the Security Council may be suspended from the exercise of the rights and privileges of membership by the General Assembly upon the recommendation of the Security Council. The exercise of these rights and privileges may be restored by the Security Council.

Article 6

A Member of the United Nations which has persistently violated the Principles contained in the present Charter may be expelled from the Organization by the General Assembly upon the recommendation of the Security Council.

CHAPTER III. ORGANS

Article 7

1. These are established as the principal organs of the United Nations: a General Assembly, a Security Council, an Economic and Social Council, a Trusteeship Council, an International Court of Justice, and a Secretariat.
2. Such subsidiary organs as may be found necessary may be established in accordance with the present Charter.

Article 8

The United Nations shall place no restrictions on the eligibility of men and women to participate in any capacity and under conditions of equality in its principal and subsidiary organs.

CHAPTER IV. THE GENERAL ASSEMBLY

COMPOSITION

Article 9

1. The General Assembly shall consist of all the Members of the United Nations.
2. Each Member shall have not more than five representatives in the General Assembly.

FUNCTIONS AND POWERS

Article 10

The General Assembly may discuss any questions or any matters within the scope of the present Charter, and, except as provided in Article 12, may make recommendations to the Members of the United Nations or to the Security Council or to both on any such questions or matters.

Article 11

1. The General Assembly may consider the general principles of co-operation in the maintenance of international peace and security, including the principles governing disarmament and the regulation of armaments, and may make recommendations with regard to such principles to the Members or to the Security Council or both.
2. The General Assembly may discuss any questions relating to the maintenance of international peace and security brought before it by any Member of the United Nations in accordance with Article 35, paragraph 2, and, except as provided in Article 12, may make recommendations with regard to any such questions to the state or states concerned or to the Security Council or to both. Any such question on which action is necessary shall be referred to the Security Council by the General Assembly either before or after discussion.
3. The General Assembly may call the attention of the Security Council to situations which are likely to endanger international peace and security.
4. The powers of the General Assembly set forth in this Article shall not limit the general scope of Article 10.

Article 12

1. While the Security Council is exercising in respect of any dispute or situation the functions assigned to it in the present Charter, the General Assembly shall not make any recommendation with regard to that dispute or situation unless the Security Council so requests.

2. The Secretary-General, with the consent of the Security Council, shall notify the General Assembly at each session of any matters relative to the maintenance of international peace and security which are being dealt with by the Security Council and shall similarly notify the General Assembly, or the Members of the United Nations if the General Assembly is not in session, immediately the Security Council ceases to deal with such matters.

Article 13

1. The General Assembly shall initiate studies and make recommendations for the purpose of:
   A. promoting international co-operation in the political field and encouraging the progressive development of international law and its codification;
   B. promoting international co-operation in the economic, social, cultural, educational, and health fields, and assisting in the realization of human rights and fundamental freedoms for all without distinction as to race, sex, language, or religion.
2. The further responsibilities, functions, and powers of the General Assembly with respect to matters mentioned in paragraph 1(b) above are set forth in Chapters IX and X.

Article 14

Subject to the provisions of Article 12, the General Assembly may recommend measures for the peaceful adjustments of any situation, regardless of origin, which it deems likely to impair the general welfare or friendly relations among nations, including situations resulting from a violation of the provisions of the present Charter setting forth the Purposes and Principles of the United Nations.

Article 15

1. The General Assembly shall receive and consider annual and special reports from the Security Council; these reports shall include an account of the measures that the Security Council has decided upon or taken to maintain the international peace and security.
2. The General Assembly shall receive and consider reports from other organs of the United Nations.

Article 16

The General Assembly shall perform such functions with respect to the international trusteeship system as are assigned to it under Chapters XII and XIII, including the approval of the trusteeship agreements for areas not designated as strategic.

Article 17

1. The General Assembly shall consider and approve the budget of the Organization.
2. The expenses of the Organization shall be borne by the Members as apportioned by the General Assembly.
3. The General Assembly shall consider and approve any financial and budgetary arrangements with specialized agencies referred to in Article 57 and shall examine the administrative budgets of such specialized agencies with a view to making recommendations to the agencies concerned.

VOTING

Article 18

1. Each member of the General Assembly shall have one vote.
2. Decisions of the General Assembly on important questions shall be made by a two-thirds majority of the members present and voting. These questions shall include: recommendations with respect to the maintenance of international peace and security, the election of the non-permanent members of the Security Council, the election of the members of the Economic and Social Council, the election of members of the Trusteeship Council in accordance with paragraph 1(c) of Article 86, the admission of new Members to the United Nations, the suspension of the rights and privileges of membership, the expulsion of Members, questions relating to the operation of the trusteeship system, and budgetary questions.
3. Decisions on other questions, including the determination of additional categories of questions to be decided by a two-thirds majority, shall be made by a majority of the members present and voting.

Article 19

A Member of the United Nations which is in arrears in the payment of its financial contributions to the Organization shall have no vote in the General Assembly if the amount of its arrears equals or exceeds the amount of the contributions due from it for the preceding two full years. The General Assembly may, nevertheless, permit such a Member to vote if it is satisfied that the failure to pay is due to conditions beyond the control of the Member.

PROCEDURE

Article 20

The General Assembly shall meet in regular annual sessions and in such special sessions as occasion may require. Special sessions shall be convoked by the Secretary-General at the request of the Security Council or of a majority of the Members of the United Nations.

Article 21

The General Assembly shall adopt its own rules of procedure. It shall elect its President for each session.

Article 22

The General Assembly may establish such subsidiary organs as it deems necessary for the performance of its functions.

CHAPTER V. THE SECURITY COUNCIL

COMPOSITION

Article 23

1. The Security Council shall consist of fifteen members of the United Nations. The [People's] Republic of China, France, the Union of Soviet Socialist Republics, the United Kingdom of Great Britain and Northern Ireland, and the United States of America shall be permanent members of the Security Council. The General Assembly shall elect ten other Members of the United Nations to be non-permanent members of the Security Council, due regard being specially paid, in the first instance to the contribution of Members of the national peace and security and to the other purposes of the Organization, and also to equitable geographical distribution.
2. The non-permanent members of the Security Council shall be elected for a term of two years. In the first election of the non-permanent members after the increase of the membership of the Security Council from eleven to fifteen, two of the four additional members shall be chosen for a term of one year. A retiring member shall not be eligible for immediate re-election.
3. Each member of the Security Council shall have one representative.

FUNCTIONS AND POWERS

Article 24

1. In order to ensure prompt and effective action by the United Nations, its members confer on the Security Council primary responsibility for the maintenance of international peace and security, and agree that in carrying out its duties under this responsibility the Security Council acts on their behalf.
2. In discharging these duties the Security Council shall act in accordance with the Purposes and Principles of the United Nations. The specific powers granted to the Security Council for the discharge of these duties are laid down in Chapters VI, VII, VIII, and XII.
3. The Security Council shall submit annual, and when necessary, special reports to the General Assembly for its consideration.

Article 25

The members of the United Nations agree to accept and carry out the decisions of the Security Council in accordance with the present Charter.

Article 26

In order to promote the establishment and maintenance of international peace and security with the least diversion for armaments of the world's human and economic resources, the Security Council shall be responsible for formulating, with the assistance of the Military Staff Committee referred to in Article 47, plans to be submitted to the Members of the United Nations for the establishment of a system for the regulation of armaments.

VOTING

Article 27

1. Each member of the Security Council shall have one vote.
2. Decisions of the Security Council on procedural matters shall be made by an affirmative vote of nine members.
3. Decisions of the Security Council on all other matters shall be made by an affirmative vote of the nine members including the concurring votes of the permanent members; provided that, in decisions under Chapter VI, and under paragraph 3 of Article 52, a party to a dispute shall abstain from voting.

PROCEDURE

Article 28

1. The Security Council shall be so organized as to be able to function continuously. Each member of the Security Council shall for this purpose be represented at all times at the seat of the Organization.
2. The Security Council shall hold periodic meetings at which each of its members may, if it so desires, be represented by a member of the government or by some other specially designated representative.
3. The Security Council may hold meetings at such places other than the seat of the Organization as in its judgement will best facilitate its work.

Article 29

The Security Council may establish such subsidiary organs as it deems necessary for the performance of its functions.

Article 30

The Security Council shall adopt its own rules of procedure, including the method of selecting its President.

Article 31

Any Member of the United Nations which is not a member of the Security Council may participate, without vote, in the discussion of any question brought before the Security Council whenever the latter considers that the interests of that Member are specially affected.

Article 32

Any Member of the United Nations which is not a member of the Security Council or any state which is not a Member of the United Nations, if it is a party to a dispute under consideration by the Security Council, shall be invited to participate, without vote, in the discussion relating to the dispute. The Security Council shall lay down such conditions as it deems just for the participation of a state which is not a Member of the United Nations.

CHAPTER VI. PACIFIC SETTLEMENT OF DISPUTES

Article 33

1. The parties to any dispute, the continuance of which is likely to endanger the maintenance of international peace and security, shall, first of all, seek a solution by negotiation, enquiry, mediation, conciliation, arbitration, judicial settlement, resort to regional agencies or arrangements, or other peaceful means of their own choice.
2. The Security Council shall, when it deems necessary, call upon the parties to settle their dispute by such means.

Article 34

The Security Council may investigate any dispute, or any situation which might lead to international friction or give rise to a dispute, in order to determine whether the continuance of the dispute or situation is likely to endanger the maintenance of international peace and security.

Article 35

1. Any Member of the United Nations may bring any dispute, or any situation of the nature referred to in Article 34, to the attention of the Security Council or of the General Assembly.
2. A state which is not a Member of the United Nations may bring to the attention of the Security Council or of the General Assembly any dispute to which it is a party if it accepts in advance, for the purposes of the dispute, the obligations of pacific settlement provided in the present Charter.

3. The proceedings of the General Assembly in respect of matters brought to its attention under this Article will be subject to the provisions of Articles 11 and 12.

Article 36

1. The Security Council may, at any stage of a dispute of the nature referred to in Article 33 or a situation of like nature, recommend appropriate procedures or methods of adjustment.
2. The Security Council should take into consideration any procedures for the settlement of the dispute which have already been adopted by the parties.
3. In making recommendations under this Article the Security Council should also take into consideration that legal disputes should as a general rule be referred by the parties to the International Court of Justice in accordance with the provisions of the Statute of the Court.

Article 37

1. Should the parties to a dispute of the nature referred to in Article 33 fail to settle it by the means indicated in that Article, they shall refer it to the Security Council.
2. If the Security Council deems that the continuance of the dispute is in fact likely to endanger the maintenance of international peace and security, it shall decide whether to take action under Article 36 or to recommend such terms of settlement as it may consider appropriate.

Article 38

Without prejudice to the provisions of Articles 33 to 37, the Security Council may, if all the parties to any dispute so request, make recommendations to the parties with a view to a pacific settlement of the dispute.

CHAPTER VII.
ACTION WITH RESPECT TO THREATS TO THE PEACE, BREACHES OF THE PEACE, AND ACTS OF AGGRESSION

Article 39

The Security Council shall determine the existence of any threat to the peace, breach of the peace, or act of aggression and shall make recommendations, or decide what measures shall be taken in accordance with Articles 41 and 42, to maintain or restore international peace and security.

Article 40

In order to prevent an aggravation of the situation, the Security Council may, before making the recommendations or deciding upon the measures provided for in Article 39, call upon the parties concerned to comply with such provisional measures as it deems necessary or desirable. Such provisional measures shall be without prejudice to the rights, claims, or position of the parties concerned. The Security Council shall duly take account of failure to comply with such provisional measures.

Article 41

The Security Council may decide what measures not involving the use of armed force are to be employed to give effect to its decisions, and it may call upon the Members of the United Nations to apply such measures. These may include complete or partial interruption of economic relations and of rail, sea, air, postal, telegraphic, radio, and other means of communication, and the severance of diplomatic relations.

Article 42

Should the Security Council consider that measures provided for in Article 41 would be inadequate or have proved to be inadequate, it may take such action by air, sea, or land forces as may be necessary to maintain or restore international peace and security. Such action may include demonstrations, blockade, and other operations by air, sea, or land forces of Members of the United Nations.

Article 43

1. All Members of the United Nations, in order to contribute to the maintenance of international peace and security, undertake to make available to the Security Council, on its call and in accordance with a special agreement or agreements, armed forces, assistance, and facilities, including right of passage, necessary for the purpose of maintaining international peace and security.
2. Such agreement or agreements shall govern the numbers and types of forces, their degree of readiness and general location, and the nature of the facilities and assistance to be provided.
3. The agreement or agreements shall be negotiated as soon as possible on the initiative of the Security Council. They shall be concluded between the Security Council and Members or between the Security Council and groups of Members and shall be subject to ratification by the signatory states in accordance with their respective constitutional processes.

Article 44

When the Security Council has decided to use force it shall, before calling upon a Member not represented on it to provide armed forces in fulfillment of the obligations assumed under Article 43, invite that Member, if the Member so desires, to participate in the decisions of the Security Council concerning the employment of contingents of that Member's armed forces.

Article 45

In order to enable the United Nations to take urgent military measures, Members shall hold immediately available national air-force contingents for combined international enforcement action. The strength and degree of readiness in these contingents and plans for their combined action shall be determined, within the limits laid down in the special agreement or agreements referred to in Article 43, by the Security Council with the assistance of the Military Staff Committee.

Article 46

Plans for the application of armed force shall be made by the Security Council with the assistance of the Military Staff Committee.

Article 47

1. There shall be established a Military Staff Committee to advise and assist the Security Council on all questions relating to the Security Council's military requirements for the maintenance of international peace and security, the employment and command of forces placed at its disposal, the regulation of armaments, and possible disarmament.
2. The Military Staff Committee shall consist of the Chiefs of Staff of the permanent members of the Security Council or their representatives. Any Member of the United Nations not permanently represented on the Committee shall be invited by the Committee to be associated with it when the efficient discharge of the Committee's responsibilities requires the participation of that Member in its work.
3. The Military Staff Committee shall be responsible under the Security Council for the strategic direction of any armed forces placed at the disposal of the Security Council. Questions relating to the command of such forces shall be worked out subsequently.
4. The Military Staff Committee, with the authorization of the Security Council and after consultation with appropriate regional agencies, may establish regional subcommittees.

Article 48

1. The action required to carry out the decisions of the Security Council for the maintenance of international peace and security shall be taken by all the Members of the United Nations or by some of them, as the Security Council may determine.

2. Such decisions shall be carried out by the Members of the United Nations directly and through their action in the appropriate international agencies of which they are members.

Article 49

The members of the United Nations shall join in affording mutual assistance in carrying out the measures decided upon by the Security Council.

Article 50

If preventive or enforcement measures against any state are taken by the Security Council, any other state, whether a Member of the United Nations or not, which finds itself confronted with special economic problems arising from carrying out those measures shall have the right to consult the Security Council with regard to a solution of those problems.

Article 51

Nothing in the present Charter shall impair the inherent right of individual or collective self-defence if an armed attack occurs against a Member of the United Nations, until the Security Council has taken measures necessary to maintain international peace and security. Measures taken by Members in the exercise of this right of self-defence shall be immediately reported to the Security Council and shall not in any way affect the authority and responsibility of the Security Council under the present Charter to take at any time such action as it deems necessary in order to maintain or restore international peace and security.

CHAPTER VIII. REGIONAL ARRANGEMENTS

Article 52

1. Nothing in the present Charter precludes the existence of regional arrangements for dealing with such matters relating to the maintenance of international peace and security as are appropriate for regional action, provided that such arrangements or agencies and their activities are consistent with the Purposes and Principles of the United Nations.

2. The Members of the United Nations entering into such arrangements or constituting such agencies shall make every effort to achieve public settle-

ment of local disputes through such regional arrangements or by such regional agencies before referring them to the Security Council.

3. The Security Council shall encourage the development of pacific settlement of local disputes through such regional arrangements or by such regional agencies either on the initiative of the states concerned or by reference from the Security Council.

4. This Article in no way impairs the application of Articles 34 and 35.

Article 53

1. The Security Council shall, where appropriate, utilize such regional arrangements or agencies for enforcement action under its authority. But no enforcement action shall be taken under regional arrangements or by regional agencies without the authorization of the Security Council, with the exception of measures against any enemy state, as defined in paragraph 2 of this Article, provided for pursuant to Article 107 or in regional arrangements directed against renewal of aggressive policy on the part of any such state, until such time as the Organization may, on request of the Governments concerned, be charged with the responsibility for preventing further aggression by such a state.

2. The term *enemy state* as used in paragraph 1 of this Article applies to any state which during the Second World War has been an enemy of any signatory of the present Charter.

Article 54

The Security Council shall at all times be kept fully informed of activities undertaken or in contemplation under regional arrangements or by regional agencies for the maintenance of international peace and security.

CHAPTER IX. INTERNATIONAL ECONOMIC AND SOCIAL CO-OPERATION

Article 55

With a view to the creation of conditions of stability and well-being which are necessary for peaceful and friendly relations among nations based on respect for the principle of equal rights and self-determination of peoples, the United Nations shall promote:

A. higher standards of living, full employment, and conditions of economic and social progress and development;

B. solutions of international economic, social, health, and related problems; and international cultural and educational co-operation; and

C. universal respect for, and observe of, human rights and fundamental freedoms for all without distinction as to race, sex, language, or religion.

Article 56

All members pledge themselves to take joint and separate action in co-operation with the Organization for the achievement of the purposes set forth in Article 55.

Article 57

1. The various specialized agencies, established by intergovernmental agreement and having wide international responsibilities, as defined in their basic instruments, in economic, social, cultural, educational, health, and related fields, shall be brought into relationship with the United Nations in accordance with the provisions of Article 63.

2. Such agencies thus brought into relationship with the United Nations are hereinafter referred to as specialized agencies.

Article 58

The Organization shall make recommendations for the co-ordination of the policies and activities of the specialized agencies.

Article 59

The Organization shall, where appropriate, initiate negotiations among the states concerned for the creation of any new specialized agencies required for the accomplishment of the purposes set forth in Article 55.

Article 60

Responsibility for the discharge of the functions of the Organization set forth in this Chapter shall be vested in the General Assembly and, under the authority of the General Assembly, in the Economic and Social Council, which shall have for this purpose the powers set forth in Chapter X.

CHAPTER X. THE ECONOMIC AND SOCIAL COUNCIL

COMPOSITION

Article 61

1. The Economic and Social Council shall consist of fifty-four Members of the United Nations elected by the General Assembly.

2. Subject to the provisions of paragraph 3, eighteen members of the Economic and Social Council shall be elected each year for a term of three years. A retiring member shall not be eligible for immediate re-election.

3. At the first election after the increase in the membership of the Economic and Social Council from twenty-seven to fifty-four members, in addition to the members elected in place of the nine members whose term of office expires at the end of that year, twenty-seven additional members shall be elected. Of these twenty-seven additional members, the term of office of nine members so elected shall expire at the end of two years, in accordance with arrangements made by the General Assembly.

4. Each member of the Economic and Social Council shall have one representative.

FUNCTIONS AND POWERS
Article 62

1. The Economic and Social Council may make or initiate studies and reports with respect to international economic, social, cultural, educational, health, and related matters and may make recommendations with respect to any such matters to the General Assembly, to the Members of the United Nations, and to the specialized agencies concerned.

2. It may make recommendations for the purpose of promoting respect for, and observance of, human rights and fundamental freedoms for all.

3. It may prepare draft conventions for submission to the General Assembly, with respect to matters falling within its competence.

4. It may call, in accordance with the rules prescribed by the United Nations, international conferences on matters falling within its competence.

Article 63

1. The Economic and Social Council may enter into agreements with any of the agencies referred to in Article 57, defining the terms on which the agency concerned shall be brought into relationship with the United Nations. Such agreements shall be subject to approval by the General Assembly.

2. It may co-ordinate the activities of the specialized agencies through consultation with and recommendations to such agencies and through recommendations to the General Assembly and to the Members of the United Nations.

Article 64

1. The Economic and Social Council may take appropriate steps to obtain regular reports from the specialized agencies. It may make arrangements with the Members of the United Nations and with the specialized agencies to obtain

reports on the steps taken to give effect to its own recommendations and to recommendations on matters falling within its competence made by the General Assembly.

2. It may communicate its observations on these reports to the General Assembly.

Article 65

The Economic and Social Council may furnish information to the Security Council and shall assist the Security Council upon its request.

Article 66

1. The Economic and Social Council shall perform such functions as fall within its competence in connexion with the carrying out of the recommendations of the General Assembly.
2. It may, with the approval of the General Assembly, perform services at the request of Members of the United Nations and at the request of specialized agencies.
3. It shall perform such other functions as are specified elsewhere in the present Charter or as may be assigned to it by the General Assembly.

VOTING

Article 67

1. Each member of the Economic and Social Council shall have one vote.
2. Decisions of the Economic and Social Council shall be made by a majority of the members present and voting.

PROCEDURE

Article 68

The Economic and Social Council shall set up commissions in economic and social fields and for the promotion of human rights, and such other commissions as may be required for the performance of its functions.

Article 69

The Economic and Social Council shall invite any Member of the United Nations to participate, without vote, in its deliberations on any matter of particular concern to that Member.

Article 70

The Economic and Social Council may make arrangements for representatives of the specialized agencies to participate, without vote, in its deliberations and in

those of the commissions established by it, and for its representatives to participate in the deliberations of the specialized agencies.

Article 71

The Economic and Social Council may make suitable arrangements for consultation with non-governmental organizations which are concerned with matters
within its competence. Such arrangements may be made with international organizations and, where appropriate, with national organizations after consultation
with the Member of the United Nations concerned.

Article 72

1. The Economic and Social Council shall adopt its own rules of procedure, including the method of selecting its President.
2. The Economic and Social Council shall meet as required in accordance with
   its rules, which shall include provision for the convening of meetings on the
   request of a majority of its members.

CHAPTER XI. DECLARATION REGARDING NON-SELF-GOVERNING TERRITORIES

Article 73

Members of the United Nations which have or assume responsibilities for the administration of territories whose peoples have not yet attained a full measure of
self-government recognize the principle that the interests of the inhabitants of
these territories are paramount, and accept as a sacred trust the obligation to promote the utmost, within the system of international peace and security established by the present Charter, the well-being of the inhabitants of these territories, and, to this end:

A. to ensure, with due respect for the culture of the peoples concerned, their
   political, economic, social, and educational advancement, their just treatment, and their protection against abuses;
B. to develop self-government, to take due account of the political aspirations
   of the peoples, and to assist them in the progressive development of their
   free political institutions, according to the particular circumstances of each
   territory and its peoples and their varying stages of advancement;
C. to further international peace and security;
D. to promote constructive measures of development, to encourage research,
   and to co-operate with one another and, when and where appropriate,
   with specialized international bodies with a view to the practical achieve-

ment of the social, economic, and scientific purposes set forth in this Article; and

E. to transmit regularly to the Secretary-General for information purposes, subject to such limitation as security and constitutional considerations may require, statistical and other information of a technical nature relating to economic, social, and educational conditions in the territories for which they are respectively responsible other than those territories to which Chapters XII and XIII apply.

Article 74

Members of the United Nations also agree that their policy in respect of the territories to which this Chapter applies, no less than in respect of their Metropolitan areas, must be based on the general principle of good-neighborliness, due account being taken of the interests and well-being of the rest of the world, in social, economic, and commercial matters.

CHAPTER XII. INTERNATIONAL TRUSTEESHIP SYSTEM

Article 75

The United Nations shall establish under its authority an international trusteeship system for the administration and supervision of such territories as may be placed thereunder for subsequent individual agreements. These territories are hereinafter referred to as trust territories.

Article 76

The basic objectives of the trusteeship system, in accordance with the Purposes of the United Nations laid down in Article 1 of the present Charter, shall be:

A. to further international peace and security;
B. to promote the political, economic, social, and educational advancement of the inhabitants of the trust territories, and their progressive development towards self-government or independence as may be appropriate to the particular circumstances of each territory and its peoples concerned, and as may be provided by the terms of each trusteeship agreement;
C. to encourage respect for human rights and for fundamental freedoms for all without distinction as to race, sex, language, or religion, and to encourage recognition of the interdependence of the people of the world; and
D. to ensure equal treatment in social, economic, and commercial matters for all Members of the United Nations and their nationals, and also equal treatment for the latter in the administration of justice, without prejudice to the

attainment of the foregoing objectives and subject to the provisions of Article 80.

Article 77

1. The trusteeship system shall apply to such territories in the following categories as may be placed thereunder by means of trusteeship agreements:

   A. territories now held under mandate;

   B. territories which may be detached from enemy states as a result of the Second World War; and

   C. territories voluntarily placed under the system by states responsible for their administration.

2. It will be a matter for subsequent agreement as to which territories in the foregoing categories will be brought under the trusteeship system and upon what terms.

Article 78

The trusteeship system shall not apply to territories which have become Members of the United Nations, relationship among which shall be based on respect for the principle of sovereign equality.

Article 79

The terms of trusteeship for each territory to be placed under the trusteeship system, including any alteration or amendment, shall be agreed upon by the states directly concerned, including the mandatory power in the case of territories held under mandate by a Member of the United Nations, and shall be approved for in Articles 83 and 85.

Article 80

1. Except as may be agreed upon in individual trusteeship agreements, made under Articles 77, 79, and 81, placing each territory under the trusteeship system, and until such agreements have been concluded, nothing in this Chapter shall be construed in or of itself to alter in any manner the rights whatsoever of any states or any peoples or the terms of existing international instruments to which Members of the United Nations may respectively be parties.

2. Paragraph 1 of this Article shall not be interpreted as giving grounds for delay or postponement of the negotiation and conclusion of agreements for placing mandated and other territories under the trusteeship system as provided for in Article 77.

Article 81

The trusteeship agreement shall in each case include the terms under which the trust territory will be administered and designate the authority which will exercise the administration of the trust territory. Such authority, hereinafter called the administering authority, may be one or more states or the Organization itself.

Article 82

There may be designated, in any trusteeship agreement, a strategic area or areas which may include part or all of the trust territory to which the agreement applies, without prejudice to any special agreement or agreements made under Article 43.

Article 83

1. All functions of the United Nations relating to strategic areas, including the approval of the terms of the trusteeship agreements and of their alteration or amendment, shall be exercised by the Security Council.
2. The basic objectives set forth in Article 76 shall be applicable to the people of each strategic area.
3. The Security Council shall, subject to the provisions of the trusteeship agreements and without prejudice to security considerations, avail itself of the assistance of the Trusteeship Council to perform those functions of the United Nations under the trusteeship system relating to political, economic, social, and educational matters in the strategic areas.

Article 84

It shall be the duty of the administering authority to ensure that the trust territory shall play its part in the maintenance of international peace and security. To this end the administering authority may make use of volunteer forces, facilities, and assistance from the trust territory in carrying out the obligations towards the Security Council undertaken in this regard by the administering authority, as well as for local defence and the maintenance of law and order within the trust territory.

Article 85

1. The functions of the United Nations with regard to trusteeship agreements for all areas not designated as strategic, including the approval of the terms of the trusteeship agreements and of their alteration or amendment, shall be exercised by the General Assembly.
2. The Trusteeship Council, operating under the authority of the General Assembly, shall assist the General Assembly in carrying out these functions.

CHAPTER XIII. THE TRUSTEESHIP COUNCIL

COMPOSITION

Article 86

1. The Trusteeship Council shall consist of the following Members of the United Nations:

   A. those Members administering trust territories;
   B. such of those Members mentioned by name in Article 23 as are not administering trust territories; and
   C. as many other Members elected for three-year terms by the General Assembly as may be necessary to ensure that the total number of members of the Trusteeship Council is equally divided between those Members of the United Nations which administer trust territories and those which do not.

2. Each member of the Trusteeship Council shall designate one specially qualified person to represent it therein.

FUNCTIONS AND POWERS

Article 87

The General Assembly and, under its authority, the Trusteeship Council, in carrying out their functions, may:

A. consider reports submitted by the administering authority;
B. accept petitions and examine them in consultation with the administering authority;
C. provide for periodic visits to the respective trust territories at times agreed upon with the administering authority; and
D. take these and other actions in conformity with the terms of the trusteeship agreements.

Article 88

The Trusteeship Council shall formulate a questionnaire on the political, economic, social, and educational advancement of the inhabitants of each trust territory, and the administering authority for each trust territory within the competence of the General Assembly shall make an annual report to the General Assembly upon the basis of such questionnaire.

VOTING

Article 89

1. Each member of the Trusteeship Council shall have one vote.

2. Decisions of the Trusteeship Council shall be made by a majority of the members present and voting.

PROCEDURE

Article 90

1. The Trusteeship Council shall adopt its own rules of procedure, including the method of selecting its President.
2. The Trusteeship Council shall meet as required in accordance with its rules, which shall include provision for the convening of meetings on the request of a majority of its members.

Article 91

The Trusteeship Council shall, when appropriate, avail itself of the assistance of the Economic and Social Council and of the specialized agencies in regard to matters with which they are respectively concerned.

CHAPTER XIV. THE INTERNATIONAL COURT OF JUSTICE

Article 92

The International Court of Justice shall be the principal judicial organ of the United Nations. It shall function in accordance with the annexed Statute, which is based upon the Statute of the Permanent Court of International Justice and forms an integral part of the present Charter.

Article 93

1. All Members of the United Nations are ipso facto parties to the Statute of the International Court of Justice.
2. A state which is not a Member of the United Nations may become a party to the Statute of the International Court of Justice on conditions to be determined in each case by the General Assembly upon the recommendation of the Security Council.

Article 94

1. Each member of the United Nations undertakes to comply with the decision of the International Court of Justice in any case to which it is a party.
2. If any party to a case fails to perform the obligations incumbent upon it under a judgment rendered by the Court, the other party may have recourse to the Security Council, which may, if it deems necessary, make recommendations or decide upon measures to be taken to give effect to the judgment.

Article 95

Nothing in the present Charter shall prevent Members of the United Nations from entrusting the solutions of their differences to other tribunals by virtue of agreements already in existence or which may be concluded in the future.

Article 96

1. The General Assembly or the Security Council may request the International Court of Justice to give an advisory opinion on any legal question.
2. Other organs of the United Nations and specialized agencies, which may at any time be so authorized by the General Assembly, may also request advisory opinions of the Court on legal questions arising within the scope of their activities.

CHAPTER XV. THE SECRETARIAT

Article 97

The Secretariat shall comprise a Secretary-General and such staff as the Organization may require. The Secretary-General shall be appointed by the General Assembly upon the recommendation of the Security Council. He shall be the chief administrative officer of the Organization.

Article 98

The Secretary-General shall act in that capacity in all meetings of the General Assembly, of the Security Council, of the Economic and Social Council, and of the Trusteeship Council, and shall perform such other functions as are entrusted to him by these organs. The Secretary-General shall make an annual report to the General Assembly on the work of the Organization.

Article 99

The Secretary-General may bring to the attention of the Security Council any matter which in his opinion may threaten the maintenance of international peace and security.

Article 100

1. In the performance of their duties the Secretary-General and the staff shall not seek or receive instructions from any government or from any other authority external to the Organization. They shall refrain from any action which might reflect on their position as international officials responsible only to the Organization.

2. Each Member of the United Nations undertakes to respect the exclusively international character of the responsibilities of the Secretary-General and the staff and not to seek to influence them in the discharge of their responsibilities.

Article 101

1. The staff shall be appointed by the Secretary-General under regulations established by the General Assembly.
2. Appropriate staffs shall be permanently assigned to the Economic and Social Council, the Trusteeship Council, and, as required, to the other organs of the United Nations. These staffs shall form a part of the Secretariat.
3. The paramount consideration in the employment of the staff and in the determination of the conditions of service shall be the necessity of securing the highest standards of efficiency, competence, and integrity. Due regard shall be paid to the importance of recruiting the staff on as wide a geographical basis as possible.

CHAPTER XVI. MISCELLANEOUS PROVISIONS

Article 102

1. Every treaty and every international agreement entered into by any Member of the United Nations after the present Charter comes into force shall as soon as possible be registered with the Secretariat and published by it.
2. No party to any such treaty or international agreement which has not been registered in accordance with the provisions of paragraph 1 of this Article may invoke that treaty or agreement before any organ of the United Nations.

Article 103

In the event of a conflict between the obligations of the Members of the United Nations under the present Charter and their obligations under any other international agreement, their obligations under the present Charter shall prevail.

Article 104

The Organization shall enjoy in the territory of each of its Members such legal capacity as may be necessary for the exercise of its functions and the fulfillment of its purposes.

Article 105

1. The Organization shall enjoy in the territory of each of its Members such privileges and immunities as are necessary for the fulfillment of its purposes.

2. Representatives of the Members of the United Nations and officials of the Organization shall enjoy such privileges and immunities as are necessary for the independent exercise of their function in connexion with the Organization.

3. The General Assembly may make recommendations with a view to determining the details of the application of paragraphs 1 and 2 of this Article or may propose conventions to the Members of the United Nations for this purpose.

CHAPTER XVII. TRANSITIONAL SECURITY ARRANGEMENTS

Article 106

Pending the coming into force of such special agreements referred to in Article 43 as in the opinion of the Security Council enable it to begin to exercise of its responsibilities under Article 42, the parties to the Four-Nation Declaration, signed at Moscow, 30 October 1943, and France, shall, in accordance with the provisions of paragraph 5 of that Declaration, consult with one another and as occasion requires with other Members of the United Nations with a view to such joint action on behalf of the Organization as may be necessary for the purpose of maintaining international peace and security.

Article 107

Nothing in the present Charter shall invalidate or preclude action, in relation to any state which during the Second World War has been an enemy of any signatory to the present Charter, taken or authorized as a result of that war by the Governments having responsibility for such action.

CHAPTER XVIII. AMENDMENTS

Article 108

Amendments to the present Charter shall come into force for all Members of the United Nations when they have been adopted by a vote of two-thirds of the members of the General Assembly and ratified in accordance with their respective constitutional processes by two-thirds of the Members of the United Nations, including all the permanent members of the Security Council.

Article 109

1. A General Conference of the Members of the United Nations for the purpose of reviewing the present Charter may be held at a date and place to be fixed by a two-thirds vote of the members of the General Assembly and by a vote

of any nine members of the Security Council. Each Member of the United Nations shall have one vote in the conference.

2. Any alteration of the present Charter recommended by a two-thirds vote of the conference shall take effect when ratified in accordance with their respective constitutional processes by two-thirds of the Members of the United Nations including all permanent members of the Security Council.

3. If such a conference has not been held before the tenth annual session of the General Assembly following the coming into force of the present Charter, the proposal to call such a conference shall be held if so decided by a majority vote of the members of the General Assembly and by a vote of any seven members of the Security Council.

CHAPTER XIX. RATIFICATION AND SIGNATURE

Article 110

1. The present Charter shall be ratified by the signatory states in accordance with their respective constitutional processes.

2. The ratifications shall be deposited with the Government of the United States of America, which shall notify all the signatory states of each deposit as well as the Secretary-General of the Organization when he has been appointed.

3. The present Charter shall come into force upon the deposit of ratifications by the [People's] Republic of China, France, Union of Soviet Socialist Republics, the United Kingdom of Great Britain and Northern Ireland, and the United States of America, and by a majority of the other signatory states. A protocol of the ratifications deposited shall thereupon be drawn up by the Government of the United States of America which shall communicate copies thereof to all the signatory states.

4. The states signatory to the present Charter which ratify it after it has come into force will become original Members of the United Nations on the date of the deposit of their respective ratifications.

Article 111

The present Charter, of which the Chinese, French, Russian, English, and Spanish texts are equally authentic, shall remain deposited in the archives of the Government of the United States of America. Duly certified copies thereof shall be transmitted by that Government to the Governments of the other signatory states.

IN FAITH WHEREOF the representatives of the Government of the United Nations have signed at the present Charter.

DONE at the city of San Francisco the twenty-sixth day of June, one thousand nine hundred and forty-five.

NOTES

INTRODUCTION

1. *Washington Post National Weekly Edition,* 15–21 December 2002.

CHAPTER 1

1. J. Robert Moskin, *Mr. Truman's War: The Final Victories of World War II and the Birth of the Postwar World* (New York: Random House, 1996), 5–7.

2. Ibid., 7–8; Walter Issacson and Thomas Evan, *The Wise Men: Six Friends and the World They Made* (New York: Simon & Schuster, 1986), 253–257.

3. Harry Truman, *Memoirs: Years of Decision,* vol. 1, *1955–1956* (Garden City, N. Y.: Doubleday, 1955), 4–7; R. H. Ferrell, ed., *Off the Record: The Private Papers of Harry S. Truman* (New York: Penguin, 1980), 14–16; Jonathan Daniels, *The Man of Independence* (New York: Lippincott, 1950), 259; Margaret Truman, *Letters from Father: The Truman Family's Personal Correspondence* (New York: Arbor House, 1981), 106 (see March 3, 1948).

4. H. Truman, *Memoirs,* 119; Alonzo L. Hamby, *Man of the People: A Life of Harry S. Truman* (New York: Oxford University Press, 1995), 12–13.

5. Hamby, *Man of the People,* 12–23; John Hersey, *Aspects of the Presidency* (New Haven, Conn.: Ticknor and Fields, 1980), 6–47; H. Truman, *Memoirs,* 271–272; David McCullough, *Truman* (New York: Simon & Schuster, 1992), 242–243, 253–254, 259–260, 286.

6. H. Truman, *Memoirs,* 6–8; Margaret Truman, *Harry S. Truman* (New York: William Morrow, 1973), 213; James Reston, "Security Parley Won't Be Delayed," *New York Times,* 12 April 1945; Robert Divine, *Second Chance: The Triumph of Internationalism in America During World War II* (New York: Atheneum, 1967), 279–280; address by T. Patrick Killough, "A Peace Made on Main Street: Private Americans Help Create the 1945 United Nations Charter," Southwestern World Affairs Institute, YMCA Center, Black Mountain, North Carolina, 26 July 1991, 20.

7. H. Truman, *Memoirs,* 9, 271; Robert Dallek, *Franklin D. Roosevelt and American Foreign Policy, 1932–1945* (New York: Oxford University Press, 1979), 522; "Latest Opinion Trends in the U.S.A.," 23 February 1945, President's Secretary's File, Franklin D. Roosevelt Presidential Library, Hyde Park, New York.

8. Anne O'Hare McCormick, *New York Times Magazine,* "His 'Unfinished Business'—And Ours," 22 April 1945; H. Truman, *Memoirs,* 11; Thomas M. Campbell and George C. Herring, eds., *The Diaries of Edward Stettinius, Jr., 1943–1946* (New York: New Viewpoints, 1975), 315–316.

9. Campbell and Herring, *Diaries*, 317–319; H. Truman, *Memoirs*, 13–17.

10. McCullough, *Truman*, 352–355; H. Truman, *Memoirs*, 22–23; M. Truman, *Harry S. Truman*, 218.

11. H. Truman, *Memoirs*, 14–16, 23–26; W. Averell Harriman and Elie Abel, *Special Envoy to Churchill and Stalin, 1941–1946* (New York: Random House, 1975), 440–442; "United Nations Conference on International Organizations at San Francisco," Secretary of State Stettinius to President Truman, 13 April 1945, Harry S. Truman Presidential Library, Independence, Missouri.

12. James Reston, "Six Problems Facing Security Council," *New York Times*, 14 April 1945; H. Truman, *Memoirs*, 28–31, 36–39.

13. Excerpts from the text of the Truman Address to Joint Session of Congress, *New York Times*, 17 April 1945; Moscow Radio report, *New York Times*, 17 April 1945.

CHAPTER 2

1. H.C.F. Bell, *Woodrow Wilson and the People* (New York: Doubleday, 1945), 253.

2. August Heckscher, *Woodrow Wilson* (New York: Charles Scribner's Sons, 1991), 533–535.

3. Ibid., 551–553.

4. Ibid., 542, 551–553; John Blum et al., *The National Experience: A History of the United States*, 6th ed. (New York: Harcourt Brace Jovanovich, 1985), 614. Lodge's fourteen reservations contained language to ensure that the United States be the judge of its own internal affairs; that the United States retain the right to withdraw from the League; that the League not restrict any individual rights of U.S. citizens; that Congress approve all U.S. officials appointed to the League; and that Congress control all U.S. appropriations for the League.

5. Blum et al., *The National Experience*, 614; Arthur Schlesinger Jr., "Back to the Womb: Isolationism's Renewed Threat," *Foreign Affairs* (July/August 1995).

6. Heckscher, *Wilson*, 589–590.

7. Senate Democrats brought up the treaty for a second vote on March 19, 1920, after organizations representing some 20 million Americans petitioned for ratification. The pact was rejected for a second time, falling seven votes short of the two-thirds required for adoption; Wilson's prophetic warning speech in Omaha, Nebraska, September 1919.

8. Arthur Schlesinger Jr., *The Crisis of the Old Order* (Boston: Houghton Mifflin, 1957), 364–365; Townsend Hoopes and Douglas Brinkley, *FDR and the Creation of the United Nations* (New Haven, Conn.: Yale University Press, 1997), 9; Georg Schild, "The Roosevelt Administration and the United Nations," *World Affairs Journal* (summer 1995), 26–34.

9. Evan Luard, *A History of the United Nations: The Years of Western Domination 1945–55*, vol. 1 (New York: St. Martin's Press, 1982), 3.

10. Ibid., 4–13.

11. Wayne Cole, *Roosevelt and the Isolationists, 1932–1945* (Lincoln: University of Nebraska Press, 1983), 23–24; Franklin Roosevelt, *Looking Forward* (New York: John Day, 1933), 254–256; Cordell Hull, *The Memoirs of Cordell Hull*, vol. 1 (New York: Macmillan, 1948), 150–153.

12. Cole, *Isolationists,* 116.

13. Arthur Schlesinger Jr., *The Imperial Presidency* (Boston: Houghton Mifflin, 1973), 95–96; R. A. Divine, *The Illusion of Neutrality* (Chicago: University of Chicago Press, 1962), chapter 2; E. B. Nixon, ed., *Franklin Roosevelt and Foreign Affairs* (Cambridge, Mass.: Belknap Press of Harvard Press, 1962), 377.

14. Arthur Schlesinger Jr., "Franklin Roosevelt and U.S. Foreign Policy" (address to the Society for Historians of American Foreign Relations, Vassar College, 18 June 1992), 5, 9.

15. Sumner Welles, *Seven Decisions That Shaped History* (New York: Harper & Brothers, 1951), 176.

16. Hoopes and Brinkley, *FDR,* 18–19; T. Patrick Killough, "A Peace Made on Main Street: Private Americans Help Create the 1945 United Nations Charter" (address to the Southwestern World Affairs Institute, YMCA Center, Black Mountain, North Carolina, 26 July 1991), 21.

17. Robert Divine, *Second Chance: The Triumph of Internationalism in America During World War II* (New York: Atheneum, 1967), 29.

18. Hoopes and Brinkley, *FDR,* 26–27.

CHAPTER 3

1. Robert Hildebrand, *Dumbarton Oaks: The Origins of the United Nations and the Search for Postwar Security* (Chapel Hill: University of North Carolina Press, 1990), 5–7.

2. Frank Weller, "Mr. 5 by 5 Handles Some Hefty Problems—and Secretary Hull," *Washington Post,* 13 August 1944; Cary Reich, *The Life of Nelson A. Rockefeller: Worlds to Conquer, 1908–1958* (New York: Doubleday, 1996), 284–285; Donald Critchlow, *The Brookings Institution, 1916–1952: Expertise and the Public Interest in a Democratic Society* (DeKalb: Northern Illinois University Press, 1985), 159.

3. Leo Pasvolsky Papers, Manuscripts Division, Library of Congress; Townsend Hoopes and Douglas Brinkley, *FDR and the Creation of the United Nations* (New Haven, Conn.: Yale University Press, 1997), 50; transcript of oral interview with James Green, 21 April 1986, U.N. Library Collection; Critchlow, *Brookings,* 74–74, 194–195.

4. Cordell Hull, *Memoirs of Cordell Hull,* vol. 2 (New York: Macmillan, 1948), 1626; Weller, "Mr. 5 by 5."

5. Hilderbrand, *Dumbarton Oaks,* 6–8.

6. Ibid., 6–9; Sumner Welles, *Seven Decisions That Shaped History* (New York: Harper & Brothers, 1951), 183; Hull, *Memoirs,* 1631–1632.

7. Hilderbrand, *Dumbarton Oaks,* 8–10.

8. Ibid., 10–12; Hull, *Memoirs,* 1630–1631.

9. Hoopes and Brinkley, *FDR,* 36–40.

10. Hilderbrand, *Dumbarton Oaks,* 12–13; Hull, *Memoirs,* 1631–1633.

11. Hull, *Memoirs,* 1632–1633; Hoopes and Brinkley, *FDR,* 45–46.

12. Hoopes and Brinkley, *FDR,* 47–51; Hull, *Memoirs,* 1634; Hilderbrand, *Dumbarton Oaks,* 14.

13. Hull, *Memoirs,* 1638–1639; Pasvolsky Papers; Hoopes and Brinkley, *FDR,* 49–51.

14. Hilderbrand, *Dumbarton Oaks,* 18–20; Hull, *Memoirs,* 1639–1640.

15. Hoopes and Brinkley, *FDR,* 45–47, 73–74; Benjamin Welles, *Sumner Welles: FDR's Global Strategist* (New York: St. Martin's Press, 1998), 332; Hull, *Memoirs,* 1642–1647; Hilderbrand, *Dumbarton Oaks,* 19.

16. Hilderbrand, *Dumbarton Oaks,* 17–18; B. Welles, *Welles,* 334–335; Hull, *Memoirs,* 1639.

17. B. Welles, *Welles,* 334–336; Hoopes and Brinkley, *FDR,* 68–69.

18. Hoopes and Brinkley, *FDR,* 32–36, 60–61; B. Welles, *Welles,* 333.

19. Hoopes and Brinkley, *FDR,* 65–69; Harley Notter, *Postwar Foreign Policy Preparation, 1939–1945* (Washington, D.C.: Department of State, 1949), 107; "Notes on a Talk with the Secretary," 19 April 1943, unknown author, Pasvolsky Papers.

20. "Talk with the Secretary," Pasvolsky Papers.

21. Hull, *Memoirs,* 1643–1647; Hilderbrand, *Dumbarton Oaks,* 23–25.

22. Hoopes and Brinkley, *FDR,* 78–82; S. Welles, *Seven Decisions,* 189; B. Welles, *Welles,* 336. The last meeting of Welles's Special Subcommittee on International Organization occurred on 26 June 1943, Department of State Report, 4 October 1944, in the Pasvolsky Papers.

23. Hull, *Memoirs,* 1647; Pasvolsky Papers; Notter, *Postwar Foreign Policy,* 170–173, 693–713 (after Hull and FDR, Pasvolsky had the most listings in the authoritative Notter study index); Ruth Russell, *A History of the United Nations' Charter: The Role of the United States 1940–1945* (Washington, D.C.: Brookings Institution, 1958), 215–217. The most prominent of the outside groups, according to Russell, were the Commission to Study the Organization of Peace; the Council on Foreign Relations; the American Association for the United Nations; the Federal Council of Churches in America; Americans United for World Organization; and the Foreign Policy Association. Thomas Connally and Alfred Steinberg, *My Name Is Thomas Connally* (New York: T. Y. Crowell, 1954), 279.

24. Hoopes and Brinkley, *FDR,* 76–78; Hull, *Memoirs,* 1647–1648; Notter, *Postwar Foreign Policy,* 170–173.

25. Hoopes and Brinkley, *FDR,* 83–109; Notter, *Postwar Foreign Policy,* 170–173; Hull, *Memoirs,* 1280–1283, 1646–1649.

26. Hull, *Memoirs,* 1649.

27. Ibid.; Hilderbrand, *Dumbarton Oaks,* 30–34.

28. Hull, *Memoirs,* 1650.

29. Hoopes and Brinkley, *FDR,* 114–115; Hilderbrand, *Dumbarton Oaks,* 30–38.

30. Hilderbrand, *Dumbarton Oaks,* 64–65; Hoopes and Brinkley, *FDR,* 112, 124–125; Hull, *Memoirs,* 1651, 1657.

31. Hilderbrand, *Dumbarton Oaks,* 71; Evan Luard, *A History of the United Nations: The Years of Western Domination 1945–55,* vol. 1 (New York: St. Martin's Press, 1982), 25; Hull, *Memoirs,* 1684; Richard Edis, "A Job Well Done: The Founding of the United Nations Revisited," *Cambridge Review of International Affairs,* vol. 4, no. 1 (summer 1992), 29–40. For British, Soviet Union, and Chinese proposals, see Foreign Relations of U.S. 1994, Vol. 1, 670–693, 706–711, 718–728.

32. Hilderbrand, *Dumbarton Oaks,* 70, 309–320; Lord Gladwyn, *The Memoirs of Lord Gladwyn* (London: Weidenfeld and Nicholson, 1972), 145, 147; Weller, "Mr. 5 Handles Some Hefty Problems–and Secretary Hull."

33. Hilderbrand, *Dumbarton Oaks,* 86–90; Hoopes and Brinkley, *FDR,* 157.

34. Hilderbrand, *Dumbarton Oaks,* 170.

35. Ibid., 123–129, 184–195, 249–252. Some British historians argue that Gladwyn Jebb proposed the compromise voting formula, not Pasvolsky. See Richard Edis, "A Job Well Done: The Founding of the United Nations Revisited," *Cambridge Review of International Affairs* 4, no. 1 (summer 1992), 35.

36. Hilderbrand, *Dumbarton Oaks,* 95–101; Hoopes and Brinkley, *FDR,* 152; Foreign Relations of the United States, 1944, vol. 1, 798–804.

37. Hull, *Memoirs,* 1705.

CHAPTER 4

1. Anne O'Hare McCormick, "His 'Unfinished Business'—and Ours," *New York Times Magazine* (22 April 1945): 5, 43–44.

2. Clark Eichelberger, *Organizing for Peace: A Personal History of The Founding of the United Nations* (New York: Harper & Row, 1977), 250–251; Dorothy Robins, *Experiment in Democracy: The Story of U.S. Citizen Organizations in Forging the Charter of the United Nations* (New York: Parkside Press, 1971), 40–41.

3. Robins, *Experiment in Democracy,* 37–39, 44–45, 62; Hoopes and Brinkley, *FDR,* 168–169.

4. Robins, *Experiment in Democracy,* 46–49, 62, 65–66.

5. Hoopes and Brinkley, *FDR,* 168–169; Robins, *Experiment in Democracy,* 5, 62; Notter, *Postwar Foreign Policy,* 378–379.

6. Harley Notter, *Postwar Foreign Policy Preparation, 1939–1945* (Washington, D.C.: Department of State, 1949), 374–378.

7. Robert Hildebrand, *Dumbarton Oaks: The Origins of the United Nations and the Search for Postwar Security* (Chapel Hill: University of North Carolina Press, 1990), 210–211; Townsend Hoopes and Douglas Brinkley, *FDR and the Creation of the United Nations* (New Haven, Conn.: Yale University Press, 1997), 152–153; Foreign Relations of the United States, 1944, vol. 1, 798–804; Robert Divine, *Second Chance: The Triumph of Internationalism in America During World War II* (New York: Atheneum, 1967), 272.

8. Notter, *Postwar Foreign Policy,* 381–384; Ministry of Foreign Affairs of the USSR, *Stalin's Correspondence with Roosevelt and Truman* (New York: Capricorn, 1965), 173–174, 178–179.

9. Notter, *Postwar Foreign Policy,* 384–386; State Department Memorandum of Conversation, "Voting Formula for Security Council," 8 January 1945, Leo Pasvolsky Papers, Manuscripts Division, Library of Congress; Hoopes and Brinkley, *FDR,* 171–172.

10. Notter, *Postwar Foreign Policy,* 380–381, 384; Cordell Hull, *The Memoirs of Cordell Hull,* vol. 1 (New York: Macmillan, 1948), 1686–1699.

11. Stalin Correspondence, 170; Anne O'Hare McCormick, "His 'Unfinished Business'—and Ours," 5.

12. Rudy Abramson, *Spanning the Century: The Life of W. Averell Harriman, 1891–1986* (New York: William Morrow, 1992), 369–372; Robert Sherwood, *Roosevelt and Hopkins: An Intimate History* (New York: Harper & Row, 1948), 85C–865; Hoopes and Brinkley, *FDR,* 174; Alger Hiss, *Recollections of a Life* (New York: Henry Holt and Company, 1988), 98.

13. Notter, *Postwar Foreign Policy,* 395; Winston Churchill, *The Second World War: Triumph and Tragedy* (Boston: Houghton Mifflin, 1953), 356; Sherwood, *Roosevelt and*

Hopkins, 854–855; Hoopes and Brinkley, *FDR,* 174–175; James Byrnes, *Speaking Frankly* (New York: Harper & Row, 1947); Hiss, *Recollections,* 122; Abramson, *Spanning the Century,* 380; Thomas M. Campbell and George C. Herring, eds., *The Diaries of Edward Stettinius Jr., 1943–1946* (New York: F. Watts, 1974/New Viewpoints, 1975), 244–245.

14. Byrnes, *Speaking Frankly,* 39–42; Divine, *Second Chance,* 265–267; Notter, *Postwar Foreign Policy,* 396–397; Sherwood, *Roosevelt and Hopkins,* 857.

15. Byrnes, *Speaking Frankly,* 38–39; Campbell and Herring, *Diaries,* 253–254.

16. Byrnes, *Speaking Frankly,* 29–33; Hoopes and Brinkley, *FDR,* 175–176; Robert Dallek, *Franklin Roosevelt and American Foreign Policy, 1932–1945* (New York: Oxford University Press, 1979), 513.

17. Notter, *Postwar Foreign Policy,* 397; Sherwood, *Roosevelt and Hopkins,* 865–866; James Byrnes, *All in One Lifetime* (New York: Harper & Brothers, 1958), 264; Dallek, *Franklin Roosevelt,* 513, 537.

18. Edward Stettinius, *Roosevelt and the Russians: The Yalta Conference,* ed. Walter Johnson (Garden City, N. Y.: Doubleday, 1949), 190–191; Divine, *Second Chance,* 267.

19. Divine, *Second Chance,* 267–268; Hoopes and Brinkley, *FDR,* 176–177.

20. Divine, *Second Chance,* 270–272; Hoopes and Brinkley, *FDR,* 179; Arthur H. Vandenberg Jr., ed., *The Private Papers of Senator Vandenberg* (Boston: Houghton Mifflin, 1952), 146–155, 158.

21. Divine, *Second Chance,* 268; Sherwood, *Roosevelt and Hopkins,* 869–874; Hoopes and Brinkley, *FDR,* 177.

22. Divine, *Second Chance,* 269–270; Hoopes and Brinkley, *United Nations,* 178–179.

23. Notter, *Postwar Foreign Policy,* 410–411; Hoopes and Brinkley, *United Nations,* 178.

24. Notter, *Postwar Foreign Policy,* 409; Evan Luard, *A History of the United Nations: The Years of Western Domination 1945–55,* vol. 1 (New York: St. Martin's Press, 1982), 38–39; Divine, *Second Chance,* 272.

25. Sherwood, *Roosevelt and Hopkins,* 875–876; Stalin's Correspondence, 197, 199–204; Foreign Relations of the United States (FRUS), vol. 1 (1945), Diplomatic Papers, The United Nations Conference (Washington, D.C.: U.S. Government Printing Office, 1967), 151.

26. Notter, *Postwar Foreign Policy,* 398–407; Hoopes and Brinkley, *United Nations,* 192–193; James Reston, "Stettinius Aides Lauded in Mexico," *New York Times,* 5 March 1945; Campbell and Herring, *Diaries,* 272; Allen Weinstein, *Perjury: The Hiss-Chambers Case* (New York: Knopf, 1978), 354.

27. Notter, *Postwar Foreign Policy,* 398–407; Hoopes and Brinkley, *United Nations,* 192–193; Reston, "Stettinius Aides"; Campbell and Herring, *Diaries,* 261–267, 283, 286–287, 309–310; Carey Reich, *The Life of Nelson A. Rockefeller: Worlds To Conquer, 1908–1958* (New York: Doubleday, 1996), 308. Rockefeller met with President Roosevelt on March 16 in the White House to press his case for renewal of U.S. diplomatic ties to Buenos Aires.

28. Porter McKeever, *Adlai Stevenson: His Life and Legacy* (New York: William Morrow, 1989), 94; Robins, *Experiment in Democracy,* 82–83, 91–96; Divine, *Second Chance,* 283–286; Dallek, *Franklin Roosevelt,* 506, 522; *Second Chance,* 283–285.

29. Divine, *Second Chance*, 285–286.

30. Notter, *Postwar Foreign Policy*, 421–422; Robins, *Experiment in Democracy*, 86–90; Ruth Russell, *A History of the United Nations' Charter: The Role of the United States 1940–1945* (Washington, D.C.: Brookings Institution, 1958), 594–596; Divine, *Second Chance*, 283–286; James Shotwell, *The Long Way to Freedom* (Indianapolis, Ind.: Bobbs-Merrill, 1960), 580; Harold Josephson, *James Shotwell and the Rise of Internationalism in America* (Cranbury, N. J.: Associated University Presses, 1975), 256–260; FRUS, 1:167.

31. Notter, *Postwar Foreign Policy*, 414–421; Divine, *Second Chance*, 272–273.

32. Divine, *Second Chance*, 272–273; Hoopes and Brinkley, *United Nations*, 180–181.

33. Divine, *Second Chance*, 273–274; Hoopes and Brinkley, *United Nations*, 180–181.

34. Sherwood, *Roosevelt and Hopkins*, 875–877; Divine, *Second Chance*, 273–276; Hoopes and Brinkley, *United Nations*, 180–181; FRUS, 1:179–180, 183–189, 196–198.

35. W. Averell Harriman and Elie Abel, *Special Envoy to Churchill and Stalin, 1941–1946* (New York: Random House, 1975), 427–428.

36. Harriman and Abel, *Special Envoy*, 429–431; Byrnes, *Speaking Frankly*, 54–56; Stalin Correspondence, 201–204, 211–213.

37. McCormick, "His 'Unfinished Business'—and Ours," 43–44.

38. Divine, *Second Chance*, 277; Sherwood, *Roosevelt and Hopkins*, 879; Hoopes and Brinkley, *United Nations*, 181–182; McCormick, "His 'Unfinished Business'—and Ours," 5; FRUS, 1:166–167; Michael Beschloss, *The Conquerors: Roosevelt, Truman and the Destruction of Hitler's Germany, 1941–1945* (New York: Simon & Schuster, 2002), 210.

CHAPTER 5

1. Thomas M. Campbell and George C. Herring, eds., *The Diaries of Edward Stettinius Jr., 1943–1946* (New York: F. Watts, 1974/New Viewpoints, 1975), 322–323; John Crider, "United Nations Conference Translates Charter into Deeds," *New York Times*, 26 April 1945.

2. William Leuchtenburg, *In the Shadow of FDR: From Harry Truman to Ronald Reagan* (Ithaca, N. Y.: Cornell University Press, 1983), 14–15; Walter Johnson, ed., *The Papers of Adlai Stevenson: Washington to Springfield 1941–1948*, vol. 2 (Boston: Little Brown, 1973), 233.

3. James Chace, *Acheson: The Secretary of State Who Created the American World* (New York: Simon & Schuster, 1998), 105–106; Dean Acheson, *Present At the Creation: My Years in the State Department* (New York: W. W. Norton, 1969), 88; Elting Morison, *Turmoil and Tradition: A Study of the Life and Times of Henry L. Stimson* (Boston: Houghton Mifflin, 1960), 612; Arthur H. Vandenberg Jr., ed., *The Private Papers of Senator Vandenberg* (Boston: Houghton Mifflin, 1952), 167–168, 191; Virginia Gildersleeve, *Many a Good Crusade* (New York: Crowell-Collier-Macmillan, 1954), 320–321; Cary Reich, *The Life of Nelson A. Rockefeller: Worlds to Conquer, 1908–1958* (New York: Doubleday, 1996), 260; Kai Bird, *The Chairman: John J. McCloy: The Making of the American Establishment* (New York: Simon & Schuster, 1992), 692–693; Michael Beschloss, *The Conquerors: Roosevelt, Truman and the Destruction of Hitler's Germany, 1941–1945* (New York: Simon & Schuster, 2002), 167.

4. Brian Urquhart, *Ralph Bunche: An American Life* (New York: W. W. Norton, 1993), 118; Nigel Hamilton, *JFK: Reckless Youth* (New York: Random House, 1992), 692.

5. James Forrestal, *The Forrestal Diaries,* ed. Walter Mills (New York: Viking, 1951), 53–54; Arthur Krock, *Memoirs: Sixty Years on the Firing Line* (New York: Funk & Wagnalls, 1968), 232–233; Averell Harriman and Elie Abel, *Special Envoy to Churchill and Stalin, 1941–1946* (New York: Random House, 1975), 455–456; oral interview with James Green, 21 April 1986, 7, in U.N. Library, New York City; Sol Bloom, *The Autobiography of Sol Bloom* (New York: G. P. Putnam's Sons, 1948), 277; Reich, *Life of Nelson A. Rockefeller,* 345.

6. Norman Graebner, ed., *An Uncertain Tradition: American Secretaries of State in the Twentieth Century* (New York: McGraw-Hill, 1961), chapter 11: Walter Johnson, "Edward R. Stettinius, Jr.," 210–211; Campbell and Herring, *Diaries,* xiv.

7. Graebner, *An Uncertain Tradition,* 211–217.

8. Townsend Hoopes and Douglas Brinkley, *FDR and the Creation of the United Nations* (New Haven, Conn.: Yale University Press, 1997), 136; Patricia Bosworth, *Anything Your Little Heart Desires: An American Family Story* (New York: Simon & Schuster, 1997), 159.

9. Harry Truman, *Memoirs: Years of Decision,* vol. 1, *1955–1956* (Garden City, N. Y.: Doubleday, 1955), 272.

10. Vandenberg, *Private Papers,* 162–163, 170; James Reston, "Majority to Rule Our Delegation at Parley: Justice Theme Gains," *New York Times,* 11 April 1945; Foreign Relations of the United States (FRUS), vol. 1 (1945), Diplomatic Papers, The United Nations Conference (Washington, D.C.: U.S. Government Printing Office, 1967), 353–355.

11. Truman, *Memoirs,* 273, 277–280; FRUS, 1:353–355.

12. Campbell and Herring, *Diaries,* 319–321; FRUS, 1:204–206, 459, 491.

13. Vandenberg, *Private Papers,* 169; Truman, *Memoirs,* 46, 49, 73, 272, 277–280.

14. Vandenberg, *Private Papers,* 171; William White, "Connally Predicts Dumbarton Shifts," *New York Times,* 21 April 1945.

15. Truman, *Memoirs,* 73; Campbell and Herring, *Diaries,* 324–325.

16. Campbell and Herring, *Diaries,* 324–325; James Reston, "Argentine Regime Recognized by U.S.," *New York Times,* 10 April 2001.

17. Harriman and Abel, *Special Envoy,* 441–443; Walter Issacson and Evan Thomas, *The Wisemen* (New York: Simon & Schuster, 1986), 260.

18. Chalmers Roberts, "Averell Harriman at 90," *Washington Post,* 8 November 1981.

19. Harriman and Abel, *Special Envoy,* 445; Truman, *Memoirs,* 37; Robert Donovan, *Conflict and Crisis: The Presidency of Harry Truman 1945–48* (New York: W. W. Norton, 1977), 37.

20. Truman, *Memoirs,* 38–39, 50.

21. Harriman and Abel, *Special Envoy,* 446; Issacson and Thomas, *The Wisemen,* 258–260; Rudy Abramson, *Spanning the Century: The Life of W. Averell Harriman* (New York: Morrow, 1992), 395; "New Russian Note Is Sent on Poland; Envoys Rush Here," *New York Times,* 19 April 1945.

22. Issacson and Thomas, *The Wisemen,* 262; Harriman and Abel, *Special Envoy,* 449–450; "Soviet Will Insist Lublin Act for Poland at Parley," *New York Times,* 17 April 1945; Lansing Warren, "U.S. Again Rejects Demand by Russia for Bid to Poland," *New York Times,* 20 April 1945.

23. Harriman and Abel, *Special Envoy,* 448; Truman, *Memoirs,* 70–72.

24. Truman, *Memoirs,* 70–72; Harriman and Abel, *Special Envoy,* 447–448.

25. Harriman and Abel, *Special Envoy,* 448–449; Truman, *Memoirs,* 70–72.

26. Campbell and Herring, *Diaries,* 324, 328; Truman, *Memoirs,* 73; Issacson and Thomas, *The Wisemen,* 263.

27. "Polish Pact Vital in Russians' View," *New York Times,* 23 April 1945; Truman, *Memoirs,* 75.

28. Truman, *Memoirs,* 75–77.

29. Harriman and Abel, *Special Envoy,* 451; Stettinius, Campbell and Herring, *Diaries,* 329; Truman, *Memoirs,* 77; Forrestal, *Forrestal Diaries,* 49.

30. Truman, *Memoirs,* 77; Harriman and Abel, *Special Envoy,* 452; Forrestal, *Forrestal Diaries,* 50; FRUS, 1:252–255.

31. Truman, *Memoirs,* 77–79; Harriman and Abel, *Special Envoy,* 452–453; Forrestal, *Forrestal Diaries,* 50–51; Martin Sherwin, *A World Destroyed: The Atomic Bomb and the Grand Alliance* (New York: Random House, 1977), 157.

32. Truman, *Memoirs,* 79–81.

33. Ibid., 79–82; Donovan, *Conflict and Crisis,* 41–42.

34. Truman, *Memoirs,* 79–82; Issacson and Thomas, *The Wisemen,* 266–267; Andrei Gromyko, *Memories* (London: Century Hutchinson, 1989), 95–96.

35. Harriman and Abel, *Special Envoy,* 453–454; Charles Bohlen, *Witness to History* (New York: W. W. Norton, 1973), 213–214, 222–223; FRUS, 1:79–82; Averell Harriman, *America and Russia in a Changing World: A Half Century of Personal Observation* (New York: Doubleday, 1971), 40; Vandenberg, *Private Papers,* 176.

36. Truman, *Memoirs,* 85–86; Sherwin, *A World Destroyed,* 160; *Stalin's Correspondence with Roosevelt and Truman, 1941–1945* (New York: Capricorn, 1965), 219–220.

37. Truman, *Memoirs,* 94–95; Anne O'Hare McCormick, "Grim War Mood Pervades Opening of Conference That Seeks Peace," *New York Times,* 26 April 1945.

CHAPTER 6

1. Cary Reich, *The Life of Nelson A. Rockefeller: Worlds to Conquer, 1908–1958* (New York: Doubleday, 1996), 322; Brigadier General Carter W. Clarke, MIS, to the Commanding General, Signal Security Agency, 10 July 1945, National Archives, Washington, D.C. Also see James Bamford, *Body of Secrets* (New York: Doubleday, 2001), 22–23: The military man in charge of the San Francisco eavesdropping and code-breaking operation indicated his own sense of accomplishment, writing in the semimonthly Branch Activity Report: "Pressure of work due to the San Francisco Conference has at last abated and the 24-hour day has been shortened. The feeling in the Branch is that the success of the Conference may owe a great deal to its contribution."

2. Thomas Campbell and George Herring, eds., *The Dairies of Edward Stettinius Jr., 1943–1946* (New York: F. Watts, 1974/New Viewpoints, 1975), 303; Sanford Unger, *FBI: An Uncensored Look Behind the Walls* (Boston: Little, Brown, 1975), 225.

3. The National Archives and Records Administration, Record Group 457 (Records of the National Security Agency/Central Security Service), "'Magic' Diplomatic Summaries," 1942–1945. The NSA declassified portions of the summaries for me on October 28, 1993, on the basis of my request of August 13, 1993, under the Freedom of Information Act. All are from 1945. The intercept numbers on the declassified portions were found in the full summaries by historian David Kahn. I will cite the sources in each

summary by "'Magic' Diplomatic Summaries," date, and page. For the organization and operation of the Special Branch, which produced and distributed the summaries, see David Kahn, "Roosevelt, Magic and Ultra," *Cryptologia Magazine* 16 (October 1992): 289–319; Unger, *FBI,* 107–108; Robert Louis Benson and Michael Warner, eds., *Venona: Soviet Espionage and the American Response, 1939–1957* (Washington, D.C.: National Security Agency, 1996), 59, copy of Secretary Stettinius's memorandum to President Roosevelt explaining his instruction to Donovan. See James Bamford, *Body of Secrets* (New York: Doubleday, 2001), 22–23, and David Alvarez, *Secret Messages: Code-Breaking and American Diplomacy, 1930–1945* (Lawrence: University Press of Kansas, 2000), 235.

4. Reich, *Life of Nelson A. Rockefeller,* 292, 302–303, 322.

5. "'Magic' Diplomatic Summaries," 10 March 1945, 8–9, and 22 March 1945, 7–9.

6. The FBI declassified certain records pertaining to the San Francisco Conference on October 27, 1998, on the basis on my request made on October 3, 1995, under the Freedom of Information Act. I will hereafter list the FBI document number and date. FBI: number 16280, 6 April 1945.

7. "'Magic' Diplomatic Summaries," 8 January 1945, 4–6; 11 January 1945, 9; 19 January 1945, 9–12; 22 January 1945, 13.

8. Ibid., 16 April 1945, 10–11.

9. Ibid., 6 February 1945, 5–7.

10. Ibid., 24 February 1945, 8–10; 6 March 1945, 8–11.

11. Ibid., 29 March 1945, 9–10; 12 April 1945, 6–8; 14 April 1945, 8–10; 5 June 1945, 14–15.

12. FBI Number: 100–69266–94, 19 March 1945; FBI Number 100–19377, 7 April 1945; FBI Number 100–69266–97, April 2, 1945.

13. FBI Number 100–69266–97, 2 April 1945.

14. "'Magic' Diplomatic Summaries," 11 April 1945, 12–13.

15. Ibid., 13 April 1945, 7–9.

16. Ibid., 7 March 1945, 6–8; 9 March 1945, 6–7.

17. Robert Hilderbrand, *Dumbarton Oaks: The Origins of the United Nations and the Search for Postwar Security* (Chapel Hill: University of North Carolina Press, 1990), 40, 120–121; "France Lining Up with Big Powers," *New York Times,* 25 April 1945; "France's Position Put by De Gaulle," *New York Times,* 26 April 1945; "France Position Still in Doubt," *New York Times,* 28 April 1945; "Hints France Asks Major-Power Role," *New York Times,* 3 May 1945.

18. "'Magic' Diplomatic Summaries," 30 June 1945, 4–6.

19. "Party Ship Is Sent to Parley by Soviet," *New York Times,* 21 April 1945; Edwin James, "San Francisco Learns About Soviet Diplomacy," *New York Times,* 13 May 1945; Memorandum released to author on 8 December 1998 by the Department of Army, U.S. Army Intelligence and Security Command, regarding FBI memo dated 18 April 1945 on Russian request for a radio line to its ship.

20. Benson and Warner, *Venona,* vii–viii.

21. Hiss, Alger, *Recollections of a Life* (New York: Arcade, 1988) 130; Allen Weinstein, *Perjury: The Hiss-Chambers Case* (New York: Knopf, 1978), 355.

22. Sam Tanenhaus, *Whittaker Chambers* (New York: Random House, 1997), 203, 226; Weinstein, *Perjury,* 346–347, 351, 359; Adolf Berle, *Navigating the Rapids,*

1918–1971: From the Papers of Adolf Berle, ed. Beatrice Bishop Berle and Francis Jacobs (New York: Harcourt Brace Jovanovich, 1973), 582–587, 598–599; Allen Weinstein, "Nixon vs. Hiss," *Esquire Magazine* (November 1975). A Herbert Feis memorandum, 8 April 1953, recorded a visit to Feis by FBI agents inquiring whether Pasvolsky might have been a Communist while at the State Department. Nothing ever resulted from this investigation.

23. Tanenhaus, *Whittaker Chambers,* 272; *Newsweek Magazine,* 8 March 1999, 56; Weinstein, *Perjury,* 346.

24. Tanenhaus, *Whittaker Chambers,* 225, 363.

25. Benson and Warner, *Venona,* 423.

26. Tanenhaus, *Whittaker Chambers,* 227; Benson and Warner, Venona, 423. In "Tangled Treason," a review of *The Haunted Woods: Soviet Espioage in America—The Stalin Era* by Allen Weinstein and Alexander Vassiliev, *Venona: Decoding Soviet Espionage in America* by John Earl Haynes and Harvey Klehr, and *The View from Alger's Window: A Son's Memoir* by Tony Hiss, *New Republic,* 5 July 1999, Sam Tanenhaus argued that Hiss was, in fact, playing a double game in that he picked and chose the issues that helped the United States and those that assisted the USSR. Hiss and others may have "functioned less as moles than as ideological freelancers, sampling various positions, trimming the differences between the United States and the Soviet Union, perhaps even priding themselves on the contradictions. These were not dual loyalties; they were negotiable loyalties." Hiss memo, U.S. State Department, 8 February 1945; Charles Bohlen, *Witness to History, 1929–1969* (New York: W. W. Norton, 1973), 194; 20 May 1949, *Defendant's Exh. Z,* U.S. District Court, Southern District of New York, 27 June 1949, 1–2.

27. Weinstein, *Perjury,* 346; James Barros, "Alger Hiss and Harry Dexter White: The Canadian Connection," *Orbis Magazine,* vol. 21, no. 3 (1977).

28. David Rees, *Harry Dexter White: A Study in Paradox* (New York: Coward, McCann & Geoghegan, 1973), 9–11, 62–63.

29. Robert Skidelsky, *John Maynard Keynes: Fighting for Britain, 1937–1946,* vol. 3 (New York: Macmillan, 2001), see Appendix: "Harry Dexter White: Guilty and Naïve."

30. Venona documents dated 4 May 1945, Telegram 230, and 5 May 1945, Telegram 235, 236, obtained by the author directly from the National Security Agency.

31. The author submitted a list of questions to Alger Hiss and received answers on May 4, 1995, transmitted by his son, Tony Hiss. Alger Hiss made clear that he knew nothing about the Army Signal Corps intercepts at the time but he guessed that President Roosevelt had authorized them to help guarantee the success of the U.N. conference.

CHAPTER 7

1. *New York Times,* 25, 27 April and 29 June 1945.

2. Oral interview with Oliver Lundquist, 19 April 1990, United Nations Oral History Project, U.N. Library, New York, 2, 4, 8, 13; Donal McLaughlin, "Origin of the Emblem and Other Recollections of the 1945 U.N. Conference," personal monograph, Garrett Park, Maryland, 1995, 3, 7.

3. Lundquist interview, 6–7.

4. Lundquist interview, 8–9; *New York Times,* 28 June 1945; Walter Johnson, ed., *The Papers of Adlai Stevenson: Washington to Springfield, 1941–1948,* vol. 11 (Boston: Little Brown, 1973), 240.

5. Ruth Russell, *A History of the United Nations' Charter: The Role of the United States, 1940–1945* (Washington, D.C.: Brookings Institution, 1958), 639–645; Foreign Relations of the United States (FRUS), vol. 1 (1945), Diplomatic Papers, The United Nations Conference (Washington, D.C.: U.S. Government Printing Office, 1967), 156–157, 174–175, 181–183.

6. Townsend Hoopes and Douglas Brinkley, *FDR and the Creation of the United Nations* (New Haven, Conn.: Yale University Press, 1997), 185–186.

7. Alger Hiss, *Recollections of a Life* (New York: Arcade, 1988), 130, 133; *New York Times,* 29 June 1945.

8. *New York Times,* 8 April 1945; McLaughlin, "Origin," 6; UN 50 Committee 1945–1995 Official Program, San Francisco, California (San Francisco: 2M&G, June 1995); Samuel Tanenhaus, *Whittaker Chambers* (New York: Random House, 1997), 385–385.

9. *New York Times,* 23 April 1945; United Nations Association of the United States, 1995 National Convention, Luncheon Program, Grand Ballroom, Fairmont Hotel, 27 June 1995, San Francisco.

10. Anne O'Hare McCormick, "San Francisco: Battlefield for Peace," *New York Times Magazine,* 6 May 1945, 9; McLaughlin, "Origin," 6; *Irish Times,* 23 March 1994.

11. *New York Times,* 29, 30 April 1945; Virginia Gildersleeve, *Many a Good Crusade* (New York: Crowell-Collier-Macmillan, 1954), 326.

12. Gildersleeve, *Crusade,* 325, 332–334.

13. *New York Times,* 10, 22, 27, 29 April 1945; Gildersleeve, *Crusade,* 335;

14. *New York Times,* 15, 25 April 1945; *San Francisco Chronicle,* 23 April 1995.

15. Linda Melvern, *The Ultimate Crime: Who Betrayed the U.N. and Why* (London: Allison and Busby, 1995), 23; *New York Times,* 26, 29 April 1945; *New York Herald Tribune,* 26 April 1945; McLaughlin, "Origin," 7.

16. *New York Times,* 25, 26 April and May 5 1945; FRUS, 1:380–384; Hiss, *Recollections,* 134; Cary Reich, *The Life of Nelson A. Rockefeller: Worlds to Conquer, 1908–1958* (New York: Doubleday, 1996), 324, cited in Stettinius Calendar Notes, 30 April 1945.

17. Hoopes and Brinkley, *FDR,* 185–186; Russell, *History of the United Nations' Charter,* 634–636; Thomas Campbell and George Herring, eds., *The Diaries of Edward Stettinius Jr., 1943–1946* (New York: F. Watts 1974/New Viewpoints, 1975), 337–340; John Blum, ed., *The Price of Vision: The Diary of Henry Wallace, 1942–1946* (Boston: Houghton Mifflin, 1973), 436.

18. Arthur H. Vandenberg Jr., ed., *The Private Papers of Senator Vandenberg* (Boston: Houghton Mifflin, 1952), 178–179; Russell, *History of the United Nations' Charter,* 635; *San Francisco Examiner,* 25 June 1995, reprint of article by John Fitzgerald Kennedy, published by Hearst Newspapers, 28 April 1945.

19. Harley Notter, *Postwar Foreign Policy Preparation, 1939–1945* (Washington, D.C.: Department of State, Publications Division, Office of Public Affairs, 1949), 435–436; Thomas Connally and Alfred Steinberg, *My Name Is Thomas Connally* (New

York: T. Y. Crowell, 1954), 279–280; FRUS, 1:218, 297–299; Porter McKeever, *Adlai Stevenson: His Life and Legacy* (New York: William Morrow, 1989), 94.

20. *New York Times,* 27 April, 3, 29 June 1945; UN 50 Committee 1945–1995 Official Program.

21. *New York Times,* 14 May 1945; William Hardy McNeill, *America, Britain, & Russia: Their Cooperation and Conflict, 1941–1946* (New York: Johnson Reprint Corporation, 1970), 592.

22. Dorothy Robins, *Experiment in Democracy: The Story of U.S. Citizen Organizations in Forging the Charter of the United Nations* (New York: Parkside Press, 1971), 200–201; address by T. Patrick Killough, "A Peace Made on Main Street: Private Americans Help Create the 1945 United Nations Charter," Southwestern World Affairs Institute, YMCA Center, Black Mountain, North Carolina, 26 July 1991, 27; Clark Eichelberger, *Organizing for Peace: A Personal History of the Founding of the United Nations* (New York: Harper, 1977), 263.

23. Robins, *Experiment,* 105–106, 110.

24. Ibid., 107, 115, 129; Killough, "Peace Made on Main Street," 22; FRUS, 1:460–472.

25. Robins, *Experiment,* 107, 115, 116, 120,129; Gildersleeve, *Crusade,* 323–324; FRUS, 1:340–341.

26. Robins, *Experiment,* 129–132, 218–221; Robert Divine, *Second Chance: The Triumph of Internationalism in America During World War II* (New York: Atheneum, 1967), 292; Address by Barbara Blaustein Hirschhorn, at the Fiftieth Anniversary Celebration of the United Nations, San Francisco, 22 June 1995, describing the role of her father, Jacob Blaustein, who represented the American Jewish Committee as a consultant at the founding meeting in 1945.

27. Robins, *Experiment,* 122–129, 216–218.

28. Ibid., 111.

29. Killough, "Peace Made on Main Street," 42; Thomas Campbell, *Masquerade Peace: America's UN Policy 1944–1945* (Tallahassee: Florida State University Press, 1973), 63.

CHAPTER 8

1. Foreign Relations of the United States (FRUS), vol. 1 (1945), Diplomatic Papers, The United Nations Conference (Washington, D.C.: U.S. Government Printing Office, 1967), 281–287, 353, 383.

2. FRUS, 1:386–402; Arthur H. Vandenberg Jr., ed., *The Private Papers of Senator Vandenberg* (Boston: Houghton Mifflin, 1952), 176–177; W. Averell Harriman and Elie Abel, *Special Envoy to Churchill and Stalin, 1941–1946* (New York: Random House, 1975), 454–455.

3. FRUS, 1:386–402, 412; Vandenberg, *Private Papers,* 176–177; Harriman and Abel, *Special Envoy,* 455.

4. FRUS, 1:386–402, 412; Vandenberg, *Private Papers,* 176–177; Harriman and Abel, *Special Envoy,* 455.

5. *New York Times,* 22, 23 April 1945; Cary Reich, *The Life of Nelson A. Rockefeller: Worlds to Conquer, 1908–1958* (New York: Doubleday, 1996), 321–323, 327.

6. Reich, *Life of Nelson A. Rockefeller,* 325.

7. Thomas Campbell and George Herring, eds., *The Diaries of Edward Stettinius Jr., 1943–1946* (New York: F. Watts 1974/New Viewpoints, 1975), 341–342.

8. Ibid., 336, 341–342; FRUS, 1:407–413; Reich, *Life of Nelson A. Rockefeller,* 325–326; Vandenberg, *Private Papers,* 176–178.

9. Reich, *Life of Nelson A. Rockefeller,* 328; Vandenberg, *Private Papers,* 177–180; FRUS, 1:413, 416–418, 483.

10. Reich, *Life of Nelson A. Rockefeller,* 328; Vandenberg, *Private Papers,* 177–180; FRUS, 1:413, 416–418, 483.

11. *New York Times,* 27 April 1945.

12. Evan Luard, *A History of the United Nations: The Years of Western Domination, 1945–55,* vol. 1 (New York: St. Martin's Press, 1982), 41; Reich, *Life of Nelson A. Rockefeller,* 328–329; *New York Times,* 28 April 1945; FRUS, 1:483; Campbell and Herring, *Diaries,* 340; Vandenberg, *Private Papers,* 180–181.

13. Campbell and Herring, *Diaries,* 340–341; Charles Bohlen, *Witness to History, 1929–1969* (New York: W. W. Norton, 1973), 214; Nigel Hamilton, *JFK: Reckless Youth* (New York: Random House, 1992), 697.

14. Vandenberg, *Private Papers,* 180–182; FRUS, 1:483; Campbell and Herring, *Diaries,* 341; Harry Truman, *Memoirs: Years of Decision,* vol. 1 (Garden City, N. Y.: Doubleday, 1955), 281.

15. Campbell and Herring, *Diaries,* 342–344; Reich, *Life of Nelson A. Rockefeller,* 329; FRUS, 1:484; Cordell Hull, *Memoirs of Cordell Hull,* vol. 1 (New York: Macmillan, 1948), 1407; *New York Times,* 28 April 1945.

16. FRUS, 1:486–487.

17. Ibid., 486–490; Secretary Stettinius telephone conversation with President Truman, summary, 28 April 1945, Edward Stettinius Papers, University of Virginia.

18. *New York Times,* 29 April 1945; Reich, *Life of Nelson A. Rockefeller,* 330.

19. Reich, *Life of Nelson A. Rockefeller,* 330; Campbell and Herring, *Diaries,* 344–345; Stettinius Memorandum to Harry Truman, 1 May 1945, Harry S. Truman Papers, Harry S. Truman Presidential Library, Independence, Missouri.

20. *New York Times,* 1 May 1945; Stettinius Memorandum to Truman, 1 May 1945, Truman Papers, Harry S. Truman Presidential Library.

21. *New York Times,* 1 May 1945; Reich, *Life of Nelson A. Rockefeller,* 331.

22. *New York Times,* 1 May 1945; Vandenberg, *Private Papers,* 179–182; Ruth Russell, *A History of the United Nations' Charter: The Role of the United States, 1940–1945* (Washington, D.C.: Brookings Institution, 1958), 639–642; Truman, *Memoirs,* 280–282.

23. John Blum, ed., *The Price of Vision: The Diary of Henry Wallace, 1942–1946* (Boston: Houghton Mifflin, 1973), 439–440; Arthur Krock, *Memoirs: Sixty Years on the Firing Line* (New York: Funk & Wagnalls, 1968), 209–211; Campbell and Herring, *Diaries,* 346–347.

24. *Time Magazine,* 14 May 1945; *Washington Post,* 1 May 1945; Walter Lippmann, *New York Harold Tribune,* 3 May 1945; Reich, *Life of Nelson A. Rockefeller,* 332; Ronald Steel, *Walter Lippmann and the American Century* (New York: Atlantic Monthly Press, 1980), 420; E. B. White, *The Wild Flag: Editorials from the New Yorker on Federal World Government and Other Matters* (Boston: Houghton Mifflin, 1946), 152.

25. FRUS, 1:501–504; Reich, *Life of Nelson A. Rockefeller*, 332–333; Vandenberg, *Private Papers*, 182.

26. Reich, *Life of Nelson A. Rockefeller*, 337; FRUS, 1:500–502; *New York Times*, 29 May 1945; Robert Divine, *Second Chance: The Triumph of Internationalism in America During World War II* (New York: Atheneum, 1967), 294; State Department memorandums of conversation, 30 April, 1 May 1945, President Truman and Secretary Stettinius, Stettinius Papers.

27. State Department memorandum of conversation, 1 May 1945, Stettinius Papers.

28. State Department memorandum of conversations, 30 April, 1 May 1945, and State Department summary of Secretary Stettinius's telephone conversation, 1 May 1945, Stettinius Papers.

29. Divine, *Second Chance*, 291.

CHAPTER 9

1. Stettinius Calendar Notes, 1 May 1945, Stettinius Telephone Log, 6 May 1945, Edward Stettinius Papers, University of Virginia.

2. Stettinius Calendar Notes, 1 May 1945, Stettinius Papers; Memorandum from Charles Noyes, Assistant to Secretary Edward Stettinius, 8 May 1945, Leo Pasvolsky Papers, Manuscripts Division, Library of Congress. Foreign Relations of the United States (FRUS), vol. 1 (1945), Diplomatic Papers, the United Nations Conference (Washington, D.C.: U.S. Government Printing Office, 1967), 116; *New York Times*, 11 May 1945.

3. FRUS, 1:116; *New York Times*, 11 May 1945.

4. Robert Divine, *Second Chance: The Triumph of Internationalism in America During World War II* (New York: Atheneum, 1967), 288; Anne O'Hare McCormick, "Abroad," *New York Times*, 9 June 1945; Walter Johnson, ed., *The Papers of Adlai Stevenson: Washington to Springfield 1941–1948*, vol. 2 (Boston: Little, Brown, 1973), 240.

5. FRUS, 1:116–118, 187, 215–216, 227–228, 232–233, 378–379.

6. *New York Times*, 27 April 1945; FRUS, 1:489; Stettinius Telephone Conversation, 4 May 1945, Stettinius Papers.

7. *New York Times*, 11, 13 May 1945; Stettinius Telephone Log, 11 May 1945, Stettinius Papers.

8. Averell W. Harriman and Elie Abel, *Special Envoy to Churchill and Stalin, 1941–1946* (New York: Random House, 1975), 456–457; Harriman interview with Arthur Schlesinger Jr., 27, 24 May 1981.

9. Harriman and Abel, *Special Envoy*, 457; Arthur H. Vandenberg Jr., ed., *The Private Papers of Senator Vandenberg* (Boston: Houghton Mifflin, 1952), 130–131; Charles Bohlen, *Witness to History, 1929–1969* (New York: W. W. Norton, 1973), 215; Ronald Steel, *Walter Lippmann and the American Century* (New York: Atlantic Monthly Press, 1980), 418–420; Walter Issacson and Evan Thomas, *The Wise Men: Six Friends and the World They Made* (New York: Simon & Schuster, 1986), 269.

10. Patricia Bosworth, *Anything Your Little Heart Desires: An American Family Story* (New York: Simon & Schuster, 1994), 159; Divine, *Second Chance*, 293–294; Harriman and Abel, *Special Envoy*, 456–457; John Lewis Gaddis, *The United States and the Origins of the Cold War, 1941–1947* (New York: Columbia University Press, 1972), 226–227.

11. Arthur Krock, *Memoirs: Sixty Years on the Firing Line* (New York: Funk & Wagnalls, 1968), 233; Johnson, *Papers of Adlai Stevenson*, 230, 234; Porter McKeever, *Adlai Stevenson: His Life and Legacy* (New York: William Morrow, 1989), 102; John Bartlow Martin, *Adlai Stevenson of Illinois: The Life of Adlai Stevenson* (New York: Doubleday, 1976), 237. Ironically, a few days after the intervention by Krock and Reston with the secretary of state, Stettinius chastised them both for a story about him in the *New York Times*, Stettinius Telephone Conversations, 11 May 1945, Stettinius Papers.

12. Johnson, *Papers of Adlai Stevenson*, 235–238; McKeever, *Adlai Stevenson*, 103; *New York Times*, "Stettinius Hailed for Part in Parley," 24 May 1945; *New York Times*, "Report from San Francisco," editorial, 29 May 1945.

13. Johnson, *Papers of Adlai Stevenson*, 237–238; McKeever, *Adlai Stevenson*, 103.

14. Johnson, *Papers of Adlai Stevenson*, 237–238; McKeever, *Adlai Stevenson*, 103; FRUS, 1:1130–1131; Memorandum by Stettinius, Meeting of Big Five, 3 June 1945, Stettinius Papers.

15. Leonard Mosley, *Dulles: A Biography of Eleanor, Allen and John Foster Dulles and Their Family Network* (New York: Dial Press, 1978), 190–191.

16. Nick Clarke, *Alistair Cooke: A Biography* (New York: Arcade, 1999), 202; Arthur Krock, "In the Nation," *New York Times*, 11 May 1945; Stettinius Memorandum of Conversation, "Meeting with Advisors," 10 May 1945, Stettinius Papers.

17. Divine, *Second Chance*, 288; Issacson and Thomas, *Wise Men*, 269; Bosworth, *American Family Story*, 160; "In Time's Eye," *Irish Times*, 23 March 1994; *New York Times*, 12 May 1945; Nigel Hamilton, *JFK: Reckless Youth* (New York: Random House, 1992), 693.

18. Divine, *Second Chance*, 287–288; Clarke, *Alistair Cooke*, 202–204; Hamilton, *JFK*, 688, 694.

19. Arthur Schlesinger, *A Thousand Days: John F. Kennedy in the White House* (Boston: Houghton Mifflin, 1965), 87–89.

20. E. B. White, *The Wild Flag: Editorials from the New Yorker on Federal World Government and Other Matters* (Boston: Houghton Mifflin, 1946), 81, 88–90, 180.

21. Krock, "In the Nation."

CHAPTER 10

1. *New York Times*, 28 April, 5 May 1945.

2. *New York Times*, 6 May 1945; Stettinius Memorandum to President Truman, 9 May 1945, President's Secretary Files, Harry S. Truman Papers, Harry S. Truman Presidential Library, Independence, Missouri.

3. Arthur H. Vandenberg Jr., ed., *The Private Papers of Senator Vandenberg* (Boston: Houghton Mifflin, 1952), 184–185; Foreign Relations of the United States (FRUS), vol. 1 (1945), Diplomatic Papers, The United Nations Conference (Washington, D.C.: U.S. Government Printing Office, 1967), 353–355; 506–509; Stettinius Memorandum of Conversation, dinner given by British Foreign Minister Anthony Eden, 1 May 1945, Edward Settinius Papers, University of Virginia; Stettinius to Truman, telegram, 2 May 1945, Stettinius to Truman, telephone call, 2 May 1945 at 6:45 P.M., Stettinius Papers.

4. Virginia Gildersleeve, *Many a Good Crusade* (New York: Arno Press, 1980), 322.

5. FRUS, 1:217–218; Gildersleeve, *Many a Good Crusade*, 323; Thomas Connally and Alfred Steinberg, *My Name Is Tom Connally* (New York: T. Y. Crowell, 1954), 279; Carey Reich, *The Life of Nelson Rockefeller: Worlds to Conquer, 1908–1958* (New York: Doubleday, 1996), 346; Stettinius Private Notes, 19 May 1945, Stettinius Papers. During the conference, Pasvolsky also chaired thirty-five meetings between the five deputies to the heads of the Big Five delegations from April 29 to June 15, 1945, in the Fairmont Hotel.

6. Ronald Pruessen, *John Foster Dulles: The Road to Power* (New York: Free Press, 1982), 241–242, 253.

7. Ibid., 255.

8. FRUS, 1:273, and see entire volume.

9. FRUS, 1:221, 224–225, 230.

10. Ibid., 255–257.

11. Ibid., 475–477.

12. Ibid., 308–309, 333–334, 400; Pruessen, *John Foster Dulles,* 243–244, 251.

13. FRUS, 1:308–309, 400; Pruessen, *John Foster Dulles,* 243–244, 251, 257; James Reston, *Deadline* (New York: Random House, 1991), 229.

14. Stettinius to Truman, telephone call, 2 May 1945, Settinius Papers; Stettinius to Truman, telegram, 2, 3 May 1945, Stettinius Papers; Thomas Connally and Alfred Steinberg, *My Name Is Thomas Connally* (New York: T. Y. Crowell, 1954), 280; Vandenberg, *Private Papers,* 185.

15. Vandenberg, *Private Papers,* 183–185; Stettinius to Truman, telegram, 5 May 1945, Truman Papers, Truman Presidential Library; FRUS, 1:555; *New York Times,* 6 May 1945.

16. Stettinius, memorandum of conversation, 3 May 1945, Stettinius Papers; Vandenberg, *Private Papers,* 183–185; *New York Times,* 6, 7, 8 May 1945.

17. Stettinius to Truman, telephone conversation, 6:07 P.M., 4 May 1945, Stettinius Papers; Vandenberg, *Private Papers,* 183–185; *New York Times,* 6, 7 May 1945.

18. *New York Times,* 5, 6, 7 May 1945.

19. *New York Times,* 8 May 1945; Stettinius to Truman, telegram, 9 May 1945, Truman Papers, Truman Presidential Library.

20. Settinius and Bidault, memorandum of conversation, 3 May 1945, Stettinius Notes for 29 May 1945, Stettinius Papers; Carlos Romulo and Beth Day Romulo, *Forty Years: A Third World Soldier at the U.N.* (New York: Greenwood Press, 1986), 9–10.

21. *New York Times,* 5, 7 May 1945.

22. *New York Times,* 7 May 1945.

23. Mary Ann Glendon, *A World Made New* (New York: Random House, 2001), 20; Anne O'Hare McCormick, "San Francisco: Battlefield for Peace," *New York Times Magazine,* 6 May 1945.

24. *New York Times,* 8 May 1945; FRUS, 1:628; Robert Divine, *Second Chance: The Triumph of Internationalism in America During World War II* (New York: Atheneum, 1967), 292–293.

25. *New York Times,* 4 May 1945.

26. Memorandum of Conversation, Stettinius and Lie, 6 May 1945, Stettinius Papers.

27. Divine, *Second Chance,* 292; *New York Times,* 9 May 1945.

CHAPTER 11

1. Memorandum of Conversation, 5 May 1945, Leo Pasvolsky Papers, Manuscripts Division, Library of Congress; Stettinius, Telephone Log, 5 May 1945, Edward Stettinius Papers, University of Virginia; Foreign Relations of the United States (FRUS), vol. 1 (1945), Diplomatic Papers, The United Nations Conference (Washington, D.C.: U.S. Government Printing Office, 1967), 614, 634.

2. Cary Reich, *The Life of Nelson A. Rockefeller: Worlds to Conquer, 1908–1958* (New York: Doubleday, 1996), 340; Memorandum of Conversation, 5 May 1945, Pasvolsky Papers; Stettinius Telephone Log, 5 May 1945, Stettinius Papers; FRUS, 1:596, 614, 634.

3. Reich, *Life of Nelson A. Rockefeller,* 340; FRUS, 1:591–593; Arthur H. Vandenberg, Jr. ed., *The Private Papers of Senator Vandenberg* (Boston: Houghton Mifflin, 1952), 186–188.

4. Reich, *Life of Nelson A. Rockefeller,* 340; Vandenberg, *Private Papers,* 186–188; *New York Times,* 7, 8 May 1945.

5. Vandenberg, *Private Papers,* 186–188; Reich, *Life of Nelson A. Rockefeller,* 341; Vandenberg to Stettinius, 5 May 1945, Pasvolsky Papers; Townsend Hoopes and Douglas Brinkley, *FDR and the Creation of the United Nations* (New Haven, Conn.: Yale University Press, 1997), 194.

6. Reich, *Life of Nelson A. Rockefeller,* 341–342; Stettinius Telephone Log, 6 May 1945, Stettinius Papers; Thomas Campbell and George Herring, eds., *The Diaries of Edward Stettinius, Jr., 1943–1946* (New York: F. Watts 1974/New Viewpoints, 1975), 349–351.

7. Reich, *Life of Nelson A. Rockefeller,* 342.

8. FRUS, 1:617–618; 620–622, 633–635; Vandenberg, *Private Papers,* 189; Ronald W. Pruessen, *John Foster Dulles: The Road to Power* (New York: Free Press, 1982), 236–257.

9. Reich, *Life of Nelson A. Rockefeller,* 343; FRUS, 1:624, 626, 639; Vandenberg, *Private Papers,* 189.

10. Reich, *Life of Nelson A. Rockefeller,* 343–344; Campbell and Herring, *Diaries,* 353–355; Stettinius to Truman, telegram, 8 May 1945, Stettinius Papers.

11. Campbell and Herring, *Diaries,* 355–356; FRUS, 1:642, 646; Stettinius Telephone Log, 8 May 1945, Stettinius Papers.

12. FRUS, 1:643, 648; Thomas Campbell, *Masquerade Peace: America's UN Policy, 1944–1945* (Tallahassee: Florida State University Press, 1973), 170; Gabriel Kolko, *The Politics of War: The World and the United States Foreign Policy, 1943–1945* (New York: Pantheon Books, Random House, 1968), 469–474.

13. FRUS, 1:644, 650–652; Campbell and Herring, *Diaries,* 356.

14. FRUS, 1:659–660; *New York Times,* 9 May 1945; Reich, *Life of Nelson A. Rockefeller,* 344–345.

15. FRUS, 1:657–660, 666; Campbell and Herring, *Diaries,* 359; Reich, *Life of Nelson A. Rockefeller,* 346.

16. FRUS, 1:666, 672, 674–686; Campbell and Herring, *Diaries,* 361–362; Stettinius to Truman, Telephone Log, 12 May 1945, Stettinius Papers.

17. FRUS, 1:691–710; Vandenberg, *Private Papers,* 192; Campbell and Herring, *Diaries,* 363–364.

18. FRUS, 1:665–670, 691–710; Vandenberg, *Private Papers,* 192; Campbell and Herring, *Diaries,* 363–364. Later some accommodation was given to preemptive attacks if the threat of assault was immediate.

19. Reich, *Life of Nelson A. Rockefeller,* 350; FRUS, 1:714–718; Campbell and Herring, *Diaries,* 364–368.

20. Reich, *Life of Nelson A. Rockefeller,* 351–352; Campbell and Herring, *Diaries,* 366–368; FRUS, 1:719.

21. Reich, *Life of Nelson A. Rockefeller,* 350–351; FRUS, 1:721–725; Campbell and Herring, *Diaries,* 267; *New York Times,* 15, 20 May 1945.

22. FRUS, 1:719–725; Campbell and Herring, *Diaries,* 267–268; Vandenberg, *Private Papers,* 192–193.

23. Campbell and Herring, *Diaries,* 368–370.

24. FRUS, 1:730–733.

25. Campbell and Herring, *Diaries,* 370–372; FRUS, 1:730–734.

26. Vandenberg, *Private Papers,* 193; FRUS, 1:735.

27. FRUS, 1:738–739; John Bartlow Martin, *Adlai Stevenson of Illinois: The Life of Adlai Stevenson* (New York: Doubleday, 1976), 237.

28. FRUS, 1:749; John Foster Dulles, *War or Peace* (New York: Macmillan, 1950), 91; *Washington Post,* 16 May 1945; Stettinius to Truman, Stettinius to Rockefeller, Telephone Log, 15 May 1945, Stettinius Papers; *New York Times,* 16 May 1945.

29. FRUS, 1:781; Dulles, *War or Peace,* 91; Ruth Russell, *A History of the United Nations' Charter: The Role of the United States, 1940–1945* (Washington, D.C.: Brookings Institution, 1958), 700–703. The key phrase in Article 51 was the following: "Nothing in the present Charter shall impair the inherent right of individual or collective self-defense if an armed attack occurs against a Member of the United Nations, until the Security Council has taken measures necessary to maintain international peace and security."

30. Kolko, *Politics of War,* 474; Evan Luard, *A History of the United Nations: The Years of Western Domination, 1945–1955,* vol. 1 (New York: St. Martin's Press, 1982), 54; Reich, *Life of Nelson A. Rockefeller,* 353–354; Benjamin Rivlin, "Regional Arrangements and the UN System for Collective Security and Conflict Resolution: A New Road Ahead?" *International Relations Journal* (1992): 95–110.

31. Reich, *Life of Nelson A. Rockefeller,* 353–354; Dulles, *War or Peace,* 92.

CHAPTER 12

1. Thomas Connally and Alfred Steinberg, *My Name Is Tom Connally* (New York: T. Y. Crowell, 1954), 282; *New York Times,* 18 May 1945; Foreign Relations of the United States (FRUS), vol. 1 (1945), Diplomatic Papers, The United Nations Conference (Washington, D.C.: U.S. Government Printing Office, 1967), 822.

2. *New York Times,* 27 May 1945.

3. *New York Times,* 5, 7 May 1945.

4. *Encyclopedia Britannica* (Chicago: William Benton, 1966), 898; *Colliers Encyclopedia* (New York: Macmillan Educational Co., 1988), 469.

5. *New York Times,* 10, 15 May 1945; FRUS, 1:420, 762.

6. *New York Times,* 19, 24 May 1945; Gabriel Kolko, *The Politics of War: The World and the United States Foreign Policy, 1943–1945* (New York: Pantheon Books, Random

House, 1968), 475–477; Evan Luard, *A History of the United Nations: The Years of Western Domination, 1945–1955,* vol. 1 (New York: St. Martin's Press, 1982), 44; Robert Divine, *Second Chance: The Triumph of Internationalism in America During World War II* (New York: Atheneum, 1967), 294–295; Stettinius to Truman, telegram, 22 May 1945, Edward Stettinius Papers, University of Virginia.

7. FRUS, 1:770, 778, 799, 799–811; *New York Times,* 19 May 1945; Ruth Russell, *A History of the United Nations' Charter: The Role of the United States, 1940–1945* (Washington, D.C.: Brookings Institution, 1958), 720–729; Arthur H. Vandenberg Jr., ed., *The Private Papers of Senator Vandenberg* (Boston: Houghton Mifflin, 1952), entry for 26 May 1945, 200.

8. *New York Times,* 20, 23 May 1945; Stettinius to Truman, telegram, 19 May 1945, Stettinius Papers.

9. *New York Times,* 23 May 1945; FRUS, 1:842–843, 917; Cary Reich, *The Life of Nelson A. Rockefeller: Worlds to Conquer, 1908–1958* (New York: Doubleday, 1996), 357.

10. *New York Times,* 23 May 1945; Stettinius to Truman, telegram, 22 May 1945, Harry S. Truman Papers, Harry S. Truman Presidential Library, Independence, Missouri; Harry Truman, *Memoirs: Years of Decision,* vol. 1 (Garden City, N. Y.: Doubleday, 1955), 284–285.

11. Truman, *Memoirs,* 286; Thomas Campbell and George Herring, eds., *The Diaries of Edward Stettinius Jr., 1943–1946* (New York: F. Watts 1974/New Viewpoints, 1975), 377–378; Secretary of State Summary of Conversation with President Truman, 23 May 1945, Stettinius Papers.

12. Stettinius to Truman, telegram, 26 May 1945, Harry S. Truman Papers; Russell, *History of the United Nations' Charter,* 720–721; FRUS, 1:876–880; *New York Times,* 26, 27 May, 3 June 1945; Stettinius to Truman, telegram, 25 May 1945, Stettinius Papers.

13. Stettinius to Truman, telegram, 26 May 1945, Harry S. Truman Papers; Russell, *History of the United Nations' Charter,* 720–721; FRUS, 1:876–880; *New York Times,* 26, 27 May, 3 June 1945; Stettinius to Truman, telegram, 25 May 1945, Stettinius Papers.

14. FRUS, 1:930–933; *New York Times,* 28 May 1945.

15. Truman, *Memoirs,* 242–243.

16. *New York Times,* 29 May 1945.

17. FRUS, 1:970, 1011–1022; Vandenberg, *Private Papers,* 200; Memorandum of Conversation, "Mr. Grew Calling Mr. Stettinius," 31 May 1945, Stettinius Papers.

18. *New York Times,* 2, 3 June 1945; FRUS, 1:1073; Vandenberg, *Private Papers,* 201.

19. FRUS, 1:1088–1089; Truman, *Memoirs,* 287.

20. FRUS, 1:1095–1099; Campbell and Herring, *Diaries,* 383–384.

21. FRUS, 1:1117–1119.

22. FRUS, 1:1152–1158; Campbell and Herring, *Diaries,* 385–387; 389–391.

23. FRUS, 1:1152–1158; Campbell and Herring, *Diaries,* 385–387; 389–391.

24. Vandenberg, *Private Papers,* 203–204; Campbell and Herring, *Diaries,* 387–388; Ronald W. Pruessen, *John Foster Dulles: The Road to Power* (New York: Free Press, 1982), 247–248; Stettinius Telephone Log, 4 June 1945, Stettinius Papers.

25. FRUS, 1:1172; *New York Times,* 5, 6, 7 June 1945.

26. Russell, *History of the United Nations' Charter,* 714.

27. Memorandum of Conversation, 4 June 1945, Stettinius Papers.

CHAPTER 13

1. Harry Truman, *Memoirs: Years of Decision,* vol. 1 (Garden City, N. Y.: Doubleday, 1955), 257–258; Robert Sherwood, *Roosevelt and Hopkins: An Intimate History* (New York: Harper, 1948), 881; George McJimsey, *Harry Hopkins: Ally of the Poor and Defender of Democracy* (Cambridge, Mass.: Harvard University Press, 1987), 373–374; Walter Issacson and Evan Thomas, *The Wise Men: Six Friends and the World They Made* (New York: Simon & Schuster, 1986), 283; Kenneth Davis, *Experience of War: The United States in World War II* (New York: Doubleday, 1965), 628.

2. E. B. White, *The Wild Flag* (Boston: Houghton Mifflin, 1946), 82; see also *Stalin's Correspondence with Roosevelt and Truman, 1941–1945* (New York: Capricorn, 1965).

3. *New York Times,* 6 May 1945; Memorandum of Conversation, Stettinius and Molotov, 8:00 P.M., 3 May 1945, Edward Stettinius Papers, University of Virginia.

4. *New York Times,* 5, 6 May 1945; Arthur H. Vandenberg Jr., ed., *The Private Papers of Senator Vandenberg* (Boston: Houghton Mifflin, 1952), 185–186; Sir Llewellyn Woodward, *British Foreign Policy in the Second World War* (London: Her Majesty's Stationary Office, 1971), 542; Memorandum of Conversation, Stettinius, Eden, and Molotov, 4 May 1945, Stettinius Papers.

5. Truman, *Memoirs,* 257–258; *New York Times,* 5 May 1945; McJimsey, *Harry Hopkins,* 378; Sherwood, *Roosevelt and Hopkins,* 885–887; Charles Bohlen, *Witness to History, 1929–1969* (New York: W. W. Norton, 1973), 215; W. Averell Harriman and Elie Abel, *Special Envoy to Churchill and Stalin, 1941–1946* (New York: Random House, 1975), 459; Rudy Abramson, *Spanning the Century: The Life of W. Averell Harriman, 1891–1986* (New York: Morrow, 1992), 397.

6. White, *Stalin's Correspondence,* 231–232; *New York Times,* 20, 21 May 1945.

7. Truman, *Memoirs,* 258–259; Alonzo Hamby, *Man of the People: A Life of Harry S. Truman* (New York: Oxford University Press, 1995), 320.

8. Truman, *Memoirs,* 259; Sherwood, *Roosevelt and Hopkins,* 887.

9. Sherwood, *Roosevelt and Hopkins,* 889–890.

10. Ibid., 893–898.

11. Ibid., 898; Foreign Relations of the United States (FRUS), vol. 1 (1945), Diplomatic Papers, The United Nations Conference (Washington, D.C.: U.S. Government Printing Office, 1967), 300.

12. Sherwood, *Roosevelt and Hopkins,* 907–910; McJimsey, *Harry Hopkins,* 383–387; FRUS, 5:304–305.

13. Sherwood, *Roosevelt and Hopkins,* 907–910; Truman, *Memoirs,* 263; McJimsey, *Harry Hopkins,* 383–387; FRUS, 5:305–307, 319.

14. Sherwood, *Roosevelt and Hopkins,* 910–912; Edward Stettinius, *Roosevelt and the Russians: The Yalta Conference* (Garden City, N.Y.: Doubleday, 1949), 321; Harriman and Abel, *Special Envoy,* 473.

15. McJimsey, *Harry Hopkins,* 386–387; William Hardy McNeil, *America, Britain and Russia: Their Cooperation and Conflict, 1941–1946* (New York: Johnson Reprint Corporation, 1970), 588.

16. Stettinius, *Roosevelt and the Russians,* 301; Robert Donovan, *Conflict and Crises: The Presidency of Harry Truman 1945–1948* (New York: W. W. Norton, 1977), 53.

17. Hamby, *Man of the People,* 321; Bohlen, *Witness to History,* 192.

18. Thomas Campbell and George Herring, eds., *The Diaries of Edward Stettinius Jr.,*
1943–1946 (New York: F. Watts 1974/New Viewpoints, 1975), 393–395; Stettinius Calendar Notes 6, 7 June 1945, Stettinius Papers; Memorandum of Conversation, 7 June
1945, Stettinius Papers.

19. FRUS, 1:1190–1195, 1210–1211; Campbell and Herring, *Diaries,* 392–395; Vandenberg, *Private Papers,* 208–210.

20. Vandenberg, *Private Papers,* 208; Stettinius Notes on Forty-fourth Day, 7 June
1945, Stettinius Papers.

21. Stettinius Notes, 7 June 1945, Memorandum of Conversation, Stettinius et al., 7
June 1945, Stettinius to President Truman, telephone call, 7 June 1945, Stettinius Papers; Campbell and Herring, *Diaries,* 394–395.

22. *New York Times,* 8 June 1945.

23. *New York Times,* 8, 9 June 1945; Ruth Russell, *A History of the United Nations'*
Charter: The Role of the United States, 1940–1945 (Washington, D.C.: Brookings Institution, 1958), 737.

24. *New York Times,* 9 June 1945; Russell, *United Nations' Charter,* 736–739;
Thomas Connally, *My Name Is Thomas Connally* (New York: T. Y. Crowell, 1954),
282–283; Memorandum of Conversation between Stettinius and Grew, Department of
State, 12 June 1945, Stettinius Papers.

25. Russell, *United Nations' Charter,* 738–739; Vandenberg, *Private Papers,* 211.

26. Sherwood, *Roosevelt and Hopkins,* 915–916; *New York Times,* 14 June 1945.

27. Woodward, *British Foreign Policy,* 554; *New York Times,* 21, 25 June, 1 July
1945; Harriman and Abel, *Special Envoy,* 470.

CHAPTER 14

1. Foreign Relations of the United States (FRUS), vol. 1 (1945), Diplomatic Papers,
The United Nations Conference (Washington, D.C.: U.S. Government Printing Office,
1967), 1148–1149; *New York Times,* 15, 19 June 1945.

2. FRUS, 1:1148, 1319–1323, 1340, 1394; *New York Times,* 18 June 1945; Thomas
Campbell and George Herring, eds., *The Diaries of Edward Stettinius Jr., 1943–1946*
(New York: F. Watts 1974/New Viewpoints, 1975), 395–396.

3. Campbell and Herring, *Diaries,* 395–397; Arthur H. Vandenberg Jr., ed., *The Pri-*
vate Papers of Senator Vandenberg (Boston: Houghton Mifflin, 1952), 212–213.

4. FRUS, 1:1311, 1328–1330; *New York Times,* 18 June 1945; Stettinius Notes, 13
June 1945, Memorandum of Conversation between Stettinius and Gromyko, 16 June
1945, Edward Stettinius Papers, University of Virginia; Harry Truman, *Memoirs: Year*
of Decision, 1945–1946, vol. 1 (Garden City, N. Y.: Doubleday, 1955), 288.

5. FRUS, 1:1311, 1328–1330; Vandenberg, *Private Papers,* 212–213; *New York*
Times, 18 June 1945; Memorandum of Conversation between Stettinius and Gromyko,
16 June 1945, Stettinius Papers.

6. FRUS, 1:1340–1342, 1353–1355; *New York Times,* 18 June 1945; Truman, *Mem-*
oirs, 288.

7. FRUS, 1:1341, 1382; Vandenberg, *Private Papers,* 214; *New York Times,* 20 June
1945; Truman, *Private Papers,* 288.

8. FRUS, 1:1382–1388; Vandenberg, *Private Papers,* 214.

9. FRUS, 1:1397–1398; Vandenberg, *Private Papers,* 214.

10. John Foster Dulles, *War and Peace* (New York: Macmillan, 1950), 79–80; Brian Urquhart, *Ralph Bunche: An American Life* (New York: W. W. Norton, 1993), 116; FRUS, 1:459–460.

11. FRUS, 1:445–452, 459–460; Evan Luard, *A History of the United Nations: The Years of Western Domination, 1945–55,* vol. 1 (New York: St. Martin's Press, 1982), 61.

12. Urquhart, *Ralph Bunche,* 118; Luard, *History of the United Nations,* 59; *New York Times,* 15 May 1945.

13. FRUS, 1:792–798; Luard, *History of the United Nations,* 62; Mary Anne Glendon, *A World Made New: Eleanor Roosevelt and the Universal Declaration of Human Rights* (New York: Random House, 2001), 12; *New York Times,* 11–12, 19, 25 May 1945.

14. Urquhart, *Ralph Bunche,* 122.

15. Ruth Russell, *A History of the United Nations' Charter: The Role of the United States, 1940–1945* (Washington, D.C.: Brookings Institution, 1958), 912; Virginia Gildersleeve, *Many a Good Crusade* (New York: Arno Press, 1980), 345; Assistant Secretary of State Archibald MacLeish to Secretary of State Stettinius, Department of State Memorandum, 8 June 1945, Leo Pasvolsky Papers, Manuscripts Division, Library of Congress.

16. Gildersleeve, *Many a Good Crusade,* 344; Sol Bloom, *The Autobiography of Sol Bloom* (New York: G. P. Putnam's Sons, 1948), 3–4.

17. Russell, *History of the United Nations' Charter,* 910–918; Stettinius Memorandum to President Truman, 30 May 1945, Harry S. Truman Papers, Harry S. Truman Presidential Library, Independence, Missouri; FRUS, 1:1363.

18. Russell, *History of the United Nations' Charter,* 900–910; Luard, *History of the United Nations,* 62–63.

19. Russell, *History of the United Nations' Charter,* 900–910; *New York Times,* 16 June 1945.

20. Russell, *History of the United Nations' Charter,* 900–910; *New York Times,* 16 June 1945.

21. Russell, *History of the United Nations' Charter,* 845–847, 852–854; Luard, *History of the United Nations,* 64–65.

22. Russell, *History of the United Nations' Charter,* 847–851; Luard, *History of the United Nations,* 64; Stettinius Notes, 13 June 1945, Stettinius Papers.

23. Russell, *History of the United Nations' Charter,* 678–680; *New York Times,* 13 June 1945.

24. Russell, *History of the United Nations' Charter,* 777–808; *New York Times,* 12 June 1945.

25. Luard, *History of the United Nations,* 66–68; Russell, *History of the United Nations' Charter,* 864–897; Truman, *Private Papers,* 286.

26. *New York Times,* 16, 17 June 1945.

27. Minutes of the Big Five Meeting, 12 June 1945, Stettinius Papers; Lord Gladwyn, *The Memoirs of Lord Gladwyn* (London: Weidenfeld and Nicolson, 1972), 162.

28. Michael Ignatieff, *Isaiah Berlin: A Life* (New York: Henry Holt, 1998), 132–133.

29. Cary Reich, *The Life of Nelson Rockefeller: Worlds to Conquer 1908–1958* (New York: Doubleday, 1996), 363–364.

CHAPTER 15

1. David McCullough, *Truman* (New York: Simon & Schuster, 1992), 293, 308; Alonzo Hamby, *Man of The People: A Life of Harry S. Truman* (New York: Oxford University Press, 1995), 305.

2. *New York Times,* 3 June 1945.

3. Thomas Campbell and George Herring, eds., *The Diaries of Edward Stettinius Jr., 1943–1946* (New York: F. Watts 1974/New Viewpoints, 1975), 398–401.

4. Ibid.

5. *New York Times,* 29 June 1945; Arthur H. Vandenberg Jr., ed., *The Private Papers of Senator Vandenberg* (Boston: Houghton Mifflin, 1952), 224–225.

6. Memorandum by Isaiah Bowman, June 24, 25, 26 1945, Edward Settinius Papers, University of Virginia; Margaret Truman, *Letters from Father: The Truman Family's Personal Correspondence* (New York: Arbor House, 1981), 253.

7. Harry Truman, *Memoirs: Year of Decision, 1945–1946*, vol. 1 (Garden City, N. Y.: Doubleday, 1955), 326.

8. Campbell and Herring, *Diaries,* 403–404.

9. Ibid., 404; *New York Times,* 28 June 1945.

10. Foreign Relations of the United States (FRUS), vol. 1 (1945), Diplomatic Papers, The United Nations Conference (Washington, D.C.: U.S. Government Printing Office, 1967), 1375–1377.

11. Stettinius Memorandum, 23 June 1945, Stettinius Papers; H. Truman, *Memoirs,* 295–296; *New York Times,* 21 June 1945.

12. Campbell and Herring, *Diaries,* 404–405; Stettinius Memorandum, 21 June 1945, Stettinius Papers; *New York Times,* 26 June 1945; oral interview with Oliver Lundquist, 19 April 1990, United Nations Oral History Project, U.N. Library, New York, 2, 4, 8, 13, 17, 18; Donal McLaughlin, "Origin of the Emblem and Other Recollections of the 1945 U.N. Conference" (Garrett Park, Md.: Personal Monograph, 1995), 8–9.

13. Virginia Gildersleeve, *Many a Good Crusade* (New York: Arno Press, 1980), 355–356; *Washington Post,* 26 June 1945; *New York Times,* 26 June 1945; *San Francisco Chronicle,* 26 June 1945.

14. *New York Times,* 26 June 1945.

15. Campbell and Herring, *Diaries,* 401; Gildersleeve, *Many a Good Crusade,* 356; *New York Times,* 26 June 1945.

16. Stettinius Memorandum, 25 June 1945, Stettinius Papers.

17. FRUS, 1:1425–1429.

18. *New York Times,* 27 June 1945; Lundquist interview, 18; McLaughlin, "Origin of the Emblem," 9; *Time,* 9 July 1945.

19. *New York Times,* 27 June 1945.

20. Ibid.

21. Ibid., 28, 29 June; Vandenberg, *Private Papers,* 216; Alger Hiss interview, 13 February and 11 October 1990, United Nations Oral History Project, Yale University

Institution for Social and Policy Studies, 48–50; Linda Melvern, *The Ultimate Crime: Who Betrayed the UN and Why* (London: Allison and Busby, 1995), 25.

22. *New York Times*, 22, 27, 28 June 1945; Cary Reich, *The Life of Nelson A. Rockefeller: Worlds to Conquer, 1908–1958* (New York: Doubleday, 1996), 346; Vandenberg, *Private Papers*, 215.

23. Norman Graebner, ed., *An Uncertain Tradition: American Secretaries of State in the 20th Century* (New York: McGraw-Hill, 1961), 222.

24. *New York Times*, 12 June 1945; George Kennan, *Memoirs 1925–1950* (Boston: Atlantic Monthly Press, 1967), 216–217; Alexander Dallin, *The Soviet Union at the United Nations: An Inquiry Into Soviet Motives and Objectives* (New York: Praeger, 1962), 25.

25. *New York Times*, 15, 24, 26 June 1945.

26. Walter Johnson, ed., *The Papers of Adlai E. Stevenson: Washington to Springfield 1941–1948*, vol. 2 (Boston: Little, Brown, 1973), 241–242, 246.

27. *New York Times*, 17, 22, 24, 26 June 1945.

CHAPTER 16

1. Robert Divine, *Second Chance: The Triumph of Internationalism in America During World War II* (New York: Atheneum, 1967), 299; *New York Times*, 15, 23, 24 June 1945.

2. *New York Times*, 27, 29 June 1945.

3. Divine, *Second Chance*, 299–300; *New York Times*, 28 June 1945; *Time*, 9 July 1945; *Newsweek*, 9 July 1945; Arthur H. Vandenberg Jr., ed., *The Private Papers of Senator Vandenberg* (Boston: Houghton Mifflin, 1952), 216–217.

4. *New York Times*, 29 June 1945.

5. Vandenberg, *Private Papers*, 217–218; *New York Times*, 30 June 1945.

6. Vandenberg, *Private Papers*, 218; *New York Times*, 30 June 1945.

7. *New York Times*, 30 June, 1, 2 July 1945.

8. Dorothy Robins, *Experiment in Democracy: The Story of U.S. Citizen Organizations in Forging the Charter of the United Nations* (New York: Parkside Press, 1971), 144–145; Divine, *Second Chance*, 302; *New York Times*, 23, 27 June 1945.

9. Robins, *Experiment in Democracy*, 143–145; Divine, *Second Chance*, 303–304.

10. Jeffrey Donaldson, *Archibald MacLeish: An American Life* (Boston: Houghton Mifflin, 1992), 387; Divine, *Second Chance*, 302; Robins, *Experiment in Democracy*, 145; *New York Times*, 1 July 1945.

11. *New York Times*, 3 July 1945.

12. Divine, *Second Chance*, 304.

13. Ibid., 305; *New York Times*, 10 July 1945.

14. Divine, *Second Chance*, 305–306.

15. Ibid., 305–306; Edward Luck, *Mixed Messages: American Politics and International Organizations 1919–1999* (Washington, D.C.: Brookings Institution, 1999), 180–181.

16. Divine, *Second Chance*, 306.

17. Robins, *Experiment in Democracy*, 148; Divine, *Second Chance*, 306–309; Ruth Russell, *A History of the United Nations Charter: The Role of the United States, 1940–1945* (Washington, D.C.: Brookings Institution, 1958), 937–938.

18. Divine, *Second Chance*, 309–310; Russell, *History of the United Nations Charter*, 947–948

19. Divine, *Second Chance*, 310–311.

20. Ibid., 311–313; Russell, *History of the United Nations Charter*, 942.

21. Divine, *Second Chance*, 312–313; Russell, *History of the United Nations Charter*, 944–945.

22. Divine, *Second Chance*, 313–314; Vandenberg, *Private Papers*, 218; Harry Truman, *Memoirs: Year of Decision, 1945–1946*, vol. 1 (Garden City, N. Y.: Doubleday, 1955), 399–400; Russell, *History of the United Nations Charter*, 947.

23. Robins, *Experiment in Democracy*, 148; Luck, *Mixed Messages*, 259; *New York Times*, 1 July 1945; Dean Acheson, *Present at the Creation: My Years in the State Department* (New York: W. W. Norton, 1969), 111.

24. Charles Kupchan, *The End of the American Era: U.S. Foreign Policy and the Geopolitics of the Twenty-First Century* (New York: Knopf, 2002), 194–196.

25. Thomas Franck, *Nation Against Nation: What Happened to the UN Dream and What the U.S. Can Do About It* (Oxford, England: Oxford University Press, 1985), 7.

26. *Congressional Record*, 79th Cong., 1st sess., November 26 1945, 10965.

27. Ibid., 10967.

EPILOGUE

1. Gabriel Kolko, *The Politics of War: The World and the United States Foreign Policy 1943–1945* (New York: Pantheon Books, Random House, 1968), 483; Evan Luard, *A History of the United Nations: The Years of Western Domination, 1945–55*, vol. 1 (New York: St. Martin's Press, 1982), 68; John Garraty, *Henry Cabot Lodge: A Biography* (New York: Knopf, 1953), 379–382.

2. Brian Urquhart, "Looking for the Sheriff," *New York Review of Books*, 16 July 1998, 49; Rosemary Righter, *Utopia Lost: The UN and World Order* (New York: 20th Century Fund Press, 1995), 41.

3. James Traub, "Who Needs the U.N. Security Council?" *New York Times Magazine*, 17 November 2002, 49.

4. Freedom House, "Democracy's Century: A Survey of Global Political Change in the 20th Century," 7 December 1999.

5. Fareed Zakaria, "Annals of Foreign Policy: Our Way—The Trouble with Being the World's Only Superpower," *New Yorker*, 14 and 21 October 2002, 78; *Time*, June 27 1955.

BIBLIOGRAPHY

BOOKS

Abramson, Rudy. *Spanning the Century: The Life of W. Averell Harriman, 1891–1986.* New York: Morrow, 1992.

Acheson, Dean. *Present at the Creation: My Years in the State Department.* New York: W. W. Norton, 1969.

Alvarez, David. *Secret Messages: Code-Breaking and American Diplomacy, 1930–1945.* Lawrence: University Press of Kansas, 2000.

Bamford, James. *Body of Secrets.* New York: Doubleday, 2001.

Bell, H.C.F. *Woodrow Wilson and the People.* Garden City, N.Y.: Doubleday, 1945.

Benson, Robert Louis, and Michael Warner, eds. *Venona: Soviet Espionage and the American Response, 1939–1957.* Washington, D.C.: National Security Agency, 1996.

Berle, Adolf. *Navigating the Rapids, 1918–1971: From The Papers of Adolf Berle.* Ed. Beatrice Bishop Berle and Francis Jacobs. New York: Harcourt Brace Jovanovich, 1973.

Beschloss, Michael. *The Conquerors: Roosevelt, Truman and The Destruction of Hitler's Germany.* New York: Simon & Schuster, 2002.

Bird, Kai. *The Chairman: John J. McCloy, the Making of the American Establishment.* New York: Simon and Schuster, 1992.

Bloom, Sol. *The Autobiography of Sol Bloom.* New York: G. P. Putnam's Sons, 1948.

Blum, John, William McFeely, Edmund Morgan, Arthur Schlesinger Jr., Kenneth Stampp, and C. Vann Woodward. *The National Experience: A History of the United States.* 6th ed. New York: Harcourt Brace Jovanovich, 1985.

Blum, John, ed. *The Price of Vision: The Diary of Henry Wallace, 1942–46.* Boston: Houghton Mifflin, 1973.

Bohlen, Charles. *Witness to History, 1929–1969.* New York: W. W. Norton, 1973.

Bosworth, Patricia. *Anything Your Little Heart Desires: An American Family Story.* New York: Simon & Schuster, 1997.

Broadwater, Jeff. *Adlai Stevenson: The Odyssey of a Cold War Liberal.* New York: Twayne Publishers/Macmillan, 1994.

Byrnes, James. *Speaking Frankly.* New York: Harper & Row, 1947.

———. *All in One Lifetime.* New York: Harper & Brothers, 1958.

Campbell, Thomas. *Masquerade Peace: America's UN Policy 1944–1945.* Tallahassee: Florida State University Press, 1973.

Campbell, Thomas, and George Herring, eds. *The Diaries of Edward Stettinius Jr., 1943–1946*. New York: F. Watts 1974/New Viewpoints, 1975.

Chace, James. *Acheson: The Secretary of State Who Created the American World*. New York: Simon & Schuster, 1998.

Churchill, Winston. *The Second World War: Triumph and Tragedy*. Vol. 4. Boston: Houghton Mifflin, 1953.

Ciechanowski, Jan. *Defeat in Victory*. New York: Doubleday, 1947.

Clarke, Nick. *Alistair Cooke: A Biography*. New York: Arcade, 1999.

Cole, Wayne. *Roosevelt and the Isolationists, 1932–1945*. Lincoln: University of Nebraska Press, 1983.

Connally, Thomas, and Alfred Steinberg. *My Name Is Thomas Connally*. New York: T. Y. Crowell, 1954.

Craig, Gordon A., and Francis L. Lowenheim, eds. *The Diplomats, 1939–1979*. Princeton, N. J.: Princeton University Press, 1994.

Critchlow, Donald. *The Brookings Institution, 1916–1952: Expertise and the Public Interest in a Democratic Society*. DeKalb: Northern Illinois University Press, 1985.

Dallek, Robert. *Franklin Roosevelt and American Foreign Policy 1932–45*. New York: Oxford University Press, 1979.

Dallin, Alexander. *The Soviet Union At the United Nations: An Inquiry Into Soviet Motives and Objectives*. New York: Praeger, 1962.

Daniels, Jonathan. *The Man of Independence*. New York: Lippincott, 1950.

Davis, Kenneth. *Experience of War: The United States in World War II*. New York: Doubleday, 1965.

Divine, Robert. *The Illusion of Neutrality*. Chicago: University of Chicago Press, 1962.

_____. *Second Chance: The Triumph of Internationalism in America During World War II*. New York: Atheneum, 1967.

Donaldson, Jeffery. *Archibald MacLeish: An American Life*. Boston: Houghton Mifflin, 1992.

Donovan, Robert. *Conflict and Crises: The Presidency of Harry Truman 1945–48*. New York: W. W. Norton, 1977.

Dulles, John Foster. Papers. Princeton University Library, Princeton, N.J.

_____. *Three Years of The United Nations*. New York: 1948.

_____. *War and Peace*. New York: Macmillan Co., 1950.

Eichelberger, Clark. *Organizing For Peace: A Personal History of the Founding of the United Nations*. New York: Harper, 1977.

Feis, Herbert. *Churchill, Roosevelt, Stalin: The War They Waged and the Peace They Sought*. Princeton, N. J.: Princeton University Press, 1957.

Ferrell, R. H., ed. *Off the Record: The Private Papers of Harry S. Truman*. New York: Penguin, 1980.

Foreign Relations of the United States. Vol. 1 (1945). Diplomatic Papers, The United Nations Conference. Washington, D.C.: U.S. Government Printing Office, 1967.

Forrestal, James. *The Forrestal Diaries*. Ed. Walter Mills. New York: Viking Press, 1951.

Fosdick, Dorothy. *Common Sense and World Affairs*. New York: Harcourt, Brace & Company, 1955.

Franck, Thomas. *Nation Against Nation: What Happened to the U.N. Dream and What the U.S. Can Do About It*. New York: Oxford University Press, 1985.

Garraty, John. *Henry Cabot Lodge: A Biography*. New York: Knopf, 1953.

Gildersleeve, Virginia. *Many a Good Crusade*. New York: Arno Press, 1980.

Gladwyn, Lord. *The Memoirs of Lord Gladwyn*. London: Weidenfeld and Nicolson, 1972.

Glendon, Mary Anne. *A World Made New: Eleanor Roosevelt and the Universal Declaration of Human Rights*. New York: Random House, 2001.

Goodwin, Doris Kearns. *No Ordinary Time*. New York: Simon and Schuster, 1994.

Graebner, Norman, ed. *An Uncertain Tradition: American Secretaries of State in the 20th Century*. New York: McGraw-Hill, 1961.

Gromyko, Andrei. *Memoirs*. New York: Doubleday, 1990.

Hamby, Alonzo L. *Man of the People: A Life of Harry S. Truman*. New York: Oxford University Press, 1995.

Hamilton, Nigel. *JFK: Reckless Youth*. New York: Random House, 1992.

Harriman, W. Averell. *America and Russia in a Changing World: A Half-Century of Personal Observation*. New York: Doubleday, 1971.

Harriman, W. Averell, and Elie Abel. *Special Envoy to Churchill and Stalin, 1941–1946*. New York: Random House, 1975.

Haynes, John Earl, and Harvey Klehr. *Venona: Decoding Soviet Espionage in America*. New Haven, Conn.: Yale University Press, 1999.

Heckscher, August. *Woodrow Wilson*. New York: Charles Scribner's Sons, 1991.

Hersey, John. *Aspects of the Presidency*. New Haven, Conn.: Ticknor and Fields, 1980.

Hildebrand, Robert C. *Dumbarton Oaks: The Origins of the United Nations and the Search for Postwar Security*. Chapel Hill: University of North Carolina Press, 1990.

Hiss, Alger. *Recollections of a Life*. New York: Arcade, 1988.

Holloway, David. *Stalin and the Bomb*. New Haven, Conn.: Yale University Press, 1994.

Hoopes, Townsend. *The Devil and John Foster Dulles*. Boston: Little, Brown, 1973.

_____. *Driven Patriot: The Life and Times of James Forrestal*. New York: Knopf, 1992.

Hoopes, Townsend, and Douglas Brinkley. *FDR and the Creation of the United Nations*. New Haven, Conn.: Yale University Press, 1997.

Hull, Cordell. *Memoirs of Cordell Hull*. Vols. 1 and 2. New York: Macmillan, 1948.

Ikenberry, John, ed. *American Foreign Policy: Theoretical Essays*. Glenview, Ill.: Scott, Foresman, 1989.

Issacson, Walter, and Evan Thomas. *The Wise Men: Six Friends and the World They Made*. New York: Simon & Schuster, 1986.

Johnson, Walter, ed. *The Papers of Adlai E. Stevenson, Washington to Springfield, 1941–1948*. Vol. 2. Boston: Little, Brown, 1973.

Josephson, Harold. *James Shotwell and the Rise of Internationalism in America*. Cranbury, N.J.: Associated University Presses, 1975.

Kant, Immanuel. *Perpetual Peace, and Other Essays on Politics, History and Morals*. Trans. Ted Humphrey. Indianapolis, Ind.: Hackett Publishing Company, 1983.

Kennan, George. *Memoirs 1925–1950*. Boston: Atlantic Monthly Press, 1967.

Kimball, Warren. *FDR: The Juggler*. Princeton, N.J.: Princeton University Press, 1991.

Kolko, Gabriel. *The Politics of War: The World and the United States Foreign Policy 1943–1945*. New York: Pantheon Books, Random House, 1968.

Krock, Arthur. *Memoirs: Sixty Years on the Firing Line*. New York: Funk and Wagnalls, 1968.

Kupchan, Charles. *The End of the American Era: U.S. Foreign Policy and the Geopolitics of the Twenty-First Century*. New York: Knopf, 2002.

Leuchtenburg, William. *In the Shadow of FDR: From Harry Truman to Ronald Reagan*. Ithaca, N. Y.: Cornell University Press, 1983.

Luard, Evan. *A History of the United Nations: The Years of Western Domination, 1945–55*. Vol. 1. New York: St. Martin's Press, 1982.

Luck, Edward. *Mixed Messages: American Politics and International Organizations 1919–1999*. Washington, D.C.: Brookings Institution, 1999.

Martin, John Bartlow. *Adlai Stevenson of Illinois: The Life of Adlai Stevenson*. New York: Doubleday, 1976.

McCullough, David. *Truman*. New York: Simon & Schuster, 1992.

McJimsey, George. *Harry Hopkins: Ally of the Poor and Defender of Democracy*. Cambridge, Mass.: Harvard University Press, 1987.

McKeever, Porter. *Adlai Stevenson: His Life and Legacy*. New York: William Morrow, 1989.

McLaughlin, Donal. "Origin of the Emblem and Other Recollections of the 1945 U.N. Conference." Garrett Park, Md.: Personal Monograph, 1995.

McNeill, William Hardy. *America, Britain and Russia: Their Cooperation and Conflict, 1941–1946*. New York: Johnson Reprint Corporation, 1970.

Meisler, Stanley. *The United Nations: The First Fifty Years*. New York: Atlantic Monthly Press, 1955.

Melvern, Linda. *The Ultimate Crime: Who Betrayed the U.N. and Why*. London: Allison and Busby, 1995.

Morison, Elting. *Turmoil and Tradition: A Study of the Life and Times of Henry L. Stimson*. Boston: Houghton Mifflin, 1960.

Moskin, J. Robert. *Mr. Truman's War: The Final Victories of World War II and the Birth of the Postwar World*. New York: Random House, 1996.

Mosley, Leonard. *Dulles: A Biography of Eleanor, Allen and John Foster Dulles and Their Family Network*. New York: Dial Press, 1978.

Moynihan, Daniel Patrick. *On the Law of Nations*. Cambridge, Mass.: Harvard University Press, 1990.

Nixon, E. B., ed. *Franklin Roosevelt and Foreign Affairs*. Cambridge, Mass.: Belknap Press of Harvard Press, 1962.

Notter, Harley. *Postwar Foreign Policy Preparation, 1939–1945*. Washington, D.C.: Department of State, 1949.

Pasvolsky, Leo. Papers, Library of Congress, Manuscript Division, Washington, D.C.

Pruessen, Ronald W. *John Foster Dulles: The Road to Power*. New York: Free Press, 1982.

Raczynski, Edward. *In Allied London*. London: Weidenfeld and Nicolson, 1962.

Rees, David. *Harry Dexter White: A Study in Paradox*. New York: Coward, McCann & Geoghegan, 1973.

Reich, Cary. *The Life of Nelson A. Rockefeller: Worlds to Conquer, 1908–1958*. New York: Doubleday, 1996.

Reston, James. *Deadline*. New York: Random House, 1991.

Righter, Rosemary. *Utopia Lost: The UN and World Order.* New York: 20th Century Fund Press, 1995.

Robins, Dorothy. *Experiment in Democracy: The Story of U.S. Citizen Organizations in Forging the Charter of the United Nations.* New York: Parkside Press, 1971.

Romulo, Carlos, and Beth Day Romulo. *Forty Years: A Third World Soldier at the UN.* New York: Greenwood Press, 1986.

Roosevelt, Eleanor. *This I Remember.* New York: Harper & Brothers, 1949.

Roosevelt, Franklin. *Looking Forward.* New York: John Day, 1933.

Rosek, Edward. *Allied Wartime Diplomacy: A Pattern in Poland.* New York: Wiley, 1958.

Russell, Ruth. *A History of the United Nations' Charter: The Role of the United States, 1940–1945.* Washington, D.C.: Brookings Institution, 1958.

Santis, Hugh. *The Diplomacy of Silence: The American Foreign Service, the Soviet Union and the Cold War 1933–1947.* Chicago: University of Chicago Press 1983.

Schlesinger, Arthur M. Jr., *The Crisis of the Old Order.* Boston: Houghton Mifflin, 1957.

––––––. *A Thousand Days: John F. Kennedy in the White House.* Boston: Houghton Mifflin, 1965.

––––––. *The Imperial Presidency.* Boston: Houghton Mifflin, 1973.

––––––. *A Life in the 20th Century: Innocent Beginnings, 1917–1950.* Boston: Houghton Mifflin, 2000.

Sherwin, Martin. *A World Destroyed: The Atomic Bomb and the Grand Alliance.* New York: Random House, 1977.

Sherwood, Robert. *Roosevelt and Hopkins: An Intimate History.* New York: Harper, 1948.

Shotwell, James. *The Long Way to Freedom.* Indianapolis, Ind.: Bobbs-Merrill, 1960.

Skidelsky, Robert. *John Maynard Keynes, Fighting for Britain, 1937–1946.* Vol. 3. New York: Macmillan, 2001.

Smith, Gaddis. *American Diplomacy During the Second World War, 1941–1945.* New York: John Wiley & Sons, 1965.

Smith, John Chabot. *Alger Hiss: The True Story.* New York: Holt, 1976.

Stalin, Josef. *Stalin's Correspondence with Roosevelt and Truman 1941–45.* New York: Capricorn, 1965.

––––––. *Stalin's Correspondence with Churchill and Atlee 1941–45.* New York: Capricorn, 1965.

Steel, Ronald. *Walter Lippmann and the American Century.* New York: Atlantic Monthly Press, 1980.

Stettinius, Edward. Papers. University of Virginia Library, Charlotsville, Va.

––––––. *Roosevelt and the Russians: The Yalta Conference.* Ed. Walter Johnson. Garden City, N. Y.: Doubleday, 1949.

Stimson, Henry, and McGeorge Bundy. *Stimson: On Active Service in Peace and War.* New York: Harper & Brothers, 1947–1948.

Tanenhaus, Sam. *Whittaker Chambers.* New York: Random House, 1997.

Truman, Harry. *Memoirs: Year of Decision, 1945–1946.* Vol. 1. Garden City, N. Y.: Doubleday, 1955.

Truman, Margaret. *Harry S. Truman.* New York: William Morrow, 1973.

––––––. *Letters from Father: The Truman Family's Personal Correspondence.* New York: Arbor House, 1981.

Unger, Sanford. *FBI: An Uncensored Look Behind the Walls.* Boston: Little, Brown, 1975.

Urquhart, Brian. *Ralph Bunche: An American Life.* New York: W. W. Norton, 1993.

Vandenberg, Arthur, Jr. Papers. Diary. Clements Library, University of Michigan, Ann Arbor, Mich.

Vandenberg, Arthur, Jr., ed. *The Private Papers of Senator Vandenberg.* Boston: Houghton Mifflin, 1952.

Wayne, Cole, *Roosevelt and the Isolationists, 1932–1945.* Lincoln: University of Nebraska Press, 1983.

Weinstein, Allen, and Alexander Vassiliev. *The Haunted Wood: Soviet Espionage in America—The Stalin Era.* New York: Random House, 1998.

Weinstein, Allen. *Perjury: The Hiss-Chambers Case.* New York: Knopf, 1978.

Welles, Benjamin. *Summer Welles: FDR's Global Strategist.* New York: St. Martin's Press, 1998.

Welles, Sumner. S*even Decisions That Shaped History.* New York: Harper & Brothers, 1951.

White, E. B. *The Wild Flag: Editorials from The New Yorker on Federal World Government and Other Matters.* Boston: Houghton Mifflin, 1946.

_____. *One Man's Meat.* Gardiner, Ma.: Tilbury House, 1997.

Woodward, Sir Llewellyn. *British Foreign Policy in the Second World War.* London: Her Majesty's Stationary Office, 1971.

ARTICLES, ADDRESSES, AND REPORTS

Barros, James, "Alger Hiss and Harry Dexter White: The Canadian Connection," *Orbis Magazine*, vol. 21, no. 3 (1977).

Burgers, Jan. "Road to San Francisco: Sankey Declaration." *Human Rights Quarterly,* vol. 14, no. 4 (November 1992).

Edis, Richard. "A Job Well Done: The Founding of the United Nations Revisited." *The Cambridge Review of International Affairs,* vol. 6, no. 1 (summer 1992).

Freedom House, "Democracy's Century: A Survey of Global Political Change in the 20th Century," 7 December 1999.

Killough, T. Patrick, "A Peace Made on Main Street: Private Americans Help Create the 1945 United Nations Charter," address to Southwestern World Affairs Institute, YMCA Center, Black Mountain, North Carolina , July 26, 1991.

McLaughlin, Donal, "Origin of the Emblem and Other Recollections of the 1945 U.N. Conference," personal monograph, Garrett Park, Md., 1995.

Polansky, Antony. "Stalin and the Poles, 1941–1947." *European History Quarterly* 17 (1987): 453–492.

Reynolds, Jaime. "'Lublin' Versus 'London': The Party and the Underground Movement in Poland, 1944–45." *Journal of Contemporary History* 16 (1981), 617–647.

Rivlin, Benjamin, "Regional Arrangements and the UN System For Collective Security and Conflict Resolution: A New Road Ahead?" *International Relations Journal* (1992).

Schild, Georg. "The Roosevelt Administration and the United Nations." *World Affairs Journal* (summer 1995).

Schlesinger, Arthur Jr., "Back to the Womb: Isolationism's Renewed Threat," *Foreign Affairs* (July/August 1995).

Schlesinger, Arthur Jr., "Franklin Roosevelt and U.S. Foreign Policy," address to the Society for Historians of American Foreign Relations, Vassar College, 18 June 1992.

Tanenhaus, Sam, "Tangled Treason," *New Republic*, 5 July 1999.

Traub, James, "Who Needs the U.N. Security Council?" *New York Times Magazine*, 17 November 2002.

Urquhart, Brian, "Looking for the Sheriff," *New York Review of Books*, 16 July 1998.

Weinstein, Allen, "Nixon vs. Hiss," *Esquire Magazine* (November 1975).

Zakaria, Fareed, "Annals of Foreign Policy: Our Way—The Trouble with Being the World's Only Superpower," *New Yorker*, 14 and 21 October 2002.

INTERVIEWS

Green, James. Oral interview by Yale researcher. United Nations Oral History Project. Yale University, 21 April 1986.

Hiss, Alger. Oral interview by Yale researcher. United Nations Oral History Project. Yale University, 13 February and 11 October 1990.

Lundquist, Oliver. Oral interview by Yale researcher. United Nations Oral History Project. Yale University, 19 April 1990.

Pell, Claiborne. Oral interview by Yale researcher. United Nations Oral History Project. Yale University, 20 February 1990.

Stassen, Harold. Oral interview by Yale researcher. United Nations Oral History Project. Yale University, 15 April 1983.

_____. Personal telephone interview by author. 19 November 1997.

INDEX